CRUSADER

By Horse to Jerusalem

D1225854

Tim Severin was born in 1940 and educated at Tonbridge School and Oxford University. He has sailed a leather boat across the North Atlantic in the wake of St. Brendan, captained an Arab sailing ship from Muscat to China, and steered the replica of a Bronze Age galley to investigate the stories of Jason and the Argonauts and Ulysses' Odyssey. He holds the Founder's Medal of the Royal Geographical Society, awarded in 1986 for outstanding service to exploration and geographic history. In 1988, the Royal Scottish Geographical Society presented him with the Livingstone Gold Medal.

When not travelling Tim Severin lives in County Cork, Ireland.

Also by Tim Severin

Tracking Marco Polo
Explorers of the Mississippi
The Golden Antilles
The African Adventure
Vanishing Primitive Man
The Oriental Adventure
The Brendan Voyage
The Simbad Voyage
The Jason Voyage: The Quest for the Golden Fleece
The Ulysses Voyage: Sea Search for The Odyssey
The Spice Islands Voyage
In Search of Moby Dick

CRUSADER

By Horse to Jerusalem

Tim Severin

Photographs by Peter Essick

PHOENIX
PRESS

PHOENIX PRESS
5 UPPER SAINT MARTIN'S LANE
LONDON WC2H 9EA

A PHOENIX PRESS PAPERBACK

First published in Great Britain
by Hutchinson in 1989
This paperback edition published in 2001
by Phoenix Press,
a division of The Orion Publishing Group Ltd,
Orion House, 5 Upper St Martin's Lane,
London WC2H 9EA

© Line drawings and Plates 1 and 24:
Bibliotheque Nationale, Paris
From Roman de Godefroi de Bouillon, Mss Fr 22495

Copyright © 1989 by Tim Severin

A CIP catalogue record for this book
is available from the British Library.

Printed and bound in Great Britain by
Butler & Tanner Ltd, Frome and London

ISBN 1 84212 278 9

Contents

CHAPTER 1

Carty

The fat horse and I stared at one another with mutual doubts. Chubby and poorly coordinated, he had tripped over his own immense feet as he squelched through the mud to come to inspect me. Just a youngster who had not yet finished growing, already he weighed three quarters of a ton. Nor could anyone have described him as handsome. His head was blocky and enormous. A pronounced Roman bump on his nose gave him a slightly comical and endearing expression as he peered at me through long eye lashes, though his eyes seemed far too small for that massive head. The huge barrel of his body was supported by four legs as thick as small tree trunks but so short that at sixteen hands he appeared to lack the height to match his massive girth and huge frame. The stiff grey hair of his mane was tangled and matted, with the consistency of a wire wool pot scourer. His tail, trimmed into a ridiculous bob, was a joke, an afterthought stuck on his fat bottom. His shaggy winter coat was a lighter shade of grey, erratically tinged with strawberry blotches and now so liberally daubed with mud smears that he looked like a minor species of woolly mammoth that had emerged, blinking, from a forgotten corner of Siberia. Indeed the skeletons of his ancestors had been dug up from Stone Age caves, and there was an obvious, if superficial, resemblance to the roly-poly horses drawn on the cave walls by Cro-Magnon man. Yet the animal I was looking at was what I was seeking. He belonged to one of the oldest surviving breeds of working horse in Europe – the Ardennes Heavy Horse – and was a reasonable facsimile of a medieval warhorse.

In our own ways both the fat horse and I were equally wary and naive.

I had only read about such awe-inspiring creatures in books, while the horse's only horizon had been the couple of hundred acres of sour bog land, meadow, and forest on a remote farm in northern France where he had been raised. Yet I was hoping that those vast hooves, now totally submerged under his great weight in muddy slop, would somehow carry the both of us from this flat dripping semi-marshland, across a continent and more than two thousand miles of road, into parched mountains where a temperature of 38 or 39 degrees was normal on a summer's day. Also I had been warned that this particular four-year-old horse was really too young to undertake the tremendous journey I had in mind. He had run free since birth, and never been trained or ridden. In fact his owners probably didn't even possess a saddle broad enough to cover him. Fat as butter, he was totally unfit, and the thick woolly coat was obviously unsuitable for a hot climate. With a little imagination I could just about picture him pulling a cart, hauling a plough, or even trotting along as a member of a spectacular Heavy Horse team attached to a brewers' dray. But if it was difficult to see him as a saddle horse, it was virtually impossible to picture him for what he ran the risk of becoming. If I did not buy him, his next destination would probably be the butcher's block, because locally the flesh of the Ardennes horse was a prized food. As the lumbering youngster was certainly not of show quality, he was likely to be turned into steaks. Anything I had in mind for his future, I reflected, could not be quite such a miserable fate.

But why did I need such an odd creature? And what had led me to this damp meadow in the borderlands between France and Belgium? The answer lay fifty miles to the northwest where the river Semois wriggles through the folds of a tough granite plateau that emerges like a craggy island from the rich agricultural lowlands of Flanders and Brabant. In the depths of that plateau the Semois coils around a steep crag of rock, and on the summit of that rock stands Chateau Bouillon. Its grey walls dominate the little medieval town that fills the river's gorge. The castle is the pride of the region, key to the routes that criss-cross the rain-soaked forest of Ardennes with its dense cover of oak and beech. Nearly nine centuries ago the seigneur of the castle had ridden from this primeval and misty land to begin a fabled journey. He had mortgaged his chateau to pay the ruinous cost of raising and arming a small army that amounted to his private brigade, and in 1096 Godfrey, Duke of Bouillon, had set out on the First Crusade to the Holy Land, vowing to reach Jerusalem. The Duke was only one among a number of Europe's leading noblemen who had pledged to liberate the Holy Land, but by the time Jerusalem was firmly in their hands some three years later, his haughty and turbulent colleagues selected him to be their Prince of Jerusalem. Less than a year afterwards he died in the Holy City, his reputation still unsullied, and the same followers buried his corpse close to the very spot where Jesus' body was laid when it was taken down from the cross. It was the holiest burial ground in Christendom and they felt that Duke Godfrey deserved this last resting place. He was their 'perfect knight'.

Duke Godfrey's reputation endured far beyond his own times. Today, in the provinces where he raised his vanished army, school classrooms are still hung with engravings of his greatest triumphs, and in the nineteenth century a statue of the Duke, on a prancing and not at all ungainly horse, was installed in a central square in Brussels. When the pioneer English printer Caxton was commissioned to print a life of King Arthur, he suggested that the Duke of Bouillon's story would be more appropriate. Arthur's reputation, Caxton ventured to his patron, was largely legendary, but the heroism and merit of the Duke of Bouillon was proven fact. Minstrels and jongleurs had composed songs to commemorate Godfrey's exploits on that First Crusade. Illuminators took care to put him in their pictures when they coloured the medieval chronicles with scenes of noble battle and distant journey, and in folklore he was ranked with King Arthur and Sir Lancelot.

Two years earlier I had added Godfrey to my personal list of semi-mythical travellers whose journeys had provided the raw material of legend. Such figures fascinated me, and in the past I had investigated the stories of St Brendan, Sindbad the Sailor, Jason and the Argonauts and Ulysses, using replicas of ancient boats to explore whether there was any truth behind their tales of distant travel.* Duke Godfrey's reputation also arose out of a great journey, but he posed a rather different sort of conundrum. Here was a real historical figure, an ordinary man, one

---

* *The Brendan Voyage*, Hutchinson, 1978.
   The Sindbad Voyage, Hutchinson, 1982.
   The Jason Voyage, Hutchinson, 1985.
   The Ulysses Voyage, Hutchinson, 1987.

3

among many, who had gone on the First Crusade. The events of the journey had made him a superhero to his immediate successors. Only a generation later stories were being told about his prodigious physical strength, his piety, his selflessness, his extraordinary feats of arms. What had happened to create such renown? Was it justified? And why had Duke Godfrey, among all the leaders of the First Crusade, been chosen for this special fame? To find the answer I proposed to follow Duke Godfrey's path to Jerusalem just as he had travelled along it – on horseback. Along that road, from Chateau Bouillon to his burial place in the Church of the Holy Sepulchre, I hoped to find some clues to the building of the legend of a man whose deeds made him one of the greatest heroes of chivalry. But I had a wider purpose, too. By actually riding a horse to Jerusalem I also wanted to come to grips with that extraordinary phenomenon, when tens of thousands of men and women, even some children too, had ventured to walk and ride across a continent, trying to reach Christ's tomb. Not just knights and soldiers had followed Duke Godfrey, but a straggling train of civilians had trudged in his wake. Untold numbers had fallen by the way; some faltered and turned back, discouraged by the hardships of the road; others died of malnutrition and disease. Every single survivor who finally laid eyes on Jerusalem had paid dearly with sweat and pain. So gruelling was the experience that, although many other Crusades would depart from Europe for the Holy Land over the next 300 years, not one of them succeeded in repeating exactly the same path. A few tried and failed, but most shunned the sections where those early Crusaders had suffered so cruelly.

Thus the First Crusade was a unique feat. Historians had dealt exhaustively with its documents and chronicles, written about its special geopolitics, causes and effects, ecclesiastical, social, diplomatic and administrative topics. But I was much more drawn to the practical details of the trip itself. It had been a stupendous journey, an achievement difficult to comprehend with our modern means of rapid travel and notions of time and distance. The Crusaders had been on the road for nearly three years, moving farther and farther away from their bases and sources of supply, parted from their homes by unimaginable distances. Warriors and civilians alike had journeyed through alien lands ruled by exotic enemies. How had they achieved it? And why? Scholarly opinion proposed variously that the First Crusade had been motivated by greed, by land hunger, by fanaticism, by ignorance, that it was the child of deliberate political manipulation between a Pope in Rome and an Emperor in Byzantium, that it was a mass migration, that it failed for Christianity but succeeded for Christendom. Only was there general agreement that the Crusade turned into the single most important phenomenon of the age. What, then, was it like to have travelled to Jerusalem in the manner of a medieval man? If I could taste that experience, even marginally, perhaps it would give an insight into the motives of those travellers and the reasons for their persistence. For me, one man brought everything into focus: Duke Godfrey of Bouillon was still the perfect symbol of the Crusade.

If I wanted to follow him, then there was a simple logic to choosing the correct type of horse I should use. Duke Godfrey recruited a major part of his army from his personal domain around Chateau Bouillon. His knights would have rallied to his banner with all manner, shapes and sizes of horses but, as the Duke's chateau lay in the heart of the Ardennes Forest, they must have brought with them at least some of the native breed – the Ardennes Heavy Horse. The breed books enthusiastically described the race as 'sober and robust . . . renowned for its toughness, its ability to withstand all types of climate, its eagerness to work and its frugal feeding.' But to Duke Godfrey and his knights, an animal weighing as much as a ton and capable of galloping at 20 miles an hour for short distances had one overwhelming advantage: in ridden combat such a monstrous charger was their day's equivalent to a main battle tank. Anyone knocked down and trodden on by such a crushing weight would have no further interest in the fight. The 'Belgian Horse', as the Ardennes and other Low Country breeds came to be known, was the most devastating mobile weapon of war known at that time. Possession of a warhorse of such dimensions was so dangerous that, a century later, it was controlled by royal edict. Kings were aware that in the hands of a rebellious vassal a squadron of Heavy Horses could mean the loss of a throne. In the winter of 1095, when the war leaders were planning their march on Jerusalem, they knew they would have to fight their way through a cordon of Muslim states before reaching the walls of the Holy City. It would have been inconceivable to them not to start out with their warhorses. Just how few of the great animals would survive the journey, they could not have imagined.

In my quest for further information about the Ardennes Heavy Horses, a listing in the British Equestrian Directory had led me four months earlier to Charlie Pinney, whose Carthorse Company appeared under the subheading 'Ardennes'. Charlie preached convincingly that farming could still be done efficiently and economically using Heavy Horses. To prove his thesis, he ran his own small farm in Devon without a single tractor, designed and built horse-drawn farm machines to do all the work on the farm, gave tuition in handling Heavy Horses, and competed successfully in horse-drawn ploughing matches where Charlie's hefty six-foot-three in gum boots, muddy trousers, well-worn canvas jacket, and long side burns must have well matched his tremendous plough horses. His enthusiasm for the Ardennes Horse was carefully researched. 'One day I wrote down a list of all the qualities I wanted in a working Heavy Horse for farm work,' he told me. 'Then I sent letters to every Heavy Horse breeder I could locate, asking for details of their breeds. When the answers came in, I put a tick against each breed, column by column for each quality. When I had finished, one breed had a tick on each line – the Ardennes.'

Charlie then took me out to a field to see his horses. He had an amazing rapport with the great beasts, constantly talking to them, scratching their stomachs so they stretched their huge bellies and almost purred with delight, picking up their massive feet, poking fingers in their mouths, and keeping up a constant flow of information. Every part of the animal seemed to have some special feature to look for. For the first time I heard about 'good black feet' that would hold horseshoe nails well, and was warned to beware too much 'feather', the shaggy tufts of hair round the hooves that would retain dirt and dried mud. 'You don't want your horse walking around with a breeze block on each foot' was how Charlie succinctly put it. I heard of the merits of good round leg bones – 'those legs won't snap off' – of the tremendous broad chests – 'perfect' – which meant the animal could pull several times its own weight in harness, and 'a back you can load without breaking'. When I asked Charlie how far one of these stately-looking creatures could walk in a day, he promptly replied that they were expected to pull '19 miles in the furrow'. This compared encouragingly with my calculation that Duke Godfrey's army must have covered an average of more than 15 miles per day. Already I had spent five months in the libraries reading the original chronicles of

6

the Crusade, not just for details about Duke Godfrey himself but to extract all the practical data of travel and to try to lay out his route, stage by stage, on contemporary maps. The difficulty was, I knew, that a neat line drawn across a map did not take into account the nature of the terrain, the detours for finding shelter or fodder, time spent fording rivers, the delays from bad weather or animal sickness, and a host of other variables. Only first-hand experience of actual horseback travel ultimately would provide that information.

For my own long journey Charlie counselled me against getting a mare – 'too moody' – but in almost the same breath he was jovially warning me that a stallion could prove even more of a handful if he saw an attractive female. Crusader Knights are always shown riding stallions but I had a sudden daunting vision of an amorous Ardennes stallion bulldozing his destructive trail through the countryside to get better acquainted with a seductive mare in a distant field. Charlie had already described how one day his inquisitive Ardennes stallion had wished to leave his field and visit the farmyard. The animal had merely walked through the field's five bar gate, which crashed off its hinges and lay bent on the ground behind him. But Charlie's enthusiasm for the Ardennes Horses allowed no second thoughts. He saw the most unexpected advantages in my choice of breed. 'Mind you, the Ardennes do fart a lot, but that could be useful in traffic,' and he laughed.

But Charlie had no horse suitable for my unorthodox venture. His handful of Ardennes were all being trained for farmwork. So to find my mount for a Crusader's ride he advised me to go to France, to a horse farm on the fringes of the Ardennes, and ask the help of the remarkable woman who ran it. 'She's among the best breeders of Ardennes horses,' he said, 'and totally dedicated to the task. Once I was walking round her farm with her, and asked why she never got married. She let out a whistle, and a moment later a huge Ardennes stallion came charging over the hill, galloped down towards us, and came slithering to a great smashing stop in front of us. Turning to me she said, "And where would I find a man who would obey me like that!"'

Charlie gave me Cecile's address, and I wrote to her asking if I might visit the farm. After a month, when no reply came back, I telephoned Cecile and was told that of course any friend of 'Charlee' would be most welcome. But nothing Charlie told me prepared me adequately for my first visit to the Ferme du Bourbeau in the melancholy borderlands between France, Germany and Belgium where every kilometre is a reminder of the bloodbaths of the First World War. Each hill has a military cemetery and every town is a garrison name.

Not far from Verdun, I found the Ferme du Bourbeau at the end of a narrow road leading through young forest. To enter the farmyard was like stepping back into an old black-and-white French film. A large, ancient cattle truck stood in the centre of the farmyard. Perhaps twenty years old, the vehicle had 'Attention Chevaux' printed on a metal plate bolted to the back of it. A part-Alsatian hound was leaping with rage at the end of its chain, barking frenziedly at my arrival, and besides the expected quota of chickens, there was a steady shuttle service of little pink pigs which trotted back and forth from the milking shed to raid the grain heap. On each sortie they were passing, at a nicely calculated radius, another hysterical part-Alsatian, no doubt a relative of the one already barking at me. Each time the dog came hurtling out to the full extent of its chain with a murderous snarling rush, but was brought up short with a strangling jerk that lifted the animal clean off its feet while the little pigs trotted on insolently to their snack. The noise was an ear-numbing combination of barking, snarling, squawking, clucking, the bawling of calves, squeals from pigs, the shrill neigh of a distant unseen horse, an unidentified clanking and clattering, and all suddenly overlaid by a piercing yell of 'Tais-toi!', directed at the woodshed dog by a short, bustling woman with close-cropped iron-grey hair who burst out of the woodshed door. She was dressed in a blue tee shirt and old blue trousers, and on her feet were what appeared to be a pair of army boots. She stumped towards me holding out a hand in welcome and simultaneously letting out a volley of abuse at the livestock. This was Cecile, Chevalier of the Legion of Honour (for services to agriculture) and doyenne of Ardennes Heavy Horse breeders.

Cecile, I later discovered, was quite accustomed to Ardennes enthusiasts visiting the remote farmhouse to inspect her horses, and refused to let such visits disrupt her routine. So I was placed at the kitchen table and told to repose myself for ten minutes with the help of a vast pot of jam, a knife with a broken handle and an extremely large and slightly stale loaf of bread hauled out from a big paper sack containing eight other such loaves. There were no niceties to farm teas here; this was every minute a working household. Cecile took two slices of bread herself as she stamped back and forth, ramming chunks of wood into the maw of the cast iron stove, crashing a skillet on the top, kicking the door shut, and muttering to herself all the time that it was impossible to look after the house and keep up with the farmwork. 'Go and look at the horses, while I bring in the cows,' she announced marching out, 'then we'll talk,' and I could hear the barrage of shouts begin immediately as she entered the cacophonous yard.

I ventured out gingerly in her wake. As the cows were brought into the milking parlour, the field gate was left open and two vast Ardennes mares took their chance to stroll in from their field looking for pickings. They plodded into the farmyard like amiable leviathans, unstoppable as they pushed their way into the barn to munch on the straw. One of them somehow managed to get herself astraddle a large rusty metal hopper, which would have taken three or four men to budge. The mare simply sent the obstacle skidding out of her way with a gentle push of a leg. Her companion must have been irritated by a fly, for she stamped her foot, and with awe I noted how the hoof had gouged a pock mark out of the hardpacked earth and stones as if the ground had been struck by a navvy wielding a sledge hammer. From time to time, as Charlie had warned, the two animals broke wind thunderously until interrupted by Cecile who bobbed back into view and gave several piercing cries of outrage so that the two horses turned slowly and walked majestically back to their field with all the unhurried certainty of a fleet of merchantmen at sea.

Nailed above the rickety barn door, by my count, were 55 prize metal plaques awarded at various horse shows for different categories of prize Heavy Horses, stallions, mares, foals, mares-with-foals, yearlings, and so forth. I feared the weight of any more plaques would bring down the rickety building in the next gale. The winners of the plaques and their progeny were scattered over the wide pastureland surrounding the farm, contentedly grazing. From a distance, they looked like hippopotami on the veldt, particularly the more pregnant mares. The fields were very big, running right up to the surrounding forest. Occasionally a Heavy Horse would emerge from the trees, its arrival heralded by a series of crashes and cracks as the creature simply shoved its way through the saplings like an earthmover. I was joined by Cecile and we strolled through the herd. Getting precise information from her was baffling. How many horses did she have on the farm? She didn't know precisely. What was the best age for a horse to go on a very long journey? There was a shrug – 'a certain age'. How much time was needed to train an Ardennes horse to the saddle? Again, a shrug. Why did all the horses have docked tails? The response was a bemusing explanation: first, it was the custom, and second, in the old days long tails were a nuisance, always getting entangled in the reins and working machinery. I suspected I got nearer the truth when Cecile cheerfully slapped the nearest horse on its huge rump and announced that the bobbed tail set off its buttock lines very well. I had to admit that for sheer rotundity, little could compete with the full billowing stern of a plump Ardennes Horse. Whereas Charlie had owned just a few animals, and trained and worked with them, Cecile raised dozens and dozens which drifted about the farm, simply growing up. She knew the name, lineage and age of every one of them, but though there was fondness there was a pragmatic limit to sentimentality. Mares were kept for breeding purposes, good stallions selected and sold or retained, poor quality animals and surplus stallions fattened up as quickly as possible and then sent to the butcher's hook. In a matter-of-fact tone Cecile told me that a young Ardennes horse would put on edible flesh more quickly than a bullock, and that according to butcher's lore a bay horse gave less stringy steaks than a roan. The Crusaders too, I reflected, had been driven to eat their horses.

After an hour's stroll we returned to the farmhouse for a tot of a ferocious plum liqueur followed by supper at the long kitchen table with an assortment of companions so strange that they enhanced the sense of being in an earlier part of the century. Half way through our meal a huge black man came staggering in. At first I thought he was a negro and drunk, but he was black with fine dust and lurching from sheer exhaustion, not alcohol. It was Cecile's brother Dédé, who as usual had been driving himself to the point of utter exhaustion, working to keep the farm afloat. He sat down heavily in the chair at the head of the table and barely had time to eat a little food before his head began to droop sleepily.

I stayed overnight at the farm so was on hand to watch the striking sight of Dédé's first breakfast, a deep bowl of powdered, chicory-flavoured coffee at daybreak, accompanied by a shot of 'le grog', cheap beet-sugar rum. This was reinforced when he reappeared after two hours of back-breaking work with a plate containing four thick slices of pig fat that had simmered in water for half an hour and then been lightly fried. Brimming with cholesterol, Dédé held out an enormous hand to wish me goodbye, and then rushed back to his toil. The previous night I had plucked up enough courage to explain the seemingly preposterous idea that I wished to buy one of their horses in order to ride the animal on the medieval road to Jerusalem. I might as well have been suggesting that I would just ride a few hundred metres around the farm. Yes, yes, he nodded and asked if I would like another pastis. Cecile was off to Verdun to run her little shop where on three days a week she sold a few pints of milk and eggs, and she was equally off-hand. There would be no problem, she said. She would find a quiet animal and when I came back Dédé would train the creature for the saddle. I drove away, wondering if my command of French was less than I had supposed.

Charlie came to my rescue. He accompanied me on my next visit to Bourbeau a couple of months later, and somehow, through his mangled French delivered in a very English accent, he was always on precisely the right wavelength. The whole family clearly adored him, and there was much banter and discussion of farm quotas, crops, milk yields, as well as the names, characters, colours and pedigrees of famous Ardennes horses. It was like listening to an arcane rite, and I merely eavesdropped as he, Cecile and I walked through all the pastures once again to try to select my horse.

As we tramped the entire round of the farm, stopping and regarding every horse in sight, I became increasingly worried. Time was running short if I was to train and learn to ride an Ardennes horse and set out in the spring: the season when the prudent medieval traveller began his journey, once the snows had melted and the muddy roads had dried. There was no chance of my going off to look for other horse farms. Bourbeau was my best and only hope. Yet every time our trio halted to inspect an animal, the odds dwindled. For a start it became clear that Cecile would not part with any of the mares, because every one of them was pregnant and carrying a foal. That eliminated ninety per cent of the horses on the farm. Among the stallions the selection was very restricted indeed. Most of them were very young, mere colts and foals, and as such quite unsuitable. There was a superb pair of four-year-olds, which I had admired previously, but they were bespoke and far too fine for what I needed. The same was true of the other stallions: they were either already sold, or spoken for or would be kept on as possible replacements for the stud farm. Perhaps it was accident or, more likely, good stage management, but after two hours walk and inspecting apparently every field, we had not seen a single suitable animal. I was really beginning to wonder whether anyone at Bourbeau had the least idea of what I wanted, or why, or that it mattered so much to me to have a genuine Ardennes for my journey.

But I need not have been so on edge. Cecile knew exactly what would suit me. She led us behind the farm, down past a spinney to a distant, soggy field containing just one forlorn horse, who looked very lonely. He was a roan, muddy and fat, and comic-looking with his Roman nose.

Charlie later told me that it was a puzzle to him why this horse had been kept on. Nothing about him was quite right for a fine Ardennes stallion. The head was wrong, the walk odd, the stance slightly askew, the 'conformation', as the horse-judging world called it, was indifferent. But there was no doubt that this particular horse had a strong character of his own – you could see it in the way he held his head and looked at us – and a horse's character, Charlie had told me a long time before, was the most important quality of all. If I was to coax a Heavy Horse into walking across a continent, the animal would need a strong character to withstand the rigours of the journey.

Quite what sort of a character the horse possessed, there was no way of knowing. And if I had guessed what lay in store, perhaps I would have thought longer before offering to Cecile to buy this, her sole, suitable horse whose grandiloquent name, it turned out, was Quarté de Bourbeau and whose lineage was fully inscribed in the Ardennes stud book as a four-year-old pure bred. Carty, as his name was instantly abbreviated, was to turn out to be stubborn, cunning, brave, greedy, affectionate, destructive, innocent, gentle, full of guile, timid, majestic, squalid, docile, fractious. He would dominate my life for the next twelve months. Like his relatives, he had been born in the foaling bay in the great barn of Bourbeau, with the help of a splendid contraption of which Dédé was very proud. Above the foaling stall was a large metal box bolted to a rafter, and from it extruded a hook. A stout rope was attached to the hook, and at the other end of the rope a broad canvas belt was wrapped around the huge girth of the pregnant Ardennes mare about to produce

12

her foal in the stall below. On the most likely night for the birth, either Dédé or Cecile would sleep on a mattress in the stable ready to assist the mare in labour. When the mare was ready, she would lie down on the straw. This pulled on the canvas belt which tugged on the rope which pulled on the hook which in turn activated a Second World War klaxon that began hooting and roused the sleeper. Thus, Carty had been born in the middle of the night to the raucous howls of a machine normally associated with war and destruction. Nothing, I was to find out, could have been more appropriate. The world had been alerted to the fact that Carty, rascal extraordinary, had arrived.

CHAPTER 2

Duke Godfrey

Duke Godfrey's lineage – on his mother's side – was Ardennes of a different sort, although no less impeccable. He was the second son of Eustace II, Duke of Boulogne, and Ida of Bouillon, daughter of the Duke of Lower Lotharingia and Lord of Ardennes. The infant was so high-born, the story runs, that when a sympathetic woman of the ducal house-hold dared to pick him up and began to breast-feed him, Godfrey's aristocratic mother was so incensed that she snatched the child away and made him vomit, declaring that anything less than her own milk risked diluting the nobility of the child.

This tale, if apocryphal, is a favourite of social historians of the early Middle Ages because it provides a glimpse of the extraordinary social pretensions of the patrician class into which Godfrey of Bouillon was born. Like several other nobles who were later to accompany him on the First Crusade, he was the lesser son of an ambitious and belligerent family of Norman warlords who had their power base in the northwest provinces of France. His father was a flamboyant figure known, because of his tremendous sweeping whiskers, as Eustace of the Moustaches, who was recognised on the battlefield by his habit of decorating his war helmet with bristling strips of whale bone.* Eustace II was knitted by parentage and marriage into a complex web of family alliances that ruled and squabbled over lands on both sides of the English Channel. Through his grandmother he was linked to the royal house of France, and via his

* It is not clear whether he chose this crest because whales were popularly considered to be terrifying monsters who swallowed ships entire, or because whale fishery was a primary occupation of the Channel port from which he took his title.

first wife — who was twice his age when he shrewdly married her — he became at one stroke brother-in-law to Edward the Confessor, King of England, and a cousin by marriage to the immensely powerful Dukes of Normandy. From the former, Eustace accepted lands and fiefs in England, while with the latter he maintained a cordial relationship which eventually led him to the battlefield of Hastings. There Eustace fought in the army of William the Conqueror against the English king, but despite all his martial advertisement the battle was not a success for the moustached warrior. He turned tail at a crucial stage in the onslaught against the Saxons, and came home with a deep arrow wound in his back, an ignominious episode in the family background of the future warrior-hero of the Crusades.

By then the future Duke de Bouillon would have been about six or seven years old. As with most of his contemporaries, there are tantalisingly few proven details about his early life. Infant mortality was so high that no-one bothered to record the events of a child's life until it was sure that he or she would survive to useful adulthood. It is not even clear whether Godfrey was born in France, his father's homeland, or in Belgium, where his mother owned large estates in her own right. There is no record of his baptism or who were his godparents, so we have only the glamorous overlay of romance and invention to account for the infancy of the boy, born about the year 1060 to the noble line of the Dukes of Boulogne and descendant of Charlemagne at eight or ten generations removed. If young Godfrey led a fairly normal life as the cadet son of a ducal household, then it was in a cold and draughty castle and it is from this stage of his life that the next tale comes. He and his two brothers, Eustace the older and Baldwin the younger, had scampered into the duke's chambers and were hiding beneath the skirts of their mother. Their father asked flippantly what was making the commotion. 'Three princes,' his wife is reputed to have replied, 'the first will be a duke, the second a king, and the third a count.'*

Ida was well qualified to talk in such vaunting terms. Her family was even more illustrious than her husband's. She too was descended from

---

* In fact Ida of Bouillon's prophecy was too modest: her eldest son became Duke of Boulogne, Godfrey was Duke of Lower Lotharingia, and youngest son Baldwin became first the Count of Edessa and then accepted the full title of King of Jerusalem.

Charlemagne. One uncle had been proclaimed as Pope (though admittedly only for a brief period, and he was never properly recognised), her brother was the Duke of Lower Lotharingia, and her father the terrible Godfrey the Bearded, after whom she had presumably named her second son. Even in an age known for its turbulence, Godfrey the Bearded was a troublemaker of renown. A chronic rebel, he spent his days in endless intrigues against his feudal overlord the German Emperor who once put him into captivity, twice stripped him of his estates and eventually forced him to flee to Italy, where with admirable resilience Godfrey the Bearded managed to win the hand in marriage of Beatrice, ruler of the richest duchy in the peninsula.

Seen from a distance of 900 years, the bickerings, manoeuvrings and private wars of the noble families of western Europe in the eleventh century have an unreal air. They seem to have been as much a matter of habit as of serious political intent. Yet they were the very tangible background to young Godfrey's upbringing and were to set the tone for the behaviour of the warlords who set forth on the long march to Jerusalem. Even when they were on the Crusade it was never certain whether the great lords would be able to work together harmoniously or whether they would quarrel. Their subordinates, the ordinary knights, were prepared to switch their allegiance from one great lord to another. The Host, as the great throng of crusaders would sometimes be called, was never coherent or disciplined. Each great noble contributed his contingent – his household retainers, his vassals, his friends and those neighbours who would follow him – but there was no overall commander until, at the very end, the Duke of Bouillon was acclaimed. It was that progression, from command of a single element of an army to the supreme leadership of the successful Crusade, which I now wanted to investigate.

But there was a more peaceable, if not exactly softer, strand to the society that young Godfrey knew, and if we are to search for the source of young Godfrey's sense of religious duty, by far the most likely candidate is his mother. Celebrated for her piety, if not her humility, the formidable Ida was considered a woman 'of great merit in the eyes of God'. She was, according to the chroniclers, deeply religious, devout, generous in her gifts to religious foundations, and a constant friend of the Church. The historical record backs up the claim. Church archives list her many gifts of land and money. Her alms-purse was inscribed, it is said, with the rather smug motto 'The more I give, the more remains.' So far as we know, Godfrey never married, and the woman who played the most significant role in shaping his beliefs was Ida of Bouillon. From her, Godfrey would have acquired a devout, if rather priggish sense of Christian duty and self-sacrifice.

From her, too, he was able to lay his claim to Bouillon's valuable chateau. The inheritance traced back to the impractical division of the enormous empire of Charlemagne and serves as another symbol of Godfrey's era because it illustrates the disastrous fragmentation of what once had been the most unified political structure of Europe since the height of the Roman Empire. At Charlemagne's death in 814, a vast realm known loosely as the 'Kingdom of the Franks' stretched from the Pyrenees to the Danube, and from the English Channel to Rome. In Godfrey's time anyone coming from this huge territory was still known as a 'Frank', whether he hailed from Bavaria and spoke German, or from the Languedoc and used Provençal, or from Brittainy and spoke Breton, in which case the three men would have been unlikely to understand one another. A generation later Charlemagne's kingdom had been shared out in three portions among his descendants. Two portions made geographic sense: the eastern part became the kingdom of Germany, and the western part evolved gradually into the kingdom of France. But the central section had no logic to it at all. A long, rambling, awkward corridor of territory, it extended all the way from the Channel in Belgium, across the Alps and into Italy, with a bulge to take in Provence. Although it included Charlemagne's ancient capital at Aix (Aachen) as well as the city of Rome, it had no natural centre. It soon snapped in half across the waist, and these halves broke up into segments. Provence broke away very early, and from both edges France and Germany gnawed away until within a single generation the kingdom-of-the-centre had disappeared.

The northerly segment of that dismembered kingdom, a broad swathe more than a hundred miles wide from the Alps to the sea, came to be divided into two dukedoms, Upper and Lower Lotharingia. Both were in the gift of the German king and could be handed out to whichever great vassal he pleased, always on the feudal obligation that it would revert to the German crown on the vassal's death. To these dukedoms, either separately or both at the same time, Godfrey the Bearded had laid persistent and troublesome claim, and by his death in 1069, he had ensured that Lower Lotharingia remained with the family of Ardennes. The German king confirmed the appointment of Ida's younger brother, another Godfrey know as the Hunchback, to the dukedom.

Thus the situation of Ida of Bouillon's second son was typical for the cadet son of a patrician family: on his father's side his elder brother Eustace would inherit the lands and titles of Boulogne and the various counties in England. Brother Eustace was being carefully groomed for this role and had been sent for his training to the court of the Duke of Normandy. On his mother's side Godfrey was related by marriage or descent to several of the most important families in Europe, and his best chance of acquiring a great estate was through his namesake and uncle, the Hunchback, who had no sons. It was hardly surprising, therefore, that young Godfrey was sent to his maternal uncle to receive his education at the ducal court, probably based for much of the time at Chateau Bouillon. There Godfrey, who in normal circumstances would have begun his apprenticeship as a noble at the age of eight, would have been instructed in the rather curious mixture of knightly skills — armed combat, horsemanship, dancing, backgammon and chess, how to present wine properly while kneeling, and how to carve meat.

Day-to-day life, by our modern standards, was a quirky mixture of discomfort and occasional luxury. Chateau Bouillon had not yet been expanded into its later size and was merely a sturdy round tower of massive stones, with several floors and a conical wooden roof that made the building look like a squat pencil stub set on end. Privacy was virtually unknown. All life took place at ground level in the circular main hall, its floor covered with rushes, bare of furniture except for a few trestles and tables. Here lived, ate and slept all the duke's immediate retainers — men-at-arms, clerks, servants, grooms, and hangers-on as well as the cluster of squires and pages. Heat and smoke came from a fire in the centre of the room which must have made life on the upper floors very sooty. Light, what there was of it, leaked in through small windows that were mere holes-in-the-wall in summer, and blocked with oiled paper or cloth in winter. Access to the upper floors, where the Duke had his personal chambers, was by a wooden stair at the side of the hall, but only privileged members of the household would ascend unless the castle was under attack: then the main defence was conducted from the top of the tower and its galleries.

Looking at matters from a traveller's point of view, however, it did seem to me that a future Crusader like Godfrey already had a lifestyle that was remarkably easy to transfer to the open road. In effect everyone, whether nobleman or varlet, was little more than camping within their castle. The tables and trestles were designed to be taken to pieces, and be swiftly put on carts. Possessions were kept in chests that could be lugged out of the hall. There was no crockery to risk breaking, just a few wooden trenchers and sturdy goblets of wood, horn or metal. Spoons were of the same materials, no forks, and everyone already carried his own knife at his belt. A castle could be stripped bare in a matter of hours, and life in a tent was scarcely different from the daily routine in the chateau. All activity began and ended with sunrise and sunset. But contrary to popular opinion the early medieval castle dweller appreciated bathing in great tubs of hot water: this was probably the only aspect of castle life Godfrey would really miss.

Young Godfrey did not, as it turned out, inherit the dukedom directly from the Hunchback who died in 1076. Instead, for what must have been eleven irksome years, he had to await his turn while the duchy was held temporarily by the young son of his liegelord, the Holy Roman Emperor Henry IV. During this interval Godfrey demonstrated his loyalty by fighting in Henry's cause in a succession of battles in Germany and Italy until finally, on the same day as the 13-year-old son of Henry IV was elevated to the title of King of the Romans, Godfrey was invested as the Duke of Lower Lotharingia. He thus came into undisputed control, though not ownership, of a duchy that extended through Flanders, Luxembourg, Brabant and Hainault. At its centre the strategic castle at Bouillon was held as a direct personal possession.

Godfrey was then 27 years old, battle-hardened and reputedly celibate. He bore one of the most celebrated family names in Europe, and in appearance was a tall, powerfully-built man with good looks and light auburn hair, according to the archbishop-historian William of Tyre who in the twelfth century composed a major account of the Crusade from contemporary documents and eyewitness accounts. Looking back on the career of Duke Godfrey, he saw his ideal warrior for Christ, He was 'a just man, generous, pious and God-fearing, correct, an enemy to everythng evil, severe and resolute in his words. He spurned the glories of this world, which is rare at this time and particularly in the trade of war.' Godfrey was 'without equivalent in general intelligence, military skill and valour in combat.' By rights, on acquiring the dukedom, this paladin should have been content to settle down and spend the rest of his life ruling one of the greatest feudal estates on the continent, siring a family to continue the proud line of Ardennes, defending the family interests against encroaching neighbours. This was the role for which he had trained and fought all his life. Instead he chose to abandon everything for a cause that promised only penury and probable death.

The single event that did most to precipitate the Crusade was a plea for help which arrived from the Christian emperor of Byzantium, Alexius Comnenus. His territories across the Bosphorus in Anatolia were coming under intense pressure from the Seljuk Turks, a Muslim people originating in central Asia, who were steadily overrunning provinces that had been in the empire since Roman times. The Seljuks were intruders not to be taken lightly. Spearheaded by flying columns of light cavalry, they pillaged the countryside, seized Byzantine towns, and then installed their own governors. The more daring of their advance patrols were cantering their horses by the shores of the Sea of Marmara. In 1071 one of Alexius' predecessors, Emperor Romanus Diogenes, had led the flower of the Byzantine imperial army eastward to put an end to these Turkish incursions. But in a quiet valley called Manzikert, deep in the Anatolian plateau, the Seljuk cavalry surrounded the Emperor's army and cut it to shreds. Romanus himself was wounded and captured, and the annihilation was total. From that moment on, the Byzantines' military self-esteem was very subdued. They opted to stay behind their city walls and deploy the more subtle means for which their diplomacy became a byword: bribes to keep the enemy at bay, secret negotiations to suborn local Turkish governors, artful schemes to foster quarrels amidst the Seljuk clan leaders, and endless prevarication to cloak a search for allies.

Seeking help, Alexius sent a delegation to a papal conference of bishops in Piacenza in 1095. His envoys asked the Christians of the West to supply soldiers to come to the aid of Byzantium. Alexius promised every facility – food, shelter, guides, military stores. He appealed to their

Turkish lord and his flocks.

spirit of Christian brotherhood. But Alexius seems to have had no spirit, nor any inkling, of crusade. Indeed the very idea was an alien concept to the eastern Church which had grown accustomed to reaching accommodation with all its various neighbours. He was interested more in defending his eastern frontier than in marching to Jerusalem. After all, the Holy City had been in the hands of the Muslims for more than 450 years, and these Muslims were far away and easy to make deals with. So Alexius was asking for one type of intervention, but he was to be given another type altogether. It was a misunderstanding which was to have momentous consequences.

The westerners saw the situation quite differently. Travellers returning from the East had been spreading harrowing tales about the mistreatment of pilgrims to the Holy Land by the Muslims. It was said that the Christians were beaten and robbed, and denied access to the Holy Places. Worse, it was claimed that the sacred shrines themselves were being defiled. Supposedly, dog carcasses were being thrown into them, and the saintly relics scattered about. Many of these reports were

The Pope travels to France (left) and preaches the Crusade at Clermont (right).

arrant propaganda, but they horrified western Europeans, for this was the great age of pilgrimage.

In every country in Europe, at every season of the year, hundreds of thousands of devout men and women went off to visit the shrines of local saints or to pray before caskets containing holy relics. Often it was no more than an excuse to travel – for a villein perhaps the only chance in his lifetime to leave his village – and there was a strong element of cult worship, certainly among the uneducated villagers whose belief had deep roots in paganism. The Church thoroughly approved. Ecclesiastical law ordained that all altars should contain relics, and encouraged every sort of pilgrimage whether a comparatively short journey to the local shrine at a church, holy spring, even a crossroads, or a major trip such as the one to go to pray at the shrine of St James at Compostella in Spain, so well-organised by the Cluniac monks. Naturally the greatest pilgrimage was the journey to the Holy Land itself; long, expensive, and arduous but guaranteed to bring spiritual reward. Indeed, anything that had the faintest whiff of the land of the Bible took on a special significance. The churches and shrines of Europe were rife with rags of cloth, splinters of wood, even pebbles, brought back from the Holy Land and possessing semi-magical associations, particularly if they had come from Nazareth or Bethlehem or Jerusalem. The West's geographers when they sketched the known world always showed Jerusalem at its very hub. The precise navel was an exact spot some thirteen feet to the west of Mount Calvary.

Thus, while Alexius looked east from his palace and saw the immediate need to push back the Turks, the westerners' gaze leapt far beyond. They were hypnotised by the vision of Jerusalem, captive to the infidel, defiled and awaiting deliverance. They would march, not for Alexius' temporal kingdom, but for the liberation of their faith. They would reopen the road to Jerusalem and, once there, rid their sacred city of all infidels. For the peaceable travellers it was the *haj*, the journey to the shrines, but for the more warlike it was the *jihad*, the Holy War with a strong sword arm.

The first public call to Crusade was preached on 27 November 1095, and the momentous harangue was made not in a great cathedral, a palace or an abbey, but from a wooden scaffolding stage erected in an open field. The town of Clermont, almost exactly in the centre of France, simply did not have a building large enough to hold the immense multitude which assembled to listen to the tall, bearded orator. Pope Urban II was himself French and, in his mid-fifties, at the height of his powers. Born Odo de Lagery and educated close to the home of his noble family at the cathedral school in Rheims, his career in the Church had been dazzling as well as exemplary. First canon, then archdeacon of Rheims cathedral, he was not yet 30 when he had made the significant decision to join the Cluniac Order who, in the words of Sir Steven Runciman, the outstanding historian of the Crusades, 'regarded themselves as the keepers of the conscience of western Christendom.'*

The crowd was told that they and all 'worshippers of Christ', present and absent, should consider setting forth in order to open the road to Jerusalem. Anyone who lost his life on the venture, either on land or sea or in battle against the infidel, would win forgiveness for his sins. This was the Pope's solemn promise. Appealing to the quarrelsome warlords, he asked 'those who have previously been fighting wrongfully in private strife' now to turn their energies to combat against the infidel. 'Let those

---

* The first volume of Runciman's three-part and magisterial *History of the Crusades* is devoted entirely to the First Crusade.

who now have been brigands,' he went on, 'become soldiers for Christ,' and 'let those who once were mercenaries for sordid hire now win eternal rewards.' With all the fervour of a revivalist meeting the Pope called on his audience to pledge themselves to the cause. There were cries from the audience of 'God Wills It!' and a leading bishop of the area, Adhémar, the Bishop of Le Puy, publicly stepped forward 'with a radiant face' and, bending his knee, asked permission to go. The Pope blessed him and announced that the Bishop would lead the host. A great fervour swept through the crowd. Volunteers thrust forward announcing they would join the movement. A messenger arrived, unexpectedly it was claimed, from a splendid grandee, Raymond of Saint Gilles, the Count of Toulouse and one of the richest men in France. The Count was hastening to the assembly, the messenger announced, and would join the great enterprise. Those who had taken the pledge began tearing up strips of cloth and sewing them in the shape of a cross to their clothes as an outward symbol of their resolve.

Probably much of this was stage-managed: the appeal was carefully planned for the final day of the Clermont conference after the more abstruse business of the clergy was out of the way. Holy wars against the Muslims were already being waged in Spain and Sicily with papal encouragement, and the previous Pope had even toyed with the idea of leading an army of 50,000 to Jerusalem. Pope Urban must have discussed the notion of a Crusade with his Churchmen and nobles long before he clambered up on the stage at Clermont. The planning was too careful for it to have been a newly-minted idea, and the timing was too apt. The speech was made in late autumn and the journey, said the Pope, was to begin the following summer. This would give the warriors – and he meant the warlords – 'time to put their affaris in order and collect what is needful for their expenditure.'

Significantly, one word never mentioned was the word 'crusade'. This was a term which later generations came to use retrospectively as a convenient way to describe the campaign for Christendom. In 1095 the Pope called on the faithful only to go on a great journey to the Holy Land in the service of the Church, and to expect to have to fight en route. Many of his hearers would talk of 'taking the cross' but never of 'crusade'. Their usual expression was simply that they would be taking 'The Way of God' and it is clear that to peasant and noble alike the path was both symbolic and real. It was the road to Jerusalem, a pilgrim's road, and the journey would not just save the Holy City, but also the travellers themselves.

CHAPTER 3

Mystery

Where was Duke Godfrey in all this? It's unlikely that he would have been at Clermont to hear the great speech. Instead, like most other nobles, Godfrey seems to have learned of the Pope's message by some mysterious sort of bush telegraph which carried news of the speech up and down the 'Kingdom of the Franks' so that it reached castles and towns in a matter of weeks. At this point something very remarkable happened: the nobility – and the commonalty as we shall see – responded in droves. Those who had bickered and squabbled now seemed to be gripped by a herd instinct. When one baron or count or duke decided to take up the cross, then his neighbour felt obliged to do the same. A chain reaction rippled through the highest level of society. The list of aristocratic subscribers to the crusade grew so rapidly during the winter months that it is impossible to keep track of just why or when each man decided to join the march to Jerusalem, until the final roll call drew from nearly every leading family of the continent.

Four major armies were eventually created. Two of these corps were raised in France, one in southern Italy, and the fourth, largely German speaking, was recruited in the northeast and followed the banner of Godfrey of Bouillon. The strategy was that, like rivulets emerging from the melting snows of winter, the minor barons and seigneurs and knights would leave in spring from their scattered fortresses and castles, and bring their individual contingents of followers and materials to their immediate overlords. In turn these forces would link up with a major commander such as Godfrey. As each army began the great journey, its route would take in other large bodies of volunteers so that eventually the four armies, like major rivers joining together, would unite in Constantinople for the Christmas of 1096 and offer their swords in the service of Emperor Alexius. He, it was optimistically – and inaccurately – felt, would then sally forth from his splendid city with his own Byzantine army and lead the combined Host all the way to the liberation of Jerusalem.

The plan was breathtakingly self-confident. It proposed a journey of at least a year's duration, with the final third of the distance certain to be contested by Turks and Arabs, known to be fiercely committed adversaries. No one had any experience of a military adventure of such length and complexity, and no one could foretell its chances of success. The First Crusade was an act of faith and hope, and of ignorance too, and the measure of the uncertainty involved was the caution displayed by those who had too much to lose. No king volunteered to join the army. The monarchs of France, England and Germany were noticeable by their absence. Prudently they stayed at home to look after their realms, as did many of the great landowners. So this was a venture mostly for younger brothers, the cadet sons, men without obvious preferment, the expendable members of a quarrelsome society. There were notable exceptions, however, the Ardennes family among them. Perhaps Ida of Bouillon, by then a dowager in her fifties, egged them on, or maybe it was from a spirit of family solidarity, but surprisingly all three sons of Eustace au Grenon – Eustace the Older, Duke Godfrey, and Baldwin the Younger – took up the cross. In terms of medieval family heritage it was an extraordinary commitment. Their action stripped their family of all its immediate male heirs.

The Pope's plan allowed six months for the nobles to prepare for the journey, and in this time Duke Godfrey had a great deal to arrange. The monks of the abbey at Afflighem record how Godfrey and Baldwin appeared at their cloisters as they crisscrossed their possessions recruiting troops and trying to raise cash for the coming journey by whatever means possible – selling valuables, calling in debts, disposing of land, raising loans. Bullion was the real need. Gold was a very scarce metal in Europe at that time so silver, in ingots or coins minted especially for the trip, was the most practical way to pay travelling expenses on the road to Jerusalem. A great lord like Godfrey was essentially the sponsor

27

for hundreds if not thousands of followers, and his costs would be enormous, the equivalent of at least three years' ducal income. It has been said cynically that the Jerusalem venture was a chance for the warlords to plunder and get rich. But for the majority it was quite the reverse. It was a cripplingly expensive endeavour, and swallowed up a great lord's inheritance. Godfrey raised money with reckless abandon. He sold the county of Verdun, together with the income of the fiefs of Stenay and Mouzay, to the Archbishop of Verdun, and — the supreme sacrifice — raised the huge sum of 1300 marks of fine silver by selling his family chateau of Bouillon to the Bishop Othbert of Liege, a prelate notorious for his good business sense and ruthless methods.

Nine centuries later, the problems of preparing such a journey by horse were somewhat different, but no less challenging. There was, for example, the difficulty of finding the correct saddle for the journey. I wanted to try using a saddle that was as close as possible to an eleventh century knight's, which, according to the history books, had a high pommel in front and cantle behind to hold the rider in place. The nearest equivalent still in use, that I could identify, was the saddle used by the *gardiens*, the cattle herders, in the Camargue region of southern France. Indeed their saddles are said to have been developed from the medieval knight's war saddle and this seemed logical as the *gardiens* prod along the cattle with long poles like medieval lances, so their saddles are designed for exactly the same action as a knight on a charger. But when I went to the Camargue to investigate I found that the Camargue horses were mere shrimps by comparison to an Ardennes horse and that I would have to have a specially broad saddle made to fit Carty. I produced a photograph of Carty and showed it to a Camargue saddle-maker, explaining that his saddle would be used to ride an Ardennes horse on the road to Jerusalem. The saddler promised to make the saddle as wide as the saddle tree would allow, but was still very doubtful. 'Poor wretch! Poor wretch!' he murmured. I thought at the time he was referring to Carty, but was subsequently to conclude that he could equally have been thinking of the discomfort of the rider.

My library research gradually built up a sheaf of notes compiled from my readings of Crusade history and a distinct feeling that Crusader literature was a bottomless pit. There were literally hundreds of learned articles, shelf after shelf of weighty volumes, and new books and studies were promised or being produced at such an alarming rate that I began to feel that unless I got started on the journey itself, I would be swallowed up in a publishing morass. I pursued several promising but ultimately unsatisfactory avenues. For example, I could not find out whether the Crusaders had shod their horses, though it seemed likely that the more valuable horses wore metal shoes to protect their hooves, and – worryingly – the timing of Godfrey's departure appeared inept. The chronicles said that he was on the road by mid-August but that seemed very late in the season. Indeed, his army corps only reached Constantinople just before Christmas and must have suffered from bad weather. I wanted to be on the road in late spring to allow plenty of spare time for mishaps and learning the technique of cross-country travel on horseback. Yet by January all I had, besides my notes, maps and a Camargue saddle on order, was the promised delivery to my home in southwest Ireland of one fat, untrained, unshod, and untried Ardennes Heavy Horse.

Carty came to my home by a roundabout route. I had to wait until a succession of bloodstock transport firms had empty lorries going in the right direction for different sections of the journey. The notion of such a large and blundering creature travelling as a 'part load' was inappropriate and, besides, Carty might have scared to hysterics the highly-strung racehorses such firms normally carried. So he travelled slowly and alone. With increasing impatience I traced his progress by a string of telephone calls from sundry stables and farms where he seemed to be having bed and breakfast in erratic stages.

'I *suppose* that's a horse,' said one sceptical voice. 'Though he's so big and ugly.'

'His pedigree is longer than any other animal you've ever carried,' I retorted huffily.

'For years I've been shifting horses,' reported another, 'and this is the first time my wife ever got out a camera and took a photograph of any of them.'

A missing health document meant a final layover on a farm near Maynooth fifteen miles outside Dublin and the home of Ireland's premier religious seminary. 'You don't suppose they're holding him for instruction,' teased a neighbour. 'Only Christian horses were allowed to go on the Crusade.'

29

Finally, in early February, Carty was dropped off at a stable in Killarney, fifty miles from home. That same day I drove over to see how he had weathered the journey. Standing in the back of a stall he looked nothing like the muddy comic creature I had first seen in Cecile's field. Someone had washed him, brushed his mane, and generally smartened him up. Quite simply he looked magnificent. Massive, barrel chested, his huge thick neck arched, and his tremendous head held proudly, he was majestic. He had been gelded at Bourbeau and was now the very image of the traditional Victorian etching of 'The Working Heavy Horse'. The only jarring note came from his head collar. Made of bright red canvas webbing it was the usual size for a normal horse. Naturally it was totally inadequate for Carty's gargantuan head. So someone had lengthened the webbing with bits of bright yellow baler twine. In effect, three-quarters of a ton of untrained animal was restrained by parcel string.

A farrier was summoned to put shoes on the monster, and there were disbelieving calculations as the size of the shoes was spelt out. Would the farrier please bring shoes nine inches in diameter? This was half as big again as anything he had in stock, and when the farrier arrived, Carty stood there placidly, looking puzzled as the farrier tugged futilely at a tree-trunk leg. There were quips about needing a hydraulic jack to lift up Carty's feet until the farrier, his reputation at stake, tapped him sharply on the fetlock with a heavy file to make him pay attention. There was no result. Finally, a shrewd kick in the same spot made Carty flinch, and the farrier took his chance to whip up the leg, and rapidly fit a shoe. Four times that happened, and each time the newly shod foot was dropped back on the floor with a metallic crash that made the onlookers wince.

'Let that land on your toe and you'll be heard all the way to Jerusalem,' muttered a voice.

The farrier departed. No one told me that the first time a difficult horse is shod, a deft farrier can get away with it by quickly putting on the shoes before the horse has really worked out what is happening. The second time, however, a cunning animal has learned the lesson, and if it is genuinely stubborn or wicked-minded then the fun really starts. Carty, as I was to discover, had the trouble-making capacity of a mischievous colossus.

I had chosen the Killarney stable because it was here I had found Mystery, Carty's future travelling companion. In theory seven-year-old

Mystery was to be the palfrey for my journey. A palfrey, according to the Oxford dictionary, was 'a saddle horse for ordinary riding, as distinct from a warhorse'. From my reading of the history books, it was evident that the travelling crusader preferred not to ride his warhorse as he went his way towards the Holy Land. Instead, the big horses were used as pack animals on the open road, and an eyewitness of the First Crusade reported how their packs were then removed before the fighting began. Presumably the knights donned their protective war armour, climbed into the war saddles and rode into the fray on the heavyweight chargers. At that, ignorant, stage in my research it seemed very logical. I supposed that the Heavy Horse was the load carrier because its strong back and tremendous muscles were designed for the job. To my cost I was to find that my thoughts did not go far enough. There was a much better reason to avoid riding a warhorse any distance.

Equally, I was naive enough to imagine that it would be easy to find my palfrey in Ireland, a land renowned for the quality of its riding horses. I soon learned differently. Horses suitable to go at a grinding pace day after day for at least 2,000 miles are not the staple product of a modern farm. A kindly friend in County Cork, a judge of Connemara ponies, began to make exhaustive enquiries for a transcontinental animal. She provided a list of the qualities to look for: the horse had to be small, had to give an easy ride if I was not to be saddle-sore, had to have good feet and strong bones, should be at least five years old, had to be docile in traffic (against the moment when some Balkan truck driver went whizzing past in his juggernaut leaving a six-inch gap), had to have stamina, had to have the temperament tough enough to undertake such a long ride, had to be an easy feeder and, not least, had to be one that I could afford. A humdrum animal of the type that I had first imagined would be a bone-shaker – 'no suspension' was the phrase – while a highbred animal was likely to run away on the road.

True to their professional tradition, local horse dealers promised paragons of equine virtue, and then produced appalling nags that even I could see were weedily unsuitable. I was taken to stables and shown horses that were limping before they left the loose box, to distant farms on the edge of peatlands where small leprechaun-like figures produced elegant leggy animals from ramshackle tin-roofed sheds and, like centaurs, put them through their paces before asking a fancy price. There were animals that were too big, too young, or had their coats clipped for hunting and could not be left out in a field. This was in addition to those creatures that seemed to be on the verge of expiring or suffering from an appalling selection of deformities or diseases, suspected, actual, and always vehemently denied by the possible vendor. My vocabulary expanded as I heard alarming words like bog spavin, glanders, staggers, and strangles. I came to understand that horses could suffer noisily from choking, roaring, wind-sucking and flatulent colic as well as quietly from constipation, diarrhoea, worms, ticks, leeches, and lice. The list was as endless as it was colourful, and I began to wonder who invented the phrase 'as strong as a horse'.

After some weeks someone finally suggested I might find the animal I was looking for at a trekking centre, where visitors hired horses to go on week-long rides. The nearest was in Killarney, and there I duly went with my horse-judging advisor to meet the proprietor.

Donie O'Sullivan proved to be one of those short, stocky, alert men who radiate energy from a compact mass. He also displayed a pace and agility of thought that makes one feel he is living one week ahead of anyone he is talking to, and nothing he said was to be taken lightly.

'What colour of horse do you want,' he flashed back at me when I asked if he had an animal to sell. It was no joke. Donie had recently sold a pair of spectacular piebalds to a German circus.

'I'm looking for a horse that can walk to Jerusalem.'

Now it was his turn to look stunned. But without a falter he suggested we should go to inspect his herd of trekking animals. It was a twenty-minute drive into the backlands because Donie stored them for the winter quite literally in a bog. When we arrived at the edge of the winter feeding grounds I could see nothing, just sedge, furze bushes, ponds of stagnant water and open space. Then Donie whistled four times, and out of the bushes ran a motley collection of nags in every assortment of size and shape. Uniformly scruffy and unkempt, to my inexperienced eye they looked as unprepossessing a group of horse flesh as one could wish. Only later did I learn that Donie knew exactly what conditions suited his tough trekking ponies and he kept them as fit and happy as riding horses pampered in the very finest of livery stables.

Squinting against the drizzle and blustery wind we peered over a sagging wire fence. All horse-buying, I reflected, seemed to be done in six inches of water on top of four inches of slime. Donie gave another piercing whistle and a further half dozen wild-looking animals came careering out of the furze, and began squabbling among themselves.

'There you are,' announced Donie expansively, 'pick the one you would like.'

It was his only slip. I turned to my expert friend, previously unknown to Donie. 'I like the look of that bay mare with the white blaze on her nose,' she said after a moment.

Donie looked thoughtful. When I got to know him better, he confessed that he was taken aback that my friend standing fifty yards away, from the other side of the fence, across a ditch, and on a wet miserable day had picked Mystery, the best horse in the bunch. Mystery was exceptional. Of all the horses in the trekking centre she was the one who could be used day after day after day, and never tire. Just fifteen hands high she was, claimed Donie, a walking machine. I bought her on the spot, trusting to luck and my friend's judgment, though I was warned that it was impossible to see what Mystery's hooves were like as they were sunk in the soggy peat. It was just as well. Some days later when Mystery was finally beached on dry land, it was revealed that she had the largest flattest feet for any horse of her size. Someone said unkindly that living in the bog had made her part-duck.

'Fat as a snail,' was Donie's succinct description of Carty as we inspected him once again in his stall. 'There's only one way for you to learn about him, and he to get to know you, and that's to break him yourself.'

Three days had passed since Carty's arrival, and I had come back to the stables to be told that he was making trouble. He had been getting restless and plunged in his stall when the training saddle was first put on his back. Everyone had rapidly scuttled out of the stall rather than share it with three-quarters of a ton of nervous Heavy Horse. Nor was Carty much better when we led him out. He porpoised across the stable yard with massive ungainly leaps, and for the first time we all understood just how strong he was. No number of powerful men could hold him back. Somewhere I had read that a robust Heavy Horse could pull seven or eight tons from a standing start. As I fumbled inexpertly with Carty's head collar, Donie's expression made it clear that perhaps his advice was

33

too optimistic. He had met enough ignoramuses at his trekking centre to know I knew next to nothing about horses. Indeed, I had very little experience with any animals. Most of my life had been connected with the sea and voyages on it, not with the land, and the only domesticated creature I remembered was my grandmother's cat.

Donie led Carty into a field and rigged up makeshift 'long reins', two 24-foot lengths of pale blue polypropylene farm rope leading through the stirrups of an old saddle and up to a bit in Carty's mouth. If Carty was looking and feeling nervous of this arrangement, his so-called 'trainer' standing behind him, ropes in hand, was feeling distinctly scared. I clicked my tongue, Carty started forward, and my worst fears were confirmed. It felt like being towed along by a Thames barge. The huge stern of the horse moved ahead of me, and when I accidentally flicked his haunch with the line, Carty twitched his skin and jumped nervously, 800 kilos of skittish power. I felt it was absurd that one was expected to control this lively behemoth with two ridiculous bits of bright blue rope I wouldn't have used to tie a small dinghy in a flat calm.

Carty plodded forward, and I meekly followed in his wake. He tried to turn left, out of the field. To correct him, I pulled on a rope – the wrong one. Carty began to panic, and so did I. The huge brute began to dance backwards at me. It was like a steam roller going into reverse, and I was standing in the wrong place. I tried heaving on the opposite rope. Even worse. Carty put his head down, and was feeling boxed in, entangled and unhappy. Behind him, I had precisely the same sensation. Whoa! Whoa! The nervousness in my voice was infectious. Carty got the message and trembled even more.

Donie appeared at my elbow and took the ropes. 'You've got him thinking he's in a corner,' he said. 'You must anticipate what he does, and make him do what you want to do. Never let him forget who's the master.' The trouble was that adolescent Carty, not me, was the boss.

We stumbled on. Gradually Carty settled into plodding round the circuit at a sedate pace. Gingerly I began to turn him, left and right without too much trouble, though it felt like steering a jumbo jet with a pair of puppet strings. Halting was more difficult. I pulled on both ropes at once. He continued to shamble forward, and I was simply towed through the mud by the taut ropes. The only way to halt him was to head him for a hedge or brick wall, and let him stop like a boat bumping its bow into a jetty. Worse came when I tried to walk him out through a gate and into the next field. He nervously twisted away with a tremendous squelching slide that would have done justice to a panicked water buffalo. Three times I tried to take him through the gate and three times I failed ignominiously. Trying not to smile, Donie took over. He drove Carty up to the gate, lined him up straight, and with a deft flick of both wrists sent the lines snapping against the massive haunches. Carty leapt forward in near-panic, shot through the gap, and Donie went hurtling after him and I was quietly pleased to hear, even from the maestro, those now-familiar cries of Whoa, there! Steady! Steady!

I was amazed how quickly Carty learned. Next morning he was obedient as a herded goose – turning surely and ponderously in response to twitches on the blue ropes. Nor was he any trouble with the saddle, and emerged from the stable without the previous commotion. He got his carrot as a reward, and within half an hour was in the habit of nudging me with his head looking for a titbit. It was like being shunted with the bucket of a mechanical dredger, but I felt that there was some hope. Carty was an intelligent horse, and there might yet be time to part-train him before setting out in late spring to ride to the Holy Land. The rest of his education could take place on the road to Jerusalem.

In late February I moved the two horses to my own village, where a local farmer generously lent me a field while I continued with Carty's training and general preparation. One of my difficulties was that there was very little information to be gleaned about trans-continental riding. I had found exactly the same gap with building and sailing historic boats: the knowledge of how to make long journeys with the original means of transport had been lost. Those who once travelled great distances rarely wrote down the practical details because they seemed so obvious. Day-to-day techniques were a part of their lives, and certainly they did not expect anyone else to have to study them. Yet I now needed to have some forewarning about the problems of how to feed the horses, what speed to ask them to travel at, what to carry in the way of equipment, and so forth.

The best modern account was still the classic book *Southern Cross to Pole Star* written in 1933 by an English schoolmaster, Aimé Tschiffley, who had ridden two horses 10,000 miles from Buenos Aires in Argentina to Washington. It was heartening to learn that his two animals were a

35

pair of unprepossessing but very tough local horses, aged 15 and 16, who had survived the two-and-a-half-year journey very well. With their 'sturdy legs, short thick necks, and Roman noses', Tschiffley wrote, they were 'as far removed from the points of a first class English hunter as the North Pole from the South'. But it was also clear to me that riding across the Americas in the 1930s was rather less complicated than riding across modern, industrialised Europe some 50 years later. Tschiffley had found farms, dirt tracks, stables, and been able to send hay ahead along his route by train. I anticipated that my journey would divide into two sectors: the first across Belgium, Luxembourg, Germany and as far as the Austrian border with Hungary would involve the problems of the modern world – motorways, border crossings, lack of stabling, few fields. The second, from Hungary to Jerusalem through Yugoslavia, Bulgaria, Turkey, Syria and Jordan would be closer to the original conditions and, paradoxically, easier for the horses. I discovered that two French sisters by the name of Coquet had successfully ridden to Israel in 1974, though their notable achievement was not entirely comparable to my own plans as they had ridden 'ordinary' horses and followed the most convenient route. I wanted to stick to the authentic trail of Duke Godfrey and his army, and this would mean wandering far off the accepted beaten track. Reading Evelyne Coquet's *Riding to Jerusalem*, I noted that although their experience of horses far exceeded anything I could hope to acquire, one of their horses had still very nearly died of exhaustion in Turkey, and both riders had suffered various falls, kicks and accidents.

During the long wait for Carty to arrive from Bourbeau I had been trying to pinpoint the correct transcontinental path to take. Duke Godfrey and his colleagues had followed the best road system of their day – the road network that the Romans had built. Luckily there were quite detailed archaeological maps of the Roman roads, and it was a simple matter to transpose the medieval route on to a modern map. But historical details of how the medieval traveller looked after his horses were much harder to find, and I was obliged to turn to the magnificently authoritative manual, *Animal Management*, prepared in 1908 by the Veterinary Department and issued to a British Army still dependent on horse transport. It distilled centuries of wartime use of horses and made thought-provoking reading. Chapter V told about 'foods, feeding and watering'; Chapter VI about 'the management of horses in the open, condition and exercise, marching, feeding, swimming, watering and picketing'; Chapter VII discussed 'Saddles and sore backs, collars and sore shoulders' and Chapter X told me how to manage 'the mule, donkey, camel and ox' if I should be driven to such expedients. What became apparent as I read of all the possible mishaps and afflictions that could befall the cavalry charger was that the armies, whether in 1908 or 1096, depended on having ample remounts. If a horse went lame or got sick, then it was changed with a spare from the available stock that accompanied the army. I, on the other hand, had just two animals and could not afford to let either of them fall by the wayside. Even a minor delay caused by, say, a saddle sore could hold up the journey for a fortnight, and throw all my calculations of distances and speeds into turmoil. It was becoming more and more obvious to me that I was going to need the help of someone who knew how to look after horses a great deal better than I did, if Mystery and Carty were to get even half the way to Jerusalem. But where to find someone with the essential skills, as well as the spare time and the inclination to accompany me on such a trek, I had no idea.

The same week that I moved Carty and Mystery to my village I happened to visit a new gourmet restaurant that had opened nearby. For company I took along a copy of Runciman's book and, as I was later told, I made a distinctly strange customer, arriving alone to read by candlelight. The observation was made by a small, slight, and very attractive young woman who ran the restaurant with her sister. Sarah had curly, dark brown hair cut short, large blue-grey eyes in a lively face, quick movements, and when she smiled, which was often, two deep dimples appeared. In her early twenties, she looked barely a teenager but I was soon aware that she took an impish delight in launching sharp barbs of sarcastic wit at anyone who underestimated her. As the proper hostess she came across to chat to me and when she told me that she had grown up with a succession of ponies and horses, I ventured to ask if she would come to look at the two horses and perhaps give me a hand with exercising them. For the fun of it, Sarah agreed to help with Carty and Mystery in the daytime hours before the restaurant opened for dinner. I didn't know how lucky I was. Sarah was not just to help me prepare the animals. She was to ride all the way to Jerusalem, though more by default than planning. Somehow, once she became involved with the project, she never seemed to find the right moment to break off. She would promise to stay on for 'another week or maybe two' and as the weeks turned into months, she became indispensible. She was the other partner in the team. Inevitably someone, noting her boyish look, remarked that I seemed to have found a page if not a squire. In view of her crisp, down-to-earth wit, it would have been more apt to think of her more as a Sancho Panza to my bemused Quixote.

Sarah's introduction to the two horses next morning was typical of the difference in our experience of horse handling. Carty and Mystery had been left in the field by themselves for three days, and in the interval Carty had reverted to his semi-wild state, boosted by a sense of power as he realised that he was much bigger and stronger than Mystery. A neighbour, going for a ride past the field, reported that Carty was charging up and down, snorting and kicking up clods of mud. Gingerly I went to investigate and climbed into the field. I had not gone ten yards when Carty saw me and reverted to pure warhorse. He whirled round and charged, hurtling straight for me at a gallop, legs flying. The sheer noise of his enormous hooves slapping into the soft ground was awesome. For a moment I didn't think he would either want to stop or be able to do so. In fact his nerve broke before mine did, and he suddenly – to my great relief – locked his feet in the mud. His huge bulk came to a lunging halt, inches away, and a splatter of mud swept over me. Then he turned sharply and let out a ponderous kick in my direction. If it had connected, I would have been knocked senseless but the movement was too slow and, it seemed, Carty was not accustomed to in-fighting. Anyone could have pictured the terrifying rush of a dozen Cartys in a medieval charge. No line of footmen, armed with axe or pike, could possibly have withstood the shattering impact. It was a glimpse of history. The real weapon in such battles was not the relatively puny knight with his lance or sword or spear, but the bodyweight of the heavy horse that smashed and trampled down the opposing infantry line.

All the while Mystery had been looking on. It was quite evident who was the boss horse. In three days the bulky Ardennes had learned the tricks of the trade that Mystery, scrabbling for existence with Donie's trekking ponies in the bog, had acquired over the years. It was not a question of technique so much as brute strength. When I offered Mystery some food and Carty came over to intervene, she laid back her ears, swung he hindquarters and waited until Carty got within range. Then, at precisely the best distance for maximum effect, Mystery lashed out with both rear feet. It was a vicious double kick delivered with all her strength, and it landed right on target. Mystery's hooves struck Carty in the chest with a cracking double thump that would have rocked a horse of ordinary dimensions. But Carty didn't even seem to notice. He stood there as if nothing had happened. Mystery dropped her head in defeat and gave ground. She knew it was useless to push an Ardennes around.

I snared Carty, buckled his new extra strength head collar on him, and attached him to a telegraph pole. But Mystery was impossible to catch. She ran away whenever I tried to get near her, and I was standing, exhausted, when Sarah arrived. She climbed over the gate, and looking like an elf in her jodphurs and boots, walked straight across the field to the disgruntled and recalcitrant Mystery. A few words, a scratch by the ears, and Mystery, who had eluded me all morning, was safely wearing her head collar and as docile as could be.

Step by step Sarah and I began to train the two horses to work together. For the first week of a grey, blustery March we merely walked around the country roads, taking it in turns to drive Carty along on his silly blue ropes. It was a hair-raising experience because we were rushing his education at a crazy pace, and were expecting this juvenile, immense animal to learn in a few days what would normally require months of careful education. We exposed him to motorbikes, braying donkeys in fields, school buses in narrow lanes, birds bursting out of hedgerows, all in the first week. Sometimes the results were dramatic. When Carty bolted, as he sometimes did, we went skimming down the roads behind him, as he thundered along with a tremendous pounding clatter from his hooves, and sparks striking up from the shoes, completely out of control. Hanging on to the ropes was like skiing downhill as a complete beginner.

Mystery found the whole process no less fraught. The first few times she went out in Carty's company she broke into a nervous sweat, and eyed his huge bulk with great agitation. He had a habit of swerving around the narrow lanes and pushing her into the ditch with his mass. Plucking up courage she would turn and bite him, or pull faces, but he rarely noticed. Mystery eventually learned that self-protection was her only course of action, and she had to skip nimbly out of the way of those ungainly nine-inch feet that flapped in all directions.

At the end of the first week we decided it was time to mount Carty. Prudently we made the attempt in a soft muddy field, and, as the person with the experience, Sarah volunteered to be the first to try. Carty stood there, as she grabbed a stirrup and climbed into the saddle. Carty made not the slightest reaction. It was as if Sarah did not exist. Sitting up on his back, Sarah looked even tinier than usual. 'I don't think he's even noticed I'm up here,' she complained, slightly miffed that there had been no fireworks. I said nothing, knowing that she would not care to be reminded of Aesop's fable when the butterfly, alighting on an ox's back, finally announced that it was leaving. But the ox had not noticed the butterfly's arrival at all, and the butterfly finished up by yelling in the ox's ear to get any attention whatsoever.

It had already become apparent that Carty did exactly what he decided, and ignored virtually any outside influence. He was incredibly strong-willed. In the hopes of making him fit, I drew up an exercise programme that steadily increased his daily mileage, but the daily distances completely depended on his whims. He refused to travel any farther than he thought necessary, and once he made up his mind there was very little that his rider could do. He stopped one day in the middle of the road and stood there for forty minutes, refusing to budge while Sarah bounced up and down and thrashed him with her whip until she was exhausted. Carty didn't even turn his head.

Even worse was trying to shoe him, and the second time Carty went to the blacksmith was a pantomime. As we arrived at the local forge the junior farrier took one look at the job and wisely remembered another engagement. He departed, leaving the task to Billy, the senior man who had been shoeing horses for more than half a century, and had long experience of dealing with the big Irish draught horses. But even he found the young Ardennes a nightmare. After four hours of frustration, Billy threw down his tools with a final curse. He had applied just two shoes and that, said Billy, was enough. He wasn't going to continue unless we rigged up some sort of block and tackle and literally hauled Carty's feet off the ground. It was that or throw the animal on its back, sit on its head, and put the shoes on feet that were held up in the air. Carty had learned his lesson from the previous shoeing, and for all his massive bulk and chunky appearance, he was a contortionist when it came to trying to get his foot free from the blacksmith's grasp. Once his hoof was up, he would begin to bend the opposite leg until he was almost kneeling, pressing his entire weight on the blacksmith's back, until finally the whole ensemble threatened to tip up. Rather than risk being squashed, the blacksmith had to drop his foot and with a tremendous clatter Carty would lurch back on his feet and look round triumphantly. It was useless to lose one's temper. Later I was to see an enraged Yugoslav farrier clout him on the ribs with the flat of a massive file. The blow made a hollow boom as it caromed off Carty's ribs, but the horse didn't even flinch. Once again, I thought, there was a historic lesson to be learned. Most normal horses would turn and bolt if they were struck by an arrow. But an Ardennes seemed to be capable of soaking up any amount of punishment. No wonder there were reports that the medieval warhorses emerged from battlefields with so many arrows sticking out of them they looked like hedgehogs.

Quite what I would do about shoeing Carty on the long journey towards Jerusalem, I did not know. Probably I would have to learn to do the job myself, but having seen his displays at the smithy I did not relish the thought of wrestling with Carty along the roadside. The army manual asserted that a set of shoes on a cavalry mount should last three to four weeks, and they had to be a special heavy weight grade, half an inch thick. But this was only an estimate. The actual wear and tear depended on quality of the road surface, the particular walking action of each horse, and how much cross country work was done. I calculated that each of our horses would need eight or nine sets of shoes. I also had been warned that good quality shoes were impossible to find beyond Austria, while the huge nine-inch shoes that Carty needed would have to be ordered specially from England, together with oversize nails to go with them. By these figures the stock of spare horse shoes would weigh over quarter of a ton. There again the original Crusaders had an advantage. Such a large body of horsemen would have been able to travel with their own farriers and blacksmiths, making and fitting replacement horseshoes as they needed them.

Through the rest of March and well into April, Sarah and I slogged on. Gradually we lengthened each day's ride, from just five miles, to ten miles, and then to the target figure of twenty miles in a day. At first Carty in his baby fat found the going very tough. Within a mile he rapidly worked up a sweat which drenched his coat and turned him a much darker red. But then he began to shed the fat, and his muscles started to show. His great fat stern changed profile as it became more heart-shaped, and he lost his portly belly while the coat began to grow lighter in colour so that the two splotches of raspberry pink stood out on his hocks almost garishly.

Finally time ran out. It was nearly the end of April and I intended that the journey should start from Chateau Bouillon on 2 May. My plan was to transfer the horses to the Chateau in a horse trailer towed by a jeep. We would cross by ferry from Ireland to France, stop off at Bourbeau to see Cecile, and be at Chateau Bouillon in time for a brief departure ceremony arranged by the town's tourist board. It was all neatly planned and I thought I had allowed ample time for loading the horses into the transport. During our excursions around the backroads we had used the trailer several times to recover the horses and bring them back home at the end of the day. Sometimes Carty was obstinate about entering the trailer, sometimes he would be reasonable. What we did learn was that if he didn't want to walk up the ramp, there was no force on this side of a bulldozer that would oblige him to do so. So at noon on 26 April we parked the trailer in the village street. It was a Sunday, a beautiful day, and all the villagers had turned out to see us off. People were wishing us luck, admiring the horses, handing in goodwill messages. Then the crowd waited expectantly to see us load up and leave. It was the ideal opportunity for Carty to show off. He knew something strange was happening, and he became pig-headed.

While Mystery watched with increasing nervousness, Carty refused to walk up the ramp. We tried to bribe him. A trail of food was dribbled out, leading up the ramp. He snuffled his way up it until he came to the top and then turned around and walked back. We repeated the technique until he had consumed a complete feed. We tried to wheedle him in with promises and sweet talk. He refused. We tried to cajole him. It was useless. We brought a huge rope from the harbour jetty and with four men each side tried to sweep him in. He simply swerved at the last moment and walked off down the village street with eight sturdy men being dangled along behind him like dolls. We were bombarded with advice. There were men in the crowd who were horse dealers. They tried their tricks — whistling, soft talk, blindfolding Carty who promptly tripped on the ramp with a crash that nearly ripped it off its hinges. There were men who regularly loaded and drove cattle lorries. They too tried their methods, waving brooms, flicking water on his rump, shifting the trailer so it stood on a downhill slope next to a wall. I forbade the use of electric cattle prods. Every single ruse was a complete failure. Carty refused to walk into the horse box, and loved every minute of the attention he was getting. He was, as Sarah observed, a horse who adored human company, and putting on a circus show in front of the intrigued crowd was his idea of bliss. Finally when the crowd had got bored and begun to drift away, he looked round, noted that he had overstayed his time, and on his own, without any coaxing, calmly walked up into the box and stood there. I could have sworn he had a smug look on his face. We closed up the tail gate at the double and I looked once again at the time. It had taken six hours to load one warhorse. At that rate it would take us a decade to get to Jerusalem.

CHAPTER 4

The Peasants' Crusade

'What a sweet and wonderful sight it was for us to see all those shining crosses, whether of silk or gold or other stuff that at the Pope's order the pilgrims, as soon as they had sworn to go, sewed on the shoulders of their cloaks, their cassocks or their tunics,' wrote an enthusiastic priest, Fulcher of Chartres. He is a key figure in the story of the Crusade because he actually heard the Pope speak at Clermont and himself decided to 'take the cross'. Starting out with the army corps forming in Northern France, he marched with them to what is now central Turkey. There he switched to the entourage of Baldwin, Godfrey's younger brother, and eventually became his chaplain. A small-town priest of modest education, Fulcher was an excellent eyewitness and, most important, he had a kindly sympathy for the experiences endured by the common people on the crusade. Through his vivid account of experiences on the way to Jerusalem, we realise how the great journey often became a nightmare for the ordinary folk. Some were to call it 'the new way of penance'.

These commoners reacted even more fervently to the crusade message than the nobility. In their thousands the peasantry also began to sell off their possessions to raise money for the trip. Guibert, Abbot of Nogent who had also been at the Council of Clermont but stayed behind in France and later wrote a history of the Crusade, noted how 'the poor were soon inflamed with so burning a zeal that none stopped to consider the slenderness of his means, neither whether it was wise for him to leave his house, his vines and his fields; and each set about selling the best things he had for a price much less than if he had found himself cast into the most cruel captivity.' The result was a crash in commodity prices as the markets were flooded with peasants' goods for sale. The value of a sheep dropped to under a denier, less than a sixth of its usual price. Guibert was sarcastic:

Truly astonishing things were to be seen, things which could not but provoke laughter; poor people shoeing their oxen as though they were horses, harnessing them to two wheeled waggons on which they piled their scanty provisions and their small children, and which they led along behind them.

This was not at all what the Pope had intended. He wanted trained fighting men to take the road to Jerusalem, not parties of civilians with their families. The papal secretariat had drafted letters carefully setting out a sensible plan for the crusade and sent them to responsible authorities such as city councils, assemblies of nobles, and bishops. Thus, monks and priests were not to go unless 'authorised by the bishop or abbot to whom they are subordinate', while 'newly married men may not take the cross without their wives' consent.' Other categories to be discouraged were the very old, men unfit to carry weapons, and women without husbands or guardians. By extension, it seems that family women were expected to join the march. Many did so, and were to play a prominent role in the later tribulations (as well as becoming scapegoats to the fire-and-brimstone priests who blamed them for causing the same sufferings). The truth was that once Pope Urban had preached his sermon, the matter was no longer under his control. The crusading message was taken up by all manner of fanatics, and self-appointed heralds began to spread their own version of his call among the lay people.

Chief of these was an itinerant preacher known as Peter the Hermit. He seems to have been one of the swarm of holy men who normally wandered from village to village, preaching to the simple peasants and attending to their spiritual needs. Runciman described him as 'a man of short stature, swarthy and with a long, lean face, horribly like the donkey that he always rode and which was revered almost as much as himself. He went barefoot, and his clothes were filthy. He ate neither bread nor meat, but fish, and he drank wine. Despite his lowly appearance he had the power to move men.'

This bizarre figure, wandering through northeast France, dressed in a

Peter the Hermit (right) on his – alleged – pilgrimage to Jerusalem dreams he is told to appeal to the Pope (left) to free the Holy Places from the Muslims.

long homespun cloak with a cowl, preached the Crusade in terms that the lay people could understand at once. Peter brandished a letter that he claimed had fluttered down from heaven, a missive direct from God that gave him authority to lead a host to the Holy Land. He asserted that he had already made the pilgrimage to Jerusalem and seen the shrines in all their defilement and neglect. In the Church of the Holy Sepulchre he had fallen into a sleep of despair and dreamed that Christ was standing over him and saying 'Rise, Peter, make haste and do without fear the tasks which have been entrusted to you, for I shall be with you. It is time that the holy places were purged . . .' This story was false. Peter had never been to Jerusalem. But his yarn was precisely the right approach to sway his credulous audience. They came to believe that Peter the Hermit, not the Pope, had devised the idea of the Crusade. Common folk flocked to him in droves, and followed him as he moved across Picardy and into Lower Lotharingia. He was so respected, observed Guibert sourly, that the ignorant plucked the hairs from his mount and kept them as sacred relics. By the time Peter reached Cologne to preach his Easter message there, he was leading a crusading force in its own right.

So while the great lords were still making their calculations about the amount of bullion they would need, drafting wills, deciding whom to appoint as guardians for their estates and children while they were away, and salving their consciences at the last minute by making gifts to religious foundations they had wronged during the earlier civil troubles, Peter and his followers stole a march on them. In April 1096 he was ready to set out for the Holy Land, three months before the nobles' contingents, and there was no one to restrain him. A handful of knights were equally soon prepared, and they provided a military core to stiffen the Peasants' Crusade, as it would come to be known. But the humble vanguard's real driving force was its fervour. They spoke of heavenly signs and manifestations, and interpreted them as divine portents that something strange and wonderful was going to happen. A great shower of meteorites had fallen in the spring of 1095, and the following February, while Peter was crossing Picardy, the moon turned red during an eclipse. The next month a great aurora appeared around the sun and the sight sent panicky congregations into the churches to pray. Seers and mystics dreamed visions of the New Jerusalem, of the millennium, and bloody conflagration. There were rumours that the sign of the cross was mysteriously appearing, etched into men's skins. In one village the population followed a goose, saying it was divinely inspired and would lead to the Holy Land. In another hamlet the pathfinder was a goat. The harvest, which had been bad for some years promised to be exceptionally good, a bumper crop. The Lord was already rewarding the faithful.

The atmosphere was ripe for hysteria, and when the crusading zeal boiled over the first victims were the Jewish populations. Why go all the way to Jerusalem to revenge oneself on Christ's enemies, the firebrands asked. The Jews had been responsible for the death of Christ and could be punished nearer to home. Jew-baiting was soon followed by robbery of Jewish homes and then by outright massacres in France. In Germany sundry warbands roamed the countryside, pillaging and looting, with the excuse of the crusade as their cover. Gradually they passed southward across the country like a wandering nightmare and reached Regensburg, the great trading city on the upper Danube and the gateway to the main corridor leading to Constantinople. There the Jewish population, cowed by reports of the atrocities further north, agreed to a mass conversion to Christianity.

One Jewish source accuses a 'duke of Lower Lotharingia' of abetting the pogroms. This could well have been Godfrey, although other Jewish sources say nothing on the subject. Godfrey seems to have been more interested in Jewish money, not deaths, for he arranged loans from the Jews of Mainz and Cologne to help pay his crusading costs. During most of the winter Godfrey dropped out of view as he made his preparations such as settling some minor matters with the monks of the abbey of Saint Hubert nearby Chateau Bouillon. Ida had given them land, and Godfrey had to confirm his mother's gift before he set out for Constantinople. In these legal and business matters younger brother Baldwin would have been a help. Extremely intelligent, he had originally been destined for a career in the church. He had therefore received a clerical training and could read and write. Whether Godfrey was literate we do not know, but under the circumstances this was not as important as his skill with languages. He spoke both French and German, and needed to be bilingual because his army corps was thoroughly polyglot. It included Walloons, Germans, French and Flemish, and they were to be joined by men from Swabia and Bavaria. The babel of tongues and dialects must have caused chaos in the military council, run by the chief nobles, that directed the endeavour.

Many of the leading warriors came from Godfrey's own duchy or the surrounding countries. Some of them did undoubtedly set out because they were bored and craved excitement or they had thoughts of material gain, to profit by lands and plunder. But the pious Godfrey was no freebooter, and many of Godfrey's knights must have joined up because they believed in the papal mission and were obeying their feudal instincts. Here, in company they knew and respected, was a cause worth fighting for, and here already was the first glimmer of the notion of chivalry, the ideal of knightly self-sacrifice in God's service. For a century the Church had castigated the knights for their unruly violence, begging them to turn their swords to a higher cause, and now it promised them rewards in heaven if they went on the mission to Jerusalem. There was a romantic streak, too. Minstrels and troubadours were beginning to eulogise the selfless deeds of warriors, often borrowing and adapting material from early folk tales, and here now was a great and real adventure. It offered all the scope of a major war epic overlaid with the colour and glamour of travel to foreign lands. It would need a hero, and one candidate was the noble duke who rode at the head of the contingent from the north.

No one knows precisely how many people were in Godfrey's army. The only figures we have are wild exaggerations, ranging into the hundreds of thousands. More realistic calculations suggest that he may have started with 1000 knights and 7000 foot, plus several times that number of noncombatants who were taking advantage of the presence of the warriors to go on the pilgrimage. Certainly the numbers were never stable. Additional groups joined up along the route, others dropped out, civilian elements were rarely taken into account and, besides, it was difficult to define whether a sturdy peasant armed with, say, a billhook was a footsoldier or a noncombatant. Normally the footsoldiers were armed with spears and axes and wore padded protective clothing. Archers carried the newfangled crossbow unknown in the distant lands, but there was no siege train. The striking arm of host, the element which held pride of place in every tactical discussion, was the cavalry. The mounted knight, as far as Godfrey's war council was concerned, was the sole arbiter of the battlefield.

Yet the knight's war equipment was still very crude. Elegant plate armour had not yet evolved, and an ordinary knight of Godfrey's household was prepared to ride into battle dressed simply in a long, supple shirt of chain mail, which reached down to his thighs. His helmet was a conical steel cap to deflect the downward slicing cut of a sword aimed at the head, with a long metal bar to guard the nose. Padded garments under the mail shirt absorbed the worst of a blow, but in general the knight was scarcely better protected than a well-equipped footsoldier. The cavalry weapon was great sword, a massive, plain iron, slashing weapon that needed a big, strong man and the height and balance of a well-seated horseman to swing it properly. His long-reach weapons, lance or even the throwing spear, were relatively ineffective. In the push and shove of battle the horse was the real weapon. Cavalry against cavalry, the quality of the horse was crucial. A fast animal was more manoeuvrable, but at close quarters killing range the advantage lay with the knight on the more stable platform, and that meant the bigger, sturdier Heavy Horse which would shoulder aside the opponent's animal, even knocking it off its feet, while the rider used both hands to swing his heavy sword and literally bludgeon his opponent to death or surrender. Infantry stood little chance. Nearly a ton of horse gave the knight the height advantage to hack downwards with his heavy sword; the horse could bring the knight quickly to the weakest point of the enemy's battleline and carry him away from the field when he was losing, so he could return to fight another day. No wonder the commoners loathed and feared the horse, called curses on the 'knights and all their horses', and in the language of the Crusaders, whether French or Italian or German, the words used for horseman or rider denoted a member of the ruling class in a society where might meant right.

In the summer of 1096, as Godfrey's army set out, every well-to-do baron or knight would have had his quota of squires and pages and retainers. Some were accompanied by their wives — Baldwin for instance took along his wife Godehilde of Tosny — others, such as the nobleman Henry d'Esch of Godfrey's household, had brothers in the same company. For the nobility it must have been a most agreeable progression, the column strung out over several days journey as it wound its way through the pleasant rolling German countryside. It was mid-August and the bumper harvest meant there was plenty of food for people and animals. The route passed through friendly lands where the aristocratic travellers could expect hospitality from the castellans, several of whom were waiting to join up. At the larger castles important leaders, such as Godfrey, would have been invited to stay. He and his barons had brought along their hawks and hounds, and there must have been much hunting and feasting along the way. The first steps of Godfrey's crusade must have felt more like a fête than a penance.

The travellers knew precisely where they were going. Indeed the army council could have consulted reasonably accurate maps of the route had they wished. Their path for the first three months had been trodden by generations of pilgrims and soldiers and merchants before them, and was described in a number of route guides. Schematic itineraries drawn out on long scrolls. At a glance the reader could see instantly how many miles lay ahead to the next city or way station, where the mountains would be met, where and when to expect to find the next river. Their road began by following the valley of the Rhine and its tributaries to the watershed with the Danube. Then it took the Danube corridor to a place called Vindabon, modern Vienna, where it cut across the Hungarian plain to rejoin the river near its junction with the Sava. Continuing to follow the Danube almost due south, the road did not branch off until it could use the corridor of its tributary, the Morava, to penetrate the Balkan mountains, and then strike southeast directly to Constantinople. Albert of Aix, the chronicler of Godfrey's army, didn't even bother to specify the route. It was so well known that he called it merely simply 'the way' or 'the right way'.*

* A canon of the church, Albert wanted to join the army, but for some reason had to stay behind. Perhaps he was refused his bishop's permission. He had to content himself with interviewing the returnees who gave up because they were sick, tired or disillusioned, or were despatched with messages and letters to the families waiting at home. Later he also included information from the veteran crusaders who stormed Jerusalem.

CHAPTER 5

Chateau Bouillon

With a lopsided horsebox Sarah and I arrived in Bouillon on 30 April, a grey and overcast day with occasional drizzle. Carty caused the slant as he weighed twice as much as Mystery. The jeep hauling the horsebox was tail down with an overload of camping gear, spare horse shoes, farrier's tools, emergency medicines for the horses, maps, buckets, coils of rope, historical reference books, and other paraphernalia. It was, I realised, all far too cumbersome and unwieldy. Even the file of veterinary documents with its multitude of certificates, customs forms, declarations of the health of the horses, results of laboratory tests on blood samples, made a book nearly three inches thick. But at that stage I had no idea of what equipment and papers would be necessary and what we could discard. I had written ahead to various riding clubs in Germany, Austria and Hungary, asking what to expect. But the answers had been inconclusive and, with the help of the Irish Veterinary Service and a local Irish vet, I had tried to cover all eventualities by assembling an impressive collection of affidavits, asserting that the horses were free from a galaxy of equine disease which I was sure few frontier officials would ever have encountered.

The plan was to spend the first month learning the techniques of cross-country travel as we rode through Belgium, Luxembourg and Germany. In the light of our experience, we would then trim our equipment. I anticipated that it was going to be difficult to find overnight stabling in the first sector of our journey as we would be crossing densely populated areas where the farming was highly intensive, and few farmers would have spare pasture or empty stables. To solve that problem, a second-hand lightweight moped was perched on a rack on the rear of the jeep. In theory I would drive forward every morning along our path with the jeep and locate a place for the horses at about twenty miles distant along the old Roman road. There I would arrange the overnight accommodation, leave the moped and return to where Sarah was preparing the horses. At the end of the day's ride I would collect the moped, ride back to the jeep where we had left it, and come forward with the equipment. It meant that I would have to cover every section of the road five times, once by horse, once by moped, and three times in the jeep. Clearly it was going to be very cumbersome and time-consuming, but I could see no other solution. A third person, just to drive the vehicle, would have had a very boring job and I wanted to keep our team as small as possible against the time when we were confident enough to leave behind the jeep and trailer and ride on alone.

On the way to Bouillon we made an overnight halt at Ferme du Bourbeau to let the horses stretch their legs, tell Cecile's family our news, and have new sets of horseshoes fitted in preparation for the serious riding. At Bourbeau nothing had altered. We arrived to the same chaos of dogs on chains, piglets, and Dédé looking exhausted from overwork. No one was getting much sleep because this was foaling time for the Ardennes mares, and there were twelve very pregnant mothers-to-be waiting in the barn, each standing with a rotund full belly and dreamy, faraway expression on her face behind the characteristic hairy forelock.

Cecile had arranged for her regular farrier to come to shoe Carty, and at seven-thirty next morning Monsieur Juillet arrived. Burly, with a shock of white hair, he was 70 years old but looked a very fit 60. His life story was that as the son of a farrier he had been apprenticed to his father but treated so harshly that he resolved to run away and enlist in the army. The very day he was old enough to volunteer without parental permission, he left the smithy, walked into the local army recruiting office and signed on. To his chagrin, after receiving basic training, he was immediately assigned to the French Army's farriery school. There he was taught all over again to shoe horses, this time the army way, and was then posted to a French cavalry depot where a team of farriers looked after the feet of 3000 cavalry horses.

Monsieur Juillet was, without the shadow of a doubt, the most experienced and professional farrier we were ever to encounter. He disapproved very strongly of shoeing *à la anglaise* as he called it, when the farrier works single-handed, holding the hoof, shaping the shoe and driving the nails all by himself. Too many young farriers in France were taking up the habit, Monsieur Juillet growled. It saved labour costs but you could never be sure of the work. The only proper way to shoe a horse was the continental method. One man held up the foot of the horse, while the master farrier trimmed the hoof, shaped the shoe and set each nail precisely. We began with Mystery and, holding up Mystery's foot, I had my first lesson in farriery, watching while Monsieur Juillet drove the nails. Then it was Carty's turn. We expected no difficulty. Monsieur Juillet had put shoes on thousands of Ardennes Horses, and Cecile's farm was specially equipped for the work. Next to the farmhouse stood a sturdy cage made of heavy iron bars deeply embedded in concrete. It was a set of Heavy Horse shoeing stocks. The idea was that the horse was driven into the cage and clamped in place so he could not budge while the farrier did the work. Coaxing Carty into the stocks was another matter altogether. Monsieur Juillet confidently took a hold on his head collar and led him forward. Carty immediately displayed his escape-artist tricks of the loading ramp, jerking away and refusing to be led. Monsieur Juillet calmly tried again. Once more Carty evaded him, and this time, with a quick snatch of his head, succeeded in bursting his head collar. Monsieur Juillet swore, and tried a third time. Once more Carty dodged. Cecile appeared, drawn by the commotion. A tirade of shouts left her bright red in the face but Carty still standing outside the stocks.

'He's spoiled, that one,' she pronounced vehemently, piqued, and stumped off to the barn, reappearing with an enormous stock whip which she cracked furiously behind Carty, ordering him forward at the pitch of her lungs and making such a racket that even the placid pregnant mares in the barn looked round in amazement. Carty skittered and swerved, cavorted and was yelled at some more but eventually we succeeded in prodding and cuffing him into the stocks. 'He's wicked, a real bad character,' was Cecile's judgment as we slid home the thick iron retaining bar behind Carty's bottom, slung two broad canvas straps under his belly and attached them to turnbars on each side of the frame and cranked the slings tight.

Finally Monsieur Juillet reached inside the frame, looped a stout rope round one of Carty's feet and yanked the foot off the ground so that he could lash the leg up to an iron bar where it was held firmly in place while he worked on it. Still Carty did not surrender. He tried his trick of bending his legs, only to find that he swung helplessly in the two belly bands like a vast cradle. He became really irate and began to wriggle and thrash. He threw himself from side to side, all feet off the ground, and the whole iron frame shook and rattled under his weight. 'Hooah! Hooah! Brute!' shouted Monsieur Juillet and gave him a smack. Carty rolled his eyes and looked thoroughly put out, then stood still. 'A trouble maker,' pronounced Monsieur Juillet, 'I wish you luck trying to shoe him on the open road.'

Even with Carty trussed up immobile, it took three hours to get new shoes on him. But he was beautifully shod when Monsieur Juillet finally released an exhausted Carty with a friendly pat. I asked how long would the new shoes last. The metal would endure one month, the master craftsman replied, and it would be two months before anyone would need to take a trimming knife to re-shape the hooves again. That was how he had worked in the French cavalry and he would guarantee the results. Even if our horses were tramping all day on the hard road surface it would not matter. Garrison cavalry regiments spent week after week clattering on the pavé, and Monsieur Juillet's job had been to keep the horses' feet healthy and well shod. But where, I thought to myself, would we find Heavy Horse shoeing stocks along our route? I did not look forward to the next time we had to put shoes on a recalcitrant Carty, and was already dreading the day when I would have to do the job myself.

The countryside around Bouillon gives a clue to the character of the men who set out in Duke Godfrey's train. To be called an 'Ardennes Head' still means to be considered stubborn, solid, phlegmatic and tough, and it is easy to see how the Ardennes plateau bred such people. It is a harsh and difficult place to make a living, the hills gashed by deep gorges, and the rock left exposed in steep cliffs and outcrops. Morning mists pour like waterfalls over the lips of ravines, or hang in the lee of the precipices, hovering like wraiths over dark green forests. There are trees everywhere, mostly oaks, which provide a dense cover for the wild boar, fox and deer. It is little wonder that the two saints most characteristic of the

Ardennes are St Hubert, patron saint of hunters, who is said to have seen a stag in the forest carrying a lighted cross between its antlers, and St Remacle, whose mule was eaten by a wolf. The frequent mist and rain reduces the horizon. Views are blocked by hill crests and endless ridges of forest, except where a gap suddenly reveals a deep narrow valley. Standing on the cliff top there is a sense of vertigo as one looks down into a pocket of farmland where a few houses stand beside water meadows. In this terrain sound matters as much as vision. The barking of a farm dog is heard clearly all the way to the next hill crest, and a distant thunderstorm echoes and re-echoes, rolling across the forests and valleys like the sounds of a far battle. Close at hand is always the noise of water: rushing streams, the dripping patter from the branches of trees, or the rustle of rain on the leaves. A dark, secretive cantonal world, it is one of the last places in Europe to hold witch trials, and as late as the 18th century the guilty were burned alive. Even today fires are lit in the spring time to drive away the evils of winter.

The inhabitants and their famous horses shared the same stubborn, heavy obstinacy. Once a project was begun, the Ardennais would see it through to a conclusion. Had they any idea, I wondered, of what they faced as they left on the great pilgrimage to the Holy Land? Could any native of that region in the 11th century have foreseen the absolute contrast from their cold, damp forests to the hot, parched lands of the Near East? Had they any notion of the change from lush green oakwoods to the yellow deserts and dun-coloured rocky hills in Asia Minor where not a blade of fresh grass remains by early summer? And what of their horses? Huge forest animals with thick coats, short legs, enormous hooves and massive muscles evolved for churning through mud. How could they survive when they had to plod through slithering sands or the heavy legs scramble over rocky mountain slopes? The thick coats and massive frames would pour with sweat; the diet deteriorate from ample green stuff to a few wisps of dry hay and leaves. The Heavy Horses of the Ardennes, like the people, would have needed to adapt. Those who did not or could not, would die.

Modern Bouillon is rightly proud of Duke Godfrey. His statue stands at the chateau entrance. There he is depicted as young, broad-browed, clear-eyed and with perfectly symmetrical features as he gazes across the

In a legendary feat of strength, Duke Godfrey lops off the head of a camel with a single blow.

gorge of the Semois river. He is the romantic image of the Crusader, pure, idealised, and not a hair out of place in the short pudding bowl hairstyle. But the portrait is imaginary. No contemporary depiction of him survives except for the small figure on a silver denier coin made for the Duke's treasury. It shows a mounted mailed knight and is so anonymous that it could be anybody. The small museum at the foot of the chateau had a section devoted to the Duke, but the offering was slim. There was an iron spur of his time, virtually indistinguishable from a modern spur, and a nearly contemporary sword, plain, heavy, with a ball-shaped pommel and a down curving guard. It was functional and sturdy, characteristic of the period. A display of faded colour slides traced the making of Godfrey's legend by the early chroniclers. Here was a picture of Godfrey setting out on horseback with his brothers, lances aslant and pennons fluttering; next he is crossing the Bosphorus to enter Asia, and in another picture he is seen using his massive sword to chop the head off a camel, after an Arab asked to witness the strength of his sword arm. The illustrations came from the chief chronicles written in the years after the First Crusade, and they underlined how much the historians had appreciated having a central hero-figure for their tale of the great endeavour. But why had they chosen Godfrey? Answers to that question, I hoped, lay not in the museum but on the road ahead.

Departure day, 2 May, was preceded by a crisis. Bernard Doffagne, President of Bouillon's Syndicat d'Initiative had provided a scrap of pasture for the animals. In the summer Bernard ran a toy train up and down the picturesque streets of Bouillon, carrying tourists. His train shed was on the outskirts of town and had a garden where we left the animals. Just as we were settling in at a hotel, a report reached us that Mystery was lying down on the ground and would not get up. We raced back up the hill. Mystery was stretched out flat and looking miserable. Sarah promptly guessed that the little mare had eaten something which disagreed with her and had a bad colic. Luckily a vet was nearby and he administered injections to help Mystery relax. But it was an inauspicious start to the journey, to have to doctor one of our horses before she had even put a hoof on the road.

Early the following morning we walked the horses up the steeply winding road to Chateau Bouillon on its crag where a modest leaving ceremony had been arranged. The main witnesses to our departure would be a couple of photographers from the local newspaper, a television crew hoping to make a documentary film of the venture who would try to rendezvous with us if and when we got as far as Bulgaria, and a handful of civic officials plus whatever citizens of Bouillon and tourists cared to stroll up the hill to see us off. There was also a photographer sent by the National Geographic Magazine in Washington. He had a roving commission, with instructions to find us on the road from time to time and try to compile a photo-record of our crusading experience.

Sarah and I and the two horses were to set out from the very heart of the chateau, the central courtyard where Duke Godfrey's original keep had stood. Since the Duke's time the castle has been extensively remodelled and enlarged so that to reach the original courtyard meant crossing a drawbridge over a deep, narrow ravine and then leading the two horses down a pitch dark, dripping tunnel driven through the outer walls. It was a spooky ordeal, with the roof barely an inch clear above Carty's head, and sparks cracking off his iron heels. I prayed he would not bolt as we groped our way through the dark, and had visions of innocent tourists being pulverised in the tunnel under the hooves of a runaway warhorse. But Carty kept calm and we emerged into the daylight at the far end to find three horses from the local riding centre waiting for us. This was to be our mounted escort for the first few miles, and the riders were beautifully dressed in trim white breeches, gleaming polished boots and cutaway coats embellished with the crest of Bouillon on the pocket badge. They even wore white gloves. Sarah and I felt rather shabby in our workaday riding gear and hard-used waxed cotton jackets.

All the riders were invited to take a glass of champagne in the Salle de Turenne, where there were short speeches from the civic dignitaries. Bouillon, it transpired, still maintained a formal link with Jerusalem. The Order of the Holy Sepulchre, a papal order of chivalry, still held occasional investitures in the chateau, and a deputation from Bouillon had recently travelled to Jerusalem with a stone from the castle parapet. To signal our departure, we were told, a cannon would be fired from the battlements. 'If Mystery takes fright,' muttered Sarah, 'we could be in Istanbul the very same day.'

The day was cloudy, with a brisk breeze that rattled the bunting hung over the castle gate and the noise made Mystery dance and fidget, as we led our horses back out through the tunnel to the grassy bank where Duke Godfrey's statue stood. More speeches, the Irish and Belgian anthems were played, then we mounted up, me on Carty, Sarah on Mystery. 'Look, look! They're riding to Jerusalem!' a child called excitedly. Maybe, I thought to myself, waiting for the cannon to boom out. When it did so, Carty didn't even stir, but Mystery, with Sarah grinning broadly, shot off down the hill at a spectacular clatter. We were off! Just two riders hoping to trace the path taken by an entire army, I thought. Some of Duke Godfrey's horses presumably had been on campaign before and knew what to expect in the way of long distance travel. But our two mounts, a juvenile Ardennes and a skittish Irish mare, could have had no inkling of just what was expected of them. As with the beginning of all expeditions, the first few days would be among the most

59

important for them as well as for Sarah and myself. After eighteen months of planning and preparation, juggling with dates and distances for our journey, I would actually have to come to grips with the practical facts of trying to ride horses across a continent. Now I would discover whether all my desk-bound theories and preparations had any value at all.

We snaked down the hill and through the town. Oddly, my first impression as of mild embarrassment. I found that riding a horse through town gives one a new perspective, and it is slightly disconcerting to find oneself looking straight in through the ground floor windows. There was nothing to do except follow our four guides from the riding club through the swirl of traffic and concentrate on keeping the horses calm. We crossed the Semois by the Pont de France, rode up the hill, and turned for one last look at the little town in its gorge. Bouillon was preparing for the tourist season, and all the window boxes were full of flowers. I could pick out the spot where, according to repute, Peter the Hermit had come to preach the Crusade in 1096; a curve of the river where in Duke Godfrey's time the citizens had the right to fish for salmon and eels. On the battlements of the dominating grey chateau the Irish flag fluttered, probably for the first time in Bouillon's long history. Then we abandoned the tarmac road, turned down a side track into the Ardennes Forest and the trees closed behind us.

Our leading guide was an official of the Forestry and Water Service. He knew the forest trails intimately and so we rode along through ranks of beech and fir and oak like a merry party of trippers. The air was full of birdsong. The overcast sky had given way to brief spells of sunshine with puffy cloud and a high haze, so that shafts of sunlight broke through the tree canopy. Our guides took it in relays with other riding club members to see us on our way. Gradually we settled down to the pace. It was obvious that Carty was our ball and chain. He plodded along sedately at his own speed, utterly oblivious of the other horses. Within the hour I was fed up with trying to coax him into a trot every three or four hundred yards so that he would catch up with the other horses. By lunch time, despite his get-fit programme, Carty was feeling the strain. His body was soaked with sweat and there were streaks of foam running down his legs. Cecile had airily told me not to worry about such signs. In the summer harvest, she said, she had seen Ardennes horses standing in the stubble so flecked with sweat that it looked as if they had been snowed on. Yet I knew we would have to keep a careful eye on our Heavy Horse and respect his needs, particularly in these early days before he had accustomed to the daily pace. The only consolation was how quickly Carty recharged his batteries. He tired very quickly, but after half an hour's rest seemed to have recouped all his energy.

We travelled just twelve miles that day, a modest distance after the late start, and our last guide left us at a small farm where an orchard was available to us. I was very stiff. The breadth of Carty's back forced one to sit with legs splayed wide apart, and although the position was not as bad as many observers feared, it was distinctly uncomfortable and made more awkward by the movement of Carty's massive shoulderbones which made the rider lurch from side to side. Not surprisingly, my back was aching, but far worse was the pain from my knees and hips. The truth was that Carty smashed each foot down on his immense iron shoe like a pile driver. There was a jarring thud each time he took a pace, and the impact hammered again and again through his huge frame into the rider. It was an excruciating ordeal, and the more Carty tired by the end of the day, the more heavily he pounded his feet. The comparison between riding Carty and riding a normal horse was the difference between travelling in a passenger car and driving the same distance on a tractor with square-shaped cast iron wheels. At a trot Carty's movement was acceptable. He managed a certain rolling consistency to the way his great feet clip-clopped forward in an almost circular rhythm. But to trot him too much, especially on the hard road surface, was unwise, since his young hooves and legs could easily be damaged. So on the road we walked. After three or four hours in the saddle, my hips and knees were aching. Take a full day's travel of, say, seven hours and there would be times when I was almost crying with pain. Later I found out that the Order of Teutonic Knights, a military order of chivalry renowned for its strict discipline, had a special punishment for miscreants: to dress in armour and ride a warhorse at the trot by the hour. Aboard Carty I was spared only the armour.

At the end of the first day's ride Sarah took a lift with our guide to fetch the jeep. Gingerly I sat down by the orchard to await her return and keep an eye on the two horses. It was lucky that I did so. The orchard had been fenced off to serve as a paddock, but only for normal horses not for an Ardennes. As soon as Carty had recharged his batteries, he began to explore his new terrain. I was brought to my feet by a tremendous rending crash of timber, and caught a glimpse of Carty's hind quarters disappearing through a gap he had bulldozed in the fence. I ran after him, caught him, brought him back to the orchard, and repaired the hole in the fence as best I could. Within five minutes there was another splintering sound, and I leaped up again to see that Carty had burst out through another self-made gap. He simply lumbered up to the rickety fence, put his chest against it and kept on walking. He was not trying to escape, merely curious to see what lay outside his field. I knew it was no use tying him up with rope since he had learned to throw his full weight back on the tether and snap it. I had tried using high-grade yachting rope of 8 ton breaking strain but all that happened was that Carty regularly snapped the top strap on his head collar, a piece of best leather, triple layered and hand stitched by a master harness maker. After Carty broke three head straps in four days I accepted that it was less expensive on harness bills if he was left to wander freely. But now the trouble was that I was running out of timber to mend the fence around the orchard. By the time Sarah returned, I was reduced to the last shreds of broken planks, hastily jamming them into the gaps as Carty wandered sublimely around seeking to investigate strange sights, sounds and smells. I tried to imagine the mayhem in Duke Godfrey's day when, presumably, several hundred Heavy Horses had all been quartered together. The resulting destruction must have been awesome if they had shared Carty's character. The Crusaders' reputation for pillaging towns and destroying cities, I told Sarah when she returned, was nothing to do with the pilgrims. It was the effect of introducing large numbers of Heavy Horse into a city. They would reduce the place to rubble in a matter of hours.

CHAPTER 6

Sarah

As Sarah and I rode onward from Bouillon, it soon became evident that Duke Godfrey's summer ride would have been a great deal more agreeable than our experience of travelling in late spring. We encountered the wettest May in forty years. The weather was atrocious. It rained so often that we wore our wet weather capes from the time we saddled up in the morning until the time we stabled the horses for the night. During one dreary spell of fifteen days we never saw the sun at all, but rode under a grey sky shut down like a lid from horizon to horizon. On several occasions hail storms caught us in the open, and for the first week the night-time temperature was close to freezing. On just the third day out of Bouillon such a foul gale blew up that we could make no progress whatsoever but were obliged to shelter in an inn, with the horses miserably huddled in the back yard.

Yet we enjoyed ourselves hugely. Everything was so fresh and vivid and unusual as we began to experiment with the best routines for watering, feeding and caring for the horses while on the move. Our first optimistic intention was to begin at first light every day but this idea was soon drowned by the appalling weather. Neither of us could summon up the enthusiasm to sally out into the six am drizzle, and the horses were as reluctant as ourselves to venture into the sodden dawn. Also we soon discovered that it took at least two hours to give the horses their breakfast, check them for any cuts or bruises, groom them properly, pick out their feet, pack our own gear, and saddle up correctly. It was time-consuming but essential. Even a crumb of dirt under a saddle might lead to back sores, and Sarah took immense pains to make sure that every item of harness was scrupulously clean and fitted snugly so there was not the least suspicion of chafe.

Finally mounted and on our way, we proceeded at a sedate walk, with occasional bursts of trotting, as we were very conscious that the horses were not yet fully fit and we did not wish to tire them. Our intention was to journey at the pace equivalent to Godfrey's army, burdened with its footsoldiers, and there was no need to hurry. So we had ample time to gaze at the passing countryside, and appreciate the advantages of the view from horseback. For most of the first full day after we had said goodbye to our guides from Bouillon, we found ourselves riding through dense Ardennes forest along bridle paths deep with russet leaf carpet. On each side the grey and green tree trunks, mostly pines in this area, stretched far back into the shadowed depths of the forest, interspersed with patches of light green elm. There was not a soul to be seen, nor any sound heard except for the talking of water when we came within earshot of the Semois. Drifts of hail lay like old snow among the tree roots, and the forest gave us shelter from the wind so that it was noticeably warmer among the trees. About midday we stopped to rest and feed the horses and ourselves. We had brought some food with us from Bouillon, and were carrying a small bag of oats for the horses, but Sarah declined to share my choice of strong, rough Ardennes sausage, preferring a double allocation of beer from the saddlebags. The horses munched their feed from nosebags. Carty's was impressively large. I had stitched it from heavy weight 18 grade sail canvas and it was about the size of a small sea anchor. As he finished eating, he banged it up and down on a tree stump to dislodge the last grains of food from the seams, and Sarah had to leap to her feet and rush to rescue the brand new nosebag as he then began blithely nibbling tree roots with the canvas still draped over his muzzle.

I was beginning to understand just how extraordinarily lucky I was to have Sarah as my companion. Her slight frame was apparently made of sprung steel for she never seemed to tire. At the end of a hard day's riding she still vibrated with energy, and over the next few weeks I was to find her unflaggingly sceptical view of life a great antidote to my aching tiredness. Her caustic observations made me laugh as she castigated life in general, the biting sarcasm usually lightened by a wicked childlike laugh of pure glee. Much of Sarah's world-weariness was a pose. Under the cynical surface was hidden a generous spirit, and when selflessness was needed, Sarah responded. However it was best not to thank her too profusely as that swiftly brought a crushing retort. The great grey-blue eyes and elfin figure made their own impression, and when Sarah approached a farmer or stable owner to ask if we could leave our horses overnight she was seldom refused. Also, she had been initiated in the freemasonry of young women who care for horses at riding stables. Sarah knew the rules of their secret society so that as soon as the stable boss had gone home, Carty and Mystery would be given extra rations of oats and hay, and reallocated to the most comfortable stalls.

Sarah was a natural traveller. It didn't matter to her which country she was in, she always found something to engage her attention, and soon she lost track of time. She did not know which day of the week or even which month it was: She readily admitted that she was not much interested in the history of the Crusades or the story of Duke Godfrey. Rather, she was absorbed by the experience of travel, the variety of the journey itself, and our daily encounters with so many different types of people.

Typically Sarah had played down her gift for foreign languages. When she agreed to come as far as Belgium, I had asked if she spoke French or German. Yes, I was told, she had a few words of each. But scarcely had we set foot in France than I discovered she spoke fluent French, and by the time we crossed into German-speaking territory I knew her well enough not to be surprised when she revealed a good command of German. All this was in addition to her extraordinary empathy with the horses. She seemed to know exactly what a horse was thinking, even before the animal knew its own mind. At the start of the day she could tell me if Mystery or Carty had rested properly, warn me if one or other was in a bad temper, even advise me to watch out – three or four minutes before it happened – when either horse was ready to shy or bolt. At the end of a long day's ride she was still alert to a slight limp or a glimpse of a stone caught in a hoof, and could slip out of the saddle and check the foot as nimbly as though it were still morning. Nor, apparently, did she need to eat. Like one of those fabled creatures of medieval geography who were supposed to subsist by inhaling the steam arising from soup cauldrons, Sarah seemed to take barely any solid food. She nibbled fruit and vegetables, washed down with copious amounts of beer which was an essential beverage. In real terms, someone remarked, she was probably the true descendant of the workaday Crusader: she understood horses perfectly, picked up languages readily, and drank with gusto.

Within a couple of days our perspective on our surroundings had changed, despite the rain and cold. We found we had become acutely conscious of everything to do with nature and the land as far as it concerned our horses. When we passed a hedgerow, for example, we treated it first as a source of food for the animals to snatch at. Second, it was a potential ambush for a dog or bird to burst out and scare the horses. Third, it was a myriad jumble of plants with their shapes, colours, flowers, and states of growth to indicate to us the progress of the season. Automatically we looked for tell-tale signs connected with our never-ending quest for food and shelter for the horses: hoof prints in the mud to show that a track was passable; farm outbuildings that might perhaps be stables; wooden fencing rather than barbed wire to indicate that someone might be keeping horses.

We noticed, too, how the constant uncertainties of the road imposed a major strain on Mystery and Carty. Horses are creatures of companion-ship and habit, and when domesticated they prefer to graze in the same familiar fields, return day after day to the same stable and be fed at regular hours on food they recognise. Now, against their natures, we were expo-sing Carty and Mystery to bewildering changes every hour. They were constantly on the move, never seeing the same stretch of road twice, never spending more than two consecutive days in the same stable, often standing overnight alongside strange and aggressive horses they had never encountered before, nor would meet again. It was completely contrary to the ways they had previously lived. Carty had scarcely left the farm where he had been born, and Mystery in her role as a trekking horse had walked the same tourist circuit near Killarney so often that she could almost have followed the road blindfold. The pair of them could no longer rely on being fed at the same regular hours, for their meal breaks depended on finding a suitably sheltered spot, and their diet was to vary in a way that would have given nightmares to a conscientious stable-manager. At first we could obtain oats and sacks of patent horse foods, but as we moved farther eastward the animals had to make do with maize, sometimes offered as loose grains but later chewed off ancient dried corncobs tossed on the ground before them or supplied as powdered meal. Next they descended to eating pig food, and finally when they entered Asia, they would be tearing the bark from trees with their teeth. By the end of a month the only fixed point in their lives would be one another, and they became inseparable. Mystery in particular would go into a frenzy if she lost sight of Carty's reassuring bulk.

Every eight or ten miles we rode through small Belgian or Luxembourgois country towns with their unassuming brick houses, but in between them much of the countryside was still thickly wooded and so deserted that large areas were used for war games. Twice we found ourselves turned aside from our track by soldiers guarding areas of manoeuvres. Then we left the bridle path and rode even deeper into the forest, skirting around the sentries as we coaxed our mounts through quiet forest so immaculately tended that scarcely a dead branch was to be seen as the foresters had cleared away the trimmings and windfalls. Occasionally we smelled woodsmoke where the workmen were burning bonfires or heard the whine of a distant chainsaw but otherwise we could have been totally alone. At such times there was a real feeling of flashback, that this was how medieval Europe must have been when Duke Godfrey rode, winding his way from castle to castle to collect recruits to join his train. One half-expected to come across a villein guarding his herd of snuffling pigs as if illustrated in a medieval book of hours.

As we emerged from each swathe of forest the open countryside was beginning to flaunt its springtime beauty. Hedges were white with hawthorn blossom, and the spring growth of grass was a particularly vivid green pinpointed with thousands upon thousands of yellow dandelion flowers. There were very few wild birds, only a handful of pigeons in a field, but we were rarely out of sight of a solitary bird of prey, wheeling over the forest we had just left. On the forest margins we saw deer, coming on them unexpectedly so that they went bounding away in alarm. Sometimes, despite the grey overcast of the sky, the landscape seemed almost artificial in its attraction. 'Any moment now,' Sarah remarked, 'Julie Andrews will come over the brow of the hill and burst out with a song from *The Sound of Music.*'

Within a few days the steel on Mystery's and Carty's feet was polished slick, and the horses slipped and slithered on the wet tarmac road surface whenever there was a steep camber. Like a lazy child Carty had the irritating habit of sliding one rear foot as he stepped forward and such was his immense weight that the half inch of steel on the heel of that shoe quickly began to be scraped away. Despite Monsieur Juillet's confident prediction of a month's wear from a set of shoes, I began to fear that we might need to stop and re-shoe Carty sooner than that. Other flaws in our equipment began to show. The cheap canvas rucksacks that served as packs on the horses had already begun to disintegrate, and with spare shoe leather from a cobbler I stitched reinforcements. There were not enough straps to attach the various items of kit to the saddles, and so I bought a dozen large size leather dog collars in a Belgian pet shop, leaving a salesman puzzling as to the breed of my sizable dog pack. But the main failure was the scheme to use the combination of moped and jeep to leapfrog the daily horse-borne march. The grisly weather was largely to blame. I came to dread the moment at the end of the day's ride when I had to mount the wretched moped and drive back to pick up the jeep. Riding the horses was one thing, but puttering on a moped fifteen or twenty miles in pouring rain every evening, when I was already tired and wet from the day's ride, my spirits sank to a very low ebb, and it was not surprising that the daily ordeal resulted in a touch of pneumonia.

On the night of Thursday, 7 May, both horses ran away. We had put them for the night in the tiny garden of a chalet at the edge of a campsite. There they were surrounded by a hedge and encircled by a portable electric fence, safe. But in the morning the garden was empty, and it was impossible to tell how they had escaped. There was no gap in the perimeter hedge, the electric fence was unbroken and still working, and the occupant of the chalet had seen or heard nothing. He had gone to bed with a huge Ardennes and a bay mare outside his window, and when he awoke there was nothing. Totally puzzled we stood in front of the chalet and wondered how it was possible to lose a horse of Carty's dimensions. We asked the farmers who drove past on their tractors but none had seen the runaways. A telephone call to the local police station brought no further news. Sarah and I looked at one another, and knew what the other was thinking. The campsite was located in the Kengert nature reserve, several thousand hectares of dense forest. If Carty had decided to be a feral Ardennes Forest horse there was not the slightest chance of finding him for days. He and Mystery would vanish like wild animals in the immense tangle of trees, bushes, ravines and cliffs. Short of organising a beaten drive, it would be impossible to flush them out.

Sarah and I began a logical search. We made a complete circle around the campsite, looking for hoof prints. But either the two creatures had walked away on tiptoe or taken flight in a balloon. Not the slightest mark was to be found. We grew more and more bewildered. We made another wider circuit of the campsite. Still there was nothing. We scouted down the road in each direction, peering hopefully into the forest. But it was impossible to see more than a hundred yards and the two horses would have been well-camouflaged. We had visions of the two delinquents happily peeping out between the oak trees, laughing at us, and gently gliding away from our pursuit. We were trudging around the edge of a field cut into the forest when we stumbled across a line of unmistakable potholes, the huge prints of Carty's nine-inch hooves sinking into the soft ground. The line of footprints led straight to the edge of the forest where, at the wall of trees, Carty had paused and turned back. I checked the direction he had taken. It was uncanny: after a week of marching, of using small sideroads with a myriad twists and turns, with no landmarks or regular routeing, Carty had set out on exactly the right compass bearing to take him home to Bourbeau. It was as if he had a built-in homing device.

Half a mile from the campsite, we came on another clue along the road. A large saucer of mud lay on the tarmac. After three months of picking out his huge hooves, I knew at once that the saucer fitted precisely inside Carty's massive foot. A few yards farther on was a single hoof print in the soft verge of the road, and very soon we were deciphering exactly what had happened in the night. Thwarted by the forest, Carty had set out to bring himself back home by re-tracing his steps of the previous day. He was the reluctant, and devious, crusader. Had he been human he could scarcely have been more circumspect. For half a mile he had walked on the hard road surface where his tracks did not show. Then, to rest his feet, he had taken to strolling along the soft grass verge. Admiringly, I cursed him under my breath. When I tried riding Carty on the verge, he was so chronically obstinate he would always insist on swerving aside to walk on the tarmac, slamming down his huge feet with spine-jarring effect. Now, left to his own devices, he voluntarily used the softer surface. The hoof prints continued to tell the story plainly. Every so often the road passed a meadow, unfenced and ankle deep in lush grass, an absolute feast for a hard-worked horse. Any normal animal would have diverted into the meadow and gorged himself and still be dallying there, ready to be caught. But Carty's hoof prints led resolutely past the meadow, never deviating as he marched sternly forward, determined to go home whatever the temptation. Mystery, however, always succumbed to the lure. In meadow after meadow was a line of smaller hoof prints where she had plunged in for the feast, walked into the centre of the field, put her head down for a minute, and then realised that Carty was marching on. Then her tracks told how she had turned and scampered back to rejoin her companion, terrified of being left alone. Finally, after four hours of searching, we saw them. Their adventure had come to an end after about five miles when a farmer must have noticed them walking past unattended, and diverted them into a cow pasture. Carty and Mystery were standing unconcernedly among a herd of cattle, with Carty pensively scratching his back against the bough of an apple tree.

We led the two runaways all the way back to the campsite, saddled up and rode on, leaving the jeep and trailer to be picked up next day. We were grimly determined to make the two horses regret their midnight escapade by insisting on a full day's ride. So at seven that evening two very tired horses plodded their way down the steep hill, clad in huge beech trees, that overlooks the border town of Echternach and the Sauer river marking the frontier between Luxembourg and Germany. Relenting slightly, we dismounted and walked the horses the last mile. But Carty was not in the least contrite. He hung back on the leading rein or veered from side to side. Sarah had to walk along behind him, flicking the long Australian stock whip we carried, which sent Carty lumbering forward in a series of ungainly surges, especially when Sarah gave an occasional wicked chuckle. At the back of Echternach we came across a riding stable, unoccupied except for a dozen horses loose in a nearby paddock who promptly stampeded at the mere sight of Carty's bulk. There was no one in attendance so ignoring the panicky galloping we opened up two stalls and drove in the horses. Carty, an exasperated Sarah announced, was a monstrous juvenile delinquent, always looking for mischief with his piggy eyes, and Mystery was a complete scatterbrain. No sensible horse, she said, would put up with Carty for five minutes, and yet it was clear that Mystery adored him. But Sarah prophesied that Mystery would learn better in due course. As usual when it came to horses, Sarah would prove to be right.

We had been advised that to pass through the German customs post we would need to produce the horses safely boxed in a trailer for inspection by the frontier veterinary officer. As this was to be our first border crossing and we did not know what to expect, we resolved to do everything correctly, if only to show off our fat volume of vaccination and equine health certificates. So next morning, while I retrieved the moped and trailer, Sarah tidied up the horses, giving them both a good wash, with special treatment for Carty whose wire wool mane and ridiculous bob tail were stiff with dirt that could only be dislodged with almost-neat washing-up liquid. Like all the foals born at Bourbeau, Carty's tail had been docked when he was a week old. Whatever was in the washing-up liquid, the unlikely effect was to make his tail hair grow, and Carty's own grey apology for a tail gradually began to lengthen until finally it became a useful fly whisk.

The stable owner, who had been quite unruffled when I tracked him down at his home and apologised for our unexpected arrival, helped us persuade Carty that his delaying tactics were no longer called for. He entered the box without demur, and early in the afternoon we drove the half mile up to the frontier post and asked for veterinary clearance to take the horses into Germany. The border guard was unhelpful, sourly telling us that we should have given twenty-four-hours' notice of arrival so that a vet could be on hand. It was no use explaining that as Carty could take five hours to enter a trailer, a precise border rendezvous was impractical. Fortunately the vet was not far away, and responded promptly to a telephone call. When he saw Carty, he upbraided the frontier guard for not calling him sooner. The guard, cowed before such educated authority, stamped our papers without further delay and twenty minutes later we were unloading the two horses once again, just inside Germany.

It had been seven days since we left Chateau Bouillon and we had learned several lessons in cross-country travel. Now I knew that I had been over-optimistic about the speed we could make in the early stages of our journey. I had not anticipated how horses were almost as weather-dependent as small boats. Rain and wind had slowed us down with late starts in the morning due to the need to dry out the equipment and the animals' backs; an entire day had been spent at a complete halt due to a storm; several afternoons' riding were curtailed by the need to find early shelter from the rain or drizzle. Effectively, we had only managed four-and-a-half-days of travel and covered but sixty miles. At that sort of speed, Duke Godfrey's footsoldiers would have had no trouble keeping up; and unlike a boat which in a spell of fine weather and fair wind can make up lost distance, a horse-borne traveller, once he loses a day, can never make it up. He cannot push his horse faster without the risk of ruining the animal. Added to which Carty marched more slowly than I had expected, and the discomfort of his gait had been a most painful surprise.

Yet nothing could be done. I had opted to try riding a Heavy Horse, and now knew why a medieval knight travelled on his palfrey. Wistfully I began to wonder if perhaps we could convert Carty to his true role as a pack horse, and consoled myself with the thought that the First Crusaders must also have had their own teething troubles. The villagers and townsfolk who left their homes and cottages to walk or ride in Duke Godfrey's train would have had very little concept of the realities of long-distance travel. Most of them would probably have never been more than a few miles from their villages. But many must have turned back within that first testing week, preferring to face the accusing looks of the stay-at-homes than the prospect of months on the move. Setting out on 'the right road to Constantinople with the prospect of a four-months' walk just to reach the haven of Emperor Alexius' promised hospitality required courage and faith. The First Crusade had usually been described in terms of its leaders' achievements, but I was starting to appreciate that the truly remarkable participants were the ordinary men and women who trudged along the path to Jerusalem, blistered, hungry, thirsty, and poorly sheltered at night. After just a few of the same obstacles and discomforts, my sympathy was with them. Later I was to understand that their commitment and fortitude must have had a vital role in the building of Duke Godfrey's heroic reputation.

CHAPTER 7

To the Rhine

The next day, 10 May, we reached Trier, the oldest city in Germany. In 1096 it lay on the borders of Godfrey's dukedom, and was by far the most important road centre of the entire region. Peter the Hermit's followers certainly passed this way, and so too, in all likelihood, would have Godfrey and his contingent as they headed towards the Rhineland. Sarah and I had not yet ridden the two horses through a major built-up area, and I was not at all sure that the traffic police of Trier would approve of Carty and Mystery clumping their way through the bustling centre of the city. But Trier was still, as it had always been, the logical crossing point of the Moselle, so I had decided we would have to tackle it direct.

A 'Roman Road' was marked on our maps and took us through a parkland of beech and ancient oaks to emerge very suddenly on the heights above the town. Another Romerstrasse led us down the steep valley face and across the railway lines where Mystery and Carty stood and snorted in puzzlement at the shiny rails until Sarah kicked Mystery on. We clattered over the long span of the 'Roman Bridge' in the middle of the town, presumably the original imperial bridging point over the Moselle, when a green and white police car drew up alongside me. The driver's colleague unequivocally gesticulated that Carty should walk closer into the gutter as his broad stern was an obstruction to passing traffic, otherwise the police had no objection: which surprised me because Sarah was finding it easier to ride on the pavement and with Mystery suffering from indigestion, a very distinctive trail was left on Trier's immaculate pavements.

It was a Sunday afternoon and Trier was looking distinctly prosperous. Streams of Sunday traffic moved along the boulevards, opulent shops sparkled with plate glass and ornate window displays of expensive goods. The few pedestrians were soberly dressed for their afternoon stroll, and much too well-mannered and self-assured to stop and point at the strange sight of an Ardennes clumping his way along their avenues. They paused to gaze at us politely, turning to watch us pass, and then swivelled back to continue their dignified promenade. We passed the rather grim arch of the Porta Nigra, the Black Gate, the city's unmistakable symbol. Ninety-eight feet high and constructed of huge blocks of black weathered sandstone held together with iron clamps, the Black Gate was the largest single gateway ever built in the Roman Empire and truly monumental. No siege engine of Godfrey's time was capable of damaging such a monster, and when Godfrey's knights began to lay siege to the cities of the East, they would never encounter anything so uncompromisingly solid and effective.

We rode down Trier's broad avenues with their signposts to the old Roman amphitheatre and the vast imperial baths, relics that, like the Black Gate, had either fallen into spectacular ruin or been included in the city's defensive perimeter by Godfrey's time. In his day the city was better known for its thrusting commercial ambition, and Trier's stone market cross, one of the very few early medieval relics to survive in Germany, had already been standing for more than a century. Suitably, the cross is now surrounded by vendor's stalls at the hub of one of the smarter shopping precincts.

On the far side of town, we saw our first Moselle vines, gaunt roots with their branches bent over in hoops, and then the inevitable advertisements for the *weinstubes* which ring the city. Here we got lost, wandering through an anonymous succession of leafy identical avenues as we searched for a path to bring us clear of the city limits. In England or Ireland it would have been a suburb where families might keep ponies for the children, so we rode on hopefully. But there were only more houses, factories on green field sites, a sanatorium, and more *weinkellers* which, when we asked, had no space for a pair of horses.

It was nearly dark by the time we found shelter in a barn in the last satellite village before we came to the open country. The family Dienst must have had a soft spot for horses, for they were farmers and their

74

stable could not have been an economic proposition. In one stall lay a foal badly injured by a gash in his chest which they were nursing, and the other stalls housed no more than a couple of animals. The Diensts themselves were like a set of cards from Happy Families. There was mother and father, uncle with a broken nose and constant smile, granny with her tightly curled hair and her apron who bustled about the kitchen stove, a son out by the stable looking after the horses, and five daughters, four of whom still lived in the immediate area. The fifth had just come home to celebrate Mother's Day, bringing her husband and two children along. Finally there were a poodle and a Persian cat. Although we had dropped in on a family celebration, two more places were laid at the table and we joined them to eat stewed pork, cabbage, fried potato and salad, followed after a decent interval by a huge cake. At that point father produced a bottle of his own home-made pear liquor, twenty years aged.

The sheer decency and hospitality of the family made a deep impression. They had lived and toiled here for generations, and by rights should have been left undisturbed. But Father Dienst still bore the scars from a terrible head wound, received on the Russian front when he had been so badly hit by shrapnel that he was left for dead. It had taken years for him to recover, and yet here, at last, he was in his rightful place, with his family around him, saying grace before the meal. 'I went to fight because it was for Germany' Father Dienst plainly stated, and I wondered if a similar uncomplicated motive would not have been just as true almost 900 years earlier when ordinary, worthy men had left this land and their families to march and fight behind Duke Godfrey and the other warlords of the Crusade. Surely it was not necessary always to search for subtle or cynical motives. Perhaps many of them had simply said to themselves 'I will go to fight for Christ'. That was motive enough.

Next morning, after I had scouted forward with the jeep and dropped off the moped at a stable twenty miles distant, the Dienst uncle offered to show us our cross-country route into the plateau of the Hunsrück. But as is common with men who have lived all their lives in the same small radius, his directions were confusing, as they depended on intimate knowledge of every minute feature of the fields. So after he had left us at the roadside we wandered uncertainly forward, losing our path, regaining it, until finally we abandoned the original directions and struck out on our own initiative.

By now we had developed an eye for the terrain. Often we could pick up the natural course of the road from the topography, guess the hidden line of the track, note where a stream cut into the plateau and so anticipate that the bridle path would make a circuit around the head of the valley, instead of descending first into the trough and then laboriously clambering up the opposite side. We rode for seven hours the first day into the plateau of Hunsrück, climbing up and down the folds of the valleys, our backs and legs soon aching from the saddle. Carty's colour darkened from light roan to deep maroon as the sweat saturated his coat. We stopped for half an hour by a stream for lunch, and rested the horses for ten minutes every two hours, but it was hard going. Now I understood another reason why the Roman road builders preferred to keep to the high ground in these parts. It was not just to avoid ambushes and clinging mud in wooded valleys. The golden rule was that height once gained was never thrown away uselessly. Nothing so wearies a horse or a person on foot as endlessly dipping up and down over hills and vales when level marching, however exposed to wind and weather, is available.

Carty's guile grew the more tired he became. He began to mince down the slopes, pretending that he was about to slip and so needed to go carefully. Really he was dawdling. He discovered that we were prepared to let the horses drink water whenever we came to a stream. So at the smallest rivulet he would gain a respite by stopping, casting around slowly for the best spot, deliberately lowering his head, and then playing with the water with his lips to pass the time, until I awoke to his ruse. His slow, sedate pace was a constant irritant. Mystery would outwalk him in a couple of hundred metres, and then I had to urge Carty forward to close the gap. It was difficult to say who used up the more energy: Carty at his slow trot, or myself digging him in the ribs with my heels, waving the stock whip menacingly and cajoling him into motion. Finally Carty would rumble forward like a juggernaut, huge hooves dishing outward in that characteristic gait until he came thundering up behind Mystery who looked nervously over her shoulder at the great lout coming up behind and threatening to tread on her heels. At the last minute Mystery would skip aside and let Carty draw level. He blundered on, totally oblivious that she did not have his bodyweight and stability. A clumsy shove from his shoulder often sent poor Mystery skittering into the ditch, and there was nothing Sarah or I could do about it. Carty responded to tugs on the bit or jabs with the heel with ponderous slowness, turning with the grace of a coal barge manoeuvring in a crowded estuary. And once Carty developed an idiosyncrasy, it was nearly impossible to dislodge. Thus he decided that he liked to be on Mystery's near side when he walked, but on her off side when he trotted. The result was that as he slowed from a trot to a walk he swerved across her tail, and once again Mystery had to pull her heels out of harm's way. As Sarah had forecast, Mystery was beginning to change her opinion of her uncouth Ardennes companion. Now, when Carty came in too close or was particularly uncouth and obnoxious, she drew back her upper lip and made a quick bite at him. Carty rarely noticed.

Late that afternoon we reached more forest, and again rode along woodsmen's tracks, steering by compass and the slant of light through the trees until we emerged at a large stable at Geilert. All four of us were thoroughly tired, and Sarah and I walked beside the horses for the last mile, glad to stretch our legs but mindful too that we should ease the animals down gently at the end of a long day's ride.

When we removed the saddles, we found that Carty's back was swelling up into bumps and lumps. Unmistakably he was developing saddle sores. If you ran your hand down his back, he arched his spine in protest and shifted from side to side with distress. A horse with a lower threshold of pain would certainly have made much more of a fuss already. It was precisely the deterioration that we had feared, knowing that Carty's back was soft and tender as it had never previously worn a saddle. If the swelling got worse or broke open despite all our precautions, we would have to halt our ride until they healed. So we began a long and anxious campaign to cure him, trying out every immediate remedy: we kept his back even more scrupulously clean, treated his bumps with patent medicines, soothed them with ointment, doubled and tripled the saddle pads, daubed on methylated spirits to toughen the skin, but nothing succeeded in reducing the swellings. Instead they grew gradually more acute. The ultimate cure, Sarah and I both knew, was to find a saddle that fitted Carty better than the Camargue saddle whose saddle tree was simply not wide enough, despite its maker's best efforts. But we had no idea where we would ever find a Heavy Horse saddle wide enough to sit on his broad back.

The steadily worsening soreness of Carty's back cast a gloom on our progress for the next three days, not helped by my own recurring bouts of coughing and shivering. We treated Carty as gently as possible and spent an extra day at Geilert to rest the animals. But the weather was against us. Thunderclouds trailed their skirts of rain across the Hunsrück and it was difficult to keep the horses' backs dry. We rode on through more hail showers, more like March rather than mid-May, and a bitingly cold north wind chilled us through our rain gear. In such conditions there was no guarantee that the horses would manage to reach their chosen destination on any particular day. It was one thing, Sarah pointed out, to go out riding in daily excursions that bring you back to a regular stable and a warm room, a place to dry your clothes, and a hot bath. It is quite another matter to ride day after day with no guarantee of where the horses would end up for the night. And the well-being of the horses always had priority. Only when we had got them stabled, and dry and fed, could we begin to find shelter for ourselves.

Sodden, we trudged along the Alte Romer Strasse beyond Kirn. Here the Roman road climbed to the whale-backed crest of the hills with forest on both flanks, and it was horrid going. We leaned into the wind and slanting rain, until finally I decided we should drop down into the valley to seek shelter. We slipped and slithered through sodden beech woods until our descent brought us to an idyllic farmhouse owned by a prosperous banker. His wife was an avid horse fancier and ran her private stable of Spanish and Portuguese riding horses, beautifully trained and lovingly cared for. It was an unforgettable moment to be welcomed in from the drenching rain, tuck up the horses, and sip whisky as we thawed out before the stove. The next night, for a contrast, we found space at a large professional stable run with a strict discipline that would have done credit to Frederick the Great. Some eighty horses stood, almost to attention, in row upon row of old-fashioned iron stables. They were so well drilled that there was not a sound, not even the rattling of the metal stall bars. Leaving in the morning I heard Sarah chuckle quietly behind me.

'You just led Carty out of a door marked "In, Stable Hands Only!",' she said. 'The groom was so startled at such a breach of discipline that he just gaped. He's probably never seen a Heavy Horse led around like a lap dog.'

But if Carty was left untended, even for a moment, there was bound to be mischief. He was not unruly, just independent-minded, insatiably curious, and virtually without fear. Every day we found to our cost that huge strength and chronic inquisitiveness make a fraught combination. In a small village on the way to Neu Bamberg in the Nahe wine-growing region, Carty excelled himself. The village was spotlessly clean and well maintained, and its quiet main street sloped so steeply that each of the flat fronted shops and houses had its own little flight of steps up from the pavement. We paused halfway down the hill to buy bread. Sarah stayed mounted on Mystery while I slid off Carty's back, handed her the reins and ran into the bakery. In less than two minutes I had bought a loaf and dashed out to take Carty again. Unfortunately in that brief interval Carty had noticed a metal rubbish bin bolted to the wall. So towing Mystery and Sarah behind him, he had simply walked over and stuck his head into the bin to see what was inside. Too lazy to back out properly, he merely lifted his head as I emerged from the bakery. The metal bin, its fixing bolts and retaining band all came away from the wall with a rending sound. Masonry and mortar dropped on to the pavement. Unpertubed, Carty stood there gazing around with the bin dangling off his nose like a giant feed bag. Then the bin slid off his face and fell to the ground with a tremendous metallic crash, tipped over, and went rolling down the hill with a series of bangs and clatters, spraying rubbish in all directions. Sarah and I shamefacedly rode out of town, trying not to look back at the damaged wall, the dented bin lying in the gutter, and the long trail of rubbish.

Now that we had travelled some 150 miles the land began to slope downwards towards the east, leading off the Hunsrück plateau as we approached the Rhine valley. The geometrical lines of crosswires and posts for the vines produced a crematorium effect like huge open war cemeteries with regiments of crosses. Pheasants crouched and scuttled between the vines. We met hares lolloping unconcernedly along, ears flopping, until they saw the horses, started up in surprise, then turned and scuttered off. As there were no hedges we could watch their bounding progress for half a mile or more. A pair of partridges whirred up from under Carty's feet without even making him falter. Bright yellow squares of oil seed rape made a garish patchwork on the distant hills, and gangs of women in flowered aprons hoeing open fields gave the scene a

Breughel effect. Their laborious handwork – they were weeding sugar beet – was a strange contrast with the huge, ultramodern and brightly painted farm machines that were parked wheel-to-wheel in every farmyard. Each village now had an obvious centre, and narrow winding streets instead of the more open pattern found farther west. But it was still difficult to find who owned the grazing. The only isolated farms tended to be converted mills standing by their original water supply, while all the other farmers lived in the villages in solid houses as sturdy as their owners.

On 19 May we covered the last few miles to the Rhine itself. The valley soil was pale and sandy, heaped up in long barrows. Men and women stooped over them like marshbirds dibbling for worms in an estuary, a long thin trowel in one hand and an implement like a mortar board in the other. With one they dug up an asparagus shoot and with the other carefully smoothed down the sandy soil behind them.

The ferry at Eich was a low, flat barge designed to carry twenty-four cars at a time. To our relief the ferry driver agreed to take the horses aboard, and we waited for him to return on the next shuttle trip when he would have fewer cars. Steel horseshoes rang on the steel deck plating with a tremendous clanging sound. The ferry revved up its engines and began to move. Carty suddenly noticed the river bank moving away from him and sliding past. He snorted in puzzlement and clumped round in a circle, keenly interested in what was going on. Mystery nervously danced and fidgeted until Sarah calmed her. We chugged across the Rhine without incident and the ferry neatly hooked on to the landing slip on the other side. The cars eased off, and finally we too could clatter away. I noticed an expression of distaste on the ferry driver's face as he peered down from his miniature bridge. Glancing back I noted two piles of manure on his steel deck, and the ticket-taker hastening to brush away the offending ordure. It began to rain again.

CHAPTER 8

Swabia

We had crossed the Rhine ten miles downstream from the city of Worms, where one of the more notorious Jewish massacres had occurred in the first year of the Crusade. In the Jewish cemetery at Worms, the oldest in Europe, three or four of the headstones date back to that bloody event. The stones can be distinguished from more recent memorials by their irregular weather-beaten shape and the ancient, less formal style of script. There is no way of knowing for certain whether they actually mark the graves of some of the 800 Jews said to have died in the Crusade pogrom, though it is possible. Today no Jews survive form the pre-war community in Worms, and the little pebbles balanced on the gravestones as mementoes of prayers of remembrance are left by visiting parties of Jews, mostly from Israel and North America. Otherwise the cemetery has a matter-of-fact, rather forlorn atmosphere, a neglected corner of the city, easily overlooked behind a nondescript wall and across from drab municipal buildings.

Our route took us across the Odenwald, Odin's Wood, where Siegfried and the Nibelungs had hunted and where every village seemed to boast a Nibelungstrasse. It was a rustic, unspoiled area of hills, heavily wooded and gentler than the Hunsrück, with a softer landscape where the villages were spaced closer together. We stopped overnight at Seeheim on the valley floor of the Rhine to have new horseshoes fitted by a young and very professional farrier, which meant another five-hour stint of wrestling with Carty, and then rode up the eastern slope into the

Odenwald. We expected the weather to improve, for the Wald has its own microclimate, with milder temperatures than the surrounding region. But there was no relaxation whatsoever in the harsh weather. On 21 May it even snowed, and there were several sleet showers. The following day was heavily overcast, and a cold wind continued to blow from the northwest.

For overnight shelter we depended on chance encounters with horse-owners, who were unfailingly hospitable. Once we stayed with the family of a Lufthansa senior pilot who kept Icelandic ponies on a farm tucked in a fold of the hills, and the next night came to a ramshackle farm which epitomised the backwater character of the Odenwald. The place was totally chaotic. Even Bourbeau would have looked modern by comparison, and we could scarcely credit that we were in modern, efficient Germany. Not a roof line of the dilapidated farm buildings was straight, every gutter and drainpipe had been repaired with odd lengths of pipe and string, the tiles had been patched and re-patched over the decades. We rode in under a covered porch where two barns met to form the sides of a large cobbled farmyard. Inside was the largest, most decomposed dung heap we had ever seen, oozing brown effluent in every direction and sprawled so wide that there was barely room to drive a tractor past. On top of the dung heap perched a splendid rooster with his collection of hens, but he dared not descend for the tyrant of the yard was an enormous red-wattled cock turkey of ferocious ugliness. This aggressive creature strutted belligerently back and forth, terrifying all the other fowl into silence, and gave Mystery a huge fright by suddenly dropping one wing tip to the cobblestones and drawing it stiffly across the ground to make a noise like a ripsaw tearing into wood. The place seethed with livestock. In addition to both white and multicoloured turkeys, there were ducks, geese – one of them lame – cats and kittens, goslings, dogs lurking under piles of roof slates or behind broken wooden pallets, calves and cows. In the farm kitchen were two dozen ducklings in one corner, rustling around in a cardboard box, while inside the oven – just being kept warm, not roasted – was yet another gaggle of goslings. The main barn, a huge wooden structure, was even more crammed. A thick fug of animal warmth and smell hung in the air, and when one's eyes got used to the dense gloom inside, you realised that every nook and cranny pulsed with animals packed in indiscriminately.

There was not an inch that was not cackling, grunting, lowing, hissing, gobbling, scratching, eating or snuffling.

Carty, of course, was in his element. A place was found for him and Mystery in yet another rickety barn, with its wooden pillars leaning at crazy angles. Sarah and I wondered if Carty would bring down the place like a card house as he nudged a vital king post in his lumbering curiosity. He was in cheeky mood and earlier that afternoon he had embarrassed us yet again. In the centre of a spruce Odenwald hamlet, he had decided to drink from the ornate horse trough in the middle of the immaculately manicured village green. The trough was more decorative than practical and probably had not supplied a thirsty horse in twenty years. He clumped across the grass leaving his tell tale nine-inch dimples in the turf, and stuck his nose in the water. Pausing for breath he lifted his head, caught his bridle under the massive brass watertap that filled the trough and ripped it off its pipe. Water shot out unchecked. Quite unperturbed he had put his mouth over the jet, sucking away happily. The surplus water gushing out of the opposite side of his lips made him look like some grotesque monumental sculpture. When he had finished, he plodded nonchalantly away, leaving the trough now a fountain, and the brass tap glittering tauntingly in the bottom of the trough under two feet of cold clear water.

Unfortunately, his back was looking worse and worse. The bumps were not shrinking, and the fur was peeling away, leaving raw pink patches. Sarah and I were growing increasingly anxious that all our attempts to cure his sore back were having little success. The horse-owners we met gave us saddle blankets, special salves, and much advice. The proprietor of a horse supply shop, herself an experienced long distance rider, sent the Camargue saddle to be re-stuffed in the hope that it would be a more comfortable fit, and meanwhile lent us a saddle of Icelandic design so that we could continue our ride. Not content with that she also loaned her own leather saddle bags to replace the canvas ones that had fallen to bits, and encouraged us to select extra leather straps, better girths, and saddle pads from her stock. She said she would send the bill later, but I knew from her tone, and the universal generosity we were receiving throughout Germany, that she would not.

Riding Carty with the loaned Icelandic saddle was worse purgatory, both for Carty's saddle sores and for the rider's comfort. It did however allow me to ride side-saddle some of the time and ease the piercing aches in hip and knee joints. Sarah volunteered to ride Carty for a while, but after 45 minutes in the saddle her face was twisted in a rictus of distress. She slid to the ground and stood there, arms stiffly out like a scarecrow and rigid with sore muscles. 'How on earth do you stand it, she groaned.

Mystery had a mishap. One morning in the last week of May when we collected the horses from a paddock Sarah noticed that the little mare had sustained a deep cut on a hind foot. We suspected that in the night Carty had stood on her foot, and his three-quarters of a ton armed with a new sharp horshoe had caused the damage. The fetlock was puffed up and very hot. But Mystery, as we had been promised back in Killarney, was an exceptional horse. Though the wound was severe enough to cripple, Mystery kept right on walking. For the next three days she limped, she hobbled, she favoured the tender foot, but by the end of each day she had still covered twenty miles.

'I wonder about Mystery sometimes,' Sarah sniffed in her usual sceptical way. 'She's so short on brains that she wouldn't even notice if her whole leg dropped off. She would simply walk to Jerusalem on the other three.'

Sarah was in her element and thriving. Glowing with health, she looked more impish every day – and somehow always managed to appear dapper and trim in a bright blue tee shirt, neat, black jodhpurs, and well-polished black jodhpur boots with a pair of vivid electric blue socks showing. With the breeze ruffling her short-cut hair and her pert grin, she looked boyish and irrepressible, and with her wicked laugh she was pure Peter Pan.

We were now in Swabia, where the population has been deeply religious over the centuries. Along the roadside were frequent calvaries and shrines, even in the remotest areas. They were positioned at crossroads or at bends in the track so that from whichever direction you approached you could see them a long way off. It gave the impression of riding from station to station in a local pilgrimage. Crucifixes were also to be seen on every hand: elevated on concrete plinths beside the road, or as small plain crosses fixed to the gable ends of farm houses, or even planted with the flowers in window boxes. Some crosses were very old. One massive squat stone one, with great square heavy arms of equal length, looked so ancient as to be pagan. Occasionally in the forest we rode past tall dolmens, each with a small window chiselled on the side facing the traveller. As you passed, you glimpsed inside yet another crucifixion scene, sculpted into the rock niche and painted in bright colours. As in Duke Godfrey's day this province of Germany was deeply committed to the faith, and had been a prime recruiting ground for volunteers who marched with him to the Holy Land.

The weather still did not improve as we travelled on. We were heading southeast across the watershed which separates the Rhine and Danube, and into Bavaria. One night the horses stayed at a small farm, the next at a private riding stable, the third evening a municipal riding club loaned us two boxes, and twice we rode for the day accompanied by local horsemen. We did not feel that we were covering more than our usual distance each day, but both times it was noticeable that the local horses were exhausted by the time they had to turn back for home. It seemed that despite Carty's sore back and Mystery's limp, our two horses were beginning to get into the rhythm of travelling fifteen or twenty miles day after day.

We passed through Ellingen, stopping off to visit the headquarters of the southern division of the German Teutonic Order, an order of chivalry which itself arose out of the Crusades. Ellingen was established as a town of the Teutonic Order in the 13th century, but by the time the palace – a florid, pompous structure – was built in 1708 the Order was largely a charade, open only to an aristocratic circle of grandees who played at being the inheritors of Crusading ideals. The corridors of Schloss Ellingen were lined with portraits of the Grand Masters of the Order, most of whom were comfortably robed Archdukes of Austria gazing upon the painter with disdainful and condescending expressions. Nothing could have been further from the hard-bitten and scruffy participants of the First Crusade.

Beyond Ellingen the Roman Road traversed a wide forest of pine trees. The road ran for miles through trees so closely planted that sometimes it was difficult to push our way through, and the branches dumped their loads of rainwater down our necks. It was impossible to see the sky above, and confusing to find our direction because the logging tracks which intersected the old Roman path were also dead straight. Strangely, we found the solution was to steer by sound. Whenever we strayed onto a logging road, the noise of the horses hooves was muffled by the thick carpet of pine needles. But when we turned back and regained the Roman track, we could tell by the distinctive scrape of the hooves cutting down through the leaf cover and scrabbling on the 2,000-year-old Roman roadstones. To confirm our track, we came upon the remains of a Roman road station, a jumbled mound of earth and mossy stones, deep in the forest where once a platoon and a change of horses had awaited the traveller. In this region the Roman Road had been built to serve the 'dry' *limes*, the long frontier wall of ditch, bank and palisade built with enormous labour to close the gap between the 'wet' *limes* of the Rhine and Danube, natural obstacles that deterred migrating German tribes from entering the imperial territory. The 'Devil's Wall' was the name given to it in Duke Godfrey's time.

By October 1096 Godfrey's crusaders were not the only army moving on the Roman roads. Far to the west two other armies were heading towards Constantinople by different routes. The Duke of Normandy and the Duke of Flanders, both rather confusingly named Robert, together with Stephen the Count of Blois, left northern France and were marching with their men to cross the Alps and travel down the length of Italy. There, at Italy's 'heel' they planned to take a ship for the short sea crossing to Durazzo in what is now Albania, and then pick up another Roman way, the Via Egnatia, which would lead them to the grand rendezvous at Constantinople. Their path crossed the track of the second corps, raised in Provence and led by Raymond, the Count of St Gilles, and Adhémar, Bishop of Le Puy. For some reason the Provençals had chosen to take the long and difficult route round the head of the Adriatic and down the Dalmatian coast, through what is now Yugoslavia. In the rugged Dalmatian mountains they were to have a hard time of it from warlike hill tribes who ambushed their stragglers. 'For three weeks we saw neither wild beasts nor birds', wrote Raymond d'Aguilers, a monk who accompanied the force.

'The barbarous and ignorant natives would neither trade with us nor provide guides, but fled from their villages and strongholds and, as though they had been badly injured by our infirm stragglers, slew there poor souls – the debilitated, the old women and men, the poor and the sick – as if they were slaughtering cattle.'

The escorting knights were too heavily armed and did not know the country so they were unable to catch and punish the bandits who slipped away into the 'rugged mountains and very dense forests'. 'Truly Slavonia is a forsaken land . . .' concluded Raymond gloomily.

But the losses in Dalmatia were more compensated for by a new, and unexpected, army that was mustering in southern Italy. The Pope's plea for the Crusade came late to the ears of the Norman warlords there. They had been busy fighting either among themselves to share out the territories won by that remarkable Norman soldier of fortune, Robert Guiscard, or in alliance with one another to wrest further lands from their neighbours. Guiscard's son and heir Count Roger was besieging Amalfi when news of the Crusade arrived, and his nephew, Bohemond, immediately asked leave to go on the Crusade. Roger could not stop him, but he could ill afford to release any troops. So Bohemond made a flamboyant gesture in front of the soldiers. Calling for men to follow him to Jerusalem, he took off his expensive cloak, unsheathed his sword and slashed the precious material in strips which he then distributed for sewing into the shape of a cross. He got his volunteers.

If there was one single group on the Crusade which can fairly be said to have joined out of self-interest, it was Bohemond and his followers from Apulia. They too claimed to be setting out to help Emperor Alexius, but Guiscard's troops – including Bohemond – had only 15 years before been fighting a bitter war against Alexius on the mainland of Greece. Tough and remarkable warriors, even by the standards of the day, they had fought in Sicily, in southern Italy's hot summer, and on the mainland of Greece. They knew the special conditions of Mediterranean warfare, its blazing heat in high summer, the lack of water, the military thinking of Arabs, Turks and Greeks. They were extraordinarily self-confident and accustomed to accepting tremendously long odds. In Bohemond they had an exceptional war leader, brave, wily, and full of initiative, while Tancred, his nephew who accompanied him, was a brilliant tactical opportunist, the perfect cavalry captain with great dash and flair, and, just as important, good luck. When Bohemond, Tancred and the Normans of Apulia took the Cross to join the march to Jerusalem, the First Crusade acquired its tempered cutting edge.

CHAPTER 9

Bavaria and Austria

On 1 June, a month after leaving Chateau Bouillon and some 300 miles into our journey, Carty began to limp. Sarah noticed the lameness immediately and we dismounted while she checked his leg, the near fore. She could find nothing obviously wrong, nor was there any problem with the shoe. We walked on gently, and the limp disappeared. We broke into a trot, and the limp reappeared. Knowing Carty's capacity to absorb pain, we realised that the limp indicated something was beginning to go seriously amiss. We consulted a local vet but he had no experience of Heavy Horses and their maladies, and could only guess at the nature of Carty's problem. Halting at the next village I telephoned Charlie Pinney in England, and asked his advice. From my description of the symptoms, he diagnosed that Carty was probably developing splints, a complaint of the sinew sheaths which could be sufferd by a young working horse. He suggested we continue gently and keep a watchful eye on the lameness to see if it got any worse. If it did, then we would have to stop for at least a week and rest Carty. This would be a blow to our schedule but I reminded myself that our entire expedition depended on the well-being of the two horses. Without them there was no journey to Jerusalem, and unlike the Crusaders we did not have spare mounts.

So I made the next day an extra rest day and gave the two horses a break from the daily grind. Our generous friend the saddle shop owner drove right across Germany to deliver the restuffed Camargue saddle, and was very doubtful about Carty's chances.

'Don't set your heart on going all the way with Carty,' she said. 'In the

Middle Ages the Ardennes horses would have been selected and raised for long-distance work. That type of breeding had been completely lost, and he was never trained for this sort of travel. It's expecting a lot of him to walk across a continent.' Even an average horse, she pointed out, should ideally have each day eight hours of work, eight hours of feeding and eight hours of rest to cover the daily distances we were expecting. A horse of Carty's bulk would require a lower proportion of work, more rest, and more food to replenish his huge frame, and that was something we could not give him on the road any more than Godfrey's knights had been able to reduce the demands on their battle chargers-cum-packhorses.

The morning of 3 June was clear but so chilly that we braced ourselves with coffee laced with brandy before we mounted up. We positioned the restuffed saddle well away from the bald spots on Carty's back. Now he wore two saddle blankets and a thick saddle pad to try to protect his withers, as well as – a recent modification – a small sheepskin on top of the saddle itself to cushion the rider. Sarah and I made our way around the industrial city of Ingolstadt, which was dominated by the tall red-and-white spires of industrial chimneys and the squat drums of a petrochemical works. At two-thirty, the sky clouded over and the rain began to fall as we came to the Danube at Vohberg, an attractive river town with an elegant bridge and a very distinctive skyline of three different spires – one onion shaped, another a tall narrow steeple and the third a buff-coloured stone square. Just before the bridge we found a track that led us into a meadow beside the river. The grass was thick and rich and dripping wet. Armies of nettles lined the hedge. Willows grew in thickets in the field and clustered on the river bank. Beside us ran the Danube, fifty yards wide and in flood. Deep and dirty green, the water was rushing past at a powerful seven knots. A noticeboard informed river users that they were 2224 kilometres from the Black Sea.

It should have been a moment for celebration. Eagerly I had been looking forward to the day we first stood on the bank of the Danube. To me the river had promised to be a symbol, the waymark that would tell us we had crossed the watershed of Europe and were setting foot in the great valley that would lead us almost to the borders of Bulgaria if all went to plan. In reality, that day was among the most dismal of the entire summer. Carty was behaving strangely. It was as if he did not care what happened to him. One moment, finding himself on the wrong side of a willow thicket from Mystery, he simply turned at right angles and blundered through the obstacle like a tank, blindly crashing his way through the branches to rejoin his partner. Then, stooping down to snatch at some grass as he walked along, he suddenly buckled at the knees and collapsed. He crashed straight forward on to his chest and belly as though he had been shot in the head by a humane killer. His collapse was so fast that I could not jump off, but remained in the saddle with Carty's huge bulk slumped beneath me. For what seemed like a full minute Carty stayed there, prone and unmoving. It was a horrible sensation to wonder if he would be able to rise again. Then he laboriously heaved himself on to his feet and, head hanging, plodded forward again to follow Mystery.

I looked around for shelter, where we could stop and rest Carty. But there was none, only a sodden meadow, a high earth dyke, and the main road running along the north bank of the river. Carty tried to catch up again with Mystery. He broke into a trot, and immediately his shoulder began to droop alarmingly with each pace as his limp reappeared. The meadow came to an end, and we were forced to ride up on the road. It was not a safe place. The road curved and twisted, following the river's line, and there was a great deal of heavy traffic. The road surface was worn and greasy, and slick with rain. I worried that a truck would skid or come too close on a corner and injure the horses; or that Carty would again stumble and fall in the roadway, and be run down. I was out of the saddle now and walking beside Carty, who was looking thoroughly miserable. His limp was now obvious even at a slow walk and I was assailed by doubts. Was he breaking down? Had I imposed too great a task on the young Ardennes? Loathing the notion that the journey was causing pain to the great horse, it was little comfort to reflect that if he hadn't set out on the expedition he could now be butcher's meat in France. For all his wiles and clumsiness, I was very fond of Carty, and I missed his antics. We walked more and more slowly. I counted Carty's paces and flinched each time he favoured the damaged leg. The trucks hurtled past a few feet away, drenching us in the spray from their wheels; I came to detest the swish of their tyres as they vanished unheeding into the murk. A black gloom descended on me as we trudged down the road and plodded over the river by the bridge at Neustadt. The rain kept spattering down, and even Sarah, normally so firmly cheerful, looked grave.

I realised we would again have to abandon our planned distance for the day. The horses needed shelter, and as soon as possible. Someone had mentioned there was a stable on the outskirts of Neustadt, and as we approached the town we met a drunk. He was wearing carpet slippers and standing in a puddle. In response to our questions about a stable, he gestured hazily that we should turn aside and cross several fields. We interpreted his alcoholic directions as best we could and followed a small side road. After half a mile we found a modest farmhouse with tables and chairs standing outside under the rain. We noticed the tell-tale signs – a horsebox tucked away round a corner, a row of tethering rings high on a wall, and half doors on the barn. It was part-farm and part-stable, for there was another hangar-like building which could have been an indoor riding school, though it had a sign advertising beer and meals. A grey-haired woman wearing an apron over her working clothes stepped out of the front door of the farm. She must have seen us from her kitchen window, plodding down the road, leading the dispirited, wet horses.

'Grüss Gott,' she exclaimed, and clucked her tongue sympathetically.

'Please, do you have space in the barn for the horses to stay over-night?' begged Sarah.

The woman displayed a smile so radiant that my spirits soared. It was such a simple, straightforward reflex. I knew that for at least one night the horses would be cared-for and dry. What is more it turned out that the farmer could rent us rooms so that in the morning we could tackle the problems without the numbing weight of fatigue. My depression started to evaporate, and the worries assumed their correct proportion.

Within the next half hour, two clean, airy stalls had been briskly prepared for the horses. Hay bales were tossed down from the loft, oats and water were provided, and a place cleared where we could spread out and dry our drenched clothing and the sopping horse blankets. Carty had his nose stuck in a manger of oats and was a hot, sweating but different animal. A couple of hours later, with a hot meal inside me from the restaurant by the riding hall, I understood just how he felt. At nightfall came a tremendous sound of croaking as the frogs in the farmyard pond began a raucous concert. 'With this weather, they probably think they're drowning,' muttered Sarah.

Next day we found another local vet to examine Carty's leg, but he too could find nothing wrong, admitting that he had no experience with Heavy Horses. He was, he said, more accustomed to looking after cows and pigs. But he administered a pain-killing injection and took the blood samples we needed to obtain medical certificates for crossing into Austria. As usual, the offer of payment was refused. I made up my mind: we would give Carty the rest he needed, and ride on with only Mystery until Carty was fit and we could have him rejoin the expedition.

What we required was a farm where there was space for him, first to rest in a stable and then to walk around taking gentle exercise, and someone to care for him. Half-a-day's easy walk beyond Neustadt we found the perfect spot. A riding club kept their horses with a Bavarian farmer whom Sarah and I immediately nick-named 'Herr Genau'. About fifty years old, with bright blue eyes and a weatherbeaten complexion, he was the calmest, most phlegmatic individual one could imagine. Slow of speech and manner, nothing disturbed him. Whatever was said to him, he replied 'Genau' – 'Indeed' – in a slow thoughtful manner, and nodded gently. When we rode up with Carty, he walked over quietly, patted the huge neck, nodded reflectively and without saying a word, simply reached for the bridle and with calm, deliberate paces walked him off to a large barn where we could unsaddle and dry off the horses. We explained about Carty's limp. We would be very grateful, we said, if he would take care of Carty for a few days: 'Genau.' We didn't know how long we would have to leave the horse: 'Genau.' We would come every day to check how he was getting on: 'Genau.' Was it possible to arrange for a horse vet to look at him and check the limp?: 'Genau.' There was nothing more to say. Herr Schuh, for that was his real name, was totally unperturbable.

At that point a cowboy walked out of the main stable building. Sarah and I looked at the apparition in amazement. From head to toe he was dressed in full Wild West regalia – high-heeled cowboy boots, leather chaps, jeans held up by a wide hand-tooled belt with a large metal buckle embossed with steers' horns, a denim shirt and a heavily fringed leather jacket. On his head, of course, was a ten-gallon hat. He was leading a pinto horse with vivid blotches and carrying a showy, silver-mounted western saddle and a brightly coloured saddle blanket. The newcomer looked as though he had walked off a Western's film set or strayed from a rodeo. He was not at all what we had expected to find in deepest rural Bavaria.

Herbert Birk was his even less likely name, and he turned out to be a construction worker who lived, ate and dreamed of the cowboy West. He drove heavy construction equipment, working overtime to save up enough money to buy his western costumes, pay for his pinto pony and take frequent trips to the American west. In consequence he spoke a curious sort of English with a strong American western twang and laced with antique cowboy phrases. Listening to him was like hearing the sound track of a poorly scripted Hollywood film with stilted cowboy conversations that repeated the same stock phrases. But he was very genuine – he would have said 'a real good guy' – and was eager to help us. He insisted on taking Sarah and me to the local town where he escorted us into Willie's Western Bar. There, to our astonishment, in the centre of a Bavarian market town was a room tricked out in all the trappings: swing doors, chandeliers, walls decorated with Confederate flags, buffalo horns and imitation Remington rifles, bursting with loud country and western music. The place was filled with Herbert Birk lookalikes, all in jeans and cowboy boots, western hats and western shirts, drinking beer from tankards. The only concession to local tastes was that the short menu, heavy on chips, substituted pork for beef steaks. We were in the den of the Bavarian cowboys.

Shouting over the clamour of the country and western singers, I told our new acquaintance about the continuing problem of Carty's sore back and how we were finding that even the restuffed Camargue saddle did not fit properly. Herbert said he would introduce us to a friend – another 'pretty good guy' – who collected old saddles. Maybe he had one that would be suitable? He was as good as his word, and the next morning we visited Carty to take a profile of the shape of his back with a length of bent wire. Reassured by more *'genaus'* from farmer Schuh, we then drove across the pleasant Bavarian countryside, until we came to the 'Ringo Ranch'. If anything it was an even more extraordinary place than Willie's Western Bar – a small German farm lovingly rearranged as if it had been located in Montana or Wyoming.

Wagon wheels decorated the driveway, rustic post-and-rail fencing penned in more pinto horses, an outbuilding with a porch was labelled 'saloon', and the *de rigeur* set of buffalo horns was nailed to the barn wall. When we arrived, Herbert's friend – in the usual cowboy costume – was stooped over the foot of a pinto pony that he was re-shoeing, very competently. We were shown up to the attic. There we found a saddlery work bench and, dumped in corners, a magpie assortment of old saddles. Naturally there were western saddles in profusion. But there were also old hunting saddles, Hungarian saddles, French saddles, pony saddles, all in a dusty jumble. I pawed through them, holding the bent wire against them to see if they matched Carty's broad shape. I came across a saddle that matched the curve of the bent wire perfectly. It seemed too good to be true, and I dragged the saddle out for closer inspection. It was broad of seat and broad of fit. I asked what sort of saddle it could be. It was, I was informed, an old German army Number Three saddle, made in the 1920s. But why was it so broad? The field artillery guns of the German army, said Ringo, were pulled by teams of four Heavy Horses, in line ahead. The first horse carried a rider to guide the team so the German army required that the saddle should fit the lead horse. I saw at once that the spread of the saddle tree was just right for Carty, the leather was of finest quality and the saddle was intelligently designed so that it could be taken to pieces in a few moments to be repaired or altered. With a few stitches I could restore the saddle to working condition. Carty's back problems, I guessed, were solved, and in the unlikely setting of a Bavarian ranch.

'Buffalo Bill', as Sarah had by now dubbed Herbert, insisted on accompanying us on the next sector. His pinto was no match for Mystery. Freed of Carty's lumbering presence she quickened her stride and when she reached the evening stable, tripped in looking eagerly for food, while the wretched pinto was shaky at the knees. Next day, with Carty still recuperating, Sarah and I took it in turns to ride Mystery and the moped. The little mare relished the pace. Instead of our usual 18 or 20 miles, we rode 30 miles, and the next day covered 40 miles without a hitch. Mystery was a walking and trotting machine which never seemed to flag or wilt, but ate up the miles like a true palfrey. Each evening we returned to see how Carty was getting on. Herr Genau told us the vet had visited him, and diagnosed an inflamed foot, the result of so much heavy work. Rest, a course of injections and some pain-suppressing drugs were prescribed. With each visit we could tell that Carty was regaining his old self, and on the fourth day we found him nosing around the corral, which was splintering under his push, while Herr Schuh unconcernedly tossed fresh grass over the rail to his favourite charge.

While Carty rested, I visited Regensburg, the city on the Danube that had been Duke Godfrey's gateway to Central Europe. By chance there was an exhibition of artwork from Regensburg's renowned school of illumination which was flourishing at the time of Duke Godfrey's expedition. The pictures challenged any notion that the 11th century society from which Duke Godfrey emerged was totally uncouth and insular. Displayed was the Royal Sacrament of the Emperor Henry II, a triumph of penmanship, exquisitely written on crisp, clean parchment, richly coloured, glittering with gold leaf. There was the German emperor, orb on knee and surrounded by scholars and teachers, with the symbols of justice, piety, law and right neatly arranged in the four corners. Beneath the imperial feet a brigand brandished a sword to threaten a kneeling man who offered up his jewels, while above the imperial head a bird, the Holy Spirit, descended from the firmament to bring the word of God to Henry the Evangelist.

Regensburg's monks had even drawn Jerusalem. The Holy City was shown schematically as the centre of a labyrinth, mankind's true goal on earth but difficult and confusing to reach, an impossible search without the guidance of the Church. The influence of Eastern art on the monkish techniques was obvious. The colours, the garments, the postures of the human figures, their clothing, the way their faces were shown, all testified how much the artists of Regensburg drew upon what elements of Byzantine style had reached them along the Danube route. They had drawn many women of the Church. An abbess in a stole held at the throat by a brooch stood with her hand raised in the preaching posture while nuns in their habits surrounded her. Another nun, her head covered with a plain cloth, knelt with hands uplifted to receive the Benedictine Order's book of rules from St Benedict himself, shown oversized with an immense black beard and a shepherd's crook. The illustrations of churchmen depicted the sort of clerics who initiated, preached, sustained, accompanied and eventually reported the Crusade. There was a striking contrast between the grand princes of the church and the ordinary preachers. The former were magnificent prelates, resplendent in embroidered vestments encrusted with precious stones,

95

and bearing jewelled crosses in their hands. Even their attendant priests, at first glance plainly dressed in simple white, had delicate bands of gold at neck and hem in tasteful contrast to their laundered robes, while their tonsures had neatness and style. On the other hand, there were the simple rough priests of tradition, barefoot, long-haired and plain of face, much more the sort who would have marched with the homespun pilgrims of Godfrey's train. These ordinary men traced their manner back to those uncompromising missionaries who had spread Christianity down the Danube valley, along the 'right way', preaching their blunt message from village to village. In the forecourt of the church of St Emmeram, Regensburg's missionary saint, was a statue carved just fifty years before the First Crusade. It depicted the itinerant preacher of the time, dressed in an ankle-length plain gown with an overmantle decorated with a cross. The long, thick hair was cut in a tonsure and there was a hint of a beard. The wide open eyes gave a slightly startled expression to the earnest face, but the figure exuded an unreserved candour backed up by unswerving conviction.

When we went with the horsebox to collect Carty from Herr Schuh, we found that five days' rest had not only cured the big Ardennes's hurt leg so that he walked without a limp, but had restored his energy and helped to mend his saddle sores. Dutifully we carried both the horses in the horsebox up to the German-Austrian border post and were glad we did so, because the Austrian veterinary authority was very strict about the horses' health documents, and insisted on a twenty-four-hour quarantine in a local stable. But this only served to give Carty extra rest and he was in splendid fettle when we saddled up and rode into the Austrian countryside. The venerable German Army saddle fitted him to perfection so that when it was removed after the first full day's ride, we found only an even patch, wet with sweat, with none of the hot dry spots that had previously marked where his saddle sores would swell. Best of all, we had the long-awaited improvement in the weather. Although it was now mid-June and the thunderclouds and sudden gusts of rain were often more like spring than summer, it was such a pleasant change to see the sun at all that everyone was in a good humour. The Austrian farmers were out in their fields, cutting and raking and turning hay by hand, and there were smiles and friendly waves as we rode by.

We had, at last, the unmistakable sensation that we were advancing into new and different terrain, a feeling the Crusaders must have shared. Far away to our right the hulking peaks and shoulders of the Alpine Foreland had begun to appear. The spectacle was unlike anything that Duke Godfrey's men from the Ardennes would have known. The hills were like a child's drawing, so steep and abrupt and sharply defined. Even at a great distance one could make out dark ridges, the spiky fringe of forest on the crests, and dramatically steep cliffs. Convection clouds were forming and shifting over them, and the play of light on the clouds produced a grey-and-white luminescence in contrast to the dark hills beneath them. It was both dramatic and definitive, because the shapes and angles of the hills gradually changed as we rode forward and thus became the first genuine gauge of our progress. Just as an observer on a ship on the featureless ocean marks his passage by the first glimpse of an island on the horizon ahead, then watches it come abeam, and finally leaves it astern, so the hills of the VorAlp produced exactly the same effect, a contrast to the weeks of travelling across the lowlands of south Germany where each day's progress could be marked on the map but gave no appreciable change on the horizon.

The Via Militaris took us over rolling countryside where the fields of maize were beginning to sprout and the wheat was well advanced. The haymaking technique was still medieval. The menfolk scythed the grass, and the women stacked it into haycocks, draped over cross-sticks thrust through a stout central pole planted in the ground. Row upon row of these haycocks marched across the sloping meadows, and riding past them in the poor light of dusk and dawn they looked like monsters from Germanic fable, shaggy shapes marshalled in field battalions. Sometimes the road shunned the muddy Danube floodplain, and climbed to more exposed ground where the drainage was better. Here Mystery sidled up the hills with her head almost upside down, trying to prevent the cold rain of the thunderstorms being driven in her ears. Surmounting each ridge, we had superb views of the Danube valley as an immense trough running right through the plateau. Poor drainage and the miasmas of the valley floor forced most settlement to the hilly slopes, and one night we stayed at a small village elevated some fifty feet above the valley floor where, as daylight faded, we could look down on the mists first rising among the alder and oak, then rolling across the fields of wheat and hay like a white tide.

Next morning was gloriously sunny and we set off, determined to enjoy the river at last. It was a complete contrast to our previous arrival on the Danube. The weather was superb, the horses in peak condition, and the countryside was idyllic. The grass was like a lawn and for the sheer joy of it we urged the horses into a gallop. Mystery shot off, and Carty put down his head, and went careering up into a thundering gallop, like a child racing home from lessons.

Soon afterwards the hills pinched in on the valley of the Danube. The old Roman Road was now a towpath passing below a steep cliff on our right, while across the river were picture-postcard views of the small river towns. On the towpath we were overtaken by the pedalling squadrons of German tourists, all in cotton peaked hats, with the men tending to singlets and streamlined cycling shorts, while the more stately women were in stretch slacks securely planted on sensible upright bicycles. For some reason the former bore heavy packs on their shoulders, while their wives pedalled sedately with empty wicker baskets on the handlebars. The towpath was banned to motor traffic so the only sound of engines came from the pushboats and motorbarges chugging up against the Danube flood. Whenever the barges passed, the waves of their wash came slapping into the revetment and made Carty jump.

Just short of Ybbs, at the end of a perfect day's travel, we roused an elderly farmer from his bed although it was not yet seven in the evening. Leaning out of his bedroom window in an enormous farmhouse, as large as a grange, he gestured that we were free to leave the horses in his paddock, provided they were well behaved. Without a qualm we assured him that the pair never tried to escape. Twenty miles farther on, at Melk's huge Benedictine abbey planted nearly 200 feet above the river on its imposing bluff, I asked to see the abbey's famous relic: the portable altar of Swannhilde, an example of the sort of transportable holy furniture which the Crusaders must have taken with them for celebrating divine office. But the altar was locked up pending restoration. Perhaps it would be on view again in four years time, they said.

The riding club at Albrechtsberg produced a farrier to re-shoe the horses, a task which was clearly overdue. The re-shoeing, the third since the admirable Monsieur Juillet of Bourbeau, was performed by another veteran blacksmith whose creed was a bottle of beer per horse to replenish sweat lost to the heat of the forge. In view of the awkwardness of shoeing Carty, this allowance was increased to a bottle of beer per shoe, and once again it took five hours to do the job. As farrier's aide and apprentice I finished up cut, bruised, exhausted, but noticeably more sober than my instructor.

At St Pölten next evening a Hungarian came to meet us. Steven Vargas worked for a Hungarian State Travel Agency that specialised in riding holidays in hungary and, hearing about our ride, had managed to track us down. 'Don't expect everything to be well organised and smooth going when you enter Hungary, he warned us jovially. 'Your will often need to improvise. But if you've got this far, you'll manage alright. And one thing is very special about riding in Hungary. In the countryside you can ride anywhere, in any direction. Don't worry about fields or roads or bridle paths. Simply go in a straight line and no one will object. If they do, just explain who you are and they'll understand.'

He swept off leaving us a treasure: a map of Hungary with the riding centres inked in neat boxes. He also promised that through the Hungarian Riding Federation he would warn the collective farms, the *economistas*, of our coming. 'Hungarians love horses,' were his last words, 'just ask for shelter at the farms and I'm sure you will be welcomed.'

Ironically, we were refused shelter at an Austrian farm that same evening. It was the first time this had happened, and was a blessing in disguise. Stoically, we went to the next farm, a long haul up a winding road to the hilltop. There, at the end of a rutted track, we found several paddocks full of horses, a line of neat stables, and a slightly chaotic farmhouse which had once been a summer home. Dogs, mostly Jack Russells, barked and scurried everywhere. A young couple ran the entire establishment with good-natured expertise. Martin was dark haired, slight and serious-looking behind his granny glasses, but possessed of a penetratingly wicked humour, his quips delivered deadpan in perfect English learned when he had worked as a jockey in England. Christa his wife was very grave and rather shy, with perfectly symmetrical features and an air of calm that made her a perfect foil to her husband's bursts of enthusiasm. Together they ran the place as a small stud farm and livery stable, combined with boarding kennels, and ran it impeccably. The horses were beautifully cared for, and Martin and Christa worked from six in the morning until ten at night to make sure their animals were healthy and content. Martin, it turned out, had long wanted to own and work a Heavy Horse on his farm. It would be ideal for the small fields and broken terrain on the hill top overlooking the Vienna Woods, and after we had extended our stay to two nights to enjoy the company of this relaxed and happy couple, Martin asked a favour. 'If you ever want to get rid of Carty,' he said, 'please contact me. I can promise you we'll give him a really good home.'

We skirted south to avoid the traffic of Vienna's conurbation, going instead by way of the Helenenthal valley and Baden to avoid the metropolitan sprawl. The weather was hot and sunny, and we rode through state forests and along pleasant valleys where meadows of uncut hay were sprinkled with summer flowers, and the villages all had tubs of geraniums and freshly painted house fronts. The names were old – Holy Cross and Cholera Chapel – and along the Helenental valley we passed beneath watchtowers guarding the strategic route into Hungary. Our goal was the Burgenland, the edge of the great Roman province of Pannonia, where begin the flatlands that had made this region of Europe the most fertile in the empire. Even today the Austrian Burgenland retains its special character with villages of single-storey houses set at right angles to the street in the traditional style and the flat fields cultivated in narrow strips. Now the ripening wheat was showing patches of pale yellow among the green, and on the tall sunflower stalks we could distinguish the shape of buds.

Here, on 28 June, our very last day in Austria, we nearly killed Carty by a mistake which had nothing whatever to do with medieval travel. Worried that he would not be able to brush away flies with his bob tail – even in its new lengthened form, the result of the application of washing-up liquid way back in Luxembourg – we decided to spray him with a proprietary brand of fly repellent we had brought from Ireland. In the morning we clipped away his excess fur, now that the daytime temperatures were rising, and Carty stood quietly in the stall as I began to spray. A trial burst on his huge haunch produced no ill effect, and I had gone on to spray almost his entire side when Sarah suddenly shouted 'Stop! Look at Carty's neck!'

The skin on the side of his huge neck was puckering up in wrinkles, contracting so fiercely that his entire head was being pulled around to the side. It was horrifying. Carty began to sway as if to faint, and we realised that, by some appalling chance, he was violently allergic to the chemical in the spray. He began to stagger. If he collapsed in the stall there would be little enough room to get such a huge animal back on his feet again. I flung down the spray bottle, and we dragged him to the yard where we turned on a hose full pressure and began to wash away the chemical. It was almost too late, the folds in his skin were deepening and the surface skin was being schorched off. He was obviously in agony. Desperately we soused him with water, and knew we had to keep him on his feet. Like walking a drunk up and down and forcing down black coffee, we dragged Carty round and round the yard, and threw buckets of cold water over him. We slapped him to keep him awake and made him trot. At all costs we kept him moving, until finally his staggering and dizziness passed. Then, weak with shock ourselves, we put him back in the stall and I buried the offending spray in a field. That, I reflected, had been a menace the Crusaders never had to encounter.

CHAPTER 10

Szarcsa

Steven Vargas had not exaggerated the Hungarians' willingness to help us once they learned we were travelling by horse. At their border post near Sopron the Hungarian veterinary official bustled through our paperwork, and then insisted on taking us around the other offices – customs, immigration, money exchange – and pressing them to give us immediate attention. In less than an hour we were clear of the formalities and heading for the first of the stables that Steven had marked on our map, the converted Chateau at Nagycenk which served as a breeding station for the National Stud. Just before reaching it, we had a shock. Around a corner came Carty's twin, pulling a farm cart. The sight was as disconcerting as walking past a full length mirror and seeing one's own moving reflection. The approaching horse was Carty's colour, the same shape, and with the same gait. Only when the horse was much closer could we see that there were some differences: the strange horse was lighter and smaller, with finer bones and considerably neater feet.

'Most of Hungary's horses perished during the Second World War,' explained the director of the breeding station. 'Afterwards the government decided to reintroduce working horses to the land because they made good economic sense for Hungarian agriculture, particularly on the smaller farms. So a government commission was sent around Europe to find the most suitable breed, and the commissioners recommended that the Ardennes Horse was ideal for our needs, and something like fifty Ardennes stallions and mares were purchased and brought to Hungary.

Most of them came from France. The horse you saw was probably descended from that shipment.'

In fact Hungary proved to be by far the most horse-conscious of all the countries we rode through all that summer. Daily we passed working horses in the fields standing patiently while their wagons were piled high with the hay crop, and in the towns horses were pulling rubbish carts or making general deliveries. The happy result was that, for once, we were not worried by motor traffic. Hungarian drivers were accustomed to passing horses on their roads, and gave us the luxury of a wide berth. But we rarely saw a horse actually being ridden, except at the stud farms and riding stables. In Hungary a horse's place was between the shafts of a cart. The sight of two riders, particularly when one was mounted on a Heavy Horse, came as a considerable surprise to most carters.

On the evening after we left Nagycenk we were riding peacefully down the road, when we noticed an empty wagon drawn by two horses approaching in the opposite direction. The driver was obviously much the worse for drink: he was slumped in the seat, oblivious to the world, head on his chest, and whip aslant in his hand. His two black horses knew their own way back to the stable and were walking along quietly, taking their master home. As they came to their turn-off, the two animals of their own accord turned purposefully to their left, across the line of oncoming traffic. There was a screech of brakes, the blare of a horn, and an angry lorry driver swerved to avoid the wagon. The din awoke the drunken carter just at the moment we drew level with him. He half-opened his eyes and was blearily looking around when he caught sight of us, not six feet away. His eyes opened wide with surprise. A look of utter befuddled astonishment swept across his face. Clutching for support, he struggled to sit upright on the seat, opened his mouth to speak to us, and twisted so he could wave a greeting. But the sudden movement of his arm startled his horses into a trot and he was caught off balance by the acceleration. In slow motion, with his mouth agape, the carter toppled gently backwards into the floor of the empty wagon. The last we saw of him were his legs waving feebly in the air like an upturned beetle as his horses drew him inexorably away down the lane, and we heard muffled halloos of greeting. In Hungary, as in Ireland, it appeared that equitation could go hand in hand with inebriation.

King Coloman, who ruled Hungary when Duke Godfrey and his army arrived at the border, is very little known outside his own country. Yet Coloman was a most unusual monarch. Trained as a priest, he had reached the rank of bishop when he inherited the throne of Hungary from an uncle. A chronicler described him as being 'of all the rulers of his time the most erudite in literary knowledge'. Nicknamed Coloman the Bibliophile, his reputation as a theologian spread as far as Rome. On the battlefield, too, Coloman was a man to be reckoned with. In the six months prior to Godfrey's arrival, a succession of pilgrim bands had been arriving on his western frontier, including that of Peter the Hermit. The first groups had been given free passage and crossed Hungary with little incident. But then three more bands of so-called 'pilgrims' had shown up, mostly Bavarians and Swabians, and including the perpetrators of the Jewish massacres along the Rhine valley. These ill-assorted groups behaved no better than brigands as they filtered into Hungarian territory, burning and pillaging. In one notorious incident the 'pilgrims' murdered a young Hungarian boy by impaling him alive on a stake. Coloman collected the Hungarian army, and descended on the interlopers like a thunderbolt. The Hungarian troops smashed the ill-disciplined mob and drove them back across the border with heavy losses. At Tulln on the Danube, Godfrey and his colleagues came across survivors who told him pitiful yarns about their maltreatment by the bloodthirsty king of the Magyars.

Prudently Godfrey halted his army near the river Leitha and sent a nobleman, Henry d'Esch, to enquire if safe passage would be granted to him and why the Hungarians had attacked the earlier pilgrims, 'Christians persecuting Christians'. Henry d'Esch was courteously received at Coloman's court where the true behaviour of the so-called pilgrims was explained to him.

'From the King Coloman to Duke Godfrey and all the Christians, greetings and most sincere regards,' began the letter Coloman sent back. 'We have heard that you are a man of power and a prince on earth, and those who know you have always appreciated your trustworthiness. This is why, knowing your unusual reputation, I now wish to meet you and make your acquaintance.' Coloman suggested that he and Godfrey should meet by the marshes of the inland sea, the Neusiedl, and discuss in person the accusations agains the Magyars. Leaving the main army, Godfrey went forward with three hundred knights to the rendezvous.

The historic meeting took place in September on a bridge near Sopron. Godfrey, with just three attendants, rode up and was embraced by King Coloman. In a short time Godfrey had accepted Coloman's invitation to go with him into Hungary.

For a week Godfrey was King Coloman's guest while the two men worked out the details of the transit of Hungary. Godfrey's army was to have safe conduct provided Godfrey gave his word that the pilgrims would behave themselves peaceably. In return the Hungarians would supply the travellers with provisions at a fair, or even subsidised price. By way of insurance Coloman added two safeguards: the Hungarian army would discreetly escort the pilgrim host, and Godfrey must deliver up a primary hostage of Coloman's choice. He named as hostage Duke Godfrey's younger brother, Baldwin, together with his wife Godehilde. They would stay at Coloman's court until the pilgrims had passed quietly out of Hungary. Coloman may have made a lucky guess, or perhaps he had been well informed by his spies, for in selecting Baldwin, as later events would show, Coloman neutralised the most dangerous man in Godfrey's army.

Baldwin, understandably, was not enthusiastic about this arrangement when Godfrey returned to the main army to announce the agreement. He flatly refused to place himself at Coloman's mercy. In that case, Godfrey answered, the only way he could keep his word to the Hungarian king was to go as the hostage himself. Shamed, the younger brother had to agree 'for the good of his brothers.'

We camped on the slope of the hill crowned by the great neoclassical Benedictine abbey of Saint Martin at Pannonhelm. It was here, according to tradition, that Godfrey stayed for his week as Coloman's guest, and in the abbey library we were shown an inventory of the abbey's possessions drawn up shortly before the First Crusade. The abbey's continuing importance in modern Hungarian life was a typical paradox of Hungarian communism. The monks of St Martin gave the impression that they considered themselves responsible, just as much as the government, for preserving and nurturing Hungary's identity. In the abbey school, the monks had educated many leading Hungarians, and in their archives they preserved documents older than any in the state collections, including the nation's birth certificate – the first document to include recognisable words in the Hungarian language. We were shown round by brother Matteus, who smiled understandingly when I confessed we were finding Hungarian an impenetrable language, and despaired of learning enough to make ourselves understood in the countryside. I proposed to carry a short note setting out our simple requirements for the horses and so, after I printed out the key phrases, Brother Matteus wrote underneath the Magyar translation. Thenceforth, in farm and village, we presented the scrap of paper like speechless aliens from another planet. It read: 'Please can you help us. Can you show us where we can keep two horses overnight, either in a field or a stable?' The second line read: 'Please can you sell us food for the horses?'

In fact the only time we were denied accommodation for the horses in Hungary had been at a riding club in the bleak town of Györ. The place was half closed, the manager away, and the elderly watchman terrified of higher officialdom. He would not allow the horses into two empty stalls without authorisation from a superior. We pleaded with him and were grudgingly given a bucket of water. Then he procrastinated for three hours until it was late enough for him to lock the stable door and scurry off, abandoning us to spend a sleepless night on a black cinder patch covered with rubbish beside the railway line, where we were tormented by mosquitos and flying insects. Like a great child Carty had skinned his knees and nose when he had tripped and fallen on the tarmac earlier that day, and I was crouched in front of him, smearing ointment on his great hairy knee when he was bitten in the rear by some insect. Without warning he leapt straight forward uttering a high-pitched squeal and landed on my big toe with his entire weight. Sarah could not conceal her mirth at my misfortune as I hopped around swearing mightily, and for the next few weeks I walked with a limp to remind me that a war horse can spring into action from a standing start.

South of Pannonhelm the little villages might have been pictures from a Victorian embroidered sampler on the virtues of country living. They had broad central avenues lined by trim cottages. In front of every cottage was a neat patch of garden with flowers and vegetables, and in the backyard a clutch of chickens or geese. Water pumps of cast iron painted sky blue stood at regular intervals along the grass verge, and the cottagers had a tendency to stand at their doorways looking content and bucolic. The land was flat and fertile, given over to wide fields of wheat and maize, with an occasional purplish patch where lavender was growing as a crop. In the fields of strawberries and black currants, peasants in singlets and shorts or floral dresses, sat comfortably on low canvas stools among the bushes while they plucked the fruit and chatted amongst themselves, shaded by wide straw hats and portable sun awnings.

Riding through such lushness was a delight. The summer had fully burst on us, and the days were long and sunny. We rode along sand tracks ideal for the horses or across maize fields with the dust puffing up from their hooves and the lines of tall dry stalks rattling off our legs. Now and again Mystery and Carty would snatch up a plant, tug it free, and walk along chewing the plant as a human might chew a grass stalk. No one seemed to mind in the least where we rode or what we did. Our noon halts were indolent and luxurious. Once, we took our lunch sprawled under a huge wild mulberry tree, picking handfuls of the squishy fruit for our dessert; the next day we were in a meadow and Carty entertained us by investigating the nearby stream. The banks were very steep and overgrown with reeds, and Carty in his curiosity went too far. The edge of the bank crumbled beneath his weight, and he slid down into the water majestically out of control, his enormous rump high in the air. Unperturbed he proceeded to slosh up and down the muddy stream bed, thigh deep in the water and grazing on the reeds like a hippopotamus. While our backs were turned to watch this spectacle, Mystery took her chance to try to roll with her saddle still on. There was a sudden oath of rage from Sarah, and I was amazed by the speed of my diminutive colleague sprinting across the meadow to where Mystery had just folded her legs and was settling on the ground, only to receive a terrific kick in the rump which Sarah delivered with the stinging accuracy of a professional footballer.

On Monday 6 July we entered the little town of Szarzentmihaily, almost our halfway point across Hungary. It was marked on our map as having a horse farm, but we never located it. Asking directions in the small grocery shop I was accosted by a very jovial pensioner, with a mouthful of stainless steel teeth and one of those bald, round and seamless heads which would look the same whichever way up they are set. He hauled us off to the front room of his house, to eat excellent cakes served by his wife, drink plum brandy and wine, and — bizarrely enough — watch Wimbledon tennis on television. Lazlo was a retired factory manager and obviously very bored. Our appearance provided the ideal excuse for us to go to see his bosom friend Lajos just up the road. Lajos, we were told, ran a farm, owned a horse, and there was no need to look farther because Lajos would be sure to take in our animals.

We were duly marched up the road to Lajos's farm, only to be told that he was up in his vineyard, working. Lazlo brightened up even more. We continued to the vineyard and found Lajos between the vines, walking along behind a stout grey mare pulling a light plough. From ten paces we could see we were going to like him. He was big and burly, with an open, suntanned face, and dressed in a sweat-stained shirt, shorts, and sandals with socks. On his head was perched a slightly comical, lightweight porkpie hat, too small for him, which he now pushed back with one hand as his face broke into an instant smile of greeting. Every sentence from Lajos, we found, was punctuated with a deep chuckle. He was one of those people who, one feels, could never be downcast by any difficulty but delights in extracting every enjoyment out of life. Then we understood Lazlo's keenness on the visit to the vineyard. The grey mare was promptly tied up in the shade of a tree and we were escorted to the small chalet beside the vineyard. Here Lajos kept his tools and stored his wine. In the cellar was the usual array of jugs, tubs, barrels, rubber tubing and funnels. A large flagon of wine was drawn off and we went outside to imbibe. Twenty minutes later another flagon was loaded, and we sat down for longer. It was nearly dusk by the time the grey mare was harnessed up to the cart for the homeward drive and we all retired to Lajos's farm, thoroughly tipsy. Lajos's generosity and good humour never faltered. Yes, he had space for Mystery and Carty in his stable. Yes, of course, he would look after the two horses for us. No, no, we were not to worry. He would feed and water and groom them too, if we needed to go away for a couple of days. If we were going away, then we must take several bottles of his wine with us for the journey, and some of his home-made sausage. Lajos, it turned out, was not just a farmer, wine-maker, and bon viveur. He was the local butcher as well.

The reason for our two day excursion was a decision that had been looming since the first day we left Bouillon with Carty: we needed a third horse. I had ridden a Heavy Horse from Belgium to Budapest and that was as painful an experience as any research would warrant. From now on I proposed to adopt a more authentic medieval method: two palfreys and a pack horse. I was confident that it would be a far more comfortable arrangement.

Steve Vargas had told us of a horse farm on the *puzta*, the vast open plain to the east of the Danube renowned for the raising of herds of horses since the days when the nomadic Magyar tribes had first ridden into Hungary. At Sarlopuzta, he said, we should find what we wanted. It was another paradox of Hungarian communism – a large riding centre rented from the state and run as a private enterprise. There, we were told, we should be able to buy a horse on the spot, whereas a state farm would need weeks to complete the necessary documentation for the purchase. So Sarah and I drove to Sarlopuzta which proved to be a large stud farm combined with a holiday riding centre for tourists. We saw no tourists, but there were hundreds upon hundreds of horses, most being raised for sale in the lucrative German market. But the animals were not what we were looking for. They were either too young and untrained, or they were so unfit that we would need weeks to prepare them for the gruelling daily slog that was our normal routine. After two months on the road since Chateau Bouillon we had a much clearer idea of the sensible, well-exercised animal that would suit our needs. I trailed along behind Sarah as she strode briskly through the horse sheds and paddock after paddock. I had never seen so many horses gathered together in one place, and was awed by her sprightly manner. She paused once or twice in her quick march to check a horse's back or legs. Usually there was something wrong, too soft, too weak, outward pointing toes, bones too light.

Finally, we came to the row of rooms where the *csikos* lived, the horse wranglers who worked at Sarlopuzta. Nearby was a small stable where they kept their own horses, the animals they used day after day to round up the herds. We went inside, and Sarah nodded approvingly.

'At least these horses are reasonably fit,' she commented. 'If they are work horses, they should have some sense too.' She pointed out a rangy bay horse, a gelding a little taller than Mystery but with the same white blaze on the nose and three white socks. 'He looks as if he might do.'

We were summoned to the main corral where the manager of the stud was waiting for us. He was surrounded by a group of *csikos*, all fit-looking types with narrow hips and broad shoulders, dressed in riding breeches, and tall boots. Clearly they were very curious which horse the long-distance riders would select. The manager was very keen we should buy a young black stallion, the pride of the stable. It would be good publicity, he said. We certainly did not want a stallion, nor could I pay the price of the splendid, fiery creature which was paraded out of the stable, rolling its eyes and giving little snorts of excitement. 'Would I like to ride him?' the manager asked me. I hastily declined the invitation. No, the lady with me was the expert with horses. The 'lady' made a face at me. But, warily, Sarah accepted the challenge. A *csikos* helped her up into the saddle, and stood clear. The animal was sweating with excitement at the strange rider, the watching audience, and clearly had too little exercise and too much food. Sarah kept control for a few walking circuits, and then the stallion took off, bucking and sprinting. She lost her stirrups, but stayed in the saddle as the animal bounced around, trying to get rid of her. The *csikos* draped over the fence beside me, murmured approvingly.

'You did say that we could buy *any* horse,' I checked with the manager. Yes, of course, he replied. 'Well, there's a bay horse with a white stripe on his nose, in the *csikos* stable, we would like to try.'

He looked puzzled. 'But he's at least twelve or thirteen years old.'

The manager was persuaded, and the horse was fetched by his rider, a tall fierce-looking horse wrangler with blond drooping moustaches' that would have made him perfect as an extra in a film about Attila the Hun. After a trial circuit, Sarah confirmed that the animal gave a quiet, comfortable ride, and would make an adequate palfrey. 'He knows a few tricks, too,' said the manager. The taciturn *csikos* took off the saddle and, bareback, rode back into the ring and murmured a few words. The animal promptly collapsed down on its side and lay flat. The *csikos* stood on its body and walked up and down. The horse only grunted. The man gave another order, and the horse heaved itself up and with front legs straight, sat on its rump. Next, the animal changed position, knelt down and began walking on its front knees. A third command and the animal was on its feet, with the rider standing balanced on top.

'That's all we needed,' Sarah muttered beside me, 'a performing horse. With Carty's antics we were half-way to being a travelling circus already.'

Haggling for Szarcsa, as the horse was named, was difficult enough, even on the semi-private horse farm. Though the horse was coming to the end of its working life on the *puzta*, the price was still very steep. But the manager had been eyeing the second-hand horse trailer from Ireland that we had laboriously towed in erratic stages from Belgium. I knew that it was impossible to obtain one in Hungary, so I offered a bargain. If the manager would drop the price for Szarcsa, I would 'lose' the trailer after we had used it to take Szarcsa back to join Carty and Mystery. We shook hands on the deal. I would telephone the stud farm to let them know where to 'find' the trailer and then it was theirs. I wondered how the stud farm management would explain to the state inspectors how they came to have a horse trailer labelled 'MacSweeney of Co Cork, Ireland', but knowing Hungarian ingenuity, I suspected there would be a suitable explanation.

Disposing of the horse trailer was a blessing. From that moment our lives became so much easier and I realised we should have sloughed off our equipment much sooner. We still had the jeep, as it held Carty's spare shoes and the stock of horse medicines, but henceforth we left the vehicle at a convenient spot, rode on ahead for several days, and then hitchhiked or took public transport back to retrieve it. The result was a totally new sense of the unexpected. We never knew from one day to the next how far we would get, whom we would meet, if we would find food for the horses, or where we would spend the night. All we depended on was our map of Duke Godfrey's route, two palfreys and a pack horse.

Professor György Györffy, doyen of Hungarian scholars, made sure that we followed the correct path. Small and neat, with white hair and spectacles, he had the alert, darting air of a small bird gathering crumbs of food, though the professor gathered historical and geographical data. Bubbling with energy and good humour, his erudition was comprehensive. Coming from a distinguished family of Hungarian scholars, he was the author of three massive gazetteers of Hungarian historical geography. No morsel of cartographic or archival material escaped his attention if it related to Hungarian geography. I had written to him before leaving Ireland, and now he invited me to his summer house set in a rather overgrown garden on the banks of the Danube.

Many years earlier he had designed the building himself, a circular two-storey structure with a conical thatched roof. It reminded me of a cross between a late Stone Age dwellinghouse and a housemartin's nest. The top floor was a single large, circular room, and it was here that the professor kept his study. From a pleasant, cluttered jumble he pulled cards from file drawers stuffed with over forty years of research, thick reference books which usually listed his own name among the contributors or editors and a blizzard of early maps.

What he wanted to make clear to me in a mixture of French, German and English – a mere fringe of his linguistic repertoire – was that the First Crusaders, and the armies of later crusades, had followed the long-established commercial and military route that led from Sopron, through Györ, and then diagonally, to avoid the great bend of the Danube, to skirt the eastern end of Lake Balaton before curving south to continue into present day Yugoslavia. This route differed, in its central section, from the track proposed by some western scholars. But Professor Györffy had identified the towns, the way stations, even the hospices built to receive sick and weary travellers. Thanks to the Professor's data, I could now ink in Duke Godfrey's trail precisely on the map of Hungary.

Our new acquisition, Szarcsa, proved to be almost a Houyhnhnm, those ultra-civilised horses described by Jonathan Swift when Gulliver is cast ashore in a land where urbane horses rule over uncouth humans. At just over 15 hands, Szarcsa had a fastidious manner that made it appear he found life a coarse and demeaning experience. His thin, aristocratic face gave him an aloof countenance, and whenever Carty was particularly gauche, Szarcsa would seem to curl his lip as if there was a bad smell under his nose. Szarcsa's manners were impeccable. He never stepped on one's foot, he was incapable of barging, and did not fight or squabble at the feeding trough. If he paused before stepping off a pavement or jumping a ditch, he did so as if to let you know that he believed such vulgar displays of activity were beneath his dignity. In truth, he was a rather timid horse, but he hid his cowardice under a cloak of good manners and world-weariness.

Converting Carty to a pack horse was a hilarious experience, as we had suspected. I stripped down the German Army saddle so that the frame would serve as a pack saddle. Luckily there were attachment points for such military accoutrements as a sabre, drag traces and spy glasses, and on these I hung two rucksacks as side panniers. The tent, feed bags, and a soft case were lashed over the top. Thus burdened and looking very splendid under his mound of luggage, Carty was set on the road. The only odd touch was that his crupper strap had chafed a sore on his rump, so I stitched up a little pad of white sheepskin as protection and he marched along looking like an enormous Peter Rabbit with a scut. Normally Sarah went in front holding the lead rope and riding Szarcsa, while Mystery and I stayed at Carty's heels urging him along with cracks of the whip. But we performed little better than two, very under-engined tugs trying to manoeuvre a super tanker with faulty steering and an uneven throttle. Carty would swerve this way and that, accelerate and slow down, and generally behave exactly as he wanted. Soon I learned that the motion of a trotting or walking horse is calculated to dislodge any burden if the balance is not perfect. The homemade packs slipped and drooped, and of course the moment the saddle was off-centre, we risked chafing Carty's back, so we had to stop to adjust and retie the load. At such halts Carty would wait until I was fully absorbed with the luggage straps, both hands full, my head butting a pannier into place. Then, as if absentmindedly, he would shift his weight and try to step on a toenail already blackened from his previous skipping effort in Győr.

Carty was so unruly on the day we left Lajos's stable, surging in every direction, that Sarah and I were obliged to ride, one each side of his head, each holding a lead rope to his bridle and treating him like a surly prisoner. We swore and shouted and cuffed him until he walked straight, and were just congratulating ourselves when Carty decided to evacuate his bowels. He stopped dead in his tracks, while our horses moved on. Abruptly we found ourselves attached to a 800-kilo living bollard. The lead ropes snapped taut in our hands, and Sarah and I toppled back in unison while with massive grunts Carty deposited a load of manure in the roadway. It was obvious that kindly Lajos had been feeding him up for departure.

CHAPTER 11

Carty's Battle

For the first mile Lajos walked beside us, leading his grey mare. When he turnd back, it was with a final barrage of happy chuckling and hugs of farewell. It was a wonderful sendoff. We were relaxed and reinvigorated the horses were well fed and rested, and we had several bottles of Lajos's wine and two kilos of his homemade suasage in the saddle bags. That night we hid the three horses in a huge, empty cattle shed as there was no one from whom to ask permission, and discreetly put up the tent in the lee of a large haystack, fearing eviction. An hour later we were discovered, but only a by a farmhand who was so drunk that he flopped down beside us in the hay, kicked off his shoes and fell asleep. At dusk we woke him with a mug of coffee from our camping stove and he lurched off, intent on stealing some pig food for the horses, a half bucket of ground-up maize that Carty and Mystery ate, but Szarcsa regarded with disdain. Next morning excessive flatulance identified the two gourmands.

The noonday sun was now hot enough to melt the tar on the roads and we discoverd why it had been sensible to have brought a stock of good quality horseshoes from Ireland. Szarcsa had been re-shod at Sarlopuzta the day we brought him, but the local metal was so feeble that the sticky road soon snapped one of his new shoes, and less than a week later all three other shoes were completely worn away. Luckily Mystery's spare shoes, with a minor adjustment, could be made to fit him, though their heavy weight and the sudden regime of route marching exhausted poor Szarcsa. He was not nearly as fit as the other two horses despite his previous work schedule with the *csikos* and, rather unexpectedly, he suffered the most from flies and insects. He stepped along a little stiffly in his heavy shoes, with a put-upon expression on his face and flecks of blood where the insects had punctured his thin skin. With time, we were confident, he would pick up the daily pace and achieve our standard twenty miles per day.

Sunday in the farming hamlets seemed to be spent tending gardens and the private plots of farmland, or it was the time when the menfolk gathered in the tiny village shops. The shelves were mostly empty but there was always a bare counter where the locals could buy cognac at twelve pence a glass, or a beer. The empty bottles were used to prop open the sash windows in the midday heat, and the customers sat on broken chairs by the pavement, watching us ride by, Carty doing a peculiar one-step as he tried to shake the melting tar from his feet. Diverting down the back streets of a small town, we came across a scene that could have been painted by Lowry — a bleak dilapidated factory building with tall chimneys and lines of broken windows set high in streaked concrete walls, a sagging entry gate, and perhaps three hundred bicycles left in an untidy grey cinder parking lot. Yet only five hundred yards farther on past the inevitable town rubbish dump and the town quarry, we were riding through great fields of ripening sunflowers, tall plants with immense round faces whose bright yellow petals almost hurt the eye as they stood in ranks like a vast silent audience dumbly gazing at the sun. We had exchanged Lowry for Van Gogh.

That day I miscalculated the length of the midday break, and we spent too long in the shade to rest the horses. As a result we were far from shelter when the sun began to set. The horses were very tired when finally, at about seven in the evening, we came to a ribbon of modest little houses along the roadside. Here we failed to find an empty barn or any morsel of horse feed until at the farthest fringe we reached the poorest dwellings of all, low crumbling bungalows, each with a standpipe for water in the front yard and a trickle of sewage flowing back down the slope. A savage-looking man in his sixties, dressed in torn baggy trousers and a stained singlet was seated on the front step of a porch spooning watery soup from a chipped bowl on his lap. Sarah stayed back, looking dubiously at this unlovely figure, as I dismounted and went over to ask, in halting German, if there was anywhere we could keep the horses for the night. Picking out fragments of chicken bone from his teeth and spitting them on the earth, he became our instant friend. Though he was genuinely trying to be useful there was something profoundly unsavoury about his brutish manner. He roared a summons for his wife, a worn-out, bedraggled woman in a torn cotton dress who sent a child a few doors down the road on some errand. He had no room for the horses, the man explained, but his son five doors down the street would help. See this, he boasted, showing me a blue arrow head tattooed on his bare arm, this he had from his German friends. It was the mark of the Fascist Brotherbond. He had served five years as a volunteer in the SS, and then eight more years in Russian prison camps. He made it clear that he had no regrets. I found it curiously uncomfortable that he was still so smug despite his very evident poverty and failure, as if he would do it all again, given the chance.

We led the horses to the son's house. The family lived miserably. A scruffy cur snarled and rattled his chain in the back garden. There was the fetid hut, squelching in horse manure, swatting the mosquitos, and trying to re-fasten picket pins driven into the crumbling earth wall. In the morning the family still helpful, offered us all the spare food they had: a quarter of a stale loaf, two wrinkled tomatoes and two chilli peppers to hot to eat. As we rode away I didn't know whether to feel the manner of the life, the yelling at the children, the ignorant incompetence of preparing the stable, the dirtiness, all grated. We passed a dreary night under the tent in the littered garden after we had picked out the shards of glass and rusty tins. The horses had no rest at all. Their makeshift stable was a hot, claustrophobic dungeon and the insects made them stamp and fidget. Carty broke loose, and at two in the morning Sarah and I heard him kicking down the mud walls. We spent an hour in the fetid hut, squelching in horse manure, swatting the mosquitoes, and trying to re-fasten picket pins driven into the crumbling earth wall. In the morning the family, still helpful, offered us all the spare food they had: a quarter of a stale loaf, two wrinkled tomatoes and two chilli peppers too hot to eat. As we rode away I didn't know whether to feel sorry for them in their wretched lives or conclude that, being so odious, there was some justice in their fate.

Following the line of a canal we found ourselves in wild, untended land, too soggy for farming or settlement and left to nature. On the ridge of the embankment the occassional trace of a narrow footpath led us forward, and by the end of the morning the only humans we had encountered were two shepherds, each with a lad to help him. The adult shepherds carried full-sized crooks, marvellously carved and decorated like a badge of office, while the assistants had only smaller versions, completely plain. Each had a wallet of food slung on one hip by a shoulder strap, and on the other a flask of drinking water because the canal water was brown and noxious. We pushed our way gently through their flocks which clustered on the embankment, the heads of the animals bobbing up in surprise with a clank of sheep bells, and a belligerent stare from a single billy goat with magnificent spiral horns.

For another two hours we saw only herons and ducks flapping up from ponded backwaters, and a covey of pheasant chicks which scurried from under the horses' feet. Small wild flowers grew in profusion, pink, white, blue, violet and deep purple. It was like riding through a nature reserve banned to visitors, and would have been a paradise but for the swarms of insects. They sprang in squadrons from the tall grass as the horses brushed past, and fastened hungrily on the animals' necks and flanks to feed until the animals were streaked with blood. The ponds seethed with so many minnows sucking down the rich feast of insect larvae that the dimples of water made it seem that raindrops were pattering down in a constant shower.

The canal system eventually brought us to the town of Szegard near the Yugoslav border. There, to my surprise, we were expected. The *economista* had received a telex from the Riding Federation to look out for us, and a man on a bicycle arrived to lead us to their stable. Outside were a dozen heavy carts used for deliveries, inside a double rank of Heavy Horses, some twenty of them. The animals were treated like lorries or buses parked for the night. The carters drove into the yard, unhitched the animals and casually led them into the stalls, and tied them up. There were a couple of ostlers filling feed bins, carrying buckets of water, cleaning up manure. The atmosphere was as workaday and casual. The great horses stamped and shifted, the ostlers pushed them this way and that, there was a tremendous fug in the gloomy, poorly ventilated building. The *economista* gave us a room for the night in their guest accommodation, a townhouse built around a central courtyard with a long verandah and high-ceilinged rooms just like an Indian or Sinhalese bungalow. At daybreak we rejoined the carters as they briskly groomed their animals, put on their harnesses in a matter of moments and were gone on their daily rounds with the carts. By contrast Sarah and I spent another two hours in preparation. Now that we had three horses to get ready we found it easier to work as a pair, loading one horse at a time with all the animal's saddlery and panniers and accoutrements. We always left Carty until last, because he was the most likely to twist his load, crush a pannier, or do some other mischief.

That mid-July day's ride took us across some of the finest countryside we had yet seen — a rolling landscape of prosperous husbandry. There were vines, and fields of wheat, sunflower and maize. The size of the fields was impressive. Some of them stretched for two or three miles. Occasionally there were paved roads, but for the most part the trails were broad paths of beaten pale yellow earth running directly across the fields. We again saw very few people, and usually only at a great distance. They would turn and wave to us as we passed. In such open country we could turn Carty loose, away from the restraint of lead rope, and herd him forward ahead of us like cattle on a drive. Occasionally he would break into a fast trot and try to outpace us, running away over the crest of a hill as we accelerated to catch up with him. 'Passenger Luggage in Advance' was Sarah's comment as the great animal disappeared over the brow of the slope, pounding along the dusty track.

Sarah's sixth sense for the horses' moods was alerted. 'I think Carty has worked out the system,' she warned me in mid-morning, 'watch out for trouble.'

Sure enough, just after lunch, the big Ardennes made a bolt for freedom. We had arrived in the bowl of a shallow valley where a minor river fed a chain of small lakes. Sarah and I delayed at the lakeside, waiting for Mystery and Szarcsa to drink their fill when Carty walked off round some bushes, put his head down and ran. It was a beautifully judged escape attempt. He ran deliberately under the stout branch of a large tree, and had calculated the height perfectly. The branch swept the luggage off his back, with a tearing of straps and bursting of buckles. Then Carty galloped. Furiously we chased him up and down the meadow for half an hour, as he dodged and doubled back and forth, nimbly diving behind trees, blundering through bushes to discourage the lighter horses.

We finally recaptured Carty, who was not the least contrite, when he was too exhausted to run any more.

Despite the wasted time we had covered 25 miles by the time we came upon the agricultural *kombinat* at Boyly. The place was impressive by any standards. The *kombinat*, or regional collective, ran an integrated complex of farms and factories, shops, public transport, workers' houses, even an agricultural museum. The showpiece of the farming division was a magnificent agricultural training centre where students could get practical experience in everything from plant research to how to train a carthorse. On the staff were a saddler, a wagon maker and a pair of master blacksmiths. To us it was like arriving in a harbour of refuge. We needed to overhaul our equipment, re-shoe the horses and check their health.

Although we arrived unexpectedly, we were overwhelmed by the help that was spontaneously offered. A squad of students prepared stalls in a gigantic barn, brought straw bedding, filled grain boxes and fetched water. Josef Werle, the undermanager insisted that we stay with him and his Czech-born wife. Another of those calm and competent men we had been so lucky to find along our route, he had worked at Boyly all his life. If there was ever a problem, he was called for. Bureaucrats and administrators sat in the central offices, but Josef was the linchpin of the establishment. It was Josef who arranged for me to spend the next day at the saddler's bench – the saddler himself was away sick – repairing our harness, and it was Josef who detailed a team of young farriers to re-shoe the three horses. The smithy echoed with cheerful laughter as they worked on Mystery and Szarcsa and gradually deteriorated into shouts of command and finally oaths as the lads wrestled with Carty. It took the five of them four hours to shoe the miscreant, and Sarah and I stayed clear of the place, except to peek in once. Carty was looking thoroughly cross, a cord twitch tied tightly round his upper lip to make him stand still and his upper lip puffed out like a balloon.

Josef, like most of the inhabitants of the region, was of German stock, descended from settlers from Swabia. And that was clearly the secret of Boyly *kombinat's* success. The Germans had brought their habits with them. Nowhere else in Hungary did we see such industry and prosperity, the land so carefully husbanded, buildings meticulously maintained, huge combine harvesters moving across the immense fields like a scene from the American wheatlands. The villages were made up of Swabian-style houses, and their churches had Swabian onion domes. It was a slice of South Germany taken up and set down on Hungary's border with Yugoslavia.

Josef, like Lajos before him, insisted that he accompany us a little distance on our road. Even the surliness of the customs inspector at the Hungarian border post could not dispel the sense of well-being that our transit of Hungary had instilled. We had been warned at Sarlopuzta that the state customs officials would scrutinise our papers for Szarcsa's purchase to see if there was any fault. If there was, we would not be allowed to take him out of Hungary. But the papers were in order, and Carty cut short the inspection with a tremendous crash. Looking up from his desk with a scowl, the customs inspector noted through a plate glass window that Carty had tipped over yet another dustbin. But this time it was one of those six-foot-tall industrial-sized bins, designed to be hoisted mechanically into a truck. The inspector angrily banged his stamp on the papers, filled in his ledger, and waved us through. 'He's always in a bad temper' apologised the Hungarian vet, an energetic woman who was obviously very popular with her colleagues. She took her own passport out of a drawer, waved cheerily to the border guards and walked across to the Yugoslav post with us. There she contacted the Yugoslav vet, introduced us, and wished us good luck. Hungary on horseback, Sarah and I agreed, had been a delight. For Duke Godfrey and his Crusaders, too, this sector of their route must have been a happy experience. Their discreet escort of King Coloman's troops ensuring them a quiet passage, the march across level countryside in late autumn with no lack of provisions, would be remembered as a pleasant contrast to the rigours that lay ahead in the hostile lands to the east.

'There are no horse facilities in Yugoslavia, and we strongly advise that you abandon your planned journey.' The letter I had received in February from the National Tourist Office in Belgrade had been blunt. 'But if you wish to continue with your programme, please contact our London office.' A more sympathetic official in London had provided me with a letter in Serbo-Croat explaining the reason for our journey. He did, however, confirm that we would encounter very few horses in Yugoslavia.

Our first impression was how ill-kempt the country seemed to be after Hungary. Even though we were crossing one of the more prosperous Yugoslav regions we found the fabric of everyday life was under much more strain. The houses were more tatty, the cottages depended on wells rather than piped water, the roads were in disrepair. People had more television sets and washing machines, but there was a hunted feeling to their lives. Inflation was a constant threat. The only families who were cushioned from the persistent decline in the value of their money were those who had sons or daughters working abroad, mostly in Germany. These emigrant workers returned home every year for their holidays, bringing their foreign exchange with them. But they never lodged the money in the banks. To safeguard against inflation, they invested in new housing, and usually did the building work themselves. So every second or third dwelling we rode past was half-finished. One year's wages might have bought the land, the second paid for the foundations, and the third financed the ground floor. Above that, the mild steel reinforcing rods still projected upwards, waiting for the next cash instalment, while the family had already moved in and was living below.

Time and again the jagged raw edge of poverty showed. On the outskirts of Osijek we rode past an encampment of tinkers living off the plastic rubbish from the nearby factory, salvaging usable tubs and jars, and washing them for re-sale. They even made the Hungarian fascists seem well-off. Suspicious dark faces peered out from under patched tents and leaky hovels as we rode past. Men, women and children dressed in rags picked over the spill of detritus tossed over the factory fence. Both Sarah and I were glad to be clear of such a sinister, desperate place. The orderliness and calm of Hungary, a little bland perhaps, had evaporated. In Yugoslavia our reception varied on individual circumstance. We might be ignored with an angry scowl or, just as likely, find a heap of grass cut and thrown down beside the tethered horses. Barely three miles inside the border we were ordered off a country lane and back on to the main road by a municipal watchman dressed in a khaki uniform and cap with a red star; half an hour later three of his colleagues visited us at our camp to ask if they could help. A householder emerged from his front door to wave us away from his fence; fifty yards farther on a farmer loading a tractor and trailer, went in search of food for the horses and refused any payment. All he could offer was a large paper bag half-full with last year's maize cobs, dried as hard as flint. Sarah tested one with several sharp blows from the shoeing hammer but succeeded in knocking off just two or three bullet-like grains. Doubtfully she threw the maize cobs on the ground before the horses. Mystery and even Szarcsa, usually rather disdainful, were so hungry that they gnawed stoutly for a little sustenance. Carty picked up an entire corn cob in his mouth, spun it round expertly in his teeth, and spat out the core neatly stripped of every grain.

Stabling was so rare that our campsites were very variable. For our third night in Yugoslavia every farm turned us away because they had only vegetable gardens or young orchards that the horses would damage. We were sent down to an isolated house standing among poplar plantations on the bank of the Danube. But the woman there refused to let us into a meadow in the woods because her husband was away. In desperation, as it was getting very late, we approached a trio of workmen sitting on a bench beside the portable cabin that was their office-cum-living quarters next to a gravel pit in the riverbank. Could we put the horses on the grass beside the cabin, and erect our tent? They had no objection, but with sign language gesticulated that we should hurry. They pointed at the sun, made flying motions with their arms and pinched their skins.

Then the night watchman appeared, carrying a broad brimmed hat with a veil, and we understood immediately. We were just too slow. At nightfall, as if a starting gun had been fired, an immense swarm of mosquitos flew in from the river swamps. In perhaps three minutes the insects were everywhere, biting so furiously that we were obliged to wrap our heads in riding jackets and wear gloves as we hurried through the last of our chores, and then dived into the tent which fortunately was mosquito proof. All that night we could hear the massed whine of insects outside the canvas. At first light, as if by magic, the insects vanished and we crawled out cautiously, our eyelids puffed and swollen from bites the evening before. The horses, thankfully, had suffered less, though they had passed a restless night and I made a mental note to stay away from river pasture in the future, if at all possible.

On 23 July came a sharp reminder of the narrow margin between a fit and a damaged horse. As an experiment I had tried placing Szarcsa's saddle bags farther forward than usual, under the saddle where the balance seemed better and the weight more evenly distributed. That evening he had a large unpleasant-looking swelling on his spine where the bags had pinched him, and I hurriedly reverted to the previous arrangement before we crippled him. As it was, we had to take an extra rest day to allow the swelling some relief. Fortunately we were taken in by a wealthy family of farmers, the plutocrats of the township. The father drove a Mercedes, and the son a Porsche, while the daughter was a lawyer in the nearby town. Everyone worked ferociously hard to maintain their lifestyle. The mother ran a bar in the front room of their house, serving beer and coffee to the local clientele, did all the cooking and clothes washing for the family, and was seen helping to push a huge broken-down tractor into the farmyard, literally shoulder to the wheel. She was overwhelmed by the notion of our journey *'Daleko put, daleko put'* she repeated over and over again, shaking her head in wonder as she bustled off to complete another task – 'a long road, a long road'.

By mid-morning the temperature now rose regularly to 35 or 37 degrees, and Sarah and I began to worry about Carty. Mystery and Szarcsa could cope adequately with the heat, but Carty's breath came in short, quick, shallow panting. He sweated massively, a regular trickle of perspiration collecting on the curve of his belly and splashing in steady drips on the ground as he walked. The obvious remedy was to start riding in the cool of the dawn. But, even so, if we were to complete a daily quota of twenty miles mostly at a walk, we were still on the open road when the sun became really hot. Then we had to take shelter in the shade, and plan to finish the distance in the late afternoon. But somehow the late afternoon never seemed to cool down sufficiently to reduce Carty's discomfort. So on 24 July I suggested that we try to speed up the pace, trot rather than walk, and complete the day's ride by noon. What I could not have known was that, by a very unlucky coincidence, that same week saw the onset of a ferocious heat wave over the Balkan peninsula. The shade temperatures rose to over 40 degrees, thousands of tourists on the relatively cool coastline suffered heatstroke, and in Greece, the province of Athens recorded 1,017 deaths, two thirds of them from the effects of heat. The main Athens cemetery, which normally handles 12 to 15 burials daily, was swamped with 60 or 70 corpses a day, and the refrigeration system could not cope with the festering bodies. Inland in Croatia the heat was stifling.

We set off at seven thirty that morning, having been up since five thirty to prepare the animals. Szarcsa's back was still sore so he carried the packs and once again I rode Carty, just for the day. Three and a half hours later we had covered about seventeen miles, mostly a a brisk trot and were feeling very pleased with ourselves. We called a halt at a featureless and dusty little village and tied the horses under some trees next to the inevitable memorial to the War of Liberation, where there was a small patch of shade and water from a standpipe. we were walking over to a small cafe to find ourselves a cold drink when, behind us Carty collapsed. He buckled at the knees and fell to the ground. The idlers at the cafe shouted and pointed. Sarah and I turned to look and after one awful moment of shock, ran back to his vast bulk. He had fallen awkwardly, front and back legs on either side of a tree. Even if he had the strength to get up, he did not have room to manoeuvre.

I shouted to the villagers to come and help. Half a dozen of us literally seized Carty's enormous torso and, rolling it back and forth to gain momentum, finally succeeded in turning him over so his legs were free. Carty gave a few massive heaves and scrabbled with his enormous legs, but he was dazed and disorientated, his muscles were no longer coordinated, and he could not get back on his feet. It was obvious that he was suffering the symptoms of heat exhaustion and sunstroke. Not knowing whether it would help or harm him, but realising we should do something, Sarah and I frantically filled buckets of water and poured them over him to try to cool him down. The dusty ground around the great horse became a slippery quagmire as we drenched his body and held up his head so he could breathe more easily. Feebly Carty tried again to rise, and collapsed back with an awful wheezing thump. His hooves were slipping on the mud, so again we manhandled him, this time swivelling him around so that his hooves would rest on drier ground. We pummelled him and shouted at him until he tried to rise again. He managed to heave his three-quarter ton upright, and stood there in a daze, weaving unsteadily on his feet. He was going to fall again and we knew it. We caught him by the head, and coaxed him away from the tree and around the back of the cafe. There, on a rough bit of land used as the village sports ground was a patch of shade and some grass. We had barely got him there when Carty flopped down again, with an awful air of finality, and lay still.

124

He lay absolutely flat. His breathing which had been so quick, was now so slow that we could barely detect it. His eyes closed, and over the next half hour his upper lip gradually drew back, revealing his teeth and gums in the rictus of death. Sarah and I both thought we had lost him. There was no hope of proper veterinary assistance. A massive stimulant injection might have helped him, but although someone had gone to fetch the only veterinary worker in the region, we knew he would have had no experience of horses. He appeared after half an hour, fresh from performing an autopsy on a dead cow, and leaped off the back of a motorcycle, arms bloody to the elbows and clutching a huge knife. 'I thought he was about to cut Carty's throat,' confessed Sarah later.

The vet looked completely out of his depth. He took Carty's temperature and shook his head. 'I don't think the horse will live,' he said. He opened his drugs bag. There was nothing inside except three vials of medicine for cows. Giving a fatalistic shrug he broke the flasks, mixed all three together and gave the entire stock to Carty in a single massive injection. Then he walked away, with an air of finality. 'If the horse is alive at midnight,' he said, 'then he may survive.'

Carty looked dreadful. Stretched out flat, he did not stir for at least an hour, and it was now the hottest part of the day. We rolled back his closed eyelid and the eye was dull and glazed. We sponged his head and mouth. There was nothing more we could do. Numbly Sarah and I squatted in the shade of the schoolhouse and watched Carty struggling to survive. Three or four times he summoned the strength to lift his head, and twice he tried to rise. But he did not even get his shoulder off the ground. His head flopped back and he seemed to give up the ghost. Even the villagers abandoned the scene. They wandered away, leaving us to wait. Had Carty been an older horse or less fit or, above all, as Sarah later pointed out, had he not been so damnably stubborn, there was no doubt he would have died. But the young, self-willed Ardennes refused to give up. He battled for his life and, though we did not realise it, was gathering his strength. He had been motionless for another two hours, lying as still as any corpse, when an inquisitive villager arrived to inspect the cadaver. He silently walked up behind Carty and gave the Ardennes a fright. Suddenly the huge 'corpse' gave a tremendous plunging heave and leapt to its feet. The stranger let out a yelp of fear and ran, never to be seen again. Carty stood there, groggy but alive. Sarah and I were overwhelmed with relief. We set up the tent and continued our vigil into the night, watching in case Carty should collapse again and need help. But he stayed on his feet and at One am the vet reappeared and by car headlights gave a second injection.

'That's a very strong animal, he commented with admiration, 'If that had been a cow, he would certainly be dead by now.' Little did he know, I thought, grateful to Carty for his incredible resilience, just how tough an Ardennes Heavy Horse could be, especially if he was as unyielding as our stubborn companion.

Carty's powers of recuperation were phenomenal. Next morning we gently walked with him a couple of miles to the next village where a kindly farmer had more suitable shelter for the horses under a lean-to. A day later it was as if the collapse had never occurred. But I had learned my lesson: trotting a Heavy Horse any distance in such heat, even in an attempt to make things easier for him, extended the animal beyond his physical limits. We would never repeat the error.

On the outskirts of the depressingly ugly city of Sremska Mitrovic we encountered a man driving a horse and a cart, a rare occurrence in that region. We asked if he could lead us to a stable. He took us to two, but the first was closed and the second was full. At the second stable we understood why there were so few work horses in Croatia. The owner made his living by collecting the last, unwanted draught horses from the outlying villages. There were perhaps forty or fifty of them at his stable, mostly broken-down old animals, but a few good ones too. All were awaiting shipment to Italy where their meat was to be minced into sausages. It reminded me that for Carty a close encounter with heat stroke was perhaps a small price to pay for avoiding a similar destiny.

Beyond Sremska Mitrovic, with the heat wave easing, we spent a strange, surreal day riding across reclaimed marshland. The crops and the hedges were so tall that we could not see the horizon. We had no landmarks to steer by, there were few people to ask for directions, and, because the area was so recently farmed, it was still a blank on the map. Effectively we were lost. No villages or hamlets had yet been established, nor were there any metalled roads or signposts. It was a totally featureless environment and when finally we reached its focus, an isolated town set down in the middle of the arable land, we might still have been riding into a weird dream. There was a railway line but no trains, not even a station, merely a siding with some empty tank wagons and, strangely enough, a vast flock of snow white geese who hissed angrily at us as we rode over the tracks. We approached some large cattle sheds to ask for shelter, only to be accosted by a watchman with a rifle over his shoulder. The man was suspicious and aggressive. He ordered us to stay where we were until an official was summoned from the mayor's office. As we waited, we realised that we had stumbled on some sort of agricultural work camp. There were barracks for workers, mostly students, and the whole place was as rigidly organised as an orthodox commune.

The town was under the control of the mayor's office. The mayor himself was absent, but I was finally summoned to his German-speaking deputy's office to explain what we were doing there. By then I was very short of patience. The horses were drooping with fatigue; they had been refused food and shelter, and we had been kept waiting for three hours at the end of a long, tiring day. I was asked to produce our documents, and they were carefully checked. The only paper in Serbo-Croat was the letter from the Yugoslav Tourist Office in London explaining who we were and what we were doing. Previously the document had been accepted but this time the deputy mayor pointed out rather nastily that the letter, though on official paper, did not have a rubber stamp at the signature. How was he to know that it was not a forgery, he asked me. He would summon the police, the *milicija*, to look into the whole matter. I was thoroughly cross. Angrily, I pointed out that any rogue could forge a rubber stamp, and that we had never met such rudeness anywhere on our trip, not in all five countries since starting out in Belgium. The *milicija* could ask their questions later, first the horses should be taken care of. The township had no concept of hospitality and should be ashamed of itself.

This last observation stung. In his expression I saw the struggle between the traditional notion of hospitality and his narrow-minded sense of bureaucratic duty. The former won. We were, of course, welcome in the town. He would give permission for the horses to be stabled overnight in the commune's machinery park and we ourselves could stay with the foreman in charge of the cattle farm. The *milicija* would investigate later. It was a popular decision with the students on the commune who were delighted to have any sort of diversion. A grinning, happy gang of them led up the horses, others ran off to steal bales of hay from the cattle sheds, ignoring the outraged shouts of the guard. We rigged up a temporary stall for the horses between some agricultural machinery, fed them and gave them water. As a final victory the mayor's office felt obliged to provide a sentry all night to watch over the animals, and the unfortunate man had to replenish their water buckets. The head cowman was mortified by the poor treatment we had been given. He and his wife lived in a small house and had very few possessions, but they produced a superb meal, and much to Sarah's embarrassment the wife brought out a bowl of hot water and, kneeling before her guest, insisted on washing Sarah's feet. The wife was very taken with Sarah, and kept on clapping her hands and saying how small and how beautiful she was. She wanted her to return on New Year's Day so she could be dressed up in rings and jewels and national costume. Sarah sat, looking lean and fit and stunned. She was utterly unused to the notion of being treated as a doll, but it was impossible to say anything in the face of such genuine kindness.

Two days later, on 29 July, we crossed the boundary of Croatia, the Sava river, which in Duke Godfrey's time had been the limit of King Coloman's territory. The king reappeared while the pilgrim army was building rafts and handed over the two hostages, Baldwin and his wife, unharmed. The crossing of the Sava must have been a delicate and time-consuming business, for it is a very substantial river and even today we found it a major obstacle. Our logical crossing point was by the great bridge at Belgrade near the Sava's outlet into the Danube, but one look at the maelstrom of city traffic and the ugly city sprawl dissuaded me. We scouted up-river and were glad to find a small and very rickety ferry for farm traffic, a flat barge with loose floorboards which was hauled across the broad river by an asthmatic launch. There was no ferry schedule so the crew sat on the river bank in a gypsy's tent, a sheet of plastic pulled over the bushes, drinking beer until they felt like moving. Chugging slowly across the brown waters of the Sava we might have been on a South American jungle ferry, until we were tipped out on the opposite shore, in the republic of Serbia.

CHAPTER 12

Serbia

The detour to avoid Belgrade took three days. We worked our way around the city in a wide sweep until we found a service bridge to take us over the *autoput*, the motorway that uses the line of the Roman Road southward towards Bulgaria. With its unheeding stream of noisy traffic the *autoput* was an artificial fence that had isolated the strip of countryside to the east of it. Just a mile from the speeding trucks and cars we found ourselves in backwater villages populated by almost-medieval figures. Outside one hamlet a flock composed of half a dozen defeated-looking sheep with downhanging heads and drooping ears, a goat, three porkers and a sow with several piglets of pink, grey and black, was being driven along by a grim-faced peasant woman who looked exactly like a witch. Even in the summer heat she wore a headscarf and a woollen jacket, and thick black wool stockings under a heavy apron. When I remarked that she could have stepped from the pages of a medieval chronicle, Sarah sniffed and observed that she would not accept a shiny apple from her.

Canny as gypsies, we now kept a look out for the verge of grass, an untended field, the open end of a tractor shed, or the cowstall where we might pass the night, with or without permission. We identified crops that might produce forage for the horses if we let them trespass. The horses had grown equally wily. They stole food without hesitation, leaning over a fence to snatch a mouthful or burrowing into pig troughs and cattle byres when no one was looking. They ate anything and everything they could. Mystery was the worst offender. The moment we halted, even for ten seconds, down would go her head as she began to ferret and browse for any scrap of food as she refuelled for that steady flat-footed pace that slapped along mile after mile. Seemingly inexhaustible, Mystery was, as Sarah had noted, totally flighty. She never learned, even after a thousand miles of the open road, still shying at chickens, hedge birds and piles of stones, and her panic if out of sight of the other horses was uncontrollable. She would skitter up and down with a drumming tattoo of her feet, crying out anxiously, and looking in every direction. She was so fit and so well muscled that it was impossible to hold her quiet. By contrast Szarcsa was always the patient ageing gentleman. He was getting wrinkles round the eyes and mouth, and was the only horse of the three to be fastidious about his food unless he was very hungry. Last to drink, he was the first to give way to the other two, with a wince of well-bred disdain.

Carty dominated them. By far the cleverest, he also had the strongest character. The others were obliged to proceed at his pace and conform to his moods. When they tried to bite him and make him hurry up, he ignored them entirely. His manners were awful. He would push the others off their food, knock over the feed bag, and snuffle around like a huge pig. With Sarah or me he could be affectionate and trusting, or stubborn and unruly. He preferred human company to the presence of other horses, and this sometimes turned out to our advantage. One afternoon a *milicija* patrol car drew up ahead of us, a sergeant stepped out, and demanded to see our papers. From the policeman's officious manner I feared we would have a difficult time. Searching for the papers, I happened to drop Carty's lead rope and to my delight, he wandered off to inspect the police car and meet its driver. He blundered around the vehicle ponderously. His haunch brushed the car, rocking it on its springs. A wing mirror was knocked askew. Then his saddle bag caught the radio aerial and bent it over. Finally Carty stuck his head in through the driver's window, and pinioned the man to his seat. Short of pulling out his pistol and putting a shot through Carty's head, the man was helpless. He called out to his colleague and the sergeant hurried back. I pulled Carty off like a reluctant lap dog, and the police patrol drove away, leaving Carty looking after them with a heavy, disappointed gaze.

We left the Danube corridor behind us. The main river would continue eastward towards the Black Sea, while we turned almost due south to follow the line of its tributary, the Morava, to take us towards Thrace and

Istanbul. Historians are unsure whether Godfrey's army followed the right or the left bank of the Morava. In the 11th century this was a remote and heavily forested area, and the chronicles refer only to a difficult march through the wilds of the 'forest of Niš'. I chose the right bank, to avoid the *autoput*, and we found ourselves riding along the slant of the hill overlooking the river. Locally the road was known as the Tsar's Road, and we passed through a chain of small towns and villages where the worn oxcarts of the older generation contrasted with German-registered Audis and Mercedes Benz that belonged to the emigrant workers home for their holidays. This was a very Christian area, and the village cemeteries displayed photographs of the dead, set as medallions into the headstones. Adapting new technology, the most recent portraits were enlarged and etched directly into the black and shiny surface of the headstones so that huge faces of the dead stared at the passerby. In one village we met a funeral led by men holding on display the portraits of the deceased. The coffin lay on a trailer drawn by a tractor, and in front walked a robed and heavily bearded priest sweating profusely in the hot August sunshine. On each side of the corpse marched the chief mourners, scarves pinned to their lapels and trailing over one shoulder. As we stood respectfully aside to let the cortege pass, an old lady appeared at the garden fence beside us, carrying a tray loaded with small cups of strong, sweet coffee and blackberries and cherries preserved in syrup, a traditional offering.

These little acts of kindness could be totally unexpected, even anonymous. The next day, 5 August, we paused in the small town of Zabari so I could search for a chain head collar to tether Carty. Exasperated with the way he snapped every item of leather harness, I hoped to adapt the chain tackle used to restrain draft oxen in those regions. We failed to find the right size of chain, but when we returned to the horses we found that they had been untied from the lamp post where we had left them, and been led away and were eating a pile of new-cut grass. Also someone had plaited Carty's forelock in strands, so that the wiry hair stood out straight between his ears in schoolgirl's pigtails.

South of Sviljanac the road veered away from the river to avoid steep bluffs where the Morava had cut into the hillside. The diversion brought us through dense woods where the villages were very isolated. This was the Crusaders' 'forest of Niš' and it must have been rough going for the pilgrims as they groped their way through a dense cover of beech and oak and tangled underbrush. The weather had turned nasty as we rode under a lowering sky·that made the woods seem exceptionally desolate, and it was nearly dark by the time we came to the only settlement, the long narrow village of Glizane strung out for nearly three miles in the narrow cleft of a forested valley. In the fading grey light it was a forbidding cheerless place with a haunted air. We rode a little way down the single street between tall, gaunt buildings with shuttered windows, interspersed with primitive farm cabins with a few chickens and pigs on the muddy earth. No one spoke to us, and the only inhabitants seemed to be incredibly old people who watched us without a flicker of expression, as though all their lives they had watched weary travellers go by. I had the feeling that eyes were watching us from the empty houses as we tried to find shelter. We went unsuccessfully from house to house, and were finally advised to go back out of the village and camp by an immense, disused cattleshed. As we turned off the road, a creaking oxcart came the other way. The two oxen were plodding along, heads low, each animal leaning in towards the other as if about to collapse. The great wheels were equally out of true, slanting inwards as they groaned on worn axles. A toothless old man lay in the straw load waving a branch as a goad, futilely as he was half-blind. A youth, doubtless his grandson, trudged along with the oxen, guiding the team. Apart from the broken tennis shoes on the boy's feet, no detail could have changed since Duke Godfrey's day – the shambling oxen, the creak of wood, the wobbling wheels, the snail-like pace of the battered vehicle.

We tethered the horses to an empty cornbin whose slats were rotten and gaping, and with thunder rolling through the surrounding hills pitched our tent inside the rotting barn. The wind billowed through massive holes in the roof above us, the entire building creaked and groaned in the rising gale like a wooden ship in a rough sea, and sections of the torn roof swayed ominously, hanging in great shreds. Nervously we wondered if the whole structure would collapse, and took care to pitch our tent away from the danger areas where the heavy earthenware roof tiles were dropping like lethal dead leaves. We had no food so walked back the length of the village only to find the single shop had been shut and padlocked hours earlier. The village bar was open, a bleak cavern of a room with small tables and hard chairs where the customers all men, sat in complete silence gazing fixedly at the television set high in one corner. They turned and stared as we entered, noted Sarah trespassing on their masculine domain, and then swivelled their gaze back to the television and continued staring in silence. We spent a shivering, spooky night in the barn which continued to disintegrate around us with the sharp explosive sound of tiles falling and shattering.

The day dawned rainy and cold, but bright enough to dispel the sinister atmosphere of the night before. As we watered the horses at a well beside a front garden, the householder invited us in for breakfast, a delicious meal which seemed all the better for our hunger from the night before: fresh biscuits and cornbread, sour cheese, butter and jam, with coffee and plum brandy. Returning to the horses, we found that they too had been given an enormous ration of hay and maize, and had stuffed themselves until they could eat no more.

We rode over the crest of the hills and found ourselves looking down once more on the broad groove of the Morava valley. The overcast sky had broken up into puffs of white cloud over the distant uplands, and the side of the valley was bathed in bright sunshine where it dropped away in front of us, planted with row upon row of young plum trees. We sat in a brand-new orchard and ate our standard lunch of peanuts and raisins, using the crown of my hat as the plate, and watched the distant glint of the river. Szarcsa was losing a hind shoe and, unwisely, I stopped in the next village to nail it back in place. Immediately a large and animated crowd gathered aroud us. Someone caught my elbow as I started hammering, and with sign language indicated that I should wait because there was a blacksmith in the town. Not wishing to give offence, I waited and five minutes later down the street walked the tiniest farrier we had ever seen.

He was another creature out of a fairy tale. About sixty years old, he could not have been more than four feet ten inches tall, and had a nut-brown skin and small, sharp features. His bow legs were accentuated by traditional Serbian breeches and puttees, and on his feet he wore carpet slippers. Stepping along with short, quick, jerky paces he lacked only a conical cap to have been a perfect companion for Snow White. 'Lucky he's not shoeing Carty,' Sarah muttered beside me, 'or he'd be flattened with a single stomp.' The man was so small that he scarcely needed to bend down to attend to Szarcsa's upheld hoof. Perching spectacles on his nose – which made him seem even more like a dwarf – he gave a few wavering blows with an ancient rusty hammer and pronounced himself satisfied. We escaped thankfully from the kindness of the village, and two miles down the road Szarcsa's other hind shoe began to clink.

We had come to detest the *autoput*. Its noise and dust polluted the countryside for miles around. For the next three days we gave it a wide berth and rode parallel to it, a mile away. Yet even at that distance the apples we took from the trees were covered with a thin film of dust settling from the distant traffic. We increased the space between ourselves and the modern road and found ourselves walking slowly up a long, sunbaked hill. It was noon, the temperature was in the mid-thirties, and it was time to seek shelter from the sun. But there were no houses or villages, just open fields and scattered woods, a distant line of the mountains on the Bulgarian border away to our left hand far ahead a small white speck at the edge of a line of trees. Hoping to find a house, we rode towards it and in a region where we had already met a witch and a leprechaun-farrier blundered into another fairy-tale scene.

As we came closer we saw that the white speck was a lonely cottage set among the trees. We rode up to the gate, and called out. There was no reply. Pushing open the gate we led the horses into the well-tended garden. There was a vegetable patch and fruit was ripening on the trees. The little low house itself was neat and trim, the windows shuttered and the door locked. We called out again, but still there was no answer. At the back of the house was a bare wooden porch and beside it, a well. Everything was in its proper place – the bucket, the rope on its windlass, the winding wheel. A yellow gourd had been left beside the bucket to serve as a dipper and drinking cup. The gourd was slightly damp as if someone had been drinking from it recently. We called again, but again there was no answer. There was some sort of outhouse behind a thorn fence. Leading Mystery, I walked over to it, and to my astonishment, as we had not seen any work horses in the area, discovered that it was a stable. What is more it was a stable for three horses, and had been made ready. There was dry straw on the ground, some hay in the mangers, and a fresh reserve of hay stuffed in the rafters over our heads. There was even a hay fork to hand. It was a complete mystery: a stable but no horses, hay and water but no animals, a damp drinking gourd but no sign of any person. At that stage, if I had found the cottage was made of gingerbread,

I would not have been surprised. Wonderingly, we put the horses in their stalls, placed extra hay before them, and then had our own lunch sitting on the shaded porch and eating plums from the garden. We stayed three hours yet no one came, and we saw no one in the distance. As we left, I rolled up a bank note in payment for the hay and stuck it in the neck of a bottle propped on the edge of the well. I only hoped that the unexplained banknote would be as much of a mystery to the owner of the cottage as it all had been to us.

But the fairy tales were not yet ended. We had still to meet the ogre in his lair. That same evening we came to a poverty-stricken hamlet set on the edge of a heath where a small river cut a deep gash in the sandy soil. We passed peasants watching over their animals grazing on the scrubland. Each person had only two or three sheep, or perhaps a single immense sow, a great grey blob peering out from under flopping ears. Sunk in the cut of the ravine, the hamlet was in almost perpetual shadow. At the tiny village shop I asked where we might be able to spend the night, and was taken across the street and down a narrow alleyway. A section of the palisaded fence was pulled aside and we led in the horses.

It was a scene of almost indescribable filth. A backyard of beaten, soggy earth was littered with piles of broken planks and agricultural rubbish. Pigs ran freely, squealing as they fought savagely over a dredge of slops poured into a large tractor tyre that had been sliced in half and lay on the ground to make a circular trough. Every surface was soiled with chicken droppings, constantly increased by a bedraggled clutch of hens and roosters. Urine dribbled out of the doors to a cowshed and added to the stream of effluent from a manure heap so pungent that the acrid stench made one's eyes water. Flies and filth were everywhere. There was a pile of old branches in one corner, waiting to be used for firewood; dirty rags and grimy plastic bags were draped here and there, and the only reasonably dry, flat area was being used to sun-dry white beans spread out on the ground.

This stomach-turning kingdom was ruled over by the roughest-looking woman we had seen. She was shaped like a potato with great thick legs and heavily muscled arms. She went barefoot everywhere, whether indoors or slithering around in the manure. She never spoke a word to us, only grunted and scowled as if she fiercely resented our presence, and communicated by brusque gestures. When we arrived, she was chopping firewood with a huge executioner-type axe. When I volunteered to help, she merely dropped the axe in the mud and stamped away to hurl more slop at the squealing pigs.

This gruesome harridan lived in a single room in the attic over the cow byre. The only furniture was a narrow grimy bed, an unwashed table, a dresser with chipped crockery, a couple of battered kitchen chairs, and a wood-burning kitchen stove with a broken oven door that had to be jammed shut with a wooden twig. In one corner a cardboard tray was full of cheeping chicks with a light bulb thrust inside to keep them warm. First our hostess proceeded to replenish their food and re-weave the strong netting that kept them in, gripping the soiled string ends in her mouth while her square ugly hands tied the knots. As she had not cleaned the tray, the heat from the light bulb spread the chicken smell through the room. For a snack she ate pears entire, thrusting the whole fruit in her mouth and biting off the stalk, which she then spat out on the bare floorboards together with any parts she did not enjoy. Though the pears were bruised and rotten she swallowed a remarkable proportion of the damaged flesh, and indicated that we should do the same, and spit similarly. She had been baking bread, crude loaves the size and shape of scooter tyres. When one was ready, she tore it in half with her bare hands and threw great chunks before us on the table as if we were animals. The bread was accompanied by large, unwashed peppers scorched on the surface of the hob until their skins were burned black, and then they too were tossed in our direction. We understood how Jack the Giant-Killer felt as he had a meal with the ogre's housekeeper.

We were still chewing our way through the tough bread when it began to sprinkle with rain. At once we all had to rush outside, hurry down the rickety wooden stair into the muddy yard, and pick up the drying beans. Darkness came on as we were still grovelling in the dirt, attempting to select individual beans from the chicken droppings. Life, I mumbled to Sarah, could be very close to the knuckle.

A retired blacksmith in the town of Aleksinac showed us how to make the horseshoes last longer. A huge, grizzled man, he welded extra lumps of metal, half an inch thick, to the toes and heels. Stojan had used the technique as a partisan in the mountains when blacksmith's metal was very scarce and the guerrillas depended on pack ponies for transport. Now 63 years old, he dusted off the ancient furnace behind his house and spent the entire day re-shoeing the horses. It was majestically thorough work, with a glass of beer as each horse was done, and when he was finished, the horses walked away gingerly on their new elevated shoes like girls in their first high heels. To a stranger the extra lumps of welded metal made it seem that they were fitted with teapot trivets.

At the city of Niš the Morava valley went on south towards Macedonia, but the route of the Crusade angled southeast into the narrow gorges that would lead through the mountains to Bulgaria. At Niš the *autoput* ended, and the old road was totally inadequate for the near-continuous stream of traffic heading south. It was the season for one of the world's newer annual migrations – hundreds of thousands of Turks migrating southward for their annual summer holidays away from their jobs in Germany. They drove vans and cars loaded to the brim with passengers, roof racks piled with electrical goods wrapped in plastic sheeting. Eager to be home in the sunshine away from their dreary work in the dull north, they sped along, loathe to spend a single unnecessary hour on the road. Unwilling to pay for overnight accommodation, they stopped only to refuel the vehicles or to eat a roadside picnic. Day and night the pace never slackened. Sometimes the same man would stay at the wheel twenty hours at a stretch. The bleary-eyed drivers shared the narrow twisting road with large intercontinental lorries grinding on towards Turkey, Iran and the Arab markets; lorries with German, Turkish, Bulgarian and even Spanish registration plates, the high-sided vehicles barely able to pass one another in the narrow unlit tunnels carved through the rock spurs. It was not a road for three horses plodding quietly along.

Four miles beyond Niš a police patrolman stopped us and advised that we leave the road. It was too dangerous, he said. The alternative track up through the mountains would be safer and quieter, and much more pleasant. He was right, though the animals had a long, stiff climb up into the highlands. We picked our way up a steep valley which closed in around us. We passed the maximum altitude where maize could be grown, and climbed beyond the last small plots of vegetables and flowers. After that there was only forest and red and grey rock. It grew notably colder, and eventually the stream we were following dried up. A forester called out directions to us, and we kept on climbing. Ahead was an apparently endless jumble of rugged mountains, bare and inhospitable, divided by deep canyons. Reaching a small hilltop village, I cursed the forester for I could see by the lie of the land that he had misdirected us. We had been going too far west. I wished I could have apologised to the horses, for they had expended their energy uselessly. We had to retrace our route, walking back down the steeply winding road for an hour, and then turn up a small side track. Here, without a doubt, was the ancient road. We passed an occasional milestone and in places glimpsed cobblestones beneath the thin skin of tar. When the tar petered out we were riding on gravel and earth. We saw no vehicles except for three army lorries loaded with infantrymen. This area was so remote that the army used it for military manoeuvres. At the crest of the long, long climb was a roadside spring. Stripped to the waist, two Yugoslav soldiers were washing there. The meadow to the right seemed a fine campsite but the soldiers stopped us. They imitated the sound of guns firing. The area was a danger zone while the troops were on exercise.

So we urged the horses through a dense hedge on the opposite verge and found ourselves in the broad sweep of a mountain meadow overlooking a spectacular deep valley. The alp curved round in a natural amphitheatre, and in the middle of the bowl was a row of wild fruit trees. We tied a rope between them, picketing the horses so they had room to graze after they had finished their nosebags, and pitched our tent under a walnut tree. As the sun went down, the slanting light changed the colours and shading of the thousand-foot rock wall facing us across the valley into a gigantic natural tableau. That night, at two o'clock, something woke me and I peered out of the tent. In the faint starlight I could make out the curve of the meadow, the outlines of the trees and the dark shapes of the horses tied beneath them. A file of soldiers on a night march was moving across the grass. The shaded torches of the leader and the last man looked like fireflies. The troops must have been puzzled to stumble on a tent and three horses in that remote highland.

Descending the far side of the mountain ridge next morning, we were forced to use the appalling main road. Cars skimmed past dangerously close, or slammed on their brakes at the last minute as they approached the horses from behind. A truck, overtaking another vehicle as it came towards us, shaved Carty so closely that we could hear the clack of the spring-loaded wing mirror as it flipped against his side pannier. In the squalid town of Bela Palanka I went to purchase supplies and left Sarah with the horses tied to their picket rope between two trees in a small, rubbish-littered park. When I returned an hour later I found her looking triumphant and giving off sparks. It seemed that scarcely had I left, than a local busybody had appeared, rudely told Sarah to move the horses, and untied the picket line. Sarah had yelled at him, snatched the rope from his hand, and ordered him to clear off. He angrily complained that the horses would dirty the park. Sarah, who had been spending her time preventing the famished horses from eating old sweet papers, empty cigarette packets, broken glass and squashed paper cups, was enraged. Kicking the rubbish with the toe of her boot she pointed out that it would be physically impossible for any creature to make such a foul place any dirtier, and the horses would have to stay where they were until I returned to help move them. Her adversary threatened to call the *milicija*. Go ahead, Sarah told him. Two uniformed and armed *milicija* men arrived. But they were neither equipped to handle the horses nor face Sarah's unabated fury. She told them to go away too and they meekly did so, saying they would try to find me and bring me back. In fact, on my shopping trip I had noticed them, standing next to me in a small shop where they were shrugging and laughing and buying a packet of cigarettes. Obviously they had no intention of returning to face 5 foot 2 inches of extremely angry Irish spitfire. I observed that Sarah was flourishing. The bounce in her stride and her quick grin, accompanied by a toss of her curls, showed that she thrived at yelling at policemen and cursing horses.

Our last three days in Serbia passed in a dismal progress from one scruffy town to the next along the main road that lay like a dirt-collecting seam in the crease of the land. At Pirot tyres had glazed the pave to a lethal sheen for metal horseshoes. Poor Carty, tired at the end of a long day, slipped and slithered like the comedian on skates in an ice pantomime, and we were thankful to get him clear of town without a serious fall. We set up camp in a plum orchard and were not surprised when the owner appeared and extorted a fee. We were near the road again and its sordid commercial rules. I paid up without a quibble, too weary to argue, but knowing that we would get value for the money as Carty had developed a craving for plums, his favourite food. We fed him stolen kilo after stolen kilo in that orchard as he crunched the plum stones between his teeth like sugar cubes and swallowed. The following night in

Dimitrograd, the last town in Serbia, a drunkenly happy *milicija* sergeant invited us to put the horses overnight in the public park, boasting that he was in charge. Unfortunately he was too inebriated to be a useful sentry. Going to check the horses, we found them shivering and miserable. To judge from the rubbish lying around them, they had been stoned by children hurling rocks and broken glass at the captive animals.

Short of sleep, riding three fractious and very hungry animals, we arrived at the border post. The building was still under construction, with sacks of cement, a half-finished roof, gangs of workmen. No one paid us the least attention. We were shooed away into the no-man's-land with Bulgaria, a broad dull expanse of tarmac road. In the distance I saw a lone figure, standing very correctly just inside Bulgaria, a yard beyond the official border stone. He was waving a greeting.

CHAPTER 13

Bulgaria

The lone figure by the frontier mark was Theodor Troev. I had first met him three years earlier in Soviet Georgia where I had gone with an expedition in the replica of a Bronze Age galley, tracing the route of Jason and the Argonauts. Theo had volunteered to be one of the crew on my next expedition, and we became shipmates when he sailed on an investigation into the wandering of Ulysses. A journalist by profession, Theo worked for Bulgaria's leading magazine of tourism, so the previous winter I had written to ask if he could help arrange our transit of Bulgaria. He had written back to ask about the precise route that I wanted to follow, the daily distances I expected the horses could cover, and a host of other details. As best I could, I answered his questions and he promised to arrange a suitable itinerary.

Now the width of Theodor's grin told me that everything was well under control. Bearded and slightly built, Theo was suntanned from a three-week archaeological visit to Greece. I introduced him to Sarah.

'I got special permission to come forward past the customs check point to meet you,' he said, 'so I'm happy to be the first person to welcome you to Bulgaria, though there's an official reception group waiting for you. Please ride up to the frontier post and take the right hand channel.'

Behind Theo's shoulder I could see the Bulgarian frontier station. Like a motorway toll station it had a canopy stretching across the entire width of the road, and several entrance lanes for approaching traffic. All the lanes, except one, were jammed with slow-moving queues of Turkish cars awaiting customs and passport controls. The right hand lane was isolated by traffic cones and empty. We clip-clopped forward past the lines of bemused motorists and entered the right hand channel. A uniformed Bulgarian officer in his glass-fronted booth cheerily waved us through, and we emerged into a reception very different from anything we had ever experienced before. Facing us was a large crowd of well-wishers and officials.

Theo began a series of rapid fire introductions: this was the senior inspector of customs, here was his counterpart in the immigration and passport control service. Both of them were ready to expedite any paperwork. A charming and efficient lady was the chief of Bulgaria's veterinary service and please could I give her the horses' vaccination papers. The man with the world-weary expression was our interpreter from the National Tourist Office. He would accompany us throughout our visit to Bulgaria, so too would the cheerful grey-haired individual introduced as a friend of Theo's. This was Lubo, a retired long distance coach driver who would drive the jeep for us as soon as I had retrieved it from Yugoslavia. Next there was a four-man deputation from the local mayor's office, plus a young man representing the Bulgarian Horse Riding Federation, which was expecting to stable our horses when we got to the capital at Sofia. Nothing had been overlooked. There was even a policeman on special assignment from the National Tourist Police who would liaise with local traffic and regional police along our route, and a historian from Sofia University who would see to it that our questions on medieval Bulgaria were correctly answered.

I had to remind myself that just a couple of miles back down the road were the stone-throwing guttersnipes of Dimitrograd and the memory of a long slog across Yugoslavia, with short rations for the horses and uncomfortable nights spent in scruffy conditions. Here, thanks to Theo and the editor of his magazine, was a reception that would have impressed even Duke Godfrey and his noble lords. Our famished horses immediately showed how much they too appreciated the reception. Standing a few paces in advance of the welcoming group were two Bulgarian girls in national costume, holding up bouquets of flowers for Sarah and myself. Mystery and Szarcsa got there first. With two quick paces and a lunge, they reached for a floral snack.

Accepting the slightly nibbled bouquets, Sarah and I observed the traditional welcome ceremony by breaking a morsel of bread from a special loaf, dipping it in salt and eating it with a draught from a cup of wine. Then Hristo the historian opened a parchment scroll and began reading a proclamation. It was a nice touch. It was an updated version of the letter that Emperor Alexius had sent to Duke Godfrey on his arrival in Byzantine territory. In his letter Alexius promised assistance to the pilgrims and warned them not to damage the people's crops or possessions. Interestingly, the one item he gave them permission to plunder was fodder for the horses. It seems that even the emperor recognised the paramount importance of the war chargers. Unfortunately no one had been keeping an eye on our own war horse, and Carty had grown restive and was looking for mischief. Very quickly he worked out that the reception committee was not used to handling horses, and he took wicked advantage of the fact. He shuffled quietly round the crowd, accepting their pats and caresses but deliberately standing on their feet. He made it look accidental, but Sarah promised me it was deliberate. More than one Bulgar limped away from the reception ceremony, and the principal and least-deserving victim was Hristo. Wearing soft shoes, he found one foot trapped under Carty's iron-shod hoof, and finished the recitation of Alexius's letter crimson with discomfort.

Off we went in grand style. First proceeded the Tourist Policeman, Stojan, who drove ahead to block off any road junctions. Even if there was no traffic we would find him standing guard at the empty intersection, with a genial smile and waving his official police baton in greeting. Then came Sarah and myself, riding along without a care in the world. Behind us at a discreet distance crept two orange cross-country vehicles of the Highway Patrol, then Theo and Lubo in the jeep, and finally a van loaded with hay and sacks of oats. Shepherding the entire cavalcade was a police motorcyclist in uniform, helmet, gloves and goggles, with a flashing blue light who peremptorily flagged down any driver bold enough to try to overtake us. Coddled within this protective shell, we came to our first halt, a roadside restaurant. There instead of our usual lunch of a handful of peanuts and raisins eaten in the lee of a hedge, we found a table prepared for twenty. While all of us enjoyed a three-course meal, a squad from the Horse Federation fed and watered the three animals outside.

After the meal Hristo led us over the shoulder of a hill to show us the clear trace of the Via Militaris running across the fields of stubble. The paving had been taken up and re-laid when the Ottoman Turks ruled the area, but they used the original stone slabs. It was a strange sensation to realise that our three horses were treading the exact same stones as the Crusaders' horses, and a little later when we passed through a canyon and heard the sound of their hooves reflected back from the cliffs I could not help wondering how many generations of riders had listened to exactly the same distinctive clattering echo. It had been arranged that we spend the night at the town of Dragoman, which had been a way-station on the great trunk route, in Roman, Byzantine, medieval and Ottoman times. 'As Britain was once the hub of the sea, so Dragoman was a hub of the land', was how the mayor proudly put it.

'The best equipment for crossing Bulgaria seems to be a strong digestion and a pair of breeches several sizes larger, Sarah observed as another gargantuan meal was placed on the table before us. With the fresh memory of going hungry in Serbia, it was difficult to resist roast stuffed lamb, salad, beans and mulberries in honey. We had just left the horses in a nearby stable. Brushing against the stable wall, a smear of whitewash had rubbed off on my sleeve and I realised that the stable had been cleaned out and freshly painted for the single night of our visit. And who, I asked our host, a retired agricultural engineer, was the imposing figure who had been hovering in the background at the stable? Dressed in a dark uniform with thin red piping, brass jacket buttons and neat cap and badge he had looked rather like a Victorian postman. That, I was told, was the regional veterinary officer. He had been on hand to inspect the horses and give them any treatment they required. What is more, he would be on standby all night long if anything went wrong. Similar veterinary assistance was to be provided at every stopping place in our crossing of the country. Duke Godfrey and his entourage, their daily stopovers arranged by the representatives of Emperor Alexius, could scarcely have been better attended.

Everything had been so meticulously arranged for our care and safety that, almost inevitably, there was now an accident. After evading countless risks from traffic and bad conditions in Yugoslavia, it was the supreme irony that one of our horses was injured because for safety's sake our Bulgarian friends did not want us to risk the city streets on horseback. Instead the animals would be taken from the outskirts of Sofia to their stable using the Riding Federation's transporter lorry which was fitted with special stalls in the interior and could contain up to nine horses at a time. We duly loaded the three horses and arranged to rendezvous at the Federation's stables. The first creature we saw as we arrived there was a strangely familiar horse being walked up and down the central exercise yard. The animal was so drenching wet it looked as if it had just been rescued from a river.

'Oh My God,' cried Sarah, it's Mystery, and look at her leg!'

A stream of blood was pumping out of her rear fetlock, and the little mare was shivering and pouring with sweat. Valentin the Riding Club representative was so distraught that he was almost as distressed as Mystery. He told us that poor, scatterbrained Mystery had panicked in the transporter. In her frantic struggles she had thrown herself sideways in her stall. Kicking wildly for a foothold, she had sliced the inside of her left hind leg with the road studs welded to the horseshoes in Yugoslavia. To judge from the depth of the wound, Mystery's travelling days were over, at least for the time being. This time it was Mystery we would have to leave behind, in the sick bay at the stables, and ride on with just Szarcsa and the seemingly indestructible Carty.

When Duke Godfrey reached Bulgaria, the country was once again a full Byzantine *theme* or province after a period as an independent nation. In the heyday of the first Bulgarian kingdom, 170 years earlier, the ruler of the Bulgars had seen himself as near-equal to the emperor of Byzantium. Victorious Bulgar armies had camped before the walls of Constantinople, and he had taken to styling himself, rather presumptuously, 'Emperor of the Romans' as well as of Bulgaria. But a vicious and protracted war in the early part of the 11th century had put an end to Bulgarian independence, at least temporarily, as Byzantine armies methodically crushed Bulgarian resistance. The same Byzantines who were soon to complain that the Crusaders were brutal and barbarous men, would conveniently forget that their own troops had practised state-sponsored savagery on a chilling scale. In 1014 after 15,000 Bulgars were captured in the upper Struma valley the Byzantine Emperor Basil II ordered that 99 out of every hundred prisoners should be blinded. The hundredth was left with his eyesight so he could guide his companions back to the Bulgar king. It is said that when King Samuel of Bulgaria saw the dreadful stumbling procession, he had a heart attack which killed him. Basil II, meanwhile, acquired the epithet 'The Bulgar Slayer'.

To Godfrey and his companions Bulgaria would have looked very familiar. The Bulgars lived in villages of plain wooden houses, often raised above ground on low posts. In their gardens they grew beans and cabbage and garlic and melons. It was a rich land, with a milder climate than the north, and the ordinary peasant probably had a higher standard of living than the Duke's followers. Bulgarian farmers could store their spare grain in underground pits, a ton at a time, and Duke Godfrey's army had no difficulty obtaining supplies. Bulgaria, with its dense forests of northern tree species, was to be the last European, as opposed to Mediterranean, country they would encounter on their great journey. Beyond, all manner of life would change. The summers would be much hotter and drier, the terrain more rocky and parched. Olive oil would replace the northerners' milk and butter, cotton take the place of wool. It was the last country where the pilgrims' thick clothes, heavy tents and baggage, as well as their dietary habits of the north, were really suitable. Just as important, after nearly a thousand miles of travel, the great horses would leave behind the conditions that suited them best, and begin to falter.

The Byzantines themselves placed the boundary between the eastern and western world in Bulgaria, rather than at the Bosphorus as one would expect. Forty miles east of Sofia the Military Road crossed a line of low hills through a col known as the Trajan Gates. It was a modest enough place where a stone wall had been strung between a series of forts and every traveller had to pay an imperial tax as he passed through. By Godfrey's time the forts had fallen into disuse and the gate was a shell, but it is here the First Crusade passed definitively into the world of Byzantium and the Near East.

Sarah and I, with Szarcsa and Carty, reached the Trajan Gates on the third day of riding after Sofia. These were days of easy, pampered progress. Our escorting convoy produced everything from archaeologists and historians to bales of hay and rations of oats. The enthusiasm was unrestrained. Each overnight stop had been planned in advance and when Carty proved too big to fit into his overnight stall in the selected farm, the proprietor cheerfully took a pick axe and smashed to pieces his cow byre to make more room for the big Ardennes. Everything was so well organised and prepared that I even began to suspect our hosts of rearranging the landscape for our benefit. We rode through a great fertile basin of land where every feature was neat and well-ordered. Over to our right in the distance a line of mountains were placed to mark the horizon. Closer to hand the foothills shaded down into pastureland with herds of plump cattle, or to geometric lines of carefully tended vineyards. Even a train chuffing across the landscape looked like a toy produced from a box and released at just the right moment to make its way across our view. Houses and trees and factory chimneys were etched in so neatly that they might have been two-dimensional drawings in a school exercise book for learning foreign vocabulary. One expected to see the Bulgarian word for each feature written in the air above them.

At our ordained campsite beyond the Trajan Gates a welcoming committee was on standby to take our packs and fetch our supper. Thirty-six people sat down to another huge picnic laid out on the grass, and afterwards we were entertained by a local folklore group with songs and dances. If our digestions were overloaded, Carty had no such qualms. He was in ecstasy. We had tied him for the night under a heavily laden wild plum tree. After he had swallowed his ration of oats, he grubbed around in long grass under the plum trees looking out for windfalls. Then he began to graze on the tree itself, sucking plums off the branches overhead. Sarah sighed and shook her head, muttering that horses were not meant to be tree feeders. But Carty was not yet done. He discovered how to barge into the tree, shaking it to dislodge a pattering rain of ripe fruit which he then vacuumed out of the grass. He ate so many plums, up to two hundred at a sitting, that I was worried what they would do to his digestive process. But the local vet assured me that the added vitamins could only do Carty good. Szarcsa of course had looked on with his customary disdain for such uncouth scavenging.

Early the following morning, half our escort were still dozing on the grass in their sleeping bags when we rode out of the camp in the chill dawn and made our way down the winding road into the little town of Vetren. The street was lined with picturesque houses of mellowed brick, each with an arbour with vines on trellises facing the road. Women and children emerged from the houses to stare at us or to applaud. Some scurried back inside and reappeared with small bunches of flowers just plucked from their gardens. I was curious to see a very old woman, dressed entirely in black, hobble out with great determination and stop Sarah in mid-street. The old woman was holding up something which she wanted Sarah to accept. I rode to where Sarah had halted and was leaning down from Szarcsa, trying to understand what the old woman was telling. The old lady was clutching three small coins in her wrinkled hand, and seemed to want us to take them. Hristo the historian came to our rescue. 'She asks if you will take the coins to Jerusalem and put them on Christ's grave,' he translated. I was deeply moved. The old lady must have heard somehow that we were going to Jerusalem, and for her it was a unique chance to make personal contact with the most important shrine of her religion, a place she could not hope to visit herself. We would be, in a sense, carrying out a pilgrimage on her behalf, just as pilgrims travelling with Duke Godfrey must have carried the offerings and mementoes of those villagers who stayed behind when the Pope's call to Crusade was first preached. Accepting the coins, I made myself a promise that if we did succeed in reaching Jerusalem those three small coins would be lodged at Christ's Sepulchre.

On 23 August Sarah went back to Sofia to check how Mystery's wound was healing. We did not want to leave the Irish horse too far behind, and due to Theo's all-embracing efficiency we were making excellent progress across Bulgaria. Sarah and I decided that if Mystery could travel we would bring her up by lorry, but heavily bandaged and sedated so that she did not panic. Sarah's departure gave our Bulgarian friends a chance to ride Carty. Both they and he loved the experience. Theo, Valentin from the Horse Federation and Hristo the historian took turns and Carty naturally relished being the centre of attention. He seemed to grin as he plodded along, doing very much as he pleased with the novices, slowing down or speeding up to annoy Szarcsa, and splashing through the mud of irrigation channels like a child, splattering himself and Szarcsa. Hristo had never ridden a horse before and had long since forgiven Carty for stepping on his foot at the frontier. Intrigued with the first-hand experience of medieval transport, he pronounced a definite similarity between riding Carty and the sensation of driving a medium tank during his military service in the Bulgarian army.

That evening we arrived at Plovdiv, the ancient Philippopolis, and were met on the outskirts of town by a deputy mayor and three more girls in national costume bearing the now customary gifts of bread, salt and flowers. It was a measure of how much better the horses were now feeling that they declined a piece of bread offered to them, and did not even sniff the flowers. After six days' convalescence in the care of the Bulgarian vets Mystery had arrived – unharmed thanks to sedation – at Plovdiv's brand new riding centre which was so immaculate and crisp that even the straw in the stalls had been raked in neat lines. Then our hosts delivered Sarah and me to a historic town house in the old quarter of Plovdiv that had been painstakingly restored. Tall double gates were pushed back to reveal a wide courtyard arranged as an attractive open air restaurant with tables and chairs, starched table cloths and gleaming china. We were taken up a broad old wooden staircase to the first floor and ushered into an enormous apartment for guests. The main reception area with its high ceilings and chandeliers was big enough to host fifty people, and had a grand piano. Besides a large private study there were two huge double rooms with carefully restored panelling in green and white and sand colours. Clutching our saddle bags Sarah and I felt dwarfed, and as soon as our hosts had withdrawn, busied ourselves with the humdrum chore of washing shirts and underwear, each in an immense bathroom *en suite*.

Next day was a rest day for the horses, so Theo took me to visit the monastery of Bachkovo in the hills to the south of Plovdiv. The monastery had been founded with 50 monks and one abbot in 1083, thirteen years before the First Crusade, and the present complex of chapels, cells, dormitories, refectory and outbuildings retained that air of sanctuary and calm so vital to the Eastern Orthodox Church. Tin cups hung by chains above double basins at the entrance so that visitors might quench their thirst, and then one entered through the gatehouse into a shady, peaceful courtyard arranged around the central church. Flowers and pot plants were everywhere, and there was an occasional glimpse of a monk in blue and purple robes passing along the balcony of a side building. The sun reflected off white-washed walls and red tiled roofs. Inside the dimly lit main church hundreds of candles flickered in brass candle holders. Overhead and all around were the rich reds and gold, the ochres and blues of every shade which created the monastery's renowned frescoes.

The effect of such a scene – which would have differed only in specific detail – on the ordinary pilgrims with Duke Godfrey must have been very disturbing. They had walked for three months to come to the aid of the Christian Church against the infidel, but the beleaguered Church they found must have seemed very alien. They had never laid eyes on such paintings and mosaics in their own lands. The identities of the saints and their deeds were recognisable enough, but the way the holy figures were depicted with stark wide staring eyes and stiff formal gestures, the robes they wore, even the colours the artists had used were unfamiliar and alien. A pilgrim from Swabia or Lotharingia would have found the Byzantine fascination with icons extraordinary. They were displayed everywhere, in churches and shrines, set in massive gilded frames and painted in ways that were exotic and off-putting to the visitors. Some churches had so many icons that the walls were completely covered with them, and there was often an icon of the month displayed on a central stand. Nor were the priests any less startling in appearance and behaviour. The Eastern Orthodox monks wore beards and, unlike their western counterparts, never used the tonsure, while the ordinary pastors, the white-clad village priests whom the pilgrims were most likely to meet, were allowed – indeed encouraged – to marry.

All this perhaps could have been put aside as superficial and irrelevant. But what must have genuinely shocked the travellers was the eventual realisation that the Byzantine Christians had no real interest in joining the Crusade. Devoutly Christian, the faith dominated their lives far more than for most people in the West. Byzantine troops invoked Christianity when they went to battle – icons were carried by the fleet and displayed to the enemy ships, and the imperial land troops charged to the battlecry of 'The Cross has conquered!' – but they had no wish to attack the infidel and carve a path to the Holy Land. They were accustomed to reaching an accommodation with the Muslims, and an Islamic mosque had even been built in Constantinople just fifty years before. A plea for the Crusade such as the Pope had delivered so successfully in Clermont would have fallen on deaf ears in Byzantium. The notion of Holy Crusade was a foreign import, and the western pilgrims were to be left to get on by themselves with their strange obsession to fight their way to Jerusalem.

We had lunch with Bachkovo's abbot, a benevolent and impressively bearded figure in an off-white robe with his medallion of office around his neck. He had joined the church at 14, as an orphan, and had known no other life. His view of the monastery's role was no different from classical

Byzantine thought. He wished only for his monastery and monks to be left alone and to run their own affairs. As in Byzantine times, the monastery was also a farm, owning large tracts of fertile land in the valley below, and the well-being of the estate seemed to be the abbot's major secular preoccupation. He pronounced himself grateful to the state for assistance with technical advice and materials on the farm as well as money and craftsmen for the restoration of the monastery itself. One had the impression of an inward-looking, passive life, a sense of quiet acceptance. I asked if anyone from the monastery ever went on pilgrimage and received a blank look. Perhaps, he said, in the 18th and 19th century, but now the only equivalent would be the rare visit to the Bulgarian monastery on Mount Athos, nothing more. I left, after a majestic, whiskery triple kiss from the abbot, and carrying his present – two bottles of a deep red rich wine flavoured with blackcurrant. The wine was full bodied, unlabelled and soporific. It seemed very apt.

Mystery's wound was ugly to look at, a deep gash just where the skin stretched over the moving joint, so it was impossible to keep the wound closed. Sarah recommended keeping Mystery on the march so as to maintain her fitness and general health while we cleaned the open wound every few hours rather than confine her to a stable and risk the joint stiffening up. Mystery, of course, was ideally suited to the treatment. She had hated being away from the other horses, and though she limped as she went she still outwalked Carty on the road. Our main worry was any unexpected knock that the wound might take. The night after we left Plovdiv we were at a hunting camp where our hosts had excelled themselves. We arrived to find three old-fashioned square tents, like small marquees, had been erected, not for us, but for each horse as an individual stable. The tents only lacked pennants flying from their peaks to look truly medieval. Even Duke Godfrey, I reckoned, had not put up his horses in such style. In the centre of each tent a fat stake had been driven three feet into the ground as a tethering point. Naturally in the night Carty uprooted his picket stake as if it was a toothpick, and I was awakened by an agitated watchman to say that one of the tents was on the move. It was Carty blundering around with a canvas cape. Of course Mystery had heard the commotion, panicked as usual, broken her head collar, escaped and tied herself in knots on a guyline, scraping open the healing wound.

But it was not enough to slow Mystery down. Two days later we were joined for our day's ride by two Bulgarian horsemen who had ridden a considerable distance to keep us company for the day. They were welcome additions to our little group as we churned our way through the thick mud of irrigated maize fields, but by lunchtime it was noticeable that the Bulgarian animals were tiring. Mystery, wounded foot and all, was pushing forward and outstripping the visitors.

As we approached the Turkish border, the countryside acquired a much more parched look. The soil was dry and sandy, the pasture scorched by the summer heat. Water buffaloes lay submerged in the stagnant village ponds rimmed by cracked mud, and in place of the tall forest, there was a dry scrubland of live oaks. Shade became ever more important, and we peered ahead for the clump of trees that might give us protection during our brief halts. There were no horses in the fields now, only donkeys, and in the blazing sun the men working in the fields covered their heads with cotton headcloths.

On our last night in Bulgaria we gave a farewell dinner for our faithful escort. It was an emotional event, with speeches from everyone, harmonica playing, a feeling of gratitude on our part and, I suspect, of some relief from Theo and his colleagues that we had been delivered safely across their country despite Mystery's bad luck. In the morning we proceeded to the border, once again to find that the right-hand channel at the border post had been specially closed off for us. Lubo the driver was in tears, Theo and the others stood waving us farewell as we were rushed through the passport formalities. The final symbolic gift was a sprig of greenery to send us on our way as we rode out of Bulgaria and into Turkey. The main impression that I carried with me was just how extraordinarily well-endowed had been all the countries we had traversed. Green and fertile, the lands from Belgium to Bulgaria had shared a natural wealth of fair climate and good soil. Across a thousand miles the country people had changed very little in their attitudes and values. With rare exceptions the Belgian, Luxembourger, German, Austrian, Hungarian, Yugoslav or Bulgar had shown us the same traits of hard work and hospitality, and a similar sense of contentment. Everywhere on a four-month journey we had witnessed the fundamental richness of Europe and the basic decency of her rural peoples.

CHAPTER 14

Byzantium

Two days before Christmas 1096 Duke Godfrey and his army arrived before the walls of Constantinople. By then they too had been more than four months on the road, and the strain was beginning to tell. In the final stages of the approach to the imperial capital, a rumour reached the Duke that a fellow crusader, Hugh of Vermandois, brother of the king of France, was being held captive by Alexius. Hugh had been shipwrecked on the Adriatic coast and sent under escort to Constantinople. If Count Hugh was not exactly a prisoner, nor was he entirely free to leave the city. He was, as matters would turn out, the first of a number of pawns which the astute Alexius would put on the board as he matched wits with the succession of Crusader armies advancing on his terrain.

Godfrey sent a message to the capital demanding Hugh's release and when he received an evasive reply from the Emperor, peevishly responded by allowing his impatient troops to pillage the area around Selymbria, modern Silivri, just a few miles down the coast from the Imperial City. This belligerence seemed to have the desired effect. Alexius sent out Hugh to meet Godfrey, who had by then moved his followers rather menacingly to a camp in front of the city walls, and invited Godfrey and his nobles to enter the city for a conference. The mass of soldiers and pilgrims, however, were to be barred from entering the city. Scarcely had this invitation been delivered than a party of strangers, fellow Franks, came secretly from Constantinople and warned Godfrey on no account to be lured into the city. The Greeks – meaning the Byzantines for the official language of their empire was Greek – were not to be trusted, said the informants.

Alexius' next move appeared to confirm the warning. To put pressure on Godfrey to attend the conference so that they could come to an arrangement before the other Crusader armies arrived, the Emperor abruptly forbade his people to sell supplies to the foreigners. Baldwin immediately countered by leading raiding parties into the surrounding countryside to seize fodder and crops. The hostility was temporarily calmed with the realisation that Christmas was meant to be a season for peace between Christians. Both sides stayed their hands sufficiently for Godfrey to remove his troops from their provocative position in front of the city walls and lodge them in the suburbs on the opposite side of the Golden Horn, the inlet of the sea to the north of the city, and along the European shore of the Bosphorus. In return the Emperor allowed traders to visit the army and sell them food. He then repeated his invitation for Godfrey to come into Constantinople, only to receive the extraordinarily tactless reply from Godfrey that 'willingly and eagerly would I come before you to look upon the wealth and glory of your household, were it not that many evil rumours, which have come to my ears about you, have terrified me.' He did not know, Godfrey went on, what to make of these reports. Were they true or were they inventions? Alexius suavely protested his innocence.

Godfrey was far out of his depth in dealing with Alexius. The Emperor was adept at cat and mouse tactics. Two weeks later, in mid-January, he abruptly shut off the supply of food a second time, and instead of the usual merchants sent boatloads of Turcopoles, Turkish mercenaries armed with light bows, across the Golden Horn. When the Franks came down to the beach, expecting to find a market as usual, they were met with a hail of arrows and several were killed. Stung into action, Godfrey overreacted. He ordered his men to leave their quarters, demolish the houses behind them, and march back to their former camp in front of the city. It was a rash decision because the only bridge across the upper end of Golden Horn was not secure, and the army could easily have been trapped. Baldwin was once again in the lead. With a picked force of 500 knights he rushed to the bridge to hold it, and promptly came under fire from the Turcopoles. Unable to fight on the bridge itself, he and his knights crossed to the dry land on the city side and were thus exposed to a sortie from the city. For the whole day, from early morning to vespers, Baldwin and his knights covered the transfer of the pilgrims. Several times the imperial troops, supported by archers, sortied from the city, and on each occasion the two sides fought to a stalemate. The Turcopoles would pick off a few Crusaders, and withdraw into the city. The Crusaders would stave off the attack but lose men and horses.

Albert of Aix noted the unusually heavy casualties among the horses, and in fact the Emperor had deliberately instructed his troops to maim the Crusader's chargers. Princess Anna, Alexius's daughter, later observed that this was the best way to deal with the knights. Anna was thirteen years old when Godfrey appeared before the walls of her father's capital, and forty years later in her biography of Alexius, she recalled how 'every Frank is invincible both in attack and appearance when he is on horseback, but when he comes off his horse, partly due to the size of his shield, and partly to the long curved peaks of his shoes and a consequent difficulty in walking, then he becomes very easy to deal with and a different man altogether, for all his mental energy evaporates as it were.' So Alexius ordered the Byzantine archers to concentrate their fire on the Frankish warhorses, loftily declaring that it would be wrong to spill Christian blood though, as he also pointed out, without their chargers the knights would not be able to pursue the Byzantine troops as they fell back into the city after each attack. That night the skirmishing ended in stalemate with Godfrey's followers unable to assault the city for lack of siege engines, and the Byzantines failing to drive away the army. For the next six days the pilgrims rampaged through the suburbs, looting, until the Emperor offered a guarantee. If Godfrey would come into the palace for negotiations Alexius would send his son John as a hostage to stay at the pilgrim camp. Once again the pilgrims withdrew and Godfrey and his nobles made ready to go into the city to parley.

Godfrey's character had nothing in it of the diplomat or schemer. In Alexius, he was now faced with a monarch who was a past master in all the arts of negotiation, flattery, bribery, half-truth, threat, prevarication, distraction, and a clear sense of purpose. Godfrey would probably have preferred to wait and consult with the Crusade's other leaders. He does not seem to have known precisely what he wanted, beyond material help from the Emperor and, paradoxically, the Emperor's personal commitment to the Crusade. If the Pope's original plan was to unfold, then the

Emperor would put himself at the head of the Crusade army, pay for its expenses, reinforce it with the Byzantine troops, and lead the host to Jerusalem. But beyond that, there seems to have been very little idea whether the Emperor's leadership would affect the Crusaders' previous allegiances to their own sovereigns back in Europe, what would happen to any territory that was reconquered, and whether the Orthodox or Roman Church would take precedence. Alexius, on the other hand, knew precisely what he wanted. His immediate objective was to make sure that the entire Crusade did not unite at Constantinople, but to get it piecemeal across the Bosphorus and safely out of range. Five months earlier he had witnessed the damage done to the suburbs of Constantinople by unruly elements of the Peasants' Crusade who had sacked and burned buildings, even stripped lead from the roofs of the churches and sold it to metal dealers. Understandably Alexius was appalled at the prospect of the influx of yet more pilgrims and Crusaders. His excellent system of spies and frontier guards was warning that thousands more were on their way. If they were allowed to combine, the massed army would represent a grave threat to the capital itself. At the same time, however, Alexius was wondering how to turn the warlike skills and the religious zeal of the Franks to his own advantage.

Godfrey and his entourage were ferried into the city in boats sent across the Golden Horn by Alexius. Only Baldwin, ever suspicious, stayed behind in the camp. The others dressed up in all their finery, intending to impress the Emperor. They wore cloaks of purple and gold, trimmed with white ermine and with marten, and after a short boat ride stepped ashore in the Queen of Cities. Though they would have landed in the commercial district along the waterfront, what they saw must have made them gape.

At that time Constantinople could claim to be the most splendid metropolis in the world. Occupying the triangular foreland where the Golden Horn empties into the Bosphorus, Constantinople was far larger than any capital in northern Europe. Fulcher of Chartres, who was to come here with Stephen of Blois, enthused:

Oh what a great and beautiful city is Constantinople! How many churches and palaces it contains, fashioned with wonderful skill! How many wonderful things may be seen even in the streets or courts! It would be too tedious to enumerate what wealth there is of every kind, of gold, of silver, of every kind of robes, and of holy relics.

Through streets of tall, brick-built balconied houses, past lavish public gardens and thriving markets selling products from as far afield as Egypt, with glimpses of elegant squares, Godfrey and his entourage were taken to the Blachernae Palace, situated close to the great outer wall at the point where it slopes down the hill towards the Golden Horn. The imperial family had moved there, it was said, to be nearer the open fields and hunting preserves outside the city walls. It may also be that the Great or Sacred Palace at the tip of the promontory had become too imposing and ornate for even their rich tastes. After more than seven centuries of additions, alterations and beautification the Great Palace had become a huge puzzle box of royal residences, offices, state chambers, baths, gardens, shrines, churches, barracks, dormitories, workshops, kitchens, stables, museums, a university, art galleries and even a zoo. It has been calculated that 20,000 staff were required to keep it running, from the silk weavers who produced the finest brocades for the imperial family to the heliographists operating the Pharos, the tower that served as a lighthouse-cum-relay station sending the imperial signals traffic around the empire.

Even the comparative austerity of the Blachernae was artfully set off with a glittering splendour that far exceeded anything that Godfrey and his knights could have seen previously. Its generous courtyards were paved with marble; there was gold decoration everywhere; and the main halls were faced with porphyry. The imperial family had amassed a fabulous collection of jewellery and other valuables, and these were carefully displayed to make the maximum impression on visitors. Byzantine rulers calculated that sufficient pomp combined with the appearance of almost limitless wealth would persuade foreigners that the Emperor was invincible: did he not have all the resources to pay great armies, bribe his enemies, hire allies, or reward his friends? By the standard practice of Byzantine court ritual, Godfrey and his barons would have been ushered into a large audience chamber and found themselves facing a magnificent curtain. Ceremoniously the curtain was drawn back to reveal a tableau. The Emperor, wearing sumptuous clothes of imperial purple thickly encrusted with gems, was seated in the centre on the wide imperial throne. On his head, if not the imperial crown used on great state occasions was, in Anna's words, 'a semi-spherical close-fitting cap, profusely adorned with pearls and jewels, some inserted and some pendant. On either side of the temples two lappets of pearls and jewels hung down on the cheeks.' Ranged on either side of the Emperor were his high court officials, many of them eunuchs, similarly resplendent in their robes of office. The colour and cut of each man's garment and his insignia, chain or belt or staff, indicated the man's station in the imperial service, which recognised as many as 18 grades in the palace hierarchy. Even the shoe colour was significant. All-red buskins or slippers were a direct imperial prerogative but there were rules as to who could wear ordinary black buskins, coloured shoes, or even – a special privilege – shoes with red spots which showed some degree of imperial connection.

To a man of Alexius's guile Godfrey and his nobles were clay ready to be moulded. The notion that the *Basileus*, Emperor of Byzantium and God's Representative on earth, would be impressed by the finery of Duke Godfrey and his nobles was laughable. Dressed in their heavy cloth and furs, they must have seemed cumbersome louts compared to the Byzantine courtiers in their elegant silk robes picked out with gold filigree. As far as Alexius was concerned, the Franks were tiresome, uncouth, untrustworthy, venal and garrulous. But there was one major problem: they were highly dangerous. Alexius had only to glance at the outer circle of the courtiers around him to be reminded of the fighting ability of the northerners. At the Byzantine court the farthest circle of royal attendants was composed of the Varangian Guard, mercenary warriors from Scandinavia, England, and the far north. Big men, handpicked for their loyalty and ferocity, the Norsemen were considered the most reliable and effective footsoldiers in the entire empire. Alexius would have known that his Varangians were not only related to the Norman Franks but that the Frankish cavalry could smash even the Norse shieldwall. Now the Varangians, like the other courtiers, stood staring meekly at the floor in respect for him.

Alexius had decided that the simplest and quickest way to cope with Godfrey and his nobles was to buy them. One by one he embraced the Frankish nobles as they approached the throne. Then, according to Albert, the Basileus made a proclamation.*

---

* Presumably in the stammering speech for which he was renowned as the emperor could not pronounce the letter 'r'.

I have heard that you are a most mighty knight and prince in your land, a man most prudent and of perfect trust. In the presence of this multitude and more to come, I therefore take you for my adopted son; and all that I possess I place in your power that through you my empire and lands may be saved.

This of course was nonsense. Either the Franks did not understand exactly what the Emperor was saying or, more likely, he was choosing his phrases to mislead them. Designing ambiguous statements that could be interpreted in any number of ways was a high art-form in the Byzantine court, and the announcement was a meaningless formula which allowed Alexius to claim that the Duke was now his vassal. Godfrey kissed the Emperor's hand, as did the other nobles, and the presents, or rather bribes, were immediately brought out and distributed. There was gold and silver for all, purple cloth, mules and horses. Every week thereafter, while Godfrey's army was close to the capital, four men went from the palace treasury to the Duke's camp carrying a sum in gold besants sufficient to pay his troops' expenses. This money, declared Albert wonderingly, the Duke distributed entirely, keeping nothing for himself. In effect the Lotharingians were on the imperial pay roll.

A month later, in late February 1097, Godfrey obediently transferred the bulk of his forces to the opposite side of the Bosphorus, and thus Alexius had got the first segment of the Crusade safely out of harm's way. It had been easily done, but then, wrote Anna acidly, 'the whole race (of Franks) is very fond of money and quite accustomed to selling even their dearest possessions for an obol.' The best she could say for Duke Godfrey was that he came from a good family, but on the whole the Franks were a 'foreign, barbaric race quite unsuitable to us'. Their most glaring fault was their rudeness. Having been brought up in a charmed circle where every member of the ruling dynasty was treated with exaggerated respect, and honorifics like 'illustrious' or 'exalted' were sprinkled on distant relatives, Anna was stunned when the foreigners were not in the least obsequious to her father. At a less formal meeting between Alexius and Godfrey's barons, a Frankish warlord strolled over and, to Anna's horror, sat down on the royal throne. Alexius said nothing, but Baldwin sharply told the man to stand up again. He did so reluctantly, muttering that he saw no reason to stand in the presence of a man who was no better than his peers.

To Anna's dismay, she learned that Robert Guiscard's son, Bohemond, was also on his way to Constantinople 'like the pungent smoke which precedes a fire'. In Anna's eyes he was the devil incarnate. 'Never indeed, have I seen a man so dishonest. In everything, in his words as well as his deeds, he never chose the right path.' Bohemond reached Constantinople about the end of the first week in April 1097, accompanied by only ten men. He had left the rest of his party along the road, said Anna waspishly, so that he could steal a march on them and ingratiate himself at a private audience with Alexius. She was convinced that Bohemond sought to seize the empire for himself, and nothing would dislodge that fear from her mind. Bohemond was so heartless and suspicious, she said, that when Alexius sent cooked food to Bohemond's lodgings in Constantinople, the Norman distributed the food to his retainers, without telling them that he feared that it had been poisoned. In the end Bohemond, with Godfrey's encouragement, also swore allegiance to Alexius, but his nephew Tancred crossed secretly into Asia, refusing to have anything to do with the Byzantine court.

About 21 April, Count Raymond of St Gilles, reached the imperial capital. Having chosen the long and arduous route through Dalmatia, his army arrived even more tired and tetchy than Godfrey's. They were particularly incensed at the bullying they had received at the hands of the military police they called Patzinaks. These were in fact Petcheneg tribesmen from the Crimea who had been hired by Alexius. They had orders to shepherd Raymond's army on its way, chivvying stragglers and protecting imperial property. So enthusiastically did this light cavalry carry out its role that the pilgrims came to regard them as worse than bandits. Even the redoubtable fighting bishop Adhémar, the Pope's personal representative, was set upon by a gang of Petchenegs when he wandered off on his own. Knocked off his mule, then beaten up, he was lucky to be rescued by a party of pilgrims who had been drawn by the commotion. The harassment by the Petchenegs grew so bad that the exasperated travellers sacked two of the coastal towns on their way to Constantinople.

Indeed Raymond was in such a foul mood when summoned before the Emperor and asked to give an oath of loyalty, that he refused. He had not come all that distance, he said, to give allegiance to another sovereign or to fight for anyone except the Lord. It was a measure of Alexius's

Using stone-throwing mangonels, Crusaders batter at the walls of a Muslim-held city.

manipulative genius that he totally won Raymond over. According to Anna, Alexius preferred Raymond to the other leaders because he 'valued truth above everything else', and he shone among the Latins 'as the sun amidst the stars of heaven'. Put more bluntly, Alexius quickly discovered that Count Raymond was as gullible as Duke Godfrey. He suborned the Count so successfully that he persuaded him to spy on Bohemond, and foil any actions that might be seen as being against the imperial interest.

So in every particular Alexius had outfoxed the Crusade's leaders, from his clever use of Hugh of Vermandois to his honeyed persuasion of Raymond. The *Basileus* had kept the Franks from formulating a common policy, sewn dissension in their ranks, bribed them individually, and hoodwinked them collectively into thinking that he was their staunch ally. Several of the Frankish nobles as they marched away from Constantinople thought they had never met such a paragon as Alexius. 'There is no man today like him under heaven,' enthused Stephen of Blois in a letter to his wife Adele.

'The Emperor received me with dignity and honour and with the greatest affection, as if I were his own son, and he loaded me with most bountiful and precious gifts. And in the whole of our army of God there is neither duke, nor count, nor any person of power whom he trusts or favours more than myself.'

In truth Alexius had not the slightest intention of travelling with the host. 'Their countless masses terrified him,' said Anna. He despatched a Byzantine general by the name of Tatikos with a detachment of the imperial army to accompany the Franks, ostensibly to reinforce the Crusade. But it soon became apparent that Tatikos was really on hand to restrain and to spy. He provided guides and siege equipment to the ill-disciplined and ill-prepared Franks, but in the actual battles against the infidel, the Byzantine troops appear to have taken little real part. In the final analysis, however, it was Alexius, not the Crusaders, who had missed the great opportunity. Ironically Alexius, for all his subtlety, had misjudged his guests. He had rated them as dangerous and venal, so he bribed and bemused them. He had totally failed to realise that many of them were driven by something more than the lust for plunder and territory. The leaders of the Crusade might be purchased but time would show that the ordinary pilgrims were the ultimate driving force of the great march. They were determined to get through to the shrine of the Holy Sepulchre, with or without the Emperor's help. Their tenacity and the fighting skill of the knights would succeed where the much more sophisticated Byzantine army had failed. When the extent of Alexius double-dealing became clear to the pilgrims, they turned against a man who they felt had toyed with them by asking for their help, then leaving them in the lurch at a time when they were marching into great danger. 'Shall I write of the most fraudulent and abominable treachery of the Emperor's counsel,' asked Raymond of Aguilers in his chronicle, 'Or shall

I record the infamous escape of our army and its unimaginable helplessness?' To the ordinary pilgrim the perfidy of the Emperor was to become a byword. They were to feel, and not for the last time, that the great and the mighty had deluded them.

CHAPTER 15

Nicaea

The clamour and noise of Turkey burst upon us. It was the seventh national frontier we had crossed, and by far the most noticeable. On one side was the orderly calm of Bulgaria, on the other the ebullience and bustle of the Turks. The same cars which a hundred yards down the road had lined up in obedient columns to present their papers to Bulgarian customs officers, exuberantly surged out into Turkey like hounds from a kennel. They jostled and swerved, switched lanes, stopped suddenly to disgorge Turkish families rushing off to buy their duty-free goods from kiosks, or parked haphazardly to submit to customs searches which in one instance was exposing seven colour television sets hidden in the back of a van. In Bulgaria everything was done by the rules; in Turkey the regulations were regarded as a source of puzzlement, delay, or dispute. The frontier officials had no notion of what to do about importing horses when I told them that we were in transit for Syria, another thousand miles of riding. There was a shrug and a smile and the horses' names were written into my passport and we were released on the promise that I would regularise matters when I got to Istanbul.

Twenty-six years earlier a hospitable Turkish family had befriended me when, by motorcycle, I arrived for the first time in Istanbul with two other student companions. Nine children living in three rooms had somehow squeezed aside to make space for three strangers, and I had never forgotten or lost touch with them. Now a delegation from 'my' family was at the frontier to meet us. Those nine children and their spouses now worked throughout a network of Istanbul jobs – used car salesmen, bank clerks, shipping offices, telephonists – and one, the youngest daughter, a nine-year-old when I first met her, was in full flight as a highly successful businesswoman. Fashionably dressed in red and black she was standing at the frontier post when we arrived, while a sister, a brother, a brother-in-law, a nephew and a pair of friends waited in the background, crammed in a car from the second-hand car dealer's stock, ready to rush us off for a meal at a roadside cafe. Official sponsorship in Bulgaria would now be replaced by an ebullient Turkish 'network' initiative, invoking friends, business contacts, friends of friends, and distant relatives, all of whom would be asked to help us. Already a young man had been produced who would drive the wretched jeep to Istanbul and relieve us of that tedious chore.

At Edirne, the first large town on our road to Istanbul, the chaos and colour and activity reached deafening proportions. A national festival was in progress and military bands were trundling down the main street on floats as white-helmeted bandsmen blew on brass instruments and thumped drums. The swarm of traffic bunched and rushed past the obstacles, horns beeping cheerfully. I was grateful that we now had three very road-wise horses, for no novice would have held its nerve in that traffic. The drivers buzzed spectacularly either side of us, hooting happily, and sped away. Shopkeepers came running across the pavement to shout and wave greetings. And when we emerged into the countryside the drivers of the big lorries would lean out of the cab windows, with one hand on the horn button and the other stuck out and raised upward in a jaunty salute of appreciation. For the first couple of hours it was very entertaining, but then it became so irritating that we deliberately steered a path out of earshot of the road.

Turkey-in-Europe was like Hungary all over again. The fields were vast, and we could travel in a straight line in any direction we wanted. The harvest was in, and we rode across mile upon mile of stubble interspersed with occasional fields of dead, abandoned maize. The farmers were burning the straw and often it looked as if a devastating army had passed that way. The horses walked over the black ash, and thin ripples of red flame stretched across the fields ahead of us. Once or twice we were obliged to pick our way through gaps in the advancing fireline. The ground smouldered under the horses' hooves as they edged through the buffeting wave of heat. The only wildlife was dense flocks of crows, which twisted and swarmed and climbed in the sky as if they were flecks of soot rising from the burning land.

It took us four days to ride from the frontier to the rim of Istanbul's conurbation. In that huge open countryside of Thrace we followed the imperial road without any practical difficulty. At night we were taken in at farm houses or by the *muhtars*, the village headmen, to whom it was inconceivable to turn away a traveller. This was rural Turkey and although the stream of cars and trucks was rushing past, loaded with modern washing machines and video tape players, the social values of the villager were firmly rooted in Islamic and Turkish tradition.

We had been on the road for four months, as long as it had taken Duke Godfrey to reach the Queen of Cities. In all that time Sarah had been caring for the horses without a break, and the strain was beginning to have its effect. She was longing, she confessed, for a change from the daily routine of grooming and watering and feeding and double checking. I, too, was looking forward to taking a worthwhile break in Istanbul, spending some time with 'my' family, but also thinking about the future of our journey. Istanbul was approximately the halfway point between Chateau Bouillon and Jerusalem, and if we continued onward at our present speed I could anticipate the very real risk that we would be trapped by the early winter snowfall in the mountains of eastern Turkey. Furthermore we did not yet have permission to ride across Syria. I began to wonder if perhaps it would be wiser to divide the long ride into two parts, take a winter break to give the horses a thorough rest somewhere in Turkey and press an application for Syrian visas, then ride on next spring. The change of plan would mean that our journey would be extended to the best part of eight months spread over two years, but then the Crusaders – delayed even more by the need to besiege a number of Muslim-held towns – had taken nearly three years to complete their trek. When I suggested the revised programme to Sarah, she agreed for the sake of the horses, particularly for Carty who had already come farther than many experts had predicted. As for her own plans, she was prepared to commit herself to go with me only as far as the winter layover point. But any riding the following year would depend on her own circumstances at the time. I did not complain. After all, officially she was still only accompanying me 'for a couple of weeks'.

On Thursday 3 September, we rode over a rise in the ground and saw ahead a distant straight line on the horizon. It was the Sea of Marmara. With a slight shock I realised that we had not seen the sea since crossing to France with Carty and Mystery, though in all that time we had been travelling steadily in one direction, southeast. The sea was a boundary. It meant we had crossed one continent, and were about to transfer to the next.

I hired a small lorry to take the horses into the centre of Istanbul, a hideous, slow journey through the stifling traffic jams of the city, lingering for what seemed like hours in the acrid fumes of the road tunnels of the motorway. We stood in the back of the lorry alongside the horses, petting them and reassuring them as they nervously looked over the low side of the lorry at the maelstrom of cars around them. Fearful that Mystery would panic once she found herself in a vehicle again, we devised a partial solution. Mystery always threw herself to the left when frightened, so we loaded her tightly against Carty, on his right, so that he served as a vast prop, like an equine bookend. He was unbudgeable on his huge hooves and each time Mystery toppled sideways, she would land against his huge bulk in a terrified huddle. After a moment or two Carty would give a massive nudge with his haunch and push her upright again. In this fashion, we proceeded without incident into the heart of the city where, for ten days, the horses rested in stables. In that time Sarah took her much-needed break from horse-tending chores but, as I knew she would, she was much too conscientious to leave the horses in the sole care of the stable grooms. Every day she went to check on their well-being and supervise their care and feeding. Meanwhile I busied myself with ordering a new Turkish-style head collar and lead chain for Carty from a harness maker in the Grand Bazaar, finding replacement saddle blankets to replace the old ones which had completely worn out, and – yet again – getting the horses re-shod, this time by the resident stable blacksmith.

But my most important task was a visit to Anakara to see the Director of the British Institute of Archaeology. Dr David French had devoted a large part of his professional life to studying the Roman roads of Anatolia. Across the length and breadth of the country he had noted Roman milestones, recorded traces of the roads, and compared the routes used by Romans, Byzantines, pilgrims and Crusaders to build up a compendious knowledge of his special topic. Now, very generously, he placed that expertise at my disposal. I came back to Istanbul carrying a folio of large-scale maps, each marked with a thin red line that Dr French had traced for me. The line indicated the track that the First Crusade had taken in a great meandering Z-shape across Turkey-in-Asia, over deserts, mountains and steppe until the pilgrims reached Antioch on the border of the Arab lands. To follow Duke Godfrey, all I needed to do was keep to that red line.

On 14 September another rented truck took the horses over the Bosphorus Bridge, which was banned to animal traffic and deposited them on the Asian shore. When Duke Godfrey and the pilgrims were ferried across the Bosphorus to continue their march to the Holy Land, they had taken the coast road, keeping close to the Sea of Marmara on their right. Today that coast road is a disaster of urban blight. Mile after mile of depressing apartment blocks alternate with offices, factories, scrap yards and building sites. This dreariness extends for almost a hundred miles along the shore. Yet it is only a thin ribbon of ugliness. Go five or six miles inland, make a short climb to the plateau and abruptly the interior of Turkey spreads out in all its immensity, covered in scrubland and nearly empty of people and settlement. It was there, in the deserted plateau, that I planned to take the horses, keeping parallel with the Roman road.

We rode only a little distance that first day in Asia. The weather was hot and, after their rest in Istanbul the horses needed to be reintroduced gradually to their work. Our target was the summer hill resort at Polonezkoy settled in the mid-19th century by Polish soldiers, mainly from eastern Poland, who served the Ottoman sultan. 'Polish Village' might still have been a cosy north European settlement. There were hedges, orchards and steeply sloping meadows which fell away to small streams draining through willow thickets, and the neat houses with their front gardens along the web of lanes gave a most un-Turkish feeling to the place. There was even a white-painted Christian church with a plain cross over the entrance to the cemetery and – most oddly in a Muslim country – the sounds and smell of pigs in a sty. The young farmer who offered a pasture for the animals told us that some 50 or 60 of the inhabitants still preserved their Polish connections. They spoke Polish in the home and, where possible, visited Poland and arranged school exchanges. But, he said, numbers were dwindling fast and all-Polish marriages were rare.

Our friends in Istanbul had asked us to be prudent about the track we followed, so as not to infringe on military zones in the sensitive areas overlooking the Bosphorus. But in the event – as everywhere in Turkey – we found that if we were discreet and kept well clear of the main army installations, no one troubled us. Next morning we rode past the radar domes that watch the approaches to the Bosphorus, but no one asked us what we were doing there, and the riding through a forest of small oak trees was magnificent. In any other country, so close to a major city, one would have met walkers or physical fitness enthusiasts. But in the entire morning Sarah and I encountered only a half platoon of soldiers laboriously digging a trench across the path to bury a telephone cable. Obligingly they filled in a temporary earthen bridge so the horses could walk across.

Military camps, army training grounds, and small dormitory towns continued in succession until we arrived at the open levels of the main plateau with its heathland. And here we came upon the birth pangs of a new town, a raw line of half-formed buildings in every stage of construction with labourers swarming over them. The fronts of the structures were ready, but the rears were still covered in scaffolding and wooden shuttering ready to receive poured concrete. Bulldozers, cranes and heavy trucks were moving everywhere. The road was potholed and rutted under their weight. Heaps of building sand, cubes of cement sacks, and piles of reinforcing rods were scattered about. But there was no sign of ordinary life, no grocery shops, bakeries, corner stores or gardens. Instead, each morsel of food was being carried in by lorries that parked under the row of trees in the main square and formed an impromptu market. We rode past rank upon rank of baths and basins and lavatory bowls stacked neatly on the ground. The start and end of the town were marked by a scatter of half a dozen little shacks, like garden potting sheds beside the road. They were land offices and, ever hopeful they all displayed signs which read 'Building Plot For Sale'.

Beyond the new town the immensity of Turkey-in-Asia opened out around us. Everything was on a vaster scale than anything we had witnessed in Europe. We were barely on the fringe of Anatolia and yet already there was the sensation of an infinite land stretching away to the horizon and beyond. Ahead, in the east, we could identify great haze-shrouded ridges, the wrinkled folds of the main Anatolian plateau vanishing into the distance. For the next thirty miles we traversed a brown wilderness of stunted oak bushes until next morning, quite abruptly, we found ourselves riding over the lip of a broad valley, a swathe of fertility hidden below horizon level and laid out beneath us with green fields, woodlands and a scatter of villages. A low tent was pitched strategically on the shoulder of the hill to look out across the magnificent scene. It was a tent out of Central Asia, low and spread out with wide wings of some sort of dark cloth. As we passed the entrance, I caught a glimpse of a woman in baggy pantaloons standing by the central pole. At first, by her rhythmic movement I thought she was churning milk, rocking it back and forth in a skin, but then we saw she was operating two huge bellows by hand, each bellow as big as a wine cask. She was pumping air steadily, and from somewhere on the far side of the tent came the sound of a hammer ringing on metal. They were nomad tinsmiths.

We rode on and there, a mile down the hill, was a small quadrangle of tents, a dozen of them pitched in such neat lines that I mistook the camp for an army patrol. But as we came closer they too proved to belong to nomads. Not a soul was visible. The entire group was sheltering in the shade, and we saw that each tent was erected directly over the owner's four-wheeled cart. It was a sensible arrangement as it kept their belongings safe and close to hand, and protected the fragile wagon wheels from warping in the fierce sun. I wondered what the tent people made of two fellow travellers riding by, with three horses, including the strange Ardennes laden with packs. On the floor of the valley we came upon the nomads' herd. Twenty or so light Turkish horses were running free in a water meadow. Even the meanest was in fine condition, much better than any horses we had seen elsewhere. Turning to look back, we saw that now, beside every tent, a man stood motionless with his arm held up to shield the sun's glare. All were staring down the valley at the strange silent riders and their unusual horses.

That night we slept at a tiny hamlet that was straight from the 18th century. Perched high on a bluff, level ground was so scarce that even the threshing floors had been carved laboriously from the near-vertical side of the slope. The houses were of mellowed brick and timber, not a post or corner true, and the upper storeys projected slightly under red-tiled roofs. The barns were of wattle and daub, covered with crude thatch pinned in place by long withes. A large communal bread oven for all the villagers stood by the central watering trough where we brought the horses for their evening drink, and afterwards a tiny imp of a girl chased away the inevitable snarling watchdogs as she led us down to a field slanting at a 30 degree angle where we were to spend the night. Walking through the village we passed a very ancient woman, her face blotched with age, sitting patiently at her cottage door in the last of the sunshine. She was watching over a sheet spread on the ground and covered with maize kernels drying in the sun. A hundred feet from where we set our tent, charcoal was being prepared in a clamp for the winter. The smell of the woodsmoke seeped up to us in a lazy blue skein which oozed out and hovered over the valley in the still air. Our feeling of contentment in such idyllic surroundings was reinforced with the realisation that in such old-fashioned, simple communities we would find everything we needed for the horses — fresh fodder, decent shelter, and an unhurried rhythm to daily routine.

At Izmit we regained the main coast road and wrinkled our noses at the rotten-egg smell from the stagnant river that drained the effluent from the tyre factory. Izmit, once the elegant classical city of Nicomedia, now has the unenviable reputation as the source for the worst-polluted corner in the Sea of Marmara, yet only five miles farther on we were riding through foothills planted with quince and plum trees that shaded upward into the forested slopes of mountains where wolf and jackal still roam wild. It was a typically Turkish juxtaposition of the new and the ancient. Our maps, for example, were officially out-of-date. They had been surveyed during the last days of the Ottoman empire and were ideal for our purposes because they indicated the old caravan tracks and bridle paths. But the names of many villages had been changed by the Republic, so the official names written on the occasional roadsigns were often different to anything on our maps. Yet when I enquired about our route into the mountains, I found that the local inhabitants had kept the old place names. Yes, I was told, there was a road through the mountains, sometimes passable for vehicles, though it depended on the depth of the mud and the rockslides. It was always open for animals. And everyone knew it was a very ancient road because when the rock slid, as happened every winter, the scar might reveal the old paving slabs hanging out of the cliff side.

Sarah and I turned up the valley trail. Groundwater dripped and trickled out of the rocks as we rode up the road notched into the hillside. The earth was a yellow clay that caught and held puddles of surface water through which the horses splashed muddily. We passed through a succession of small mountain villages, the houses all built of pine boards and mud. They had gardens and fruit trees and small plots of maize hand-cleared from the surrounding forest. Carty was by far the biggest living creature that these hill people could have ever seen. They had horses, dozens of them in every village, but they were tiny creatures, no more than fine-boned ponies some 13 hands high, although their stamina and strength was prodigious. The foresters used them to carry timber down from the mountain slopes. Some 300 kilos itself, each animal might carry up to 150 kilos of logs and branches, strapped in an untidy bundle on each flank. Under these huge loads the delicate legs scrabbled and slipped along mountain paths that would have been difficult for a human to pass. Yet the little pack ponies made four round trips of four or five miles each day, and appeared to flourish.

We discovered for ourselves just how hardy they were when along the narrow hill track we met a pony stallion, escaped and loose upon the road. He was challenging all passers-by, and the sight of three strange horses twice his size did not deter him in the least. With a whinny of defiance he charged into the attack, and to our chagrin our three horses fled. Sarah and I found ourselves breathless with laughter, clinging on as the three full-sized horses bolted up the track in undignified flight. Our stroll into the mountains became a galloping rout as the little stallion kept up a running attack, lashing out with his hooves and biting. We pulled our animals to a stop and tried to drive him off, but it was useless. The little brute even had the audacity to attack Carty, who was standing looking puzzled by all the commotion. The Ardennes was totally taken aback by the onslaught until the stallion impudently turned and lashed out with its rear hooves. Then Carty responded. With ponderous deliberation an immense half-kick was unleashed and caught the stallion in the chest. The huge hoof lifted the smaller, very shocked, animal clean off the ground, all four legs in the air, and it landed in a heap. But to the creature's credit it struggled back upright and limped back to the attack until finally I was able to lasso it and shut it up in a tiny roadside field. There we left it imprisoned and fuming with rage until we had got clear.

We were now close to the spot where the Peasants' Crusade met its bloody end while Duke Godfrey was still marching across eastern Europe. In August 1096 the followers of Peter the Hermit had confidently ventured past Constantinople and established their winter camp at a place called Civitot on the south shore of the Gulf of Nicomedia. It was an extraordinarily rash move – just 25 miles inland lay Nicaea, headquarters of one of the most dangerous Seljuk generals, Kilij Arslan, who had declared himself sultan over the region. There are two versions of what happened next. The first is merely that the Turks marched across the mountains and surprised the pilgrim camp. The sleepy defenders were butchered. Survivors either leapt into the sea or ran off into the heavily wooded mountains. One contingent barricaded themselves in an abandoned fortress on the seashore and the Turks tried to burn them out. Luckily the wind changed and the flames injured some of the Turks. But the fortress eventually surrendered, and these men too were sold into slavery.

The second version, from Albert, is much more detailed and seems to have been based on the reports of survivors. According to Albert, Kilij Arslan's patrols fanned out through the mountains between Civitot and Nicaea, and whenever they caught gangs of marauding Christians they beheaded them. News of the reprisals reached the camp at Civitot and instead of alerting the pilgrims to their peril, caused a heady uproar. There were calls for a immediate military excursion to punish the Turks. A handful of knights knew it was madness, and refused to leave camp without first consulting Peter the Hermit. But he was away in Constantinople negotiating with the Emperor. The warmongers accused the knights of cowardice. Stung by these taunts, the chivalry swore they were ready to fight, even if it meant going to their deaths. Every able-bodied man in the camp sallied out of camp, and only non-combatants were left behind, women and children, invalids, and those who were so destitute they did not have weapons.

Kilij Arslan was waiting for them. He had carefully brought his forces over the mountain so that they lay concealed in the thickly wooded slopes overlooking the valley road that led inland from the camp at

Civitot. To their amazement the Turks heard the Christians carelessly enter the woods, making as much noise as though they were on a peacetime stroll. As the two leading divisions of Christians emerged from the trees they came face to face with Turkish mounted archers who promptly attacked with their customary arrowstorm. The hail of Turkish arrows scattered the Christians, and Kilij's horsemen followed up by charging through the pilgrim ranks. Many of the Christian soldiers never even got to leave the shelter of the trees but stood huddled in fright on the narrow paths. The Christian vanguard with its handful of mounted knights was separated from the main body of pilgrims by the Turkish attack and obliged to turn round in its tracks and fight its way back to the main army. It was here that the Turks sustained their only significant losses. The massed charge of the few horsemen, supported by footsoldiers, killed 200 Turks 'in a moment'. But the Turks identified the risk and directed the arrow fire at the battle chargers, then picked off the unhorsed knights. The leading knight, Walter Sansavoir, fell, riddled with seven arrows in the chest.

The Turkish ambush then became a rout. The pilgrims streamed back towards their camp with the Turks hacking and slashing at their backs. For three miles the chase continued, and then the Turks swamped the undefended camp. They cut down the cripples and feeble, the clerics and elderly. Young men and women were taken alive, as valuable prisoners to sell later. The Turks tore down the tents, and carried off every movable item, money, valuables, clothing, horses and mules to Nicaea.

So perished the Peasants' Crusade in total and utter disaster. In a few hours of ambush and slaughter the Turks had disposed of Peter the Hermit's following. Peter himself was alive, shocked but undeterred in Constantinople. A few of his knights and footsoldiers had escaped, but the vast majority lay dead in the ambush valley near Civitot where, it was said, succeeding generations would notice great heaps of mouldering bones.

Duke Godfrey would have heard the full details of the disaster from the battered survivors whom he met at Constantinople. During the winter Peter the Hermit attached himself to the new combined host, as did many of the refugees, but their traumatic experience seems to have instilled very little caution into the high-born commanders of the new Christian army. Godfey and the other leaders were thirsting for action –

Godfrey's corps from Lotharingia had been kicking its heels on the shores of the Bosphorus all winter – and to add to their crusading zeal, they were now keen to avenge the deaths of Walter Sansavoir and his colleagues.

So in the early summer of 1097 the Host straggled along the coast road, Godfrey leading the vanguard. He found the mountain road overgrown and sent gangs of pioneers to hack a route through the forest and improve the track. Iron and wood crosses on shafts were planted as waymarks for those who followed. It was one of the very few examples of sound management that the Christian army was to show during the entire campaign and one suspects that the accompanying Byzantine staff officers under Tatikos may have had some hand in this simple device.

Without waiting for the others to catch up, the vanguard crossed the watershed and descended upon Nicaea. The Turks promptly withdrew behind the massive fortifications of the city, shut the gates, and awaited instructions. Kilij Arslan had been campaigning in the east and was now hurrying back with his army, and in the meantime his garrison felt reasonably secure. They had good reason to. By any standards Nicaea was a difficult city to assault. An imposing perimeter wall of Roman origin, complete with a shallow moat, had been strengthened and heightened. It was said to contain 200 defensive towers and they were so placed that their stone-throwing catapults had intersecting fields of fire. 'No one could move near them without peril,' said Raymond d'Aguilers, 'and if anyone wished to move forward, he could do no harm because he could easily be struck down from the top of a tower.' These superb walls protected the entire circuit of the city. Furthermore, on the west, Nicaea had its back guarded by the waters of Lake Ascanius where the city wall rose directly out of the shallows. On this side no enemy could even get near unless he was equipped with a lake fleet, and until then the defence could send messages in and out by boat, and bring in supplies and reinforcements.

On 6 May Godfrey's contingent took up its position opposite the northeast corner of the city. To their left were Tancred's Normans from south Italy reinforced by Byzantine troops under general Tatikos. Bohemond, who had been arranging with Alexius for a proper supply line to feed the troops, arrived a few days later. So they sealed off Nicaea from two sides, the east and north, but – incredibly – the southern gate was left open. This portion had been assigned to the Provençals of Count Raymond and the French contingents led by Robert of Normandy and the Count of Blois, who had not yet arrived. That the troops of Godfrey, the Byzantines and Bohemond as well as contingents under Robert of Flanders and Hugh of Vermandois were insufficient to invest the city, gives the lie to the huge figures which the chroniclers claimed for the First Crusade. Princess Anna said that Godfrey alone brought 10,000 horses and 70,000 foot with him. It could not have required more than 30,000 fighting men to surround Nicaea, yet it was only after Raymond reached there, on 16 May that the city was properly closed in on its three landward sides.

For ten days, while Godfrey and Bohemond waited for Count Raymond's forces, the defence profited from the gap to the south. They moved in men and supplies through the southern gate, and sent out a stream of messengers to Kilij Arslan urging him to hurry. Then two of the Sultan's couriers bringing back his reply were caught by the Christians and forced to talk.

There is no reason to fear the barbarous and wretched people who have laid siege to you [ran the Sultan's message of encouragement, according to William of Tyre]. I am in your neighbourhood with a strong force and awaiting the arrival of further reinforcements which are due very soon. Together we will take the Christian camp by surprise. From your side be ready to support my attack with a general sortie. Do not be discouraged by the enemy's numbers. They have come from distant countries where the sun sets; they are worn out by their travels, and they do not have horses capable of sustaining the demands of battle.

The interception of this message was the first real stroke of luck for the Christians, just as the timing of Kilij Arslan's initial attack was singularly unfortunate for the Turks. The first elements of Kilij Arslan's relieving force attempted to slip into Nicaea through the unguarded southern gate on the very day that Count Raymond, in response to urgent pleas to hurry, arrived with his Provençals. The two forces clashed in front of the city and in a sharp fight the Turks were beaten back. 'Duke Godfrey and Bohemond did not curb their horses,' reported Albert glowingly, 'but flew with loose reins through the midst of the enemy, piercing these with lances, dismounting these others, and all the while urging on their allies.'

When the Turks finally withdrew, corpses from both sides littered the level ground to the south of the city. But the Turkish relief attempt had failed, and Kilij Arslan had to abandon the city to its fate. 'Act for the future in whatever way you think best', was his last message to the beleaguered garrison as he withdrew. Jubilant, the Christians cut off the heads of their enemies. Then loading them in their catapults, hurled the grisly relics over the walls.

The Christian army now adopted the correct posture for a formal siege of the city. In theory they should have been experts at the work. Siegecraft was a well-developed art in Europe, with all manner of technical equipment for the attackers. There were *petrariae* for lobbing stones, *ballistae* for hurling spears and rocks, mobile towers on wheels to be rolled up against the defence walls, battering rams to demolish foundations and footings. Unfortunately none of these cumbersome items could have been hauled on the long march, and though the Byzantine contingent supplied some machinery – with typical adulation Princess Anna promptly claimed that her father actually invented some new gadgets specially for the occasion – the bulk of the war engines had to be built on the spot. So the pilgrims went into the forests to cut down the standing trees and trim them into heavy logs. One device to be tried was a 'sow', an armoured device like a mobile shed inside which soldiers could hack away the lower courses of the defence wall. In Nicaea's case they were mostly composed of huge blocks of Roman stone, and it would have been a difficult task at the best of times. But the sow never even got into position. Twenty knights and two barons volunteered for the honour of working the machine, and a crowd of pilgrims offered to push the engine forward under its protective cladding of leather and wickerwork. But as the machine creaked forward, it came under heavy bombardment from the *ballistae* of the defence. The hail of rocks and boulders was so accurate and dense that the machine tipped over on the uneven ground, and collapsed ignominiously. Everyone within it was crushed to death.

If this show of technical incompetence was not enough, a squad of sappers then mismanaged their attempt to breach the walls. Protected by covering fire from archers and crossbowmen, they succeeded in getting close enough to the wall to dig a mine beneath a weak section. Using standard siege practice, they propped up the foundations of the wall as they worked, using baulks of timber. In theory they would then set fire to the props which, burning away, allowed the wall to collapse and the assault to enter the breach. Such was their lack of expertise, however, that the team set fire to the props at the wrong time. The wood burned out at nightfall, and the wall fell during the darkness. At dawn when the attackers were ready to charge, they discovered that the Turks had had plenty of time to fill the gap. The wall was as strong as before.

For the rest of May and well into June the siege beat vainly against Nicaea's walls. The main consolation was that the pilgrim host did not go hungry. An efficient supply line managed to bring the Emperor's shipments of food over the mountain and the army had all the necessaries of life. Unfortunately so too did the Turks in Nicaea. They supplied the city through the watergate, bringing up provisions by boat. The fighting reached a stalemate with the occasional bloody episode, usually the result of Crusading impatience. a frustrated knight from the Duke of Normandy's household rushed the walls on his own. Clambering through the moat he shouted his defiance and, protected by his shield, began to batter at the wall, hoping his lead would inspire his own side. But they hung back and the garrison smothered him with a well-aimed rock barrage. To the anguish of the watching army, the Turks then lowered grapnels on the end of ropes and managed to hook up the corpse which they stripped of its armour before tossing the body back to the ground.

During another fierce attempt at knocking a hole with a battering ram, a Turkish defender was seen to take several direct hits from at least twenty arrows. Mortally wounded, he threw away his protective shield and continued to storm up and down the ramparts, hurling rocks at the enemy with deadly accuracy. According to Albert,

Duke Godfrey, seeing that this most warlike and cruel man was raging, and did not falter with so many arrows sticking in him, but that more of the faithful were dying from his missiles, seized his bow and standing behind the shields of two of his comrades, he struck that Turk through the vitals of his heart. And so the man was dead, and he prevented him from any further fearful slaughter.

After nearly six weeks of this futile endeavour the army realised that something had to be done about closing off access to the city across the lake. A request was made to Alexius and he supplied a number of light, shallow-draft boats. These were drawn overland on carts and launched on Lake Ascanius. However Alexius had done much more. Without informing the Crusaders he had been in secret negotiations with the Turkish garrison in Nicaea even before the siege began. A Byzantine general by the name of Butumites had actually been sent ahead of the Crusaders and been received inside Nicaea. There he was negotiating with the Turkish captains about the possibility of their switching sides. Sooner or later, Butumites warned, the Christians would break through the walls and there would be looting and massacre. If the garrison would hand over the city to Alexius, he would see to it that the city was not harmed and that the Turks were suitably rewarded. It was a typical Byzantine ruse, and Anna was very proud that her father had seen how to use the westerners for his own profit. Butumites eventually sent a message to say that the surrender of the city had been successfully arranged. All that was required was to dupe the Crusaders into thinking that the city had fallen by storm, not by intrigue, for custom had it that a captured city belonged to the first group to plant its banners on the walls. Godfrey, Count Raymond and the others were persuaded to launch a general assault, promising the full participation of the newly arrived Byzantine troops. By clever timing it could be made to appear that Butimites' troops had entered the city first. Then, by the rule of war, the Byzantines would have won the prize.

The stratagem worked admirably. The entire pilgrim host assembled for an attack, and seeing this, the Turks opened the lake gate to Butumites who brought his men into the city, so that when the Christians were about to launch their attack, they saw that imperial standards were already flying from the battlements.

The finesse dawned upon the ordinary Crusaders when they learned that they were not to be allowed into Nicaea. As at Constantinople, they were banned from entering the city. Only small groups, a handful at a time, were to be allowed in to look around. Nor was there to be any looting. Instead the Emperor issued each man a special ration of food and some bronze coins. The great leaders, however, were summoned to meet Alexius who had cautiously ventured out of Constantinople only as far as the north shore of the Gulf of Nicomedia, and he gave them splendid gifts. Most of the Frankish nobles felt handsomely rewarded. The same,

By land and water, Crusaders encircle the enemy.

however, could not be said for the rank and file. The largesse to the barons and dukes might filter down to the troops in their employ, but the ordinary pilgrim felt he had been cheated outright. Many must have been pinning their hopes on the spoils from Nicaea to help pay their onward expenses. They had to find the money for their own food and shelter and clothing along the march, and the cost was far beyond their own resources. No pedestrian could seriously have expected to carry bulky loot, valuables or clothing, all the way to Jerusalem. It was to be bartered or sold to camp traders for cash to pursue the great journey. Alexius had promised the princes and the people of the Franks that he would give them all the gold, silver, horses, and goods within [the city], commented Raymond bitterly.

Accordingly the Franks, placing faith in these promises, approved the surrender. And when Alexius had received the city, he afforded the army such an example of gratitude that, as long as they live, the people will curse him and proclaim him a traitor.

CHAPTER 16

Sarah's Accident

Nicaea, William of Tyre had written, 'has the best of fields and fertile soil'. Today the rich silt around the fringes of Lake Ascanius is watered by a very successful irrigation scheme, and we approached the city, its name now adapted to Iznik, through flourishing market gardens and vineyards. Some bygone Roman governor, eager to commemorate himself, had erected in his own honour an obelisk whose tall shaft soared up from the middle of the vines. Wild ducks bobbed in the ripples along the shallows of the lake, moorhens paddled jerkily among the stalks of tall spiky reeds, and we passed a line of sheds for storing the fruit crop. Then, abruptly, for there were no suburbs, we were riding under the massive sandstone courses of the same north gate that Duke Godfrey had blockaded in the early summer of 1097.

We found that Nicaea had grown old with grace and style. On three sides of the city the splendid circuit wall with its garland of towers still stood, and by a happy chance the present population had barely spread beyond the medieval boundary so the place kept its original scale. The grid pattern of the streets was largely unchanged. An unassuming and overgrown ruin near the central square was where the Council of Bishops in 325 AD had shaped the future of Christianity when they formally established its doctrines in the Nicene Creed, and children played casual hide-and-seek among walls and crenellations that Romans, Byzantines, Crusaders and Turks had defended or attacked. At this season of the year the setting sun eased down the length of the lake and into a notch in the distant hills as accurately as into a gunsight, so that each evening the sunset cast an almost contrived-looking red glow across the lake. Only the waterline itself had changed, receding a fraction, so that a pleasant shoreside esplanade had been built at the point where Butumites' lake flotilla had approached the western wall to infiltrate his mercenaries through the watergate. Here, in a small hotel, we rested for three days, while the horses cropped the grass in the shade of the ancient city's defences.

Nicaea's lake moderated the evening chill, but in the mountains the night-time temperature was near freezing. It was now the second half of September and in the eastern Anatolian plateau the average temperature would soon start to plummet. It was time to find a place to winter the horses. We had actually come farther, by some two hundred miles, than Godfrey's first season's march. Our daily distances were the same as his, but by starting our journey earlier, in late spring, we had been able to spend more time on the road. Yet there was a limit to what our horses could do. Bone tired, they were showing signs of the constant strain of travel, despite the ten-day respite in Istanbul. Carty's hooves, in particular, were beginning to break up from the pull of the nails holding on the heavy road shoes and the repeated removal and fitting of replacements. All three animals badly needed a major rest, and so did we. Sarah and I were tanned and fit, but we had both lost weight. At nine stone I was 20 pounds lighter than when I started, and both of us were still irked by the inevitable minor sores and stiffness from long hours in the saddle. We were beginning to feel stale and lacklustre. My Turkish family had been making enquiries on our behalf, and located a retired jockey living along our route near the city of Eskişehir. A farmer now, he had promised he would take in our animals and care for them during the winter months if we would bring them to him.

Eskişehir was on Duke Godfrey's path, but the route he took to get there was our last puzzle for that year's ride. The standard version is that between 26 and 28 June 1097 the great host of pilgrims and soldiers broke camp and began to march eastward towards the town of Lefke. At a bridge over a certain, but unnamed, river the army split in two, and the mounted archers of Kilij Arslan attacked the leading division under Bohemond, taking them utterly by surprise. There followed the most crucial engagement of the entire campaign in Anatolia, but exactly where the battle took place has never been decided. Princess Anna said that it was fought at the ancient Roman city of Dorylaeum, now Eskişehir, and that is how the battle is known. But critics have objected that to reach Dorylaeum after four, or at the most five, days' march from Nicaea was impossible. From first hand experience Sarah and I agreed. We had a shrewd idea of how far each day the army could have travelled with horse and foot, and the distance by the road from Nicaea to Eskişehir through Lefke is simply too great. I wondered if there was a shorter, more suitable route.

Dr David French had suggested an alternative. He had pointed out to me that it was illogical for the Crusade to have taken the Roman road from Nicaea to Lefke because it did not lead to Eskişehir at all, but to Ankara, well to the north. A more sensible route, he suggested, would have been if the army went directly south from Nicaea and spent the night beside the river Kocasu. Crossing the river by bridge, the army could have split into its two divisions in the early-morning darkness, and marched across the rolling countryside towards the narrow mountain pass between the towns of Pazarcik and Bozüyük. This pass, now called the Pass of the Black Village, seemed to be the one fixed point in the itinerary. It offered the only practicable access for a large army climbing up into the plateau. Everywhere else the terrain is far too rugged. Kilij Arslan had already shown with his successful ambush of the Peasant's Crusade at Civitot that he used topography intelligently, trapping the peasants in the killing ground where their road entered the bottleneck of a valley. If the Turkish commander followed the same tactics, he would have waited to attack the Christians in or near the pass at the Black Village.

So we left Nicaea on 24 September determined to try out this alternative route. But we were soon in difficulties. As we approached the first range of foothills, a farmer put us on the wrong track. We emerged on the higher slopes, well to the east of our intended path. It was wild and rugged territory slashed with precipices and canyons. High ridges piled up one behind the other, and in the next two hours of laborious riding we had covered little more than two miles in the right direction. On the shoulders of the ridges we came across flocks of sheep, guarded by huge mastiffs, five or six in a pack, all wearing massive iron collars studded with sharp three-inch metal spikes to protect them against the wolves that even in summer caused trouble. At our arrival the dogs assembled in stiff-legged gangs to drive us off, unless a shepherd appeared from under his shade tree and called back the brutes. One shepherd redirected us, but he was a mountaineer and had no notion of the sort of terrain that a horse could cover.

We found ourselves riding into a breakneck ravine, coaxing the horses down steep slopes where the rock and soil crumbled beneath their hooves. Eventually we came upon a zig-zagging goat track, but the corners were so acute that the horses found it awkward to make the turns. It was hot and glaring, the air trapped and stifling between the surrounding cliffs, and the animals ran with sweat from the heat and the sheer physical effort of keeping their footing. Mystery, with her leg wound partially healed and her experience of trekking across rough hill tracks in Ireland, took the conditions phlegmatically, while Szarcsa picked his way with the usual aloof disdain. But I wished that the doubters could have seen Carty. Supremely fit and confident, he would put his massive hooves down delicately on a path scarcely wider than his foot, carefully pick up his back legs to clear the rocks and boulders and then give a little wriggle and skip to clear the obstacle. To watch him negotiate a tight corner on the path made one close one's eyes in anticipation of an accident. Occasionally the ledge gave way beneath his three-quarters of a ton, but he did not panic at the notion of falling down the slope. Unflustered, he locked his legs, leaned back, and kept his balance as he skied down from zig to zag in a slither of rock and shale.

Arriving in the trough of the ravine, we began to thread our way along the dried-up stream bed. But we came to where a rockfall had dropped across the river, blocking the canyon. There was nothing for it but to turn back and work our way out on the opposite slope, scrambling up the mountainside until eventually we came into gentler land. We chanced upon twenty or thirty women from a remote village, laundering rugs and carpets in a mountain stream. The newly washed items had been spread on bushes to dry, and the bright Turkish colours made them look like immense exotic flowers. The women overcame their initial astonishment at our unexpected appearance from the depths of the ravine and set us on our correct path to their village. And there we did come upon the road we sought, running paved and dead straight across the hills to the south. It must have been the Roman road, for it kept to the high ground, giving us a magnificent view on either hand as we rode along it until we dropped off from the final spur of the highlands and directly into the little village of Karabahadur.

The village was our introduction into deepest rural Anatolia. It literally blended into the soil. The houses were made of daubed mud that matched the surrounding earth. Their low, smooth outlines hugged the contours of the land, with thick walls designed to keep out the sun in summer and the intense cold of winter. Each cluster of farm buildings was the same, with its low square residence, tractor shed, barn and a long cattle shelter with a small end window for the dung to be ejected into the fan shaped pile. Gates were rickety affairs of planks, and beside every front entrance the thickness of the mud wall was pierced for a bread oven, a smudge of black soot around the fire hole. Life here was very close to the soil, solid and heavy.

We rested for the night, putting the horses in a lean-to shed, and then next day came to the river Kocasu and rode along it searching for the possible site of the bridge where the Crusader host might have divided. There was no lack of choice. Indeed there were three bridging points with the remains of earlier bridges. Any one could have been suitable, and they all lay the correct distance – one day's ride – from Nicaea. Across the river the ground sloped upward easily. Here, too, the topography suited what had happened. There was no single route southward. The ground was open and sufficiently inviting, like rolling parkland, for the two divisions of the army to move forward on parallel paths side by side, but out of touch with one another.

Once again it was delightful riding, and Sarah and I were in good spirits as we travelled all day through the now-familiar scrub of oak bushes which covered the sandy soil of the hills. We saw few people and turned aside to take our lunch break in a tiny hamlet that was immaculately swept and clean. The mud houses had been freshly white-washed and the mosque was the tiniest we encountered – a single-room cottage embellished with a doll's house turret fixed to one corner. We watered our animals at the stream in the village square and as we sat and rested, it was not two minutes before a farm gate creaked open and, without a word, a girl carried out a tray with glasses of milk and water whisked together as a refreshment for the travellers. By now our life had taken on a quiet, unhurried rhythm. We knew we were ending the first main sector of our ride, but there was no sense of urgency. We had come to accept the minor events of the road: the farmer running from his orchard holding out fruit he had picked for us, the curious stares of the men in their cafés when we rode into a small town and stoped to let the horses drink at the water trough in the main square, the noonday rest in the shade of a tree, the erratic stops and starts to balance the packs or give the animals a breathing space after we had slogged up a long hill.

Finding a suitable campsite was still our greatest uncertainty. We had learned that it was best to stop riding at least two hours before nightfall to give us time to scout for a suitable field or shed, and that evening we happened to pick a village called the Place of the Leeches. Despite its name it was an attractive spot, the usual cluster of weathered houses and, some little distance off, a dell where three separate springs gushed out of the hillside and were caught in troughs for animals. We waited there until the shepherds and cowherds had brought their animals to drink, and the last of the women of the village had toiled back up the slope, two pails of water on yokes across their shoulders, and then we picketed the horses on the bright green, slightly marshy floor of the dell and pitched our tent on the hillslope. As we ate our supper of village bread and cheese a forest guard, dressed in a brown uniform, came to join us. His job, he told us, was to stop the villagers cutting the forest. It was a protected area. Were there any wild animals in the forest, I asked in fledging Turkish. Oh yes, he replied, wild boar, fox and wolf and bear. I was sceptical and thought he was trying to impress me. Are there really bears? I enquired. Of course, he said, they like to feed on wild honey, and the surrounding forest was famous for its bees. The bears had also become fond of the sunflower seeds the farmers spread on sheets on the ground to dry. In the night they came to the villages to steal the seeds and were a great nuisance. It was forbidden to harm them so they had to be chased away with loud noises. I was unconvinced. When did you last see a bear? I asked him sceptically. He thought for a moment and replied 'Three days ago.' And where was that? 'Right here,' he said, 'at this place.'

The next day, 26 September, brought our accident. In the late afternoon we were riding through Pazarcik, relaxed, confident, only a day away from winter quarters. As we left the last houses of the town behind us, Sarah was in the lead on Szarcsa. Suddenly, without any warning at all, Szarcsa slipped. His shoes were worn and slick, the road

Duke Godfrey of Bouillon, hero of the First Crusade, setting out in 1096. Illustration taken from William of Tyre's *History of Deeds Done Beyond the Sea*.

Carty the Ardennes Heavy Horse, descendant of medieval battle chargers, in County Cork, Ireland.

2 May, 1987, the day of departure: Carty and Mystery before Chateau Bouillon.

Riding through the Ardennes Forest on the first stage of the eight month journey to Jerusalem.

Tim Severin and Sarah Dormon in rainswept Germany, near Kirn.

Above: Shaping new horseshoes for Carty's 9 inch diameter hooves, Austria.

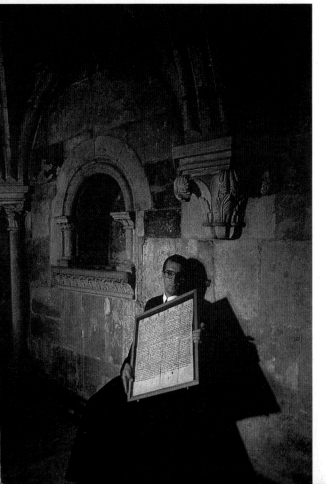

Left: At the Benedictine Abbey at Pannonhelm, a Hungarian monk holds the 11th century inventory of the abbey possessions. According to tradition, at Pannonhelm Duke Godfrey negotiated the safe passage of his army across Hungary.

Above: Herd of horses on the *puzta*, the great Hungarian Plain. When crossing Hungary, the expedition purchased a third horse for the team – Szarcsa.

Right: Tim Severin mending harness in Boyly's *kombinat* (regional collective), Hungary.

Above: An Orthodox monk walks the monastery gallery at Ljubostinja, Serbia. Wide differences between Orthodox and Western Christianity meant that the Byzantines had little enthusiasm for joining the Crusaders.

Below: Reception committee at the Bulgarian border, where a modern version of the welcoming letter to Duke Godfrey from the Byzantine Emperor is read out.

Above: Bulgarian Summer Folk Festival.

Right: Duke Godfrey was badly injured while rescuing a pilgrim from the claws of a wild bear. Nearly nine hundred years later, a gypsy's bear in Bulgaria dances to the tune of a *gadulka*.

The walls of Iznik, ancient Nicaea, still stand. Here the Crusaders first laid siege to a Muslim garrison and, according to his legend, Duke Godfrey established his reputation as a crack shot with the bow.

Above: Leaving the Turkish city of Eskişehir.

Above right: A Turkish woman planting seed on a chilly spring morning in Anatolia, as her husband ploughs with his ox.

Below: April 1988, the start of the second season's ride. Remzi, a retired Turkish jockey, had looked after the horses during their winter stopover.

Right: Lightning strike on the central steppelands of Anatolia. To the footsore Crusaders, the electrical storms were God's signs leading them on.

Fortified hilltop citadel of the Turkish city of Afyon.

Overloaded to the point of collapse, a wood-gatherer's donkey in the Turkish mountains en route to Yalvaç.

Sheep flocks on the great Turkish steppelands, east of Konya.

Wool spinning in a farmyard, central Anatolia.

Breakfast: Tim Severin and Sarah Dormon at camp in central Turkey.

With his usual instinct for self-preservation, Zippy the pack pony lies down to rest while eating from his nosebag.

Above: Cirit, an exchange of lances from horseback, was originally war training for the Turkish light cavalry, opponents of the Crusader knights on their heavy chargers.

Right: Turkish shepherdess.

Kilim (woven rug) frame in a Turkish village.

The last surviving Christian woman of the ancient Armenian community in Kayseri.

Crossing the Anti-Taurus Mountains where the Crusaders encountered the 'Mountain of the Devil'.

Turkish nomad adapting Zippy's pack saddle for a better fit.

Negotiating the rocky passes of the Anti-Taurus Mountains.

Evening hospitality in a tent of the mountain nomads.

Antioch's circuit wall, medieval state-of-the-art fortifications. The siege and ultimate capture of Antioch gave the Crusaders their most celebrated victory.

After Mystery's death, Tim Severin tries out her replacement, Yabangı, at the carters' stables in Antioch.

Left: 'The Watcher', the Crusader castle at Markab, Syria.

Below left: Leading the horses into Markab castle for overnight camp.

Below: Washing at the underground reservoir in the central courtyard.

Zippy on the desert road to Damascus, wearing stylish ear protectors and a fringe to protect him against flies.

Jordanian Arabs wave to the passing riders after more than 2,500 miles on the open road.

Refugee children outside their tented home in Jordan.

The Old City of Jerusalem, sacred to Judaism, Christianity, and Islam, with the golden Dome of the Rock.

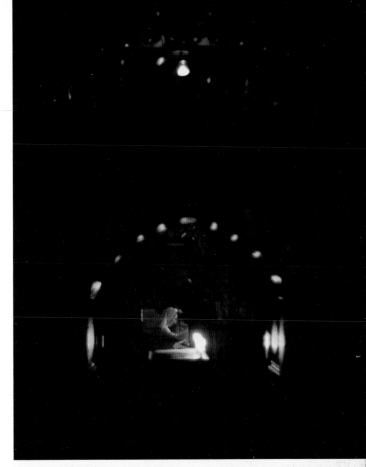

Right: Candle-lit entrance to the Tomb of Christ in the Church of the Holy Sepulchre. The most sacred shrine in all Christendom, the Crusaders had vowed to wrest it from infidel hands. Close by they buried their captain and 'perfect knight', Godfrey Duke of Bouillon.

Below: A Franciscan monk with the 'sword of Duke Godfrey', still kept as a relic in the Church of the Holy Sepulchre and now used to dub knights of the Order of the Holy Sepulchre.

Duke Godfrey in his siege tower leads the Crusaders as they storm Jerusalem on July 15, 1099.

greasy, and the camber steep. At one moment the tall Hungarian horse was stepping along quietly, half asleep. The next instant all four feet had shot out sideways from under him, and he fell flat as a board on his left side on the tarmac road. As he crashed down, his bodyweight smashed on Sarah's left leg. The speed of the fall had thrown her partly clear of the saddle, and her stirrup, a stout leather one, partially protected the foot, for later I found the stirrup crushed out of shape and threw it away. Szarcsa heaved himself clear, leaving Sarah curled up in agony on the road. I dismounted and ran to pick her up and carry her clear of any traffic. She was white with pain and shock, but quite certain of the immediate remedy: 'In my saddlebag,' she announced between gritted teeth, 'you'll find a bottle of gin. I hope it hasn't smashed.'

I rounded up the three horses and made camp by the roadside. Sarah's lower leg was so swollen that it was difficult to remove her riding boot and impossible to replace it next morning. By then, after she had endured a very painful night, it was obvious that she had done more than bruise the leg. Typically, she volunteered to ride on, but it was more important that she had medical attention. My Turkish family had already sent a driver with the jeep to bring us back from Eskişehir, and Sarah was delivered to the hospital there. There the Turkish doctor found that she had broken several small bones in her foot and in the afternoon sent her back on crutches with a large plaster cast.

After nearly five months in the saddle I felt I could handle three horses by myself for the final day of their journey. Riding Mystery and leading the other two, one on each side, I rode through the pass of the Black Village and into the town of Bozüyük. Even Carty sensed he would have to behave himself under the circumstances and was uncharacteristically docile though his shoes were equally worn. He too slipped and fell in a heap on the polished road, but he went down like a huge soft baby, rolling back on his feet unhurt, padded by the new winter coat he was beginning to sprout, then meekly followed on his lead rope without a pause. The late afternoon sun was beating off the pale dust as I finally turned south and rode into the hills. I reached the first crest and there ahead of me was the broad shallow valley where the horses would spend the next six months. A ribbon of dark green in the middle distance marked the tree line by the small river, squares of paler green indicated fields of crops, and close at hand the tiled turquoise spire of the mosque at

Kovalcı village where Remzi, the retired jockey, lived. I rode down the hillside, with Mystery mincing unhappily with each flat-footed step as though her shanks were hurting her or she was suffering from corns. Even she, the exceptional long-distance horse, was all used up.

I had a sense of relief mixed with regret and determination. I could accept that the horses could not go any farther that season and that the first, major section of the great journey was over. But I also knew very clearly that I had to go on. More than ever before, I realised, I wanted to complete the entire 2,500-mile journey to Jerusalem. To my surprise I diagnosed that I had become emotionally drawn into the story of the Crusaders themselves. I had begun to appreciate something of the hardships that they had undergone to reach Anatolian Turkey, and I could not abandon them there. To do so would be a betrayal of their achievement. Now I wanted to see for myself those same monuments in the Holy Land for whose redemption they had left their homes and suffered so cruelly. I was aware that ahead lay the most difficult sectors of the First Crusade: the Taurus mountains and the deserts of Syria. Practically, it was by no means certain that I could get official authorisation either to ride across Syria, or to cross the frontier from an Arab state into Israel. But I was determined to press for permission to complete my quest. It had become more important than ever for me to try to understand what had been the mental state of those original pilgrims. Had they felt rewarded when they reached Jerusalem, or were they disappointed? What had been their attitude during the final stages of their journey? I was beginning to suspect that Duke Godfrey's extraordinary reputation was somehow linked to the popular mood of the Host as the Crusade reached its climax. There was only one way to find out, and that was to go all the way through to the Holy Places. Kovalcı village was by no means the end of our journey. It was only a pause on the great trek.

On 27 September I entered the little village with the three horses. A man was beckoning me from the steps of the *muhtar's* office to follow him. He hurried ahead, turned up a lane, and into a tiny yard behind a small house. Remzi and his wife did not even greet me. They were hurrying back and forth, wheeling barrows of mud bricks, building a new cow byre. They had already converted their old cow shed into a winter stable for Carty, Mystery and Szarcsa, and it was standing ready. After the final barrow load, Remzi straightened up and came over to shake my hand. He was a small brisk man, with a strong hatchet face like an American Indian's, and calm deep set dark eyes that missed nothing. He had a natural poise and dignity, and a sense of theatre as well. He cocked his head on one side to inspect the three horses standing tiredly under the tree in his yard, marched across, and circled each animal, gazing critically without saying a word. He touched Mystery's wound, felt Szarcsa's forelegs, and then stood back. They are very, very tired, he announced. Their sinews are stiff and must be massaged every day. Then he went over to Carty and began to knead the shoulder muscles of the great horse. The horses, I felt, were in good hands. It was time to halt.

CHAPTER 17

Zippy

The battle of Dorylaeum was exactly what the most hawkish of the Frankish knights had dreamed of – a head-on fight with the infidels. Among its participants was an anonymous knight in Bohemond's brigade, who wrote an account of the campaign usually known as the *Gesta Francorum* (The Deeds of the Franks). The sudden appearance of Kilij Arslan's army was, according to him, a complete surprise. 'Our men could not understand whence could have come such a multitude of Turks, Arabs, Saracens and other peoples whose names I do not know, for nearly all the mountains and hills and valleys were covered with this accursed folk.'

On the other hand Fulcher of Chartres among the civilians in the baggage train said Frankish scouts had seen groups of Turks in the distance the previous evening, and the Christians doubled their precautions, setting extra sentries around their camp. So there is just a suspicion that the splitting of the host into two parts on the march from Nicaea was a deliberate ruse to draw in the Turks by deceiving them into underestimating the numbers of their opponent. More likely, however, it was a genuine bungle which turned out to be a tactical masterstroke.

Kilij Arslan's mounted archers engaged the leading division of the Crusade under Bohemond at about eight o'clock in the morning on 1 July. In the rear of the Christian army there was pandemonium among the civilians. Word came back to unload the pack animals and pitch tents, freeing the pack horses for use as battle chargers. A makeshift camp was hastily set up beside a marsh, and the wagons dragged into position as a temporary laager. The long tail of stragglers hurried to get in, but the

Turks, moving fast on their light horses, had already circled around behind the pilgrims. Remorselessly they began cutting down the laggards and loosed showers of arrows at the civilians clustered around the baggage train. An enterprising raiding party of Turks managed to find a dry passage through the marsh and suddenly appeared among the tents, looting and killing anyone in their way. It seemed that the massacre of the Peasants' Crusade was about to be repeated. 'Stunned and almost dead and with many injured,' wrote Fulcher, 'we straightaway turned our backs in flight. Nor is this to be wondered at since such fighting was unknown to any of us.'

The ordinary pilgrims, men, women and children, were in utter panic. Abruptly the road to Jerusalem seemed to lead straight to death. 'All of us huddled together like sheep in a fold, trembling and terrified, were fenced in by the enemy on all sides, so that we could not turn in any direction.' In their fear and anguish, many pilgrims were convinced that this was punishment for their sins. They wailed with fear and dismay, and ran to the priests who, dressed in their vestments, were taking confessions from their hysterical flock and calling upon the Lord for help and mercy. 'They sang weeping,' said Fulcher, 'they wept singing'.

Meanwhile Bohemond had been trying to fend off the Turkish attack. He was a very experienced and professional field commander and knew that his best hope was to hang on until the rest of the army could be brought up. He was also battle-hardened enough to know that the greatest asset of the Frankish heavy cavalry, their headlong courage, was also their potential weakness. Thirsting for action and glory, western knights had a habit of charging on their own initiative, and once they launched their charge there was little chance of regrouping them for a second assault. After bursting through the enemy line they usually went careering off on their own, partly through sheer momentum of their heavy weight and partly from lack of discipline and eagerness to loot the enemy baggage train. So Bohemond now ordered his knights to dismount and form up into an armoured defensive position, so preventing the hotheads from galloping into the enemy on their own initiative and getting into trouble.

This was the first time the Crusaders had encountered the Seljuks on an open battlefield, and the Turkish fighting spirit impressed them profoundly. 'What man, however experienced and learned, could write of the skill and prowess and courage of the Turks,' observed the *Gesta* knight. 'They have a saying that they are of common stock with the Franks, and that no men, except the Franks and themselves are naturally born to be knights.' Kilij Arslan's mounted archers were typical warriors of the central Asian tradition. Lightly armoured, they depended on the speed and agility of their horses to keep them out of trouble, and a rapid fire from their short, deeply curved bows to strike the enemy. These bows were specially designed for mounted warfare. Constructed from sandwiched layers of springy wood and horn they could be dismantled into sections and tucked into a rider's boot when travelling. In the hands of an expert their tension was sufficient to send an arrow a killing distance of eighty yards, and they were neat enough to be manipulated at a gallop by a skilled rider. So the standard Turkish manoeuvre was to race up to the enemy line, loosing off an arrow storm, wheel around and gallop away from any counter attack, often with time to turn in the saddle and send a final cluster of arrows to discourage pursuit.

The range and accuracy of the Turkish archers came as an unpleasant shock to the Christians. 'The Turks came upon us from all sides, skirmishing, throwing darts and javelins and shooting arrows from an astonishing range,' reported the *Gesta* knight who was standing alongside his fellow Apulians in Bohemond's army corps. Against this rain of arrows the best the Christian forces could offer was counterfire from their crossbows. Princess Anna called the crossbow a 'devilish invention' and said they were previously unknown to the Byzantines, so they must have been a novelty to the Turks too. But the arbalesters, the crossbowmen, worked dreadfully slowly. Anna wrote:

He who stretches this warlike and very far-shooting weapon must lie almost on his back and apply both feet strongly against the semicircle of the bow and with his two hands pull the string with all his might in the contrary direction. In the middle of the string is a socket, a cylindrical kind of cup fitted to the string itself . . . and through this arrows of many sorts are shot out. The arrows used with this bow are very short in length, but very thick, fitted in front with a very heavy iron tip. And in discharging them the string shoots them out with enormous violence and force, and whatever these darts chance to hit, they do not fall back, but pierce through a shield, then cut through a heavy iron corselet and wing their way through and out the other side.

Unfortunately by the time an arbalester had shot his first bolt, and reloaded his weapon, the Turkish archer had fired several times and galloped out of range.

So the knights suffered. Their shields and chain mail were stout enough to stop or deflect most of the arrows, but not all. 'Scarcely a Christian escaped without receiving serious wounds. Protected by their breastplates, helmets and shields, our men resisted as best they could,' wrote William of Tyre, 'but the horses and those who had no arms were felled to the ground without distinction.' There was very little the knights could do. Some remounted and tried several charges, but the Turks dodged the main weight of the cumbersome Frankish attack and then closed in on the scattered knights. As the day drew on and the one-sided fight continued, some of the footsoldiers grew so discouraged that they filtered back to the civilian camp and tried to take refuge in the tents. The unexpected result was that the Turkish looters, mistakenly thinking the newcomers were thirsting for action, fled.

Everything depended on the galloper that Bohemond had sent to find the second half of the army. He was lucky to come upon the main force barely two miles away, and still not out of camp. According to Albert, 'Duke Godfrey, who had come forward some distance from the entrace of the tent in order to inspect the allies, spotted him in the distance hurrying at a fast pace, and looking pale with a gloomy expression.' The messenger told 'the bitter and painful news' that Bohemond and the other pilgrims were fighting for their lives. Unless help arrived soon, they would be overwhelmed.

Godfrey ordered the war horns to sound the general alarm. It is not known whether Duke Godfrey, Count Raymond of Toulouse and Bishop Adhémar had time to hold a brief conference to coordinate their tactics, but there was obviously no time to wait for the footsoldiers. They were told to catch up as fast as they could, and the knights then poured out of camp heading pell mell for the battlefield. The accounts agree that it was Godfrey and a squadron of his knights who thundered off first, and Albert's description catches them in full flight, the very picture of chivalry at a gallop:

Already a very clear day had dawned, the sun was shining with brightest rays, and its splendour flashed on the golden shields, and the iron mail. The standards and flags, shimmering with jewels and purple, raised on high and fixed on spears, were fluttering. The swift horses were urged on with spurs, nobody was waiting for companion or friend but each going as fast as he could, they pressed on their way to the assistance and revenge of the Christians.

The arrival of the Frankish knights to succour Bohemond's hard-pressed force was certainly not as romantic as that picture, but it immediately tipped the scales against the Turks. Albert claims that with just fifty knights the impact of Duke Godfrey's arrival forced Kilij Arslan to pull back to a nearby hillcrest. Then Godfrey launched such a fierce direct assault that the Turks broke. More professionally, the knight of the *Gesta* records how the reinforced Frankish line formed up to deliver the famous massed charge. On the left were the battle-weary Apulians of Bohemond and the troops of Robert the Duke of Normandy who by then had been fighting for nearly six hours. They were strengthened by fresh cavalry under Count Raymond. The right of the line was composed of the mounted German knights of Godfrey, with the Frenchmen under Hugh of Vermandois and the Lowlanders of the Count of Flanders. This was the moment for which the Frankish knights had ridden 1500 miles, but even then they might not have had such a convincing win if Bishop Adhémar had not appeared with his horsemen in just the right place – to the rear of the Turks. Using dead ground the fighting Bishop had 'come round by the other mountain' and now cut off the main line of a Turkish retreat. Kilij Arslan's army was held in place, ready to receive the shattering impact of the heavy charge. The message passed down the Christian line was 'Stand fast all together, trusting in Christ and in the victory of the Holy Cross. Today, please God, you will all gain much booty.' Then the knights charged.

The battle was decided. No troops in the Muslim world could withstand the shocking collision with a well-coordinated division of Frankish knights hurtling forward on their battle horses. It was a lesson that Muslim generals, Arab or Turk, would respect for more than a century after the battle of Dorylaeum, and it altered the style of Near East warfare. The momentum of thousands of knights cantering or galloping as a great inchoate mass was unstoppable. Together each horse and rider might weigh in excess of a ton, and the chivalry, travelling forward shoulder-to-shoulder, amounted to a cataract of muscle and bone, iron and steel. There was nothing refined or sophisticated about the manoeuvre. The horses knocked down opposing footmen or barged into

Mounted warfare: Crusader knights versus Saracen cavalry.

the enemy mounts. Each knight thrust first his lance and when that was torn from his grasp or he had come to close quarters, he swung his heavy sword. Unless his opponent was similarly mounted, the contest was very one-sided. The sweep of the great sword depended on a stable platform, and the larger and steadier the horse the more formidable became his rider. The Christian knight was able to bludgeon, if not hack, his opponent to death or surrender. In strategic terms Dorylaeum was the military climax for the First Crusade. That day, as never again, there were more knights assembled, more battle horses, more cohesion and more vigour than at any other time on the great journey.

The tremendous charge disintegrated the Turkish ranks. Under-armoured and overwhelmed, the Turkish horse archers wheeled away and scampered for safety, swerving over the rising ground and 'through unfrequented places and the rough dangerous ways of the mountains where they knew the paths.' Groups of Frankish knights hammered along in pursuit, dodging the arrows that the Turks fired from the saddle.

Back in the baggage train Fulcher was still confused. For him the battle ended abruptly and inexplicably. All that happened was that 'suddenly we saw the backs of the Turks as they turned in flight.' Plucking up courage, he said 'Shouting fiercely we pursued them over mountains and through valleys. Nor did we cease to rout them until our swiftest men came to their tents.' There the victors found all the goods and wealth that Kilij Arslan had taken with him on campaign — gold and silver, embroidered tents, horses, asses, oxen and sheep. There was even a troop of camels, creatures which the Crusaders had never seen before but which they did not hesitate to load up with their booty and drive back to camp. The notorious exhortation before the battle, 'Today, please God, you will all gain much booty', has often been cited as an example of the rapacity of the Crusaders. But their hunger for booty that day had another, far more practical purpose. The spoils from the victory of Dorylaeum replaced the missing plunder of Nicaea and would pay for the next section of the long march to Jerusalem.

Three times that winter I returned to Remzi's farm to check on the well-being of the horses. Sarah had taken a secretarial job in London, and I spent most of my time in Ireland organising the notes of the trip so far, poring over maps of the route ahead, composing letters to the Syrian, Jordanian and Israeli authorities asking for visas, and trying to devise ways of stretching the slim budget for the trip which was being financed entirely by writing a book and magazine articles. Each time I went to Turkey I tried to puzzle out the most likely site for the great battle of Dorylaeum. The clues were imprecise. The description of the topography is too vague to pinpoint the battle, and there are more than enough alternative marshes and rivers, suitable hills to hide Bishop Adhémar's force, and areas of dead ground for the Turks to have assembled a major army without being noticed by the Christians to make it a difficult task. The battle had to have taken place along the line of the main road leading to Eskişehir from the pass at the Black Village, and at no more than three days travel from Nicaea. The best candidate was the valley of the Sarisu river where perhaps history had repeated itself in very similar circumstances eight centuries later during the Turkish-Greek War. The commander of the Turkish nationalist forces in this zone had anticipated that the invader would have to use the same pass. So he stood his ground in the Valley of the Sarisu, before the little town of Inonu. This time the victory went to the home army.

Remzi was doing a splendid job with two of the horses. Each time I visited him, he would lead first Mystery and then Szarcsa out of the former cow byre for inspection. The two horses positively glistened with health. Daily Remzi exercised, fed and massaged them. He would click his tongue and mutter to them and they would obey his instructions like pets. I was standing in the yard one December day, admiring Mystery, when Remzi slipped off her head collar and standing behind gave a great shout. Mystery nearly leapt out of her skin. She sprang forward and went tearing away down the lane to the village at full gallop with the mud flying up from her hooves. Remzi stood there, arms akimbo, and waited. Three minutes later I heard the slap of hooves in mud and Mystery came rocketing round a different corner, still going full pelt. She had circled through the village, and was racing for all she was worth. Remzi gave another wave of his arm, and she shot off on another circuit, completely free without halter or head collar, enjoying every minute of it. Three or four times Remzi sent her off, before she trotted happily back into the stable blowing and puffing. Szarcsa was the same. Even the sedate Hungarian horse careered round the village lanes like a colt, bucking and prancing.

But Carty was a different matter. Whatever Remzi tried, the big Ardennes was utterly miserable. He stood dejectedly in the far corner of Remzi's stable and languished. He sweated constantly, even when there was snow outside, and began to look not so much a horse as a great tatty stuffed animal. Remzi worried ceaselessly over him. He tried massaging Carty, fed him special food, exercised him, but with no noticeable improvement. Carty was distressed and out of his correct environment. Already, watching Carty perspiring in the previous summer, I had suspected that Carty had gone far enough. He had done splendidly to walk to Turkey and prove that a Heavy Horse could make the distance to the field of Dorylaeum. But I saw no point in having him suffer the increasing heat that we would surely encounter on the next stage of the journey on the way through eastern Turkey and Syria. If I took him onward, very likely he would perish just as the vast majority of the original horses of the Crusaders had died on the long march through the hot lands. Mystery and Szarcsa, I believed, were adaptable enough to go the full distance, but Carty was not. So I contacted the friendly stable owner we had met on our way through Austria, who had offered to take in Carty, and I made a present of the great horse to him. In January 1988 he drove down to Remzi's farm, collected Carty, and took him back to the Vienna Woods, where the irrepressible Ardennes settled in happily. In due course Carty was to appear in the Vienna Horse Show as 'the horse that went on the Crusade', his rider wearing medieval costume and carrying a hawk on his wrist. He was, as always, a great success.

Finding Carty's replacement was a quest in itself. We needed a pack horse tough enough to walk to Jerusalem, and I thought I knew where to find such an animal. Ever since we had been chased by the pack pony stallion in the mountains near Iznik, I had been impressed by the durability of the ponies that the foresters used for carrying timber. So on each visit to Turkey that winter I scoured the mountain villages for a suitable pack pony that was for sale. But I made the mistake of looking for a mare, believing she would be less troublesome than a stallion, and in the mountains nearly every horse was male. I tried to find out where the mares were kept, but only received disinterested shrugs. The wood-cutters bought their ponies from professional dealers who came through the villages driving herds of ponies for sale. Where the dealers bred their ponies, no one could tell me. All I did discover was the delightful fact that a horse dealer in Turkish was called a *cambaz*, and looking up the meaning of the word in the dictionary I discovered that is also meant '(1) a trick rider or acrobat in a circus, and (2) a swindler.' Horse dealers obviously had the same reputation worldwide.

Eventually I did track down a *cambaz* in the little town of Armutlu. He promised he could provide a superlative animal, capable he said of 25 miles day after day under a full load of timber. It was dark by the time we drove into Armutlu and found the *cambaz* waiting for us. To my puzzlement he led us down a narrow lane between townhouses rather than to a farm. Stopping at a street door he knocked and the owner appeared and promised to fetch the horse. I could see no stables, so imagined a long delay. Instead the owner walked three yards to the side of his house, opened the little door leading down to the cellar, and like Alice in Wonderland disappeared downwards. From the bowels of the house he then appeared leading a small pack pony who, it seemed, would be quite accustomed to climbing up the rungs of a ladder if asked to do so. This was the paragon we had been promised. The little creature was pocket size: Barely 13 hands high and not more than a third of Carty's bulk. It stood there meekly with head hanging down, tiny hooves dutifully together as if to attention, its dappled grey coat reminding me precisely of the rocking horses I associated with Victorian attics. All he needed was a pair of curved rockers attached to his hooves and we could put him in a toy shop. Was this really the horse that could carry 150 kilos every day? Yes, it was, the *cambaz* promised. He would guarantee the horse. Once again, we did not have much choice. We had seen no other animal more suitable, and at 300 pounds sterling the creature was a reasonable price. I bought him, declined the huge pack saddle that would have been added to the bargain for another forty pounds, and arranged for Zeynep, as he was called, to be taken to Remzi's farm to be trained up and introduced to Mystery and Szarcsa.

I later learned that when Remzi first laid eyes on Zeynep, he was appalled. To substitute this fragile looking little waif for the enormous Carty seemed like a bad joke. Indeed at first he refused to have Zeynep in the stable at all, and ignominiously sent him off to be lodged with a neighbour. But when he did give Zeynep house room Remzi changed his opinion. Zeynep, he discovered, really could keep up with the other horses on exercise. What is more he had an apparently limitless appetite. The little pony would eat every scrap of whatever food was put in front of him and was a born survivor. At the slightest opportunity, even when feeding, he would fold up those delicate legs and take a rest, curling up on a few wisps of straw like a cat, husbanding his strength. After a month with Zeynep, whom we renamed Zippy, Remzi reckoned that the little pony would do very well — though he would have to take two steps to every pace by Mystery and Szarcsa.

The long winter layover brought two items of very good news. Permission arrived from the Syrian authorities for Sarah and me to ride across Syria. A kindly Irish diplomat posted to Damascus as the representative of the Common Market had interceded on our behalf and managed to persuade the Syrians that we were serious in our endeavour. Almost simultaneously we heard from the embassy of Israel that if we presented ourselves at the Allenby Bridge, arriving from the Kingdom of Jordan, we would be allowed to cross the frontier and ride up to Jerusalem. That was more than I had dared hope. Normally no animal was permitted to cross, in either direction, between the territories controlled by Israel and the Arab lands. It seemed that, officially speaking, the road to Jerusalem lay open.

Sarah and I reported back to Remzi's farm in mid-April, just before the start of the new travelling season. The kit we brought with us showed the lessons of experience. We travelled much more lightly than when we had set out from Chateau Bouillon nearly a year earlier, and the bulk of our luggage was devoted to the care of the horses. We arrived with stout saddle pads two inches thick, and used two on each horse to protect their backs from sores. Sarah was to ride in the Camargue saddle on Szarcsa, and I had a French trekking saddle. Both were fitted with good leather bags and pouches, and behind our saddles we tied a sleeping bag and a raincoat. Zippy was to wear a small pack saddle attached to him by a complicated webbing of twin girths, breast band, and crupper straps. Unlike Carty, he stood patiently while he was trussed into this contraption, and then loaded up with our lightweight tent, a soft bag containing our clothes, and two side packs. These contained torches, a tiny portable stove for heating water, nosebags, collapsible water buckets, spare needles, thread and leather for running repairs to harness and clothing, and a basic medical kit for the horses with syringes, salves for saddle sores, tar for wounds and antiseptic powder for bites and cuts. We hoped to solve the chronic problem of spare horseshoes by carrying a spare set for each horse – Zippy's tiny feet needed mini-shoes small enough to slip in a pocket – an ample quantity of nails, and a couple of hundred pins of hard tungsten. These I proposed to hammer into the toes and heels of the new shoes when we re-shod the animals, so the tungsten would take the main abrasion and extend the life of each shoe. Finally, the most bulky of our new acquisitions were four canvas tubes, each about four feet long and closed with a zip. They were feed bags designed to carry 13 kilos of grain each. Draped across the horses, two on Zippy and one each on Mystery and Szarcsa, they allowed us to carry enough food for four days' travel independent of resupply. This, we anticipated, would be important when we entered the bleak high country of the eastern mountains. As for the despised jeep with its stock of spare horse medicines and small library, we would leave it at Remzi's until we came to a convenient city at, say, three weeks' distance, then catch the bus back to get it.

From exercising the animals each day in the winter snow, Remzi looked as fit and deeply tanned as any ski instructor. It had been impossible, he said, to leave the horses out in the fields, for fear of wolves. Now to get the three horses used to travelling as a team and to strengthen their stamina, he took us riding day after day through the valley of the Sarisu, steadily increasing the daily mileages. The far side of the valley was marked by tall bluffs and rounded granite hills, which led away in the distance to the grey mountains of Bursa. The bird life was extraordinary. The bluffs were home for nesting eagles, merlins and a species of large hawk that showed little fear as we rode along the line of the river, the great birds flapping up lazily from the stumps of trees. Cranes stalked the soft mud of the fields, landing like supersonic airliners with huge wings outstretched to slow their flight and long thin legs poking forward for the impact of landing. Swallows darted out of the banks of the irrigation channels and pestered the horses, flittering around their heads and making aggressive passes at their muzzles so that Mystery jerked her head in surprise and irritation. Once we saw a sudden apparition of tortoises emerging by the dozen from their winter hibernation and lumbering out into the sunshine to begin their mating rituals. The horses were fizzing with energy. As Sarah observed, Remzi had trained them up like racehorses, and the animals buzzed with excitement as we rode them out. Unused to Zippy whom we swiftly nicknamed 'the brat', the larger horses bullied and menaced him. But the fragile-seeming pony gave as good as he got, flicking his tail in Mystery's eyes, and when we came to a ditch, Zippy out-leaped them all. Even under the weight of his packs, he would spring over the obstacle in a comical arc much higher than the others, promptly earning another nickname – 'the flying flea'.

In the evenings we would return to Remzi's neat mud-walled house and tie the horses under the pear tree in his yard. Unsaddled, the animals would be massaged before being led away to their stable. Then Remzi would ceremonially invite us indoors and we would thaw out in his living room, sitting before the wood-burning stove that stood in the centre of the room with its long metal chimney pipe rising straight up and then turning at a right angle to carry away the smoke and radiate extra heat. On the whitewashed walls hung pictures of lakeland scenes, photographs of Remzi's two sons, and a faded picture, taken with a telephoto lens, of Remzi as a jockey winning a race. Everything was kept spotless and neatly ordered, and Remzi would sit there stiffly, very much the formal host, straightbacked and hands on knees while his wife served us tea or coffee, appearing in a bell skirt, blouse and with a shawl over her head so that she looked like the figure in a Dutch painting.

'What will you do when the horses have gone,' I asked Remzi. 'How will you fill your time?'

He shrugged. 'I will take some rest. And then there is my farming for the new year.' He was, I had learned, 64 years old, though he looked at least ten years younger.

'I bet you Remzi buys another horse after we've gone,' Sarah wagered. She was right. A month after we left Kovalcı, Remzi bought a mare and foal. Horses were in his blood.

CHAPTER 18

Desert Ordeal

On a cool Friday morning with bright sunshine and thunder-clouds, we set out from Remzi's farm to begin the second half of our journey. Mrs Remzi, who was in tears, gave Sarah a small hand-embroidered scarf to remember her by. Remzi was looking stern and serious. He hugged me as we said goodbye and asked me to take good care of the horses. Go slowly for the first two days, Remzi begged us, and afterwards we would have no trouble all the way to Jerusalem. He had admitted that ever since the first day we rode into his farm, Mystery had been his favourite. Szarcsa was a fine horse but Mystery, and here he patted her and ran his hand across the breadth of her chest, had a great heart. As for Zippy, half-submerged under his packs, Remzi cuffed him lightly on the head. 'Now you will have to work!' We rode away, down the lane from his farm and across the fields behind his house. Remzi watched us go, a small, solitary figure, slightly bow-legged and, as always, very upright.

Sarah and I were far more relaxed than when we had set out from Bouillon almost exactly a year earlier. We felt we knew our business much better — how to manage the horses, what the daily routine required — and that we carried the right equipment, including the heavy rain gear that, once again, we were wearing to keep us warm at the chilly start of a journey. Characteristically, Sarah had refused to confirm until after Christmas that she would continue the journey with me, but had contradicted her apparent indecision by attending a course of evening classes in Turkish. Already she spoke it better than my self-taught variety. We still had the portfolio of Ottoman maps marked with the precise route we should follow, and both of us were genuinely looking forward to our ride through Anatolian Turkey. We knew that, in stark contrast to last year's travels through modern Europe with its problems of towns and traffic, we would be travelling through a land where most farms had stables and byres, where every village had working watering troughs for the sheep and cattle, and where unmade tracks instead of motorways meandered across the countryside. We felt in our bones that we were going to enjoy ourselves.

The first night was typical of the welcome we were to receive. At a distance of only ten miles from Remzi's farm, we halted at a small, unassuming village and tied our horses to some young willow trees beside the village common. An elderly farmer appeared from his house and asked us to make sure the horses did not eat the bark from his precious shade trees, but he was diffident, even embarrassed, to ask even this small request from a traveller. Half an hour later three young men appeared and beckoned us to lead the horses into a low-roofed sheep shed for the night. They had cleared space specially for the horses, and wanted us to stay in their house, but as we had already pitched our tent, we said we would prefer to remain where we were. They apologised that they could not yet offer us to share a meal with them because it was the season of Ramadan and they were fasting until sunset. The evening was very damp and cheerless, and by the time dusk fell, we were already in our sleeping bags. I heard a footstep on the grass outside and a low voice called out softly 'safalar olsun' – may it be enjoyable. Crawling over, I pushed open the tent flap, but there was no one outside. On the ground in front of the tent lay a tray of hot food, which someone had set down and then discreetly withdrawn, presuming we did not wish to be disturbed.

Next morning, life began slowly in the cold foggy dawn of an Anatolian village drowsing halfway between winter and spring. At seven there were the first sounds of movement, and an hour later a very battered van came past, collecting milk from the farms. Breakfast was another tray of mild cheese and hot milk, delivered unasked from a nearby building. At half past eight farm gates began to open and small clumps of sheep were driven out, waiting to join the main flock that trotted past, bells clanking, and disappeared into the grey murk as they climbed the distant hillslope to pasture.

We took two hours to groom and saddle up the horses, dawdling with the hope that the day would warm up. To our chagrin we noticed that after barely half-a-day's ride, Szarcsa's chronically tender skin was already puffing up where a rolled up sleeping-bag behind his saddle had lightly touched him. Zippy's pack for some unknown reason seemed to topple to the left. It was very rare to get the balance of the two side packs right first time, however carefully one shared the load between them. I found that the best method was to saddle and load Zippy as evenly as possible in the morning, and walk for half an hour until the load began to shift, then to stop and rearrange everything precisely, using heavy iron picket pins as mobile weights to get the balance perfect.

Skirting Eskişehir, now a thriving city of nearly a million inhabitants, we stopped to eat at a roadside snack bar and tied the horses to a railing. Immediately we were swamped with hordes of children curious to stare at the strangers, until the adults appeared and strictly told them not to pester us. It was the sort of consideration which we were to find all across Turkey, though on this occasion Zippy was so full of vim that he reinforced the warning by kicking one small boy. Later that afternoon as we rode along a dirt trail beside the railway track, Szarcsa was half-asleep and stumbled, giving himself such a fright that he bolted. To our amazement the irrepressible Zippy took the opportunity to launch an attack on the Hungarian horse. Accelerating up alongside Szarcsa, the 'flying flea' leaned across then delivered a series of smart bites, racing at a full gallop, his little matchstick legs going lickety split. Stung, Szarcsa ran even faster and the trio of horses, completely out of control, tore along, legs and hooves flying. To my satisfaction the pile of luggage on Zippy did not shift a fraction despite the pounding and, as we hurtled round a corner, we came upon a Turkish farmer, driving his tractor across a level crossing. He was left open-mouthed at the sight of two laughing riders and a tiny flying pack horse thundering southward – a rodeo of the insane.

At day's end we rode over the shoulder of a hill to catch sight of the thin spike of a minaret, which now served as our beacon towards shelter, just as church spires had guided us in Christian lands. Crossing the orchards that surrounded it, we entered a small Turkish town on a cold evening in Ramadan. There was not a soul to be seen. Every house was shuttered and silent. At the street junctions we could look each way and still see nothing, not a person, nor an animal, nor even a parked vehicle except for a small bus, empty and waiting at the edge of the main square. The place might have been awaiting the arrival of the last trump. Hoof falls echoed off the mud walls as we rode our solitary way down two more streets. Then, as if prearranged, a man in a dark brown uniform and a cap like a bus conductor's appeared behind us, walking along the pavement. We halted and when he caught up with us I said in my elementary Turkish vocabulary 'We are travellers. We need a house for the horses–' Before I had even finished, the man nodded, pointed at the horses and turned on his heel. There was no pause, no need to explain or repeat the request; the arrival of three horses was taken as calmly as if we were motorists asking our way to a service station.

The brown uniform was the costume of the *bekçi* or town watchman, and without a word he led us to a disused stable and stood aside. I peered in, decided the place was too small, and shook my head. Still without saying a word he took us another three blocks and showed us another stable. Here was enough room for the horses so Sarah and I began to unsaddle. The *bekci* watched us undo the myriad straps and buckles on Zippy, off-load our saddlebags, and then silently he picked up the baggage and took us once more down the street. It was uncanny. No one else had appeared, and it was as if the man was the porter in some vast, unoccupied hotel. He brought us back to the mosque whose spire we had seen from the hill. Beside it was a small square house, obviously the *muhtar*'s office and, as it turned out, the village guest house as well. The *bekçi* opened the door and led us inside. A large open room was surrounded on all sides by a low bench, covered with rugs and cushions. This was where the village council met for their discussions, and where travellers could stay. In the middle of the room stood the inevitable iron pot stove, already loaded with twigs. The *bekci* lit the stove, waited to feed the roaring flames with coal, and then withdrew leaving us to ourselves, while the room warmed to a pleasant fug.

A short while later, there was a tap on the window. We opened it to find, balanced on the sill, another tray. The time of fasting had not ended, but a neighbour had prepared a simple meal of rice, spinach, bread and yoghurt. We were eating when the *bekci* reappeared followed by two men carrying every single item of our saddlery and the other kit we had left at the stable. They lugged all the equipment into the room, neatly stacked it in one corner, and when I protested that it was really not necessary and the bags could have stayed with the horses, the *bekci* muttered mysteriously 'in case the gypsies come to steal'.

After evening prayers, the *muhtar* himself appeared. A jovial, chunky man, he was elderly, with a grizzled beard and nut-brown face, but full of vigour. He was wearing a faded overcoat and a knitted wool hat that he did not remove although the room was by then roasting hot. Sitting down on a hard chair, he asked a string of questions that we were to hear again and again over the next two months. What was our homeland? Where were we going? By what route had we arrived? Which road would we follow next? How did we like Turkey? They were the questions of long-standing ritual, and our replies were more than just politeness. They were payment for the hospitality given us. In the humdrum routine of the community the passage of strangers, especially foreigners riding tall horses, was a lively event. The information we gave in our answers would be savoured, repeated, discussed and remembered for months to come. I had the impression that exactly the same questions had been asked of travellers over the centuries. As if to underline the timelessness of our situation, I was caught unawares by the *muhtar* asking whether I knew Ibn Batuta. I had to think twice before I realised he was asking about a medieval Arab traveller who was the Marco Polo of Islam and had journeyed through Turkey in the 15th century. To my delight the *muhtar* began to quote by memory from Ibn Batuta's writings, what he had said about Turkish towns, who had helped him, the animals he had used for his travels. Cheerfully the old man apologised that he could not read nor write, so he was citing Ibn Batuta from the traveller's tales he had heard as a child and repeated ever since. Were we not travelling the old road, the Silk Road, with our horses? Again, he was astonishingly well informed. Part of our Crusade route did indeed overlap a branch of the Silk Road, but how could I explain to this keenly intelligent but unsophisticated town *muhtar* the purpose of our journey in terms he would understand? We were making the Christian *haj*, I suddenly said, the pilgrimage to Jerusalem in the historic way. There was a church in Jerusalem where Christ was buried and it was the holiest shrine of the Christians, like the sacred stone at Mecca. The answer was more than satisfactory. 'Of course', he said, 'Kudüs [Jerusalem] is holy for the Christians, as it is also for the Muslims.' Throughout our journey we were to find that no one we met, whether Turk or Arab, would show any bigotry. To be a pilgrim, Christian or Muslim, was enough, and to make the journey to Jerusalem in the traditional style, on horseback, met with unqualified approval.

At Eskişehir our route had veered south, heading towards Turkmen Dagı, the Turkoman's Mountains. We depended on the compass or advice from the farmers and shepherds to keep in the right direction. 'Travel towards that mountain', advised a cowherd, indicating the highest peak in the distance, and we turned trustingly up a narrow track which led into pine forest. For four hours we walked without seeing a living creature except for two flocks of sheep guarded by unaccompanied packs of dogs. There were no shepherds, no houses, and only an occasional tyre track in the soft ground of the road. The soil was a gluey mud that clung to the horses' hooves and tired them unduly. Mid-afternoon we passed through a half-abandoned village, a place so remote that the population had moved away and all but a handful of houses were tumbled down and lay in ruins. The surviving inhabitants were foresters who wandered in, axes in hand, to find us resting the horses in an abandoned garden. Hospitably they scavenged chaff for the horses after we had filled their nosebags with barley from the long canvas tubes.

Next morning, the sun was shining and it was warm enough to ride without our jackets. The forest was silent and delightful, and we set out to continue the trail that traced the line of a pleasant mountain brook. Primroses flowered beside the path, crows flapped out of the trees, and a hawk gazed down at us from the ledge of a cliff. From time to time we noted small hoof prints in the mud, foresters' ponies, and so we kept climbing. It was an easy mistake to fall into, lulled by the beauty of our surroundings, but we should have turned back. The track wound upward, on and on. Each succeeding mile made it even more difficult to throw away all the effort made by the horses in the long ascent. We kept imagining that the next ridge or turn in the path would bring us to the pass. For three hours the horses laboured until finally we came to a high clearing among the pine trees where shepherds had established a summer camp. Now the place was abandoned as the altitude was so great and the season far too early. There were some roofless huts and a swampy patch of grass where the sheep trough, a hollow log, had been knocked askew so that the water trickled out over the ground saturating it to a bog. We had to stop. The animals were exhausted. They were too tired even to require a proper tether. They barely ate their nosebags and Zippy, who for some reason had refused his breakfast, stood with his head and tail hanging down, utterly spent. He looked as though if you pulled his tail, his head would wag up and down like an articulated toy with internal strings.

We were in a classic dilemma. We did not know how far was the next settlement although the uphill climb did seem to be levelling off finally. Should we go on or turn back? I decided it would be better to risk going forward, and although the path did begin to descend, it was another two hours before we came to a village. There I was chagrined to discover that we had wandered off our correct road. We had a suspicion that Zippy was limping on his near foreleg, and so we checked how far it was to the next village. Only four kilometres, came the reply. It seemed close enough and we rode on, but the information was wrong. The next village was at least twice that distance and the far side of yet another high ridge. By the time we crossed it and were descending the far side, Zippy was in a bad way. He was limping heavily on his near foreleg, in severe discomfort and moving with heart-rending slowness. Sarah and I took off as much as possible of his load and carried it on the other horses. We discussed removing his saddle and leaving it beside the road as well, but it was likely to be stolen. Furthermore, it was so light that we felt it would have made little difference to Zippy's condition. It was the same problem that we had experienced with Carty in Bavaria. The little pack pony had been pushed beyond his limts. Not even his previous work, hauling massive loads of timber in the mountains' had been as severe as this.

I calculated that we had gone nearly thirty miles and tackled a mountain barrier as well. But I did not want to stop. There was neither water nor shelter for the animals, and the night would be bitterly cold at that altitude. When we finally reached the next village, tired and depressed, with Zippy hobbling pitifully, the place made a dreadful impression with its air of utter poverty and decay. There were more empty and half-ruined houses than inhabited ones; a man winding up a bucket of water from a well was so hideously deformed that we were too embarrassed to ask his help; the next villager ignored us entirely as if we were lepers. Finally a young man, disfigured by a terrible gum disease, led us to a small outhouse he thought was fit for a stable. But it was wretchedly small and there was no hope of squeezing either Szarcsa or Mystery under the lintel. It was a problem that we were to encounter often during the next two months: Turkish horses were so much smaller than our own that the doorways to stables were simply too low for the European horses to enter.

Just as we were faced with black despair there came the sound of a tractor. The village was so poor that this was the only machine in the place. It came bouncing to a halt and the driver leapt down and strode over with the quick, confident steps of authority. He was a man of about thirty who, we later learned, was the most hale man in the moribund community, and had been appointed its *muhtar*. He was determined that his village would not wither away, and he had that special gift of cheefulness and decision that made him a natural leader. He took command briskly. We were to bring the exhausted horses to his farm, where we could put them in the cattle shed.

No sooner had we led them in and unloaded than Zippy collapsed. He was totally and completely worn out. We managed to get him back on his feet so that he snuffled in the manger for ten seconds, but then decided that he was too tired and distressed to eat, folded up his legs and slumped back to the floor. Villagers appeared and gazed on his recumbent form. 'Çok, çok hasta' – very, very sick – they diagnosed, and heads were shaken gloomily. Indeed Zippy looked appalling. He lay flopped out, white patches around his eyes and seemingly about to expire. The villagers prodded him and levered him up to his feet, but immediately he fell again. A kindly farmer began to massage the pony's gut. 'He must relieve himself, or he will die,' he said. The *muhtar* brought out a plastic shopping bag half full of ancient veterinary medicines and suggested we should give Zippy an injection. We checked the medicines, but they were out-of-date antibiotics that would do no good. Sarah watched Zippy give a few dramatic spasms, kicking with his legs, and was more sceptical.

'Zippy must have been reading the veterinary manual. A dying horse is meant to give those last few kicks,' she said. 'He's exhausted, I'm sure, but I think he's trying for an Oscar. If we let him rest, he'll be alright.'

With gloomy memories of Carty's suffering in south Germany, I went to the *muhtar*'s living room where we were served what seemed like a miraculous meal of roast kid and vegetables. Sarah and I had not eaten all day and were almost as fatigued as the horses. As I ate, I reflected that after less than a week on the road, we were already faced with a problem, even with three very well-prepared horses. It just went to prove that when embarking on cross-country travel on horseback, nothing could be taken for granted, and a crisis could develop at any time. When the *muhtar*'s shy 23-year-old wife, her brother, mother and sister, and sundry members of the family had all packed into the room, it seemed that most of the village were present, talking and laughing, lighting up cigarettes the moment that fasting was over. It was clear that without the drive and energy of the *muhtar* the place would fade away. The people drew their strength from him, and even his children were the future hope of the community. His youngest infant was a tiny baby, completely swaddled in cotton bands so that the creature looked like a small Egyptian dummy or an oversized fruit gum. Lovingly the little scrap, totally rigid and immobile, was passed from hand to hand like a parcel, and when the distance was too great, nonchalantly flung across the room like a miniature caber. On the wall hung the *muhtar*'s badge of office, an ancient rifle issued to him by the government to chase off brigands and wolves. More to the point, he said, he had a shotgun to kill rabbits for the pot. Apart from soap, cigarettes and diesel oil for his tractor there was nothing that his people bought from the town, thereby avoiding the ravages of an inflation that was running at 70 per cent. He took his firewood from the forest, built his house of mud, straw and timber, and ate his own eggs, wheat, barley, chick peas and vegetables. What about a doctor or medicine? I asked. The *muhtar* scooped up his two-year-old daughter who was scampering about us. Look, he said, showing us the child's arm which had a violent red weal. Two weeks ago she fell against the stove and burned herself severely. There is no doctor, and it would have been too slow to take her into town on my tractor. So we dipped her injured arm in milk. That was all the cure we had.

After two hours, Sarah and I excused ourselves and went to check on Zippy. To our enormous relief he was standing up on all four legs and gently nibbling his supper. A damp patch beneath him revealed that all was well with his bladder. A day that had begun so well, then degenerated into pain and discomfort for Zippy, had ended happily. When we told the villagers the distance we had come, they were very impressed. To have travelled so far in a single day and crossed the mountain too, was a feat. They were full of praise, but I promised myself not to fall into the same trap again. I had been wrong to press the horses so hard. Next time, even if the horses had an uncomfortable and hungry night on a mountain, we would stop and make them rest after a reasonable distance.

✳

After the Crusade's great triumph of Dorylaeum the entire host rested for three full days beside the river at the Field of Flowers, enjoying the pleasurable memory of total victory. The boost to their confidence and self-esteem was tremendous. Everyone, warriors and pilgrims alike, felt that they had fought and conquered for the Cross. A rumour circulated that two heavenly horsemen, mounted on fiery steeds, had been seen just before the battle. God was indeed on their side and the future was assured. No mention was made of general Tatikos and his Byzantine troops, and indeed the chroniclers did not even say whether they had played a useful role at the great battle. From now on the Christians felt that they, on their own, were quite capable of deciding their destiny, and did not need any help from the despised Emperor. In the euphoria of their success they agreed very sensibly that, from now on, the army should not divide up but march as a single unit for its better self-protection.

As the Host advanced eastward, a deep feeling of comradeship at this stage flourished among the ordinary pilgrims. According to Fulcher 'if one lost any of his possessions, he who found it would keep it carefully for many days, until by inquiry he found the loser and returned the article to him.' This, he concluded, 'is fit and proper for those who make the pilgrimage in the right spirit.' Such selflessness, among the common people at any rate, was soon to be put to the test because the defeated Turks were laying waste the land as they retreated. The enemy 'burned or destroyed everything that might be useful or helpful to us as they fled in great terror at our approach' noted the *Gesta* knight, describing how, in trying to come to grips with the fleeing enemy, the army blundered into wastelands. 'We pursued them through a land which was deserted, waterless and uninhabitable, from which we barely escaped alive, for we suffered greatly from hunger and thirst and found nothing at all to eat except prickly plants which we gathered and rubbed between our hands.' The heat and lack of fodder had a disastrous effect on the European-bred animals. Many of the nobles were still travelling with their private collections of hunting hawks and hounds, just as they had done in Europe, and these creatures perished in climatic conditions for which they were totally unfit. 'Delicate birds, soaring hawks and falcons, with which the nobility is wont to take delight when hunting and hawking, breathed forth their lives notwithstanding the care lavished upon them,' recorded William of Tyre. 'Keen-scented dogs trained for hunting, the pets of their lords, deserted their masters whom they had ever faithfully followed and panting from thirst, succumbed along the route.' But the most disastrous loss was, of course, among the horses, vital for the success of the expedition. Both the ordinary pack animals and the irreplaceable battle chargers died in large numbers. 'We lost most of our horses,' observed Fulcher sadly, 'so that many of our knights had to go as footsoldiers, and for lack of horses we has to use oxen as mounts, and our great need compelled us to use goats, sheep and dogs as beasts of burden.'

Precisely where the army suffered the worst torments of the arid lands is difficult to pinpoint because so much of that region of Turkey has now been irrigated and developed into good farmland. According to Albert, the host tried to take a short cut and entered a region of rocky defiles where there was no water, either for the men or the animals. On the worst day some fifty people died from thirst even though the daily stages of march had been shortened because of the intense August heat. The worst suffering was endured by the pregnant women. 'Their throats dried up, their wombs withered, and all the veins of the body drained by the indescribable heat of the sun and that parched region, [they] gave birth and abandoned their own young in the middle of the highway.' After describing how the pilgrims tried ineffectually to suck in the morning mist to slake their thirst, Albert wrote that many perished when they finally reached a river. The travellers pressed forward in a great crush, plunged their faces into the water, and 'set no limit to their drinking until very many who had been weakened . . . died from drinking too much.'

Exhausted and weak, the host emerged from the desert ordeal in dire need of a safe haven where they could recoup their strength. The place they chose was a fertile bowl, hidden behind mountains and safe from the Turks. They called it Pisidia, today's Yalvaç.

CHAPTER 19

Pisidia

It took Sarah and me nine days to ride the distance from Eskişehir to Yalvaç, including a rest day to follow Zippy to recover from his exhaustion. The little pony revealed impressive powers of recuperation. A few hours in the sunshine next morning to warm his strained shoulder muscles, some massage and a good feed, and Zippy was as sprightly as ever. It was now early May and the weather was rapidly warming up as Anatolia enjoyed its brief spring before the baking heat of a continental summer. By easy stages we rode on across a rich and variegated countryside where villages with red tiled roofs and white-washed walls of clay could have been basking in the sunshine of Tuscany, but for their ever-present mosques. The character of each settlement was distinct. Here was a village of horse breeders, clusters of foals grazing on the surrounding pasture land, their mothers the typically Turkish narrow-chested, bay crossbreeds. Ten miles farther on was a cattle town set in dun-coloured flatland where the inhabitants and beasts seemed equally plodding and bovine.

While we waited for a village elder to show up, a long line of women, fat and bland, queued at the village pump and pondered us without a flicker of expression. When the headman did arrive he proved to be a good-hearted slob, whose office on the upper storey of the village meeting house was an unswept mess of dead cigarette butts on a grimy bare floor. The nicotine-stained walls were decorated with three ancient posters of the founding father Ataturk in his various guises as general, statesman and warrior, two obsolete maps of Turkey and a yellowing poster for cattle drench. The only telephone in the village sat on a table, out of order and the white plastic handset jaundiced with age. It was obvious that the headman had no intention of getting an engineer to repair it. An air of deep lassitude hung over the place and yet, as always, we were shown every kindness. The mayor and his cronies were reluctant abstinents in Ramadan and waited irritably for the evening call that announced the end of fasting. The voice of the muezzin was still quavering the air when they fell to with shovelling gusto on the trays of food that their families had sent in. The food was excellent and ample, but it was better to ignore the spatter of crumbs and bits of debris which flew across the table and were then brushed onto the floor by the idle janitor who smeared the table top with the same smutty rag he used for holding the lid to the battered stove. We spread a groundsheet on the floor to insulate ourselves from the dirt when we went to sleep, and next morning woke with fierce sore throats from the accumulated cigarette smoke in the air.

Zippy had recovered sufficiently to have spent the night energetically kicking Szarcsa after the pony discovered that the ceiling of their stable was so low, an inch above Szarcsa's haunches, that the bigger horse could not life his rump to kick back. Thereupon Zippy had welted the haplass Szarcsa repeatedly. The Hungarian horse was Zippy's chosen victim, possibly because it was Sarah on Szarcsa who normally held Zippy's lead rope. Previously the little pony had hung back, tugging on the lead, or crept up and suddenly sunk his teeth into the larger horse. But then Szarcsa's good manners had finally shredded and he had learned to kick back at Zippy while Sarah smacked the culprit with the free end of the lead rope. So with consummate intelligence Zippy now devised a new way of infuriating the Hungarian horse. He pretended to like him so much that he had to stay very close. It was the perfect ruse. Zippy would walk right alongside Szarcsa, deliberately bumping his side pack against the bigger horse and throwing him off balance so that Szarcsa had to walk or trot, leaning at an uncomfortable slant. This drove Szarcsa wild with annoyance, but because Zippy was in so close it was impossible to deliver a punishing kick. And however much Sarah might shout and swear and whack Zippy on the head, the little brat would come creeping back five minutes later and commence the torture all over again.

We traversed a landscape where stark outcrops of rock had been weathered into strange contorted shapes. Some stood alone on knolls like ancient dolmens, others in clusters reminiscent of Easter Island's statues. Their shapes were so bizarre that it was automatic to check whether they had been artificially carved. But the only human traces were when enterprising shepherds had enlarged natural caves into shelters for their flocks. At the little town of Dor we knew we were on the ancient road because we came upon a vast caravan shelter or han, built in Ottoman times to provide shelter for passing caravans. A massive square building, it was abandoned, with storks nesting in the chimney pots and a rusting truck blocking the door.

Hospitality never failed, whatever the resources available. One night we stayed at a large and prosperous farm run by several brothers. Wealthy men, they had a large herd of cattle, at least a hundred sheep, horses and tractors all housed in a large, efficiently run complex of buildings. They even had their own guest house, a spotlessly clean cottage where we ate our meal with a forest guard and the village bekci. At the other end of the scale we were received with equal kindness by a man so poor that he had just one chicken. He lived on the top floor of an abandoned mud brick building and insisted that we stable the horses in the entrance hall below, and stay in a room above them. He was struggling to establish a roadside café and invited us to go there for our supper. We found a bare room with a dozen worn tables and some chairs, and it was obvious that he could afford only a gas ring and a kettle. A pane of glass was mended with sticky paper tape for lack of funds to buy a replacement. Our host could not even arrange for running water, so from time to time had to dash out to fill a jerrycan. Yet he was the soul of attention, indomitably cheerful. We bought four eggs at the next-door shop and a morsel of bread and with pride he cooked and served us the first meal of his establishment.

On 6 May we passed through Afyon, a small city much reduced in importance from the time when the Crusade marched this way. High above the city the coxcomb of a mountain crest was encircled by the curtain wall of the ancient citadel, which had been a major Byzantine fortress, though now Afyon was little more than a pleasant regional capital busy with its agricultural market. We rode in a hooting, grinding sclerosis of traffic, our horses unconcerned with such distractions. Zippy was saving his energy for the next morning, when at the edge of the next broad expanse of open ground he suddenly came to a dead stop. It was a new trick which took Sarah entirely by surprise. The lead rope was whisked from her hand as Szarcsa plodded forward heedlessly, and the moment that Zippy felt the tension go, he whirled about and scampered off in a quicksilver bid to escape. Cursing but with a certain admiration for his sense of timing, we watched the little rascal bolt for freedom. In a flash he had changed from a meek-looking pack pony into a jaunty tearaway. A minute earlier he had been trotting along beside Szarcsa with his head low, obedience in every line of his small body. Now he had his head and tail high, his ears up, and defiance in each gesture. Racing off, he kicked and bucked athletically in an attempt to rid himself of the packs. Luckily they were well secured and stayed firmly in place, so Zippy then galloped flat out to put as much distance between himself and us. We rode after him, circling round to head him off. There was an irrigation ditch which looked helpful. Perhaps we could corner him against it, but Zippy came racing up to the ditch, and in a single leap became again the flying flea, sailing over the gap as though the packs weighed just a few ounces. With another exuberant double buck he scuttled onwards and away. After a half hour chase we did finally catch him, but he was totally unrepentant, and Sarah put forward a theory that all pack animals sooner or later develop the same outlook. Without a rider on his back to exert direct control, and led day after day beside the other horses, Zippy, like Carty before him, had time to ponder on his situation and develop a spirit of independence. Small Turkish pony or massive Ardennes, as pack animals they both became knaves at heart.

At Afyon the caravan road turned eastward once more to skirt the foot of the Sultan Dağları, 'Mountains of the Sultan'. The marsh flats on our left were the remains of an ancient salt lake, while to our right the land rose steeply to high ridges still covered with winter snow. The strip of land between lake and mountain was intensively cultivated, and lines of brilliantly dressed women, their baggy trousers, shawls and headscarves of every bright colour, were stooped over the young crops. With light hoes the women were breaking the soil, or squatting on their haunches plucking up weeds by hand. For hour after hour they worked patiently, seemingly tireless. Some groups were laughing and chatting among themselves, and these stood upright leaving off their work to watch us. But other work gangs were so bowed down with the mind-numbing drudgery that they scarcely turned their heads as we rode by, not ten feet away. They seemed condemned to labour at the soil. Their menfolk were nowhere to be seen.

Beyond, the mountains reared up, stark and forbidding. The Crusaders had crossed them to reach their resting grounds at Pisidia, yet I was surprised that none of the chroniclers had mentioned the difficulties of the approach. We could see the scar of a mountain road snaking upward to the higher slopes of steel-grey rock and shale which were pocked here and there with patches of snow. Mindful of Zippy's collapse on our previous highland excursion we tackled the ascent very gently, winding our way up from the last valley settlement, past village women washing clothes by a grove of poplars where a river was born from a gash in the mountain flank, and then up the increasing grade to where the thin patches of sheep pasture finally gave way to bare rock. Here we paused to rest the animals, sheltering in a corrie, away from the cutting mountain wind. Looking back the way we had come, there was a magnificent panorama out over the valley with its string of foothill villages and to the blue heart of the great Karamik marsh with its edges shading into the pale brown of millions upon millions of tall reeds.

With the wind keening between the rocks, we came to the saddle of the mountain pass in early afternoon. It was still a moonscape of boulders and crags, and the road was broken and treacherous. Loose stones shifted beneath the horses' hooves, and it was wiser to ride close to the mountain side where the hairpin bends of the track skirted the gulleys, and sometimes the edge of the path had crumbled away. At this altitude only thorny scrubs grew and they were blackened and dead with the winter cold. Coming round a sharp corner in this bleak and desolate land we came upon the scene which might almost have been a re-enactment from an ordinary pilgrim's crusade. A man and three women had come into the mountains to gather brushwood. They had dragged the thorny branches down to the rocky track and strapped enormous bundles of them to the backs of two small donkeys. Grossly overloaded, one of the little animals had collapsed under the weight and lay folded up, its head barely visible under the great mound of firewood. It was easy to understand the frustration of the peasants. They must have scrambled for hours in the cutting wind about the rocks and crags laboriously assembling the load, and now they were faced with discarding the results of all their efforts. They were belabouring the donkey hysterically, the women screaming in high-pitched voices to get it on its feet. But the unfortunate animal was so crushed that it could not stir. In a rage a woman stood on each side and, stooping over, lifted the firewood in the air literally hoisting the donkey to a standing position, from which it was just able to totter forward like a moving bush.

Half a mile farther on we emerged on a spur of rock and there below us lay Pisidia, the resting place of the Crusade. Even from our height the land looked bountiful. We could see a sprinkling of villages surrounded by orchards, dark red patches of ploughed land, and the deep green pools of distant crops stretching away across the undulating floor of a broad fertile bowl caught between the mountain ranges. Here, in this beautiful hideaway, the Crusaders had recuperated from the rigours of the waterless rocky gorges and, ironically, Duke Godfrey nearly died in a hunting accident.

The episode was to be added to the Duke's reputation for selfless gallantry though it reflected little credit on his skill as a swordsman. 'Duke Godfrey and the rest of the nobles pitched their tents all over the delightful meadowlands, considering the district fitting and agreeable,' wrote Albert. 'Finding a wood most suitable for hunting they took up bow and quiver, girded on their swords and went into the woodland pastures near the mountains to see if anything would appear which they would be able to shoot and chase.' The Duke became separated from his companions and chanced upon an enormous bear in hot pursuit of 'a helpless pilgrim out gathering twigs'. Drawing his sword, the Duke spurred to the rescue but the bear

suddenly drove its curved claws into the Duke's tunic and bringing him to the ground, embraced him in his forepaws as he fell from his horse, and hastened to tear his throat with his teeth. The Duke therefore in great distress, remembering his many distinguished exploits and that he had up till now markedly escaped from all danger, indeed was lamenting that he was to be choked by this bloodthirsty beast in an ignoble death, and seizing the sword which had got entangled in his own legs in the sudden fall from his horse and the struggle with the frenzied wild beast, and holding it by the hilt aimed swiftly at the beast's throat, but mutilated the calf and sinews of his own leg with a serious cut.

As the Duke struggled to hold off the attack of the angry bear, a man called Huscechinus arrived on the scene, drawn by the shouts of the peasant and the roaring of the bear. He attacked the bear with his sword and, together with the Duke – an 'unstaunchable stream of blood pouring from his leg' – managed to kill the animal. The Duke, faint from pain, was placed on a litter and brought down to the camp 'with a great lamentation and grief of the men, and howling of the women, summoning the most skilled doctors to heal him. The wild beast, by the way, they divided among them, saying that they had never seen anything like it in size.'

Wild bears were last seen in the mountains of Yalvaç some fifty years ago. Today the high forest has been stripped for timber so their natural habitat has gone. Instead, crossing the barren mountain ridge produced a sensation that we were entering another province of Turkey. The hill people of the high slopes were very distinctive, dark-skinned and wild looking, quite different from those on the western side of the mountains. The first settlement we came to was an untidy place of much-battered mud houses whose collapsing walls exposed frameworks of wooden poles. Anywhere else the decay might have struck us as sad, but here the atmosphere was vibrant and cheerful. The reason was the women. Barefoot and swarthy they had boldness and panache. As we rode through the narrow street, they inspected us openly, waved and smiled, and even – extraordinarily – called out cheerily. They were dressed in the gaudiest colours, with bright turbans instead of the usual headscarves, and over their pantaloons wore a jaunty short overskirt of a scotch-like plaid which made them seem like stage gypsies. We found that the eastern villagers still used the old names for the settlements on the far side of the hills, and did not seem to know that forty years earlier all those villages had changed their names. They never visited them, and they had no interest in them.

Perhaps the local climate was milder in this protected bowl, but as we descended into Pisidia everything did seem more lush. The trees were more leafy than elsewhere, the orchards more fruitful, and the soil a rich dark loam. We had become accustomed to a countryside where every sliver of pasture had been eagerly sought and used by wandering sheep and goats, but here we could turn aside from the road and find a sheltered glade under trees where tall reeds grew unharvested beside a brook. In this favoured valley life was easy, an impression strongly reinforced at Korcular, the first town we entered. To our astonishment, as it was still the month of abstinence, the men were lazing around the café tables in the central square and openly drinking tea and smoking cigarettes, blatantly disregarding any rule of self-denial. The mayor was a portly figure, dressed in a rakish pale green suit and with the self-confidence of a small town political boss who enjoyed the good life to the hilt. Jovially he informed us that, as a farmer, he need do very little work. His crops did well, his fruit trees flourished, and he and his colleagues brewed alcohol from the fruit.

He asked if we would like to eat fresh fish for our supper and unwisely I agreed, out of curiosity to know how he would manage such a miracle a hundred miles from the sea. After dark, six of us packed into a car and we drove 30 miles through the night at high speed, radio cassette blaring, along winding mountain roads to the shores of an inland lake to find the vaunted fish. As we drove there was much shouted discussion of which was the best fish restaurant to go to, but because it was Ramadan we found the lakeshore restaurants shuttered and closed. This did not deter the mayor in the least. At the first restaurant, darkened and silent, our car drew up and he dispatched a minion to pound on the door to demand that the sleepy owner open up the place. The unlucky man came to the door, torch in hand, to say he neither had any fresh fish nor electricity because of a power failure. But the mayor was not to be thwarted or abashed, and directed our driver to the only establishment which had any signs of life. It turned out to be a shack which combined the functions of bar, restaurant and rendezvous for the ladies of the night. The landlord was outrageously sleazy, wiping his hands on a filthy rag, bowing and scraping to the mayor, and swabbing off a table. His only other customers were a party of visitors from the local town, roaring drunk and singing maudlin songs while they took it in turns to fondle two very raddled whores. Undeterred the mayor ordered us fresh fish, which actually proved to be quite palatable, and proceeded to gulp down glass after glass of *rakı*, the aniseed-flavoured alcohol, as if it was distilled water. One of the neighbouring drunks knocked over our *rakı* bottle and, failing to notice it was already empty, graciously replaced it with a full one. That too was drained without the mayor showing any ill effects whatsoever.

We stayed three days in the valley, leisurely making our way to market at the main town of Yalvaç. There in a side street we saw what looked like chunks of white fluffy cloud cut out and laid on earth. It was teased-out new wool ready to be beaten into pure felt. A foot thick, the fleece was hammered and pounded down into a three-quarter-inch thick blanket of interlocking fibres and sold to make shepherds' cloaks. We bought two large squares to turn into replacement saddle pads and threw away the old blankets which had worn out. Then we made our way back out of the valley by another long climb through hills where we were so high that the flocks of sheep and goats grazing on the slopes below us seemed like lice creeping across the hillside.

Descending from the ridges which guard Pisidia, back on to the great central plain, the heat was suddenly oppressive. Summer had come to central Anatolia and, as Sarah remarked, it was the same sensation as emerging from a plane at the airport when arriving in a hot country on winter holiday. That evening we reached a little town called Uchüyük, and again the place was so utterly different from any other settlement we had visited before that we might almost have been in another country. It had a long unpaved central street with two-storeyed mudbrick houses joined together in a continuous line on each block. The upper storeys had wooden balconies which overhung the street and apart from the unsightly wires of the electricity supply drooping between their poles, there was not a vestige of modern life. There were horse troughs at each corner; the only wheeled traffic was an occasional light farm cart drawn by a pair of horses; and the people walking the dusty yellow road were dressed in traditional clothes. The place could have been a film set for a medieval town.

The guest house proved to be in character. A low mud building with barred windows, there was a gaily painted cart parked in the porch. It had two doors side by side, one led directly into a stable for three horses, and the other into an adjoining raftered reception and sleeping room. Just inside this door a small area had been partitioned off by a low rail. Here on the smooth stone floor we were asked to leave our saddle bags, and showed niches where we could store our smaller belongings. A man poured cool water from a clay amphora over our hands, the waste water draining away through a small hole in the lower wall. Everything was perfectly arranged for the traveller. Hand towels hung from pegs in the wall, a stove filled with twigs and logs stood at one end of the room should the night grow chill, and a janitor was busily sweeping the already clean mats for us to sleep on. The walls of the building must have been nearly three feet thick and were pierced with small windows guarded by wooden shutters. Outside we could hear the rush of the town's stream flowing past the windows.

Once again the consideration and kindness of the Turks was evident. We were given tea, and then after their fast was broken, a huge vegetarian meal of yoghurt, pasta boiled in milk, spinach, unleavened bread, and a porridge of boiled wheat they called *bulgur*. The room was not large enough to hold all the interested townsfolk so they arrived in relays. First were the children, while we ate, so they could run errands, fetch and carry the plates. When they left with the trays, they were replaced by the village elders, each man making his separate dignified arrival into the room and taking up his formal position alongside the wall, before asking the well-rubbed litany of questions. At the evening call to prayer the greybeards all left to go to the mosque, and after a short interval the young working men of the community entered as a group, just returning from their jobs in the city on the mini-bus service. They too were delighted to talk with us, asked the same rote of questions, and were eager that we should feel honoured guests. Sarah was not feeling well, so the minibus driver took her into town for a night at a hotel, and I was left wondering whether I would ever get some rest that evening from my visitors when, as if impelled by some sixth sense, the entire company rose politely to its feet, wished me goodnight and withdrew, showing me how to lock the door from the inside.

The Ramadan drummer woke me briefly at two in the morning as he marched up and down Uchüyük's streets, rattling his drum to wake the citizens so they could eat their meal before sunrise began the daytime fasting. Then I slept on until dawn when a concentrated ringing of hammers on metal just outside the window proved to be a travelling band of tinsmiths who had set up their workshop in the guest house porch. They were busily mending and re-tinning the community's cooking pots, while I fed and groomed the three horses. By the time Sarah returned from town, I was replacing nails in Szarcsa's shoes.

We rode on our way eastward along the foothills, keeping to the farmland between the hills and the modern main road which is surperimposed upon the original Roman track. By now we appreciated rural, traditional Turkish life so much that we found it unpleasant to stray back into the modern world. Near Kadınhanı we made the mistake of diverting to a roadside truck stop, and found it most disagreeable to be reintroduced to engine noise and plastic rubbish, oil stains and the empty tired faces of the drivers watching a vapid video programme blaring from a distorting oversize television screen at midday. The truck stop menu, too, was revolting, a greasy meal of stale food that bore no comparison to the plain but palatable fare that we were given by the villagers.

As if to express his disgust, Zippy spent the entire meal break lying down in the squalid rubbish-littered mess of a garden behind the truck stop. He had been limping slightly and we were worried about his health. Our sympathy was totally misplaced. We had mounted up and scarcely started riding again when we came to a small irrigation ditch. Sarah on Szarcsa jumped the ditch but Zippy, quite deliberately, lagged behind. Once again the lead rope was jerked from Sarah's hand. Zippy spun about and made a run for it. Furious, we chased after him across a mile of open wheatfields, before Sarah finally caught him. At that point we lost patience. The next time he ran off, we decided, we would simply leave him to himself and ride on with the other horses, abandoning the baggage. Alone in unknown territory, Zippy might realise that he was better off in company. So, an hour later when Zippy next broke free, Sarah and I simply kept riding forward across the fields. The system worked. Zippy, after his initial break for freedom, slowed as soon as he realised no one was chasing him, put down his head to graze, and when he saw that his companions were disappearing in the distance, trotted after us. From that day on, he never made a serious bid to escape again.

Even with delays for Zippy and his mischief we had been making rapid progress. Our daily distances were regularly in excess of 25 miles, much farther than the previous year, and we were ahead of our schedule to reach Konya, the largest city we would see until we came to Syria. But the sun was very hot at midday now, and on Saturday 14 May Sarah complained of feeling unwell. She was white and fevered, her legs felt rubbery, and she started to suffer abdominal pains. The most likely cause was sunstroke, aggravated by straightforward physical exhaustion. She had refused point blank to wear a hat so I felt both exasperated and concerned. I feared that, because daily routine had taken over so quickly and smoothly at the start of this season's travel, I had fallen into the error of taking Sarah's participation too much for granted. We had ridden for hour after hour in companionable silence. At any moment in the day's chores each would know precisely what the other was doing, what particular strap or bag to hold to help one's companion, where to stow each item of equipment so it could be instantly found by the other person. It came as a shock to me to realise that I had overlooked the harsh physical demands made upon Sarah by riding 400 miles across what was sometimes very rough terrain. My colleague, pert, bronzed and caustic, was genuinely sick. Unless she had a chance to rest up, I could see that Sarah might abandon the journey as altogether too unrelenting. And to proceed across Anatolia without Sarah was a gloomy prospect.

CHAPTER 20

The Steppes

We delayed five days in Konya to give Sarah a chance to recover from the illness. The break should have been longer, but she was an indifferent patient, short-tempered and despondent, and when it became obvious that any improvement was going very slowly, it seemed better to continue our ride rather than stay wretchedly in the city, with Sarah's morale sinking. Her fever and vomiting eased but was replaced by attacks of severe coughing which left her gasping painfully for breath like an asthmatic. And she continued to suffer from diarrhoea. Much as I disliked the option, I wondered to myself if it was wise for her to go on.

East of Konya, the great flatlands of Turkey begin. At the time of the First Crusade this had been desert, in bad places deteriorating into salt lake. Surface water was so scarce that when the army left Konya the citizens advised the pilgrims to carry a day's emergency water supply in skins. Remembering their previous sufferings from thirst, they took the advice seriously and without mishap managed to reach a river on the second day's march. No longer was the army at full strength since Baldwin and Tancred had branched off to try their luck with independent sorties. Probably the slow pace of the advance, hampered by its civilian 'tail' and the wounded Godfrey, was altogether too frustrating for the younger contingent. But what in normal circumstances would have been a fast-moving flying column of the fittest most energetic knights was nothing of the sort. After the rigours of the march, their horses were in such poor condition that they could not carry the weight of their riders any distance. The raiders walked south towards the coast, leading their tired animals.

The Konya desert has now been ploughed and irrigated with artesian water to make immense dead-flat wheatfields, Turkey's granary, but the climate has not improved. As Sarah and I rode eastward, the midday temperatures were in the middle to upper 30s, and the air shimmered over the long straight dirt road so that distant objects became indistinct blobs hovering above the horizon. By noon there was no shade left. The sun was high enough so that only a razor edge of black shadow fell beside the walls of the plain square houses, and even these tiny strips of shelter were already claimed by livestock, sheep and goats crammed together in a solid panting mass, heads in the shade or tucked beneath one another's bodies as they sought to stay cool, and gasping for air. In the mornings small furry creatures, a kind of Turkish prairie dog, would sit up alert and whistle warnings as we rode past, but by mid-afternoon they had vanished into their underground burrows to avoid the heat. Not a soul was to be seen as we arrived in the baking villages. Yet as we dismounted and slumped against a wall to rest, a gate or door would swing open and someone would always emerge to give us a hand to pump water into a cattle trough and, invariably, carry out glasses of cool *ayran*, the milk and water mixture. Poor Sarah, mindful of her tortured guts, could only sip a cautious mouthful.

In a land so numbingly flat, nearly every village added 'hüyük' – knoll – to its name even if it had no more than a slight swell of the ground. From ten miles off, through the glare, we would see the fringe of scrawny trees and above it the white needle of a mosque which marked the next settlement. In these parts the crops had long since been harvested, and the fields lay bare, parching under the sun, empty of people and activity. Only at the occasional irrigation canal did we find farmers at work, tending the roaring engines of stationary pumps or parked tractors which were sucking water from the canal through plastic pipes and squirting it over the thirsty land. We kept to the canal side wherever possible for here was some sign of life. A shy white bird like an egret with a pale brown back occasionally burst out in panic from the reeds – after half a year on her transcontinental travels Mystery had finally settled down enough not to shy at such surprises – and from time to time small snakes swam across the slow-moving water, weaving their path between the bits of flotsam and brown froth.

Finally there were no more canals, and they were replaced with the diagonal spars of cantilever wells, the *serens*, dotted here and there across the exposed countryside. To water the horses, we would stop and haul down the long wooden arm so that the dangling bucket, ingeniously made from a truck tyre turned inside out and rivetted, disappeared down the well shaft. Lifting back the loaded bucket with the help of the counterweight on the long wooden arm, we tipped out the water on the lip of the well. A groove carried it down to the sheep trough carved in a stone slab, broad and shallow and so hot to the touch that the water was lukewarm by the time the thirsty horses drank.

We crossed the whitish sands of the barrens over which the Crusaders carried their skins of water, and came to the shallow river where they had replenished their supplies. Here the Roman road must have been carried on a causeway for the river water ponded up into an area of quaking marsh, where tall reeds grew from spongy peat-like soil. The inhabitants had cut away most of the reeds to roof their box-shaped mud houses, and we rode through an outer zone of brittle root stumps where the horses flinched at the sharp stubs until the ground became so soft and boggy that we were forced to detour around the mere. In the midst of this dry land it was strange to find a bright green core of living reedbeds and a small lake with water the colour of pale caramel. Stranger still was the sight of sea birds, cormorants fishing and a fluttering tern splashing as it dive-bombed for the fish, all so far from the sea. Frogs croaked heedless of the presence of their predator, a large snake, whose head left a sinister telltale v-ripple in the water.

The names of the villages told the origins of the people. Beyond the marsh we came to 'Middle Nomad Camp', followed by 'Far Nomad Camp' and then 'Hasan's Camp'. This was the great steppe of Turkey, settled by herding tribesmen out of central Asia who had found the vast, dry flatlands very reminiscent of their ancestral grazing grounds. The land stretched away as if it was limitless in its immensity. The sweep of the horizon was only emphasised by the stark outlines of the hills. It was an enormous dramatic landscape suitable for the pyrotechnics of nature, and magnificent thunderstorms occasionally rolled in from the southwest with threatening banks of black cloud and the harassing flicker of lightning arcing between them. As at sea, we could make out the distinct curtains of heavy rain that hung below the moving thunderheads, and we tried to calculate whether and where we would be caught by them, feeling tiny and helpless beneath the tremendous spectacle of raw nature.

In this wide land it was easy to feel lost. At one point we were puzzling whether we had missed the only village marked for miles on our map, when we rode over a low undulation in the ground, a dip we could barely detect from fifty yards away, and suddenly found spread before us thirty or forty tiny square houses, all earth-coloured from the soil of which they were made, all with flat roofs of earth piled on reeds, all with tiny windows to block out the heat, and each house scarcely nine feet high. The entire place was hidden in a wrinkle in the ground, and looked as if it had been there since the dawn of time.

Farther on we passed abandoned farm buildings whose mud walls were crumbling back into the soil out of which they had been created, and then a few fields of sparse green wheat told us that we were nearing habitation again. A distant clump of poplar trees announced a village and as dusk gathered prematurely in the shadow of a great mass of thunderclouds we headed at a trot for the settlement. 'Where are you from? Where are you going?' The usual cry from a young man running up from where he had been tending to a young horse tied beneath a tree. But we were in a hurry. Already the first sprinkle of rain was falling and we wanted to find shelter.

'Where is the *muhtar*,' I asked, rudely ignoring his question.

'I will take you to him,' the young man replied, running alongside us, 'but please come to my house first.'

This hijacking proved to be a blessing. Osman was the only son of a well-to-do farming family and he insisted that we stay with him, not the *muhtar*, and it made a refreshing change to join his parents and six sisters rather than the usual all-male company of the village guest house. The family looked after us royally. None of the sisters, who ranged in age from eighteen to their mid-twenties, were married and they took huge delight in vying with one another to spoil us. The village was famous for its food – fruit preserved in its own juice, a delicious yoghurt soup, lamb and even a sort of meat loaf we had never tasted before – and we were given a feast. A fire was lit in the stove in their tiny bathroom so that we could take it in turns to wallow in the steamy sauna atmosphere, drenching ourselves from great jugs of hot water, and when Sarah emerged coughing, the girls massaged her so vigorously with ointment that she groaned aloud. Everyone was so enthusiastic and welcoming that I did not hesitate to accept their invitation to stay an extra day and join them in their daily chores.

In the morning all of us, plus several neighbours, scrambled into a farm trailer to be delivered out to the sheep range to tend the flocks. We assembled by the well, where the eldest of Osman's sisters sprang up on the stone surround, called us to take hold of the rope and threw down the oversized bucket. The water table must have been at least sixty feet below the surface, for after the bucket splashed down and filled we marched off along a walkway towing the rope behind us until the brimming bucket finally surfaced to a warning yell from the eldest sister. She tipped out the water, we turned and ambled back, and the bucket again descended. Time and again we hauled and turned, hauled and turned, for there were nearly three hundred sheep to be watered. It was obvious that the family could have afforded a motor pump to do the same job in a quarter of the time, but that was not their style. Companionship, as much as water for the flock, was the reason for their labour, so everyone chattered and laughed, hauled and gossiped, sharing the work as a team.

When the sheep had drunk, they were driven into a low mud walled corral where the sisters and their colleagues began to line them up for milking, squatting down athletically behind each woolly tail and stripping two or three cupfuls of milk into a small tin pail. They insisted that Sarah try the same, but she found that it took strong hands and forearms and a lifetime of practice to get more than a few drops of milk. There was much laughter when Sarah drily informed them that now she knew why, when they had massaged her the previous evening after the bath, it felt as if she was being torn apart limb from limb. For five months a year this was the daily routine for the sisters, until winter came and the flocks had to be brought in from the range. What did they do then? I asked their father. Embroidery, needlework, and they make carpets, he replied, but they are so industrious that I have to say stop! stop! no more carpets or we won't have any more space in which to live. They sent us off from their farm with cheese and bread, handmade socks, yet another headscarf for Sarah, and a promise that when we returned they would have a carpet for us as well.

Sarah had begun to feel a little better as we moved on, though the weather did nothing to help her recovery. This was the season of sudden torrential thunderstorms and two or three times a day we were soaked by massive downpours that simply vanished into the thirsty soil. The horses loathed the storms. They were obliged to stay in barns with rainwater gushing in through broken roof tiles, or plod along in the open lashed by the wind and rain. One afternoon the wind and driving rain was so brutal that they refused to advance another step. They turned their tails and stood there miserably until the tempest was past. Another day we found ourselves struggling through a raging gale which set the trees of some surrounding orchards roaring and flailing like the ocean. Fortunately the wind was blowing across our path or the horses would have been stopped in their tracks. As it was they had to walk at a slant, leaning into the wind, and Zippy looked as if he would be blown away but for the weight of the packs. Wisely he tucked himself in Szarcsa's lee to avoid the worst of the gale.

The little pack pony had lost his earlier sparkle. At the end of each day he was more tired than he should have been, and often lay down as he ate his nosebag of barley. We took it to be his usual sense of self-preservation which had been called into play at several villages when he was chased by packs of dogs, one creature even succeeding in snapping off a part of Zippy's tail. But his withers, just where the front of the pack saddle rested on his shoulders, were puffy and swollen. After a month of riding we thought little of it. We rubbed in lotion and kept the swelling clean, for it did not seem chronic. Nor was Mystery at her best. On certain days, and for no apparent reason, she would be off her feed, hang her head, and shamble as she walked. We put it down to occasional colic, and because she perked up after these bouts, we again paid little attention to the warning signs. Only Szarcsa, haughty as ever, seemed on peak form, stepping along crisply as if he was shedding the years.

By now we had diverted towards the northeast, the wrong direction for travelling towards Jerusalem which lay southwest beyond Syria. But this had been Duke Godfrey's path and historians had long puzzled why the Crusade made this huge, time-consuming detour away from the

231

direct road to the Holy Land. Travelling by horse we now saw one simple explanation: away to our right were the forbidding ramparts of the Anti-Taurus and Taurus mountains. They rose from the vast plain like a great wall, seemingly impenetrable. Baldwin, Tancred and the cavalry had found a way through, it is true, but the ordinary pilgrim and his footsore companions marching over the flat, easy going of the plain must have been tempted to go on and on, hoping to turn the end of that great barrier rather than endure the rigours of a mountain crossing. But there was no easy way. The straggling mass of the main army was only straying farther away from their goal. Sooner or later they would have to tackle the mountains.

The other reason to veer northeast may have been the army's hope of finding friendly Christians among the Armenian communities who had established semi-independent principalities deep in Anatolia. At Eski Gümüsler near the town of Nigde we visited an abandoned monastery of the Armenians, a smaller version of the more famous rock cut caves of Göreme and Ürgüp. For defence, it seemed, a natural courtyard was hidden within a low cliff, and all around it the monks had hollowed out a complex of chapels and meeting halls, store rooms and living chambers. They had burrowed like teredo worms, going from gallery to gallery, driving shafts upward to the surface to bring light and air into their subterranean world. Even when the monks died they did not leave their rock home, for they had been buried like insect larva, each corpse laid in his tomb chiselled from the rocky floor. The puzzle is why, if the First Crusaders had sought to contact the Armenian Christians, did they make no reference to finding them as they marched through these lands. The monastery at Eski Gümüsler lay less than three miles from the Roman road, yet the chroniclers never mentioned it. Was it abandoned at that time or did the pilgrims plod past, heads down, quite unaware what lay right beside their path?

Beyond Nigde the Roman road entered a dramatic canyon. It was an early evening in late May and the slanting rays of sunshine lit up the cliffs, turning them the colour of dried blood. To our left the outlines of conical shafts and pillars of sandstone with their delicately balanced cap rocks were back-lit into fantastic and weird shapes — castles and block houses, monsters, anthills, bubbles of rock, caves like eye sockets dripping like molten wax. We detected a tiny square window cut high up in the vertical cliffs, a black rectangle with no apparent means of access, too high for ladders, and too far below the crest to be reached by any internal gallery. It remained a mystery. Was it an ancient lookout post, or had it once been the home of a solitary anchorite? There was no one to ask, the canyon was uninhabited. The road twisted and dipped, climbed and turned again, keeping to the base of more cliffs and beetling crags. Mystery was again flagging. She had managed to get loose the previous evening in a village stable, stole some chicken food and was suffering the pangs of indigestion. She slowed us down so badly that we were still within the canyon when night fell, and we were obliged to camp at the foot of a great concrete barrage built across a tributary valley. There was a slightly menacing feel to spending the night with millions of tons of backed-up water looming over us. The dam's overspill came past us as a pleasant stream where we could water the horses, but it was a quiet, unnatural place. Sarah listened to the horses in the darkness, interpreting their noises, and when Zippy gave a sudden snort of fear, she nudged me awake. Was it strange animals or a snake from the stream? I was too tired to care, and had nightmares of intruders in the camp.

Next morning we emerged from the canyon to find Mount Erciyes ahead of us, the second highest mountain in Turkey and all the more impressive for standing alone in the plain with snow-covered upper slopes, a plume of cloud streaming off the peak. It took us two days to ride to the foot of the mountain and around its base until we came to Kayseri, the ancient Caesaria where we hoped to rest the horses as they deserved another break, having covered 225 miles since Konya. For most of the first day a salt lake lay between us and the mountain, the colour of the water and crystals changing from milky white to pale blue according to the sunlight. By contrast, on the second day we might have been on English downland, for we crossed a broad expanse of green turf where the horses could stretch their legs at a gallop. The distinctly non-English features were herds of water buffalo grazing beside the irrigation canals and a group of women vigorously washing fresh sheepskins by clubbing them in the shallows with long staves.

We spent the intervening night at Incesu, an ancient caravan town whose older section lay within such steep valley that the houses had been built up against the cliffs, rising in steep tiers. The facades of the houses were boldly constructed in massive blocks of the local volcanic stone, with balconies and ornate carving, while on the higher levels each building was cut back into the cliff face to gain extra rooms. A shopkeeper invited us to stay with him, and we found ourselves stabling the horses in a vaulted cave driven into the cliff face at ground level. From there we ascended by a staircase hollowed within the cliff to his living room perched out on a ledge over the valley, while the kitchen behind was again a cave. A third storey was completely formed of caves burrowed out of the cliff face, and joined by tunnels. It was strange to find electricity and water laid on, the former with surface wires stapled to the living rock while, as plumbing with concealed pipes was impossible, the water trickled down from the kitchen through a network of surface grooves in the rock to emerge into the cobbled street by way of the cattle byre. Crammed into the ground floor cavern were several sheep, four milking cows and a donkey as well as all their fodder. It was a living example of how livestock would have been kept within a medieval town even when under siege.

We entered Kayseri over a low spur of Mount Erciyes's foothills, riding down into the city through orchards and gardens that offered no shelter for the horses. We had been told we would find municipal stables at the market place, but were misinformed. The centre of Kayseri was a dull grid of modern commercial streets and we were hesitating there when we were befriended by a carter fetching huge sacks of chaff to take to his cowstalls on the edge of town. He led us to a small stockyard in the very poorest suburbs where the only free accommodation was a ramshackle shed with a gaping hole in one mud wall and a narrow door wide enough for a donkey. But Mystery and Szarcsa were now skilled contortionists and our three horses squeezed through the gap and enthusiastically attacked their ration of chaff and barley. The carter solemnly padlocked the door behind them, ignoring that the hasp was held on with string and that we could see Mystery peering out through a gaping hole in the stable wall.

In Kayseri I wanted to visit the Church of St John the Forerunner, as it was the last functioning Armenian church in central Turkey. The city, according to Armenian tradition, had been settled by Armenians since the days of Hagg, the legendary forefather of their race, and the Greeks had even called the region 'the First Armenia'. The picture is confusing because Kayseri was variously under the control of the Byzantines, the

Seljuks or their rivals the Danishmends, and by the time the First Crusade passed that way, seems to have been intermittently the headquarters, or at least the refuge, of an Armenian Catholicos or Archbishop. The arrival of the Crusade, which entered the city in late September 1097, must have been regarded by the Armenian Christians as yet another chapter in their long and tortuous struggle to survive foreign domination, while the reaction of the Crusaders towards the Armenian Christians proved to be entirely negative. Their chroniclers took to describing the Armenians as false allies, treacherous, greedy for gain and untrustworthy. They were the same adjectives which had been applied to the Orthodox Greeks back in Byzantium, and the truth was that the farther the pilgrim army advanced eastward and the more effort and suffering was expended, the more rigid and isolated became their outlook. Already ardent in their beliefs when they took up the cross in Europe, by the time they reached the land of the Armenians they were well on their way to becoming fanatic.

The leading Armenian in modern Kayseri was Artin Celik, the knife grinder, a man in his early sixties, thin and tired looking, dressed in a worn grey three-piece suit with a watch chain hanging across its waistcoat. His chief interest was cock fighting, and a very knocked-about fighting cock with scarcely any tail feathers on its rump was cooped up in a pen beside the shop door. The walls of his tiny workshop were hung with medallions won at cock fighting competitions interspersed with his stock in trade of knives and scissors. Artin was the last surviving Armenian male in a city of nearly 400,000 population. The only other Armenian was an old woman, sick and crippled, who lived within the compound of their Church and acted as a caretaker. All the other Armenians had moved to Istanbul or emigrated, especially to North America. Once a year the Istanbul Armenians organised a group to come back to Kayseri to hold a service in the church.

The building itself was set in a church yard which we entered through a large iron-sheathed door from the street. Artin showed us around. Once gilded and grand, the church was now cracked and shabby. Plaster was falling in great flakes from the ceiling, and a scatter of rubble lay in lumps upon the threadbare carpets. There was a smell of decay and damp everywhere. On the raised dais before the altar was an Armenian bible, covered by a cheap embroidered shawl to protect it from the rain of debris. Artin opened the parchment pages to show us the handwritten text, but confessed that he could not read Armenian script. Behind him the old lady hovered nervously, leaning on her stick. It all seemed so futile and empty, not even a shadow of the old religion, and it was a relief to emerge back into the sunshine of the churchyard. Artin locked the door behind us with an enormous key which he had designed to be shaped like a cross, and moved on to show us the grounds. Here, finally, the old lady became enthusiastic. Among the tombs of former parish priests she was growing a life-giving crop of onions and tomatoes, and it seemed that here, at least, the last Armenian church was providing her with a final sanctuary.

We did not spend as long as we had intended in Kayseri, for the stabling was very poor, and Sarah was worried that the horses might pick up some sort of infection from the mixed batches of cows and calves which stayed overnight at the stockyard on their way to market. So after two days rest, long enough for the swelling on Zippy's withers to begin to subside, we headed on around the foot of Mount Erciyes. Ahead of us we could see more snow-capped mountains, this time lying directly across our path, and we knew exactly how the original pilgrims must have felt as they marched out of Kayseri: after 1500 miles on the 'path of penance' they must have come to the numbing realisation that to reach Jerusalem, the army would have to climb the great ridges of the Anti-Taurus and Taurus ranges. The mountains could not be avoided.

CHAPTER 21

The Mountains

The *Gesta* knight recalled very vividly the horrors of the journey through the mountains. Between the towns of Göksun and Maraş he had to cross

a mountain of the Devil which was so high and steep that, on the path across it, not one of us dared to go before another. Horses tumbled headlong into the ravines, and one pack animal pushed over another. On every side the knights showed their dismay and, from sadness and grief, smote themselves with their hands and asked themselves what they should do with themselves and their weapons. They sold their shields and their best breastplates, together with their helmets, for just three or five pence, or whatever they could get. Those who could not sell them threw them away for nothing . . .

The precise location of the 'Devil's mountain' has never been established though there is no lack of suitably breakneck terrain between Göksun and Maraş. The region lies within the general complex of the Taurus and Anti-Taurus mountains which rise to 12,000 feet in a confusion of peaks and ridges, gorges and canyons. Above 9,000 feet the mountains are permanently covered in snow, and seen from a distance they present a glistening barricade that can sometimes be awesome and beautiful, but mostly is hostile and grim. From the village of Akmescit where Sarah and I stayed on the night of 3 June, the impression was of an impenetrable obstacle. Though we had often glimpsed the mountains at a distance as we rode eastward from Konya, it still brought a pang of anxiety to see them now, lying so directly across our path. Unless we found a pass or valley, it was clearly impossible for the horses to get across, and we scanned the looming mass to see if there was an obvious entry to the terrific jumble of snow and rock. But there was nothing. Ahead lay an apparently unbroken mass of mountains, rank upon rank extending to the farthest horizon.

Our first obstacle, even as we began to climb the foothills, was a gorge where a river had cut through a protective layer of hard rock to gouge a 200-foot-deep gash in the soft earth underneath. Twenty-ton rectangular lumps of rock had broken away from the lid and fallen on to the soft scree slope below, where they lay like stranded toboggans waiting to slide farther. Mystery was sluggish as we descended the slope. She moved awkwardly and the moment we reached the valley floor and found a meadow, she lay down, not to roll, but to curl up looking thoroughly ill at ease. We coaxed her back on her feet, but she did not want to stand. A minute later she buckled at the knees and dropped down again on the ground with an unhappy grunt. Zippy was hardly more enthusiastic. He had flopped down on the grass and was lying flat. We went over to check on him and lifted up his head, but when we let go, he let his head fall back limply like a doll empty of stuffing. We had no idea what the matter was, or what to do. After the recent rest interval in Kayseri, the animals should have been fit and well, and there was no sign of a colic. We began to worry that they had contracted some disease, and so after lunch crept on gingerly. Zippy seemed to be feeling better, but Mystery was too ill to be ridden and for the next few miles I trudged along beside her while the poor little mare plodded miserably, head sagging and distress in every line of her body.

Once again I was painfully aware how little we could do. There was no shelter anywhere, so we could not stop, and veterinary help was unobtainable in such a remote part of the world. As we dragged our way out of the gorge and back on to the level, still heading towards the mountains, a strong wind blew up and whisked fine dust and sand into our faces. By the time we reached Taf, the little town at the foot of the first hills, we were all short-tempered, weary and spitting dust. In the town no one seemed to be able to offer shelter, until a kindly bus driver took us into his home. Nearly two hundred years previously, he told us, an entire caravan had been trapped nearby by a blizzard early in the season. Men, women, children, horses and pack animals, had all perished.

Some had been smothered by the snow, others had found refuge in nearby caves only to starve to death. In the spring the local villagers had found not one person alive, only the corpses where they lay. 'There's much gold to be found there, claimed our host, 'but the police and the gendarmes forbid anyone to search and dig.'

This hope of finding gold, either buried treasure or raw nuggets in the mountains, fascinated the country folk everywhere we went in Turkey. Repeatedly we heard rumours of lost gold mines in the hills or hidden caches of bullion. The villagers loved to believe such tales, and there was always a tremor of excitement whenever we produced our copies of the old Ottoman maps. 'Do they show where gold is found?' we were asked again and again, and they would eagerly pore over the maps, confident that in olden days men had marked gold mines on their maps. We had to explain that this was not so, but there was never any real disappointment. The villagers were always happy to discover when their own little hamlet was marked on the map, and doubly thrilled if it was given its original Ottoman name.

In fact there must have been some gold-bearing ore in the mountains because soon after we left Taf and began to penetrate the foothills, we came across four men standing in a river bed, laboriously scraping up the gravel with shovels. Over the rush of water they did not hear the slip and clatter of horses' hooves, as we were riding up the riverbed itself, and they reacted guiltily, wondering who we could be. Their leader, a tall dark-skinned man with a gold tooth and jet black hair, at first pretended not to know any Turkish. He may have been a Kurd or perhaps an Arab-speaker from the south, but we eventually prised out of him the lame excuse that they were 'gathering stones for building material' an obvious fiction as no truck could possibly have penetrated into such a remote spot. Anyway, the men had been working far too delicately, sifting through each shovelful of sediment, obviously looking for grains of alluvial gold.

The river water was beautifully clean and limpid, and at first I thought it owed its clarity to new meltwater draining down from the mountain snows and glaciers, but as we rode around the next corner we came upon the birth of the river itself. By a geological freak it emerged direct from the mountain flank. The opposite bank was a nearly vertical wall of slate, and from fissures in the rock the entire river foamed out, thousands of gallons every second, gushing out and tumbling down the slope in a roaring cascade of suds.

We clattered on up the stream bed which was merely a trickle above the waterfall, then scrambled up the bank and across a long slope through the last of the mountain hamlets, half-abandoned and in ruins. Beyond that point there was no permanent settlement, only the summer huts of shepherds. As we rode along the flank of the mountain, again a chill wind was gusting from the south and driving into our faces. We had to squint to see the way ahead, and the horses snorted to clear the dust from their nostrils. To our left the dry riverbed we had recently followed, had deepened and narrowed into an impressive abyss and, level with us across the open gap about half a mile in a direct line, we could see a single file of cattle being driven diagonally across the opposite valley face on their way to pasture. If we had shouted, we might have been heard by them, yet to walk to that same point, down into the gorge and up the far slope, would have taken two or three hours of toil. Our own path, littered with half-buried rocks, seemed an unlikely place for any road, yet we noted occasionally the grooves of wheel ruts worn in the rock where generations of travellers before us had used this same corridor.

At lunchtime we sheltered in a small, rocky bowl, away from the wind. Sarah was again sickly, with the result that her usually cheerful, if caustic, remarks had turned to plain rudeness, even to strangers, and her temper flared easily. In a black humour she rode along as if the mountains were the last place on earth where she wanted to be, and I wondered whether she would quit the journey when we came to the next town. After less than half a mile we came upon half-a-dozen black and dark brown tents pitched along the edge of a great sweep of mountain pasture. They were the homes of the Hatay nomads, pastoralists from the hot lands near the Syrian border a hundred miles away. Year after year they brought their cattle and sheep to the same grazing grounds that they rented from the villagers living in the foothills. The men all wore baggy trousers, suit jackets and the commonplace cloth flat hat of workaday Turkish male dress, while the women were much more colourful in bright pyjama pantaloons, heavy shirts and turbans. Their children scampered around, some of them clutching, like living soft toys, three-day-old lambs. The ringmarks of cooking fires and hearths speckled the turf where the tents had been pitched in the same favoured spots year after year, and for the entire summer they would stay on the *yayla*, the high pasture, grazing their cattle and sheep, shearing wool, and – at this early part of the season – raising lambs and milking the ewes to make a soft white cheese that would be found on sale in every city in Turkey. The shepherds, armed with shotguns, worked in shifts to watch over the flocks and herds, the women gossiped, gathered brushwood and tended the cooking fires, youths gathered to play football in a dell. The cheesemakers set up their boiling cauldrons, trays and stocks of empty square tins by a stream where they could cool the whey. Very occasionally someone would have to go into town to collect drums of diesel fuel for the small tractors and trailers they used to haul water in tubs to their flocks, but otherwise the nomads were self-sufficient. There was no post, no television, no hospital, no tax collectors, no government officials of any kind.

There was much interest as we unsaddled the horses and began to set up the little lightweight tent in a gap between two of the big tents. 'That won't keep out the rain,' observed one critic as I erected the inner canopy of mosquito netting on its hoops, and the others cluckled. But when I flipped over the waterproof cover, and they realised it had taken no more than three or four minutes to pitch, they clustered round to finger the cloth and see how the tent was constructed. It was an ideal moment to ask for expert advice about Zippy's swollen withers, because the nomads constantly used pack animals and might know what was wrong.

I pointed out Zippy's bloated shoulders which had begun to look really grotesque, and a small, squat man, obviously the head of one of the families, turned over the little pack saddle and felt the edge of one of the cross bars. Clearly he thought it was too close to the saddle pad, and he wanted me to shave away the wood. After I had whittled it down to his satisfaction, he sent his wife to the tent to fetch a strip of felt, a length of string and a six-inch pack needle. Kneeling over the saddle he stitched an extra pad of felt to the suspect cross bar, and assured me that the saddle would now fit Zippy. I was not so confident, the swelling was so bad that the pack saddle was bound to press on the tender flesh. Yet there was no sign of a boil or a centre to the infection that I could lance. The ridge of Zippy's shoulder was ballooning up from what was obviously a deep-seated infection, close to the bone. Gloomily I had checked the veterinary manual which told me that Zippy's problem was 'Fistulous withers: a very serious complaint, and the veterinary surgeon should be called in immediately. He may be able to remove all the diseased tissue by operation. Neglected cases are often impossible to cure. The external application of poultices or blisters is useless.'

When we had picketed the horses, Sarah and I were invited into one of the great black tents. Inside it was as large as a good-sized living room, carpeted and with cushions stacked around the outer wall. A fire burned on a patch of bare earth near the entrance, and since the tent lacked any chimney, the rising smoke oozed out through the coarsely woven fabric giving the eerie impression from the outside that the entire structure was on fire. Two or three new-born lambs nestled in dark corners of the tent, cooking utensils and miscellaneous packages were tidied away in a corner, and we were once again cross-questioned about our journey, our homeland, the reason for our travels. It turned out that the nomads had arrived only ten days earlier, and this was the beginning of the *yayla* season. Twenty years ago they would have walked with their flocks for two or three weeks, exchanging the stifling heat of the southlands for the cool pastures of the mountains. Now they hired a convoy of trucks and travelled in a day and a half, with all the sheep, goats, cattle and donkeys, tents, and chattels they would need for a five-month stay in the high pasture.

They kept us talking until long after nightfall, and when, finally, we felt we could tactfully return to our own tiny tent, it was impossible to sleep. A brace of half-wild mules resented the intrusion of strange horses. Every twenty minutes they came rushing out of the dark to attack our animals with a great braying and squealing. Attached to picket pins our horses were at a disadvantage, especially Mystery who was puzzled as to what was happening. Zippy could take care of himself despite his small size, but best of all was Szarcsa. In the moonlight I glimpsed the superb sight of his elderly black shadow, head down and lashing out with both heels like a three-year-old. The racket was appalling: eeh-hawing of mules, screaming of horses, a baby woken and crying in the nearby tent, bleating of sheep, donkeys braying in sympathy, and the frenzied barking of the huge guard dogs with their spiked iron collars. There was no peace in the *yayla* that night.

The nomads had told us that by following the Dry River, their name for the deep valley, we would find a way through the first range of mountains. It was a memorable ride. With mountain crests towering up on each side, the gorge was so narrow that often we were forced to ride in the shallows, splashing in and out of the stream bed. Whenever there was level ground on the banks, we passed small herds of cows, guarded by boys who had so little to do, for the animals could not possibly escape from the narrow valley, that the lads lay on their backs fast asleep or went swimming in the pools. A shepherd crossed the stream ahead of us, using rocks as stepping stones. Draped over his shoulders he was carrying a lamb. He looked as if he had walked straight from a stained glass window depicting the good shepherd and the rescued lamb.

The track was so narrow that it was difficult to believe this had been a Roman road. Legionnaires, Byzantine troops and the Crusaders after them could not have marched more than four abreast through the narrowest defiles, and an army would have been strung over several miles, slipping and stumbling over the boulders. Yet just beside the trail we found a Roman roadmarker, a broken column that had once stood beside the track to advise the passerby that this section of the road had been repaired and improved in the second century AD.

The Dry River carried us through the most difficult range of mountains and we emerged into hill country where isolated valleys were ploughed for crops. Here we passed more Hatay people, some of them with herds of splendid black goats with long glossy hair. At one secluded spot a poacher was washing the markings off a stolen sheep. Each animal was marked on its back with a daub of coloured paint as an owner's brand, and this poor creature had fallen into the wrong hands, for it was being held down in the shallows while its captor briskly tried to scrub off the paint with a handful of gravel. He then rinsed the animal by swishing it back and forth in the water despite its alarmed struggles. When the job was finally done, the poacher released his victim the right way up and it staggered off, weighed down and soggy, on wobbly legs.

We passed through Sar, and as if Roman road markers had not been enough, found the little town had a Roman temple on the outskirts, a Roman theatre by the river, and a Roman forum with tall ornate columns. Leaving the town we startled two peasant women who unexpectedly turned out into the narrow lane from a gate ahead of us. The lane was very deep-set with high banks, and as the two women chatted they did not hear the horses coming up right behind them. At the last moment they sensed our presence and turned to find the alarming sight of two outlandish riders and the three horses looming over them. Where we could have come from must have been a mystery because behind us were only the wild mountains. Alarmed, the two women shrank back against the earth bank, and as we passed I heard one hiss to the other, with awe and horror in her voice, 'Yabangı!' – 'foreigners'. We must have seemed like aliens from the wilderness.

The town of Göksun, the Crusaders' Coxon, was a rough-hewn place which gave the impression that everyone in town was either a hard-boiled local or someone passing through, and no one ever halted for more than a single night. The single main street was lined with the shop fronts of grain stores, dry goods shops, a shabby hotel, the bakery and various groceries and several nondescript eating places. At the main crossroads a cluster of horse-drawn carts waited, their drivers hoping for hire. Zippy's withers were looking ever more gruesome. On previous days the hump over the abscess had reduced in size during each day's walking, only to puff up to its grosser shape during the night. Now, despite his reshaped saddle with the extra padding, the swelling had barely gone down at all during the day, and he winced and squirmed as I probed gently to find the centre of the infection. We had already reduced his load to a minimum, and, when we could, sent his saddle and the packs ahead by road so that he could walk along with a bare back. The shelter in Göksun for the animals was a tiny low stable so hot and stifling that during the night the warmth brought Zippy's boil to breaking point. In the morning we found the abscess had burst. A streak of yellow pus was running down his side from a seeping split in the hump. When I touched the flesh, gobbets of blood and putrefaction gushed out, and poor Zippy went wild with the pain.

Now was the time to try to clean the wound and try to mend him, whatever the veterinary manual warned about the difficulties of curing such a deep-seated and major abscess without expert help. The manual had been written before the days of antibiotics, and if we could find the right drug we might be able to control the infection once the wound was thoroughly clean. The problem, of course, was that Zippy was hard to control. If anyone approached his painful withers, he spun about and lashed out with his heels. If Sarah held his head and picked up a hoof to immobilise him, he thrashed about frantically until he broke free, or circled around and crushed me against a post. But we had to clean out the wound at all costs and so we wrestled with him for half an hour with only partial success. The quantity of pus was appalling, and Sarah did well to prevent herself from throwing up at the sight. However much we worked, there still seemed to be more putrefaction to come out and, as the manual had warned, the position of the abscess made it virtually impossible to bring the poison upwards to the surface.

The logical solution was to turn Zippy upside down, or at least lie him flat, to get the discharge to drain. Tipping up our poor little brat required the help of two burly Turks and the horse-handling techniques of a carter who appeared with a soft, thick cotton rope. They stood Zippy in the yard, tied the rope around one hindfoot, and then led it diagonally forward to loop it around the opposite forefoot. Next they pulled smoothly on the rope until the hind front was drawn forward, and swiftly looped the rope tightly around the second forefoot. Zippy now stood balanced precariously on three legs. Then the horse-handler cast a turn of rope around the remaining free hindfoot and tugged. All four feet came together and Zippy bent at the knees and folded to the ground in much the same motion as a horse would normally lie down. A Turk dropped across him at each end, at head and tail, pinning him to the ground despite his athletic wriggles and heaves, and I was able to remove what seemed like a cupful more of pus from his abscess. When I was satisfied we had done the best we could, we let Zippy scramble back on his feet. He was rumpled, offended, and covered in dust and sported a black eye, but the relief from the constant pain was evident.

After a minute or so, he perked up and happily accepted an extra feed of barley. From a government veterinary depot for treating cattle we managed to obtain a course of antibiotic injections which we gave him for the next three days, and the cure gradually worked. For four days the wound stayed open, a deep hole as thick as a pencil, and we could hear the air whistling in and out of the cavity. We cleaned it half a dozen times a day, covered it with gauze to keep away the flies and for as long as possible avoided putting a saddle on his back. The hole gradually mended and, though there was a minor scare when a subsidiary boil swelled, we lanced that easily and by the time we entered Syria, our irrepressible pack pony was back to full health.

The simplest way to search for the *Gesta* knight's 'mountain of the Devil' was to ask the carters and hauliers of Göksun about the mountain roads on the way to Maraş, the Crusade's next stopover. They told me that everyone now used the modern highway which, for the most part, was an improved version of an old route through the mountains. But there was, they said, an even older, more direct path though it was 'cok sor', very difficult, and they were not at all sure it still remained open. If we wanted to test it we should seek the Söğütovası, the Vale of the Willows, and follow along it to the village of Çukurhisar. There we would cross a final ridge and rejoin the motor road. For the first ten miles the Söğütovası route seemed much too easy. We quickly identified the old caravan trail which took us over a col and into the Vale of the Willows. I wondered why the carters had been wary of the route, and checked our Ottoman maps. They too marked an animal track following the little river, and so we proceeded confidently. We saw no one, not even a farmer though there were one or two cultivated fields. It was evident that very few people came this way because the wild animals were not the least frightened. A pair of the large brown and white ducks, the same species as we had seen way back in Kovalcı, jumped from a patch of grass, and then circled around us again and again, quite unafraid. A large snake casually wriggled between the horses' legs as they stood in the little river to drink. Ahead was a tall rock wall that seemed to close off the end of the valley, though the river had to find some sort of passage through it because it flowed directly towards the rockface, before curling round a spur of rock and vanishing from our sight. As we approached the rock spur the footpath along the river bank petered out and we had to ride the horses into the river and once again use it as our trail. The situation seemed little different from the passage of the Anti-Taurus along the riverbed there, and as we turned the corner I fully expected to find a canyon to lead us through the ridge. We heard a roaring sound and I wondered if we would come upon another waterfall. Instead we rounded the corner, the horses belly deep in the stream, and found ourselves in a dead end. Ahead and to each side sheer cliffs rose to form a box canyon. In front of us the river ran straight towards the rock wall and then abruptly vanished. It dropped vertically down a great crak in the rock, a swallow hole. The roaring we heard was the sound of the water falling into a subterranean chasm. It was awesome and impressive, and it was a complete dead end.

Baffled, we turned the horses and retreated back up-river. I thought I had detected a goat track leading to the left up through a jumble of rocks. Leaving the horses with Sarah, I explored the track on foot. It was some sort of path, though very awkward with huge boulders and narrow gaps that an animal could only just squeeze through. Some herders had used it, for crossing a small natural amphitheatre in the naked rock, I noticed donkey droppings. On the far side of the amphitheatre the path seemed to continue. I scrambled between two large rocks and cautiously proceeded down a groove which had been cut with steps to prevent the traveller slipping on the naked rock and sliding downward as if on a fairground helter-skelter. The steps were very worn and treacherous, and in my iron-shod boots I felt extremely insecure. The last few yards I resorted to crawling carefully on hands and knees, and was glad I did so. I emerged at the very lip of a precipice and had a momentary sense of vertigo as I peered over the edge and found myself looking down at a nomad tent pitched in a rocky corrie perhaps 600 feet directly below me. If I had lobbed a pebble, it would have dropped right through the coarse brown cloth. Looking to left and right, I tried to spot the continuation of the footpath, but could not see anything that I would risk. The precipice fell away at each side, broken here and there by rock falls but seemingly unscalable. Yet the Ottoman map marked a footpath, and the carters in Göksun had told me that this was the track. If this was it, I decided, then it would take braver riders than Sarah and I to risk our necks on such a precipice. This had to be my best candidate for the Mountain of the Devil, but I was not going to kill our horses to pass across it.

I eased myself back from the edge of the cliff, and walked to where Sarah was waiting. 'We'll have to find another way out of the valley,' I told her. Away to our right, high up towards the crests we glimpsed the far dot of a human figure. It looked like a nomad woman picking her way through the scree. 'Let's try to catch up with her and ask if there's another way out of the valley.'

We urged our horses up the steep slope but were too late. By the time we were halfway up the mountainside the woman had vanished. Now we had no choice but to explore our own path out of the Söğütovası. It took us almost five hours of near-lethal travel. We picked our way through rocks, zig-zagging upwards towards another razor crest. As we clambered upward we worried that the horses would slip or twist and break their legs. Much of the time we had to dismount and lead them through the jumble of scree. It seemed inconceivable that we were on a travellers' path, and yet when we eventually reached the crest and found two makeshift shepherd bivouacs, we asked the way to Çukurhisar and the two women in the camp pointed straight down the mountainside as if it were a superhighway. I looked incredulously in the direction they pointed, and then saw what might just have been a section of goat track. Was that the right way? The two women nodded casually.

There was no question of riding even a yard of that track. So Sarah and I prepared to lead the horses down. The path was so narrow and tortuous that it was impossible to walk beside the horse's head. The only way was to go in front, holding the reins and scrambling downward, hoping that the horse would not slip and come slithering down on top of you. Zippy, of course, had to be turned loose. There was simply not enough room for him to walk beside either Szarcsa or Mystery. The only system was to let him find his own way down, hoping that he had the good sense to follow directly behind the other horses in the safe track. So we clambered downward, wobbling and slithering, grabbing rocks and tree roots to stop ourselves falling, flinching at the scrape and clatter of hooves directly behind us and occasionally dodging a large stone which a horse had dislodged and kicked down on us, as if to start a small rockslide. This was when the months of living constantly with the horses paid off. If the animals had not had total confidence in us, they would certainly not have gone down the mountain. They would have baulked, and with good reason. As it was, they followed us obediently, squeezing between the rocks, calm even when the stones began to slide away beneath their feet. It was an impressive display of their adroitness, for though Zippy was small and nimble and designed for mountain work, the other horses, and especially Szarcsa, were really too large and lanky for such conditions. Remembering Carty's spectacular agility in the mountains south of Iznik, I wondered if our huge Ardennes would have coped. It was just possible, but a large Crusader force with perhaps hundreds of horses of every sort and character, would have suffered heavy losses. If any of the army's Heavy Horses had survived this far, which was already unlikely due to the heat, the chances of their crossing that terrain were very remote. Then, too, I understood how the walking pilgrims must have felt: their shoes in tatters, legs trembling with tiredness, their only baggage whatever they could carry in their back packs because no wheeled vehicle could ever have used those paths. Winter was coming on, and – after more than a year on the road – there was no immediate prospect of reaching Jerusalem. Greed for plunder? Dream of empire? Neither had any relevance in those raw mountains. What kept them going, planting one foot wearily in front of the other, had to be something much more profound. It had to be their faith.

Sarah was superb. Gone was any trace of complaint or tiredness. She led the way confidently, without a moment of hesitation. I could only admire her courage and tenacity as she negotiated a path down the hazardous mountainside, occasionally murmuring encouragement to Szarcsa or swearing at him if he trod on her heel. I realised that when the going became tough, Sarah blossomed. When travelling was easy, Sarah had time to grouch, but if conditions became really exacting, she rose to the challenge. When we finally emerged into the far valley floor and found a village where we could stay the night, I realised that we had been on the gruelling trek for eight hours since leaving Göksun and that Sarah had never once faltered or been less than totally committed to finding our path across the mountains. I knew that I could not have had a more suitable colleague with whom to face the final 700 miles of the pilgrims' way to Jerusalem.

CHAPTER 22

Mystery's Death

The headman of Çukurhisar village was the least engaging of all the *muhtars* we met. He had a grumpily down-turned mouth under a small white moustache and, about 50 years old, was tall and thin, with a long sour face. Other *muhtars* had usually been rather jovial figures who ran their communites by consensus, or men of natural authority, but this new *muhtar* ruled by overt bullying. He was crusty and authoritarian, and given to shouting at the men who came to see him, so that their discussions degenerated into open quarrels, which seemed very strange to us after witnessing the usual smooth running of village politics. But then the valley of Çukurhisar was a peculiar place altogether. It was isolated and inward-looking, far off the normal track. Every winter it was cut off by snow, which usually came in late November, and the single road snaking over the pass then did not reopen until mid-April. For five months the valley and its half dozen villages were sealed off, and this may have accounted for the signs of in-breeding among the population, with their slightly grotesque features.

The winter blockade had obviously taught the inhabitants to husband all their resources, for nothing was wasted or thrown away. Every scrap or rag was kept stored, and even the thin plastic shopping bags were stitched up with thread when they ripped. There was a sense of claustrophobia and tension. The men went armed as they worked the fields, and that evening to our astonishment as the *muhtar* prepared for bed he made a point of taking down the official village rifle from its peg on the council-room wall and laying it beside his mattress. Only the three of us – Sarah, myself and the *muhtar* – were sleeping there, and he had already impressed us by taking off his trousers and revealing a dazzling set of boldly striped pyjama trousers underneath, which was apparently his normal underwear. The *muhtar* then rummaged into his small satchel and produced a dainty little automatic which he tucked under his pillow. Sarah and I looked at one another in wonder and she had just asked me, jokingly, whether I thought the *muhtar* was going to shoot a few croaking frogs if they disturbed him in the night, when there was a loud rifle shot from the valley. There was a flurry of alarm, with everyone running out and staring down into the valley before the household settled down for the evening.

My own opinion was that the most likely candidate to assassinate our host was his teenage son, whom his father openly humiliated before all the villagers. The boy had to fetch and carry his father's shoes, bring his food and clear the plates, fetch his cigarettes and lighter, and all the usual menial services, but the worst came at the end of the meal when the *muhtar* groped inside his mouth and pulled out his false teeth. These he handed to his son, peremptorily ordering him to wash and return them, whereupon they were stuffed back in his mouth.

We actually stayed two days with this unprepossessing figure, to give the horses an extra rest after the rigours of the mountain crossing, before we climbed our way out of the valley and back to the main road to Maraş. I now realised that when the First Crusade passed through the mountains, they were under pressure of time. Duke Godfrey and the others must have been told by the Armenian inhabitants that they had to hurry. The army was crossing the mountains in early October, and if they had dawdled and been trapped by the snow they would certainly have perished. It was imperative that they reached Marash with all speed, and then descended to the warmer lands of the Mediterranean coast before winter set in.

It was at Maraş that Duke Godfrey's sister-in-law Godehilde died. 'After her bodily ills had grown daily worse, and after being entrusted to Duke Godfrey, [she] breathed her last and was buried with Christian rites.' Wife of Baldwin, Godehilde was the most high-born of the women we know went on the great journey, and was probably worn out by its rigours. Albert describes her as English, but she seems to have been from an Anglo-Norman family with estates on both sides of the English Channel.

Today there is no trace in Maraş of Godehilde's tomb. Maraş is now an energetic, attractive city whose people seemed bent on enjoying life to the full. We arrived on a Sunday afternoon and met picnickers crammed into farm trailers, buses and a hazardous type of motorcycle sidecar much favoured in that locality. Strapped to the side of ancient motorcycles, these contraptions were carrying as many as ten passengers crammed one on top of the other, while in a single farm trailer I counted thirty people, jolting along with their plastic jerrycans of water and picnic baskets. When it began to rain, there were shrieks of laughter, the cavalcade halted to allow the women to pull plastic sheets over themselves while the men all jumped overboard and dived under the trailer for shelter. No one carried raincoats or umbrellas, and it was obvious that the showers could be guaranteed to be short and the rain warm. We had, we realised, entered another climatic region entirely. Platoons of combine harvesters were reaping the wheat, and at the edges of the villages golden and yellow cones of grain waited to be collected by the millers' lorries.

There were vineyards, too, and in them we surprised black snakes, five or six feet long, and of exceptionally nervous disposition. They would go streaking through the furrows of the vines at a tremendous pace, seeming to flow over the earth in sinuous panic and travelling as fast as our horses could canter. The villagers knew that the snakes were not poisonous, but if they trapped one they still stoned the animal to a wretched broken-backed death, citing a thoroughly medieval super-stition that if the animal became angry it could whip a man to death with its tail. In some of the villages the people were noticeably thinner and swarthier than the Anatolian Turks we had grown used to. We were passing through the fringe of the Kurdish speaking region, and the Kurdish men dressed in sombre black baggy pantaloons, jacket and flat cap, while most of the women hid inside the black *chador*.

On 16 June we reached the town of Islahiye, and in so doing had completed the summer transhumance in reverse, for this was the same town from which our acquaintances, the *yayla* nomads, started when they went up into the hills. In Islahiye we passed the holding yards and stockpens, now empty, where they gathered their sheep and cattle for dispatch to the markets of Saudi Arabia and the Near East. That night we had an idyllic campsite, high on the shoulder of a hill, under a fig tree where the farmer had terraced out a small ledge. Below us was a shallow artificial lake, and a stream issuing from a small cave in the hill slope behind us dropped down through the hollow shell of an ancient dead plane tree, and then trickled away through boggy soil to join the lake. As we sat on the ledge and watched the light fade, the owner of the field was driving in his flock. The animals climbed up the slope towards us, pausing to drink at the stream and nibble the bright green patch of grass on its banks. Then the shepherd was beside us, politely asking our news. He assured us we were welcome to stay, and before he collected up his flock and passed farther up the hillslope he sent his lad to fetch us branches of wild mulberry with the berries just ripe, and a sprig of flowers from a pomegranate tree.

The following evening we found ourselves a good campsite beside a river where a hillock would give us some shelter if the wind got up in the night, and three or four gnarled oak trees were arranged in a circle around the firestones of a shepherd's hearth. It was uncanny how from half a mile distant we were now able to identify the chance of a patch of flat land for our tent, a hint of grazing, the essential water supply and reasonable seclusion. Then, riding over, we would invariably find that we had selected a spot the shepherds already used, and discover the traces of their camp fires and the droppings of their flocks. It was a superb evening with the first bats skimming over the river to feed, a chorus of frogs, pale fawn and bright green, and the sun disappearing over the mountains to the west of us, leaving the ridge in smoky back lighting. It had been another excellent day's travel, more than twenty miles covered smoothly and comfortably for both horses and riders, and ahead lay the agreeable prospect of level riding along the valley to Antioch.

We awoke at five-thirty to a brilliant dawn and the promise of a splendid day, warm and clear. But as I opened the tent flap, I found Mystery lying on the ground beside the picket rope, and she was very sluggish rising to her feet. We fed the horses from their nosebags, and noticed that Mystery would not touch her food. Nor did she drink water when offered it from the canvas bucket. Sarah was worried, but not unduly. She suspected that Mystery had some sort of colic, perhaps had eaten something that disagreed with her digestion. Her droppings from the previous evening were unusual, irregular and small, and covered with a slimy mucus. Sarah groomed the horses as usual while I struck camp, and we loaded the animals. Everything was routine, except for Mystery's lack of energy. But she had been off her food on previous occasions, and recovered after a day or so. So we dawdled, giving Mystery time to perk up, and it was not until almost 9 am that we finally left the camp. In the first hundred yards I noticed that Mystery was walking in a daze. Gradually she fell behind the others horses. I was puzzled. Normally Mystery insisted anxiously on staying close to the other two, and would never allow herself to become separated. Now Sarah found Mystery's indifference to the other horses much more worrying than anything else. Rolling back the little mare's eyelid, she was dismayed to find that the white of the eye was a deep pink. We agreed that we would walk the horses at Mystery's slow pace, and not hurry her. But it was difficult. Mystery just went slower and slower and Szarcsa, going his normal pace, began to whinny as if urging her to catch up. By then I no longer felt I should be a weight on Mystery's back. I slipped out of the saddle and walked slowly alongside her as she plodded forward. She barely seemed to notice whether I was there or not.

Two miles down the road we arrived at a small village where there was a drinking trough. Szarcsa and Zippy bustled forward and drank eagerly. But when Mystery was led forward for her turn, she just stood and lowering her head to the water, barely wetted her lips. Sarah and I feared that if she had a colic, it was a very bad one and needed help. We kept a small bottle of liquid paraffin in the saddlebags for just such an eventuality, so we filled the barrel of the plastic hypodermic syringe which we used to administer Zippy's anti-biotics. Sarah held open the little mare's jaws, while I shot a jet of the paraffin down her throat. After five or six squirts, followed by massaging of her neck, we judged we had got a sensible dose into Mystery, though it was a messy business and we were oily to the elbows. If she was suffering from a severe colic, then the wise course was to keep her walking and not let her lie down. So we proceeded down the road at a snail's pace. Once again, the horses became separated, and Mystery fell farther and farther behind. She seemed to be semiconscious. Half a mile ahead Szarcsa would stop and keep looking back, and keep calling. Mystery never acknowledged him.

The weather was perfect, and the road should have been a pleasure. We were travelling parallel to the foothills of a long, low mountain ridge to our right. A chain of villages was strung along the highway, set back a little distance from the road. On each side were fields and orchards, and an occasional copse of trees for shade. Every time we came to a stream we tried to coax Mystery to drink. But she only played with the water with her lips, and a sheen of paraffin oil floated away, mixed with flecks of white foam. Now Sarah and I began to fear that Mystery had been poisoned, perhaps by some chemical on a plant that she had eaten. But in that case, why had the other two horses not been affected? Rolling back her eyelid again we noted that there was no longer any white to the eye at all. The entire surround was now a vivid bloodshot red.

At five o'clock I decided that we should stop early for the night. In the eight hours since we had left camp, we had walked for perhaps five. The rest of the time we had been at a standstill to treat Mystery or simply to rest her in the shade. We had covered less than seven miles. To our right was a very promising campsite where a fast-flowing stream had cut a gulley into the hillside. It was a lovely spot, with the rushing water, a picturesque jumble of rocks, and oleanders blossoming pink along the sides of the gulley. On the opposite bank was a patch of grass beside some bushes. Sarah, leading Zippy, rode Szarcsa down the bank, through the ford and up the other side. Mystery dutifully followed. To keep my feet dry I got back into the saddle as Mystery stepped into the rushing water. I halted her, hoping she would drink, or that the flow of cool water on her legs would do her good. But again she refused to drink, and I noticed she was trembling. After a short pause Mystery heaved herself up the opposite bank, and I dismounted. Sarah helped me to remove the saddle and then we led Mystery to a soft patch, free of rocks and stones where she could lie down. I had not even had time to take off the extra saddle pad from Mystery's back when the mare folded up at the knees and sank to the ground. Sarah noticed the glands behind Mystery's jaw. They had swollen up grotesquely, like half-inflated balloons.

'That's no stomach illness,' she said anxiously, 'We have to fetch a vet.'

She hurried away, down the rocky stream bank and off on the side road to get a ride into the nearest town. What sort of vet she would find, we could not guess but we knew there was no hope of finding someone skilled in treating horses. Veterinary horse specialists simply did not exist in that part of the world.

After Sarah had gone, I returned to the stream with a canvas bucket to try to fetch water for Mystery. By the time I had struggled back up the bank with the water, Mystery was lying flat on the ground, not on her stomach as she usually rested, but laid out quite horizontal, oblivious that her outstretched neck was resting on a sharp boulder. I got behind her and began to prise away the boulder to give her extra room. Mystery tried to rise, but made a mess of it. She simply did not have the strength to lever herself upright, and kept on trying pitifully. She came to a halt, half upright, her head twisted sadly down towards her stomach. To ease her, I gently pressed her flat again, then found her body blanket and laid it over her to keep her warm. Zippy and Szarcsa were hungry and bored, and growing restless, and I went to check their tethers. As I did so, I heard a commotion and turned to see Mystery trying once more to get back on her feet. But this time as she lost strength, her front legs buckled under her in an awful, ugly, way as she fell back in an ungainly heap. I knew then that something was terribly wrong. I had never seen a dying horse, Carty lying motionless in Yugoslavia while he regained his strength had been quite different from this piteous heaving and struggling, and I knew that Mystery was an animal who would never give up. She had shown the most powerful tenacity all the way through Europe and Turkey. Whether it was a cut foot or a pain in the gut, Mystery never faltered. Remzi had said, rightly, she was a horse with a great heart. Now it was clear that though her spirit was still there, as determined as ever, there was no strength or control left over her body.

I ran back to her as she tried once more to rise, and encouraged and coaxed her, but it was hopeless. She did not even get as far as her previous effort, and flopped back once more on the ground. I fetched more water and crouched by her head with the canvas bucket. She put her mouth in the bucket, but once again was unable to drink. Her head slumped back, and the best I could do was dab water on the tongue. Suddenly all four legs shot straight out rigid, and she gave a tremendous convulsion with her whole body, as though her entire belly was writhing. I recalled Sarah's words back in central Turkey when Zippy gave a similar kick as he lay exhausted on the stable floor at the end of a long day. She had said that a dying horse gave that sort of kick, and joked that Zippy must have read the veterinary manual. But brave little Mystery was no Zippy with his play-acting. Mystery really was dying. Her entire gut seemed to be heaving and convulsing, and in desperation I tried to massage it as I had seen the Turkish farmer do with Zippy.

'Come on! Come on! Good girl now, good girl.' I dabbed more water on her tongue. But it was now lolling out of the side of her mouth and there were flecks of dried foam on her lips. Her huge liquid eyes were totally blank. Suddenly there came another heaving convulsion, then snorts and whistling sounds in her throat. I knew that she was going very, very fast. An ear flickered. I put my hand to her muzzle – by now I was on my knees beside her – and felt barely any breath. I reached for her heartbeat and found only a tiny tremor. By the time I put my hand back to her muzzle there was no breath left to stir the fine hairs by the nostrils. Mystery was dead, struck down barely twelve hours after showing the first symptoms of sickness.

I was numbed and distracted as I rose to my feet. A part of my mind was firmly telling me that the loss of a horse was understandable, that the Crusaders had lost horses and continued, and that I had always known there was this risk. But another part of my mind was asking – why had it to be Mystery, our best and most gallant horse which had died? I had never once imagined that *she* was the one who would perish. She had always seemed too strong, too hardy, to break down. I had a vivid flashback to the day when I had stood in an Irish bog on a rainswept day and selected a woolly-looking little mare from Donie O'Sullivan's herd of trekking ponies. I blamed myself for bringing Mystery from such ideal surroundings to die in the mountains of Eastern Turkey. How would Donie react or feel when he heard that his horse had died, and above all, what would Remzi feel? Remzi had adored that little Irish horse and lavished affection on her. He would be very deeply distressed. Also I was appalled at the speed of Mystery's death. Was there anything else we could have done to save her? What disease had struck her down so quickly, in less than ten hours? I remembered the hundreds of miles she had led the way, from Chateau Bouillon all the distance across Eastern Europe, setting the pace for Carty and travelling tirelessly. It was so typical that she had walked on, even to the very end without a falter. For several minutes I remained standing there despondently, sensing that something irreplaceable had been lost.

Only then did I understand that Mystery's death had broken a link, a break that obliged me to rethink my view of why we were travelling. Neither of the horses that had set out from Chateau Bouillon would go the entire distance of the First Crusade. Carty was now happily ensconced on his Austrian farm; Mystery's corpse lay stretched beside a Turkish stream. Up to that point, I realised, I had been thinking of the expedition largely in terms of the horses. Contrary to the experience of the Crusaders who had lost horses and replaced them with remounts bought or captured as they proceeded, I had thought of the horses, Sarah and myself as an indissoluble team which would try to go all the way, equal partners. It had been muddled thinking: I had always suspected that Carty would have to be retired from the journey before it became too much for him. So unconsciously I used Mystery as the symbol of the entire achievement of a horseback journey to Jerusalem. Rashly I had planned ahead, and imagined her living out the rest of her life on a horse farm in Israel. Indeed I had already made arrangements for her to be placed with a trekking centre near the Sea of Galilee. There, I intended, she would be petted as the horse that had walked from Europe, be cared for and valued, and free to carry on the work she was accustomed to. Mystery was no splendid thoroughbred, though she had suspect registration papers that claimed she was. She was just a perfect family horse, gentle and willing, and her death brought home to me the fact that our journey was not so much to do with horses, as it was about the people who had set out on the great endeavour, whether the pilgrims and knights or, centuries later, Sarah and myself.

And how would Sarah react when she learned that Mystery was dead? One thing was sure. Neither of us would want to spend the night near Mystery's corpse. So I untied Szarcsa and Zippy and led them away. They had to edge past Mystery's body where it lay across the footpath to the ford, and although Zippy did not seem to mind, Szarcsa fidgeted nervously and twitched his nostrils as he passed the corpse. I took the horses back across the stream and down to a bare, bleak campsite on an exposed patch of scrubland. Automatically I hammered in the picket pins, and put up the tent. All the while Szarcsa kept whinnying plaintively, circling his picket pin at the length of his rope, and looking back up the slope to where he had last seen Mystery.

One hour later Sarah arrived. She had found two vets and brouth them back to attend to a sick horse. When she saw Zippy and Szarcsa and the little tent, she halted their car. I walked across the field, wondering how to break the news. But I think she half-guessed from the look on my face.

'Where's Mystery?' she asked.

'I'm afraid she died soon after you left. I'm sorry.'

Sarah turned abruptly, a little quick movement, and put her hands over her face in distress. For a moment or two she stood there, turned away and head down, then she straightened up. The two vets were watching us. They must have realised what had happened. 'I want to have a look at Mystery's body,' Sarah said firmly.

'Are you sure? There's no need,' I asked hesitantly.

'Yes,' Sarah replied, 'we've got to try to find out what killed her. For our own information as well as to be able to check on the other two horses. They might have the same problem.'

But the vets could tell us nothing. They did not have experience of treating horses, and though they tried their best, they had no notion of a diagnosis. The horse they pronounced had died of an 'infection'. I asked if it was possible to arrange an autopsy, just in case Mystery had contracted a contagious disease which might show up in Zippy and Szarcsa. But the vets smiled apologetically. An autopsy was out of the question. The nearest laboratory was in Ankara and the results would take months to prepare, by which time we would probably be outside Turkey. They were polite and courteous but clearly puzzled by all this fuss over a dead horse. Horses died, and that was a matter of everyday life. The corpse should be buried, they said, but the local villagers would arrange that. Was there anything else they could do? I thanked them, and they were driven back to town.

In silence, Sarah and I went about the routine chores of the campsite. I suppose it was a sign of just how close we had become, how well we understood one another, that within half an hour I was able to say to her, without any sense of intrusion, that if the loss of Mystery meant that she wanted to give up the expedition and return home, I would quite understand. Though I had ridden Mystery for all the summer, it was Sarah who had the real empathy with the horses, understood them, cared for them and cared about them. In the past she might have cuffed Mystery and complained about her lack of brains, but it was Sarah who at every opportunity showed kindness and concern for the mare, fed her titbits, petted her, chatted to her, scratched under her chin. If she now felt the price was too high for our journey, she had every right to go home. Her reply meant a great deal to me. 'No, not at all,' she said, 'Mystery's death has only made me all the more determined to go on. I think that if we had gone straight through last year, and not stopped for the winter, Mystery would probably have been the only horse to make it. The others would not have kept up the pace, but Mystery could have done it. Now I want to go on and make the whole journey if we possibly can.' Then she added, 'Remember, we've always done the best for the horses. We've always put them first.' It was the most consoling remark she could have made.

We spent a miserable sleepless night, each thinking silently about Mystery and listening to Szarca's whinnies which continued long after dark. In the morning I contacted my Turkish family to arrange for a driver to bring the jeep to collect Mystery's saddle and the extra kit. The plan had already been for the jeep to take back to Istanbul our spare equipment as we left Turkey to go into Syria, and now the driver was able to escort us the day and a half's ride into Antioch, while we took it in turns to ride Szarcsa. We stopped off at the vet's house to collect a death certificate which we might need to show to Turkish customs at the border when we left the country. On the certificate the cause of death was stated as 'acute bronchitis', but this was an obvious fiction, and try as we might, we could not identify a realistic cause. Even the chief regional vet was vague when I went to see him at the border veterinary control centre. Could it have been African Horse Sickness? I asked. What would have been the symptoms?

'There's only one symptom for that disease,' he answered flatly, 'rapid death.'

It seemed that there was no known prevention nor cure. So for the next month Sarah and I continued to fuss over Szarcsa and Zippy, anxiously checking to see if they showed any of the same warning signs as Mystery before she died. But they did not, and it was only several months later, back in Ireland, that I learned the most likely cause of Mystery's sudden demise was an acute intestinal disorder or blockage. So ironically it turned out that the paraffin we had squirted down her throat was the best chance we could have given her with our limited resources. It made me feel a little better that the manner of Mystery's death probably had nothing to do with her great journey that had taken us 2000 miles, four-fifths of the way from Duke Godfrey's castle to Jerusalem.

CHAPTER 23

The Siege of Antioch

Antioch was to provide the major trauma of the entire Crusade. The great leaders – Godfrey, Bohemond, Raymond, the two Roberts, Stephen of Blois, Hugh of Vermandois and Bishop Adhémar – agreed that the capture of the city was vital. If left alone, its Turkish garrison would harass the Christians in their winter quarters, and be poised to take them in the rear should Muslim armies arrive from the east. To the ordinary pilgrims, however, Antioch was simply one of the three holiest cities of Christendom, along with Jerusalem and Rome, and it was unthinkable to leave it in infidel hands. St Peter's original see had been Antioch and had preached here in a cave used as a temporary chapel. He had coined a new name for those who believed in the teachings of Christ, previously called 'Nazarenes', had been described for the first time as 'Christians'. St Luke was a native of Antioch and it was here he had written the Acts of the Apostles. As a result of its long association with the foundation and spread of Christianity the place had more than its fair share of Christian churches and monasteries, the most important of which the Turks had blasphemously converted into mosques. So in some ways the capture and liberation of Antioch was a dress rehearsal for the relief of Jerusalem itself.

Every effort was put in hand for its capture. By late October 1098 the main army was approaching the city, which lies a few miles inland from the northeastern corner of the Mediterranean. The Christians needed every soldier and every horse that could be mustered, so the roving captains – Tancred and the others – were called in to swell the ranks of the main army. Only Baldwin, far away in Edessa, was allowed to stand aside. No one doubted that the Turks would defend Antioch fiercely.

The Host camped a mile from the city walls and took stock of their situation. Even from that distance the city's defences were awesome. Antioch's perimeter wall was said to contain 360 towers, nearly one for every day in the year, and within its circumference enough room to pasture the warhorses of a small army. Immediately behind the city rose Mount Silpius, a rocky peak which was incorporated into the defences and crowned with a citadel that was claimed with some justification to be impossible to storm. Even the sight of the stiff climb to the summit was enough to take one's breath away. From the mountain-top citadel the boundary wall followed the ridge eastward, and was carried across a narrow gorge to the neighbouring peak. From there it dropped spectacularly down the mountainside almost to the bank of the river Orontes and turned to run parallel to the river, at times built right on the bank so the Orontes would serve as a natural moat. This massive wall was made of 'huge stones held together with an unknown and unbreakable mortar' and it continued until it completed the circle by climbing the slope of the mountain back up to the citadel.

Compared to Antioch's defences, Nicaea was an open city, and it had taken the army, when it was fresh and much more numerous, six weeks to capture Nicaea. Little wonder that there was some talk among the Crusaders that it would be wiser to leave the siege of Antioch until the following spring, when the army had rested and 'the horses also would be improved by the winter's rest and feeding.' William of Tyre, who like the other chroniclers habitually over-estimated all numbers, calculated that of seventy or eighty thousand horses that had set out, only two thousand were left alive by the time the army reached Antioch. And that included mounts captured after successful engagements like the battle of Dorylaeum. More realistically, it has been calculated that the cavalry had perhaps 200 horses left, and that in the bloody battles under the walls of Antioch most of the knights walked into the fighting. Others, William observed, rode asses and mules for want of chargers.

But the leaders themselves still retained enough confidence after their victories against the Turks to reject the notion of any delay. They wanted to finish the affair before the Muslims counterattacked from Aleppo or Damascus, so the war council ordered siege positions to be taken up without delay. The Christians were puzzled that 'the blare of horns, the neighing of horses, and the crash of arms intermingled with the shouts of men', produced no reaction whatsoever from the Turkish garrison. 'An utter silence prevailed in the city. Not a sound or noise of any kind was heard from it.' Antioch might as well have been empty of defenders.

Yaghi Siyan, the Turkish governor, was watching to see how the besiegers would spread themselves. It was physically impossible for the Christians to surround the city, even ignoring the lofty Mount Silpius side which was too rugged to blockade. Instead the Franks decided they had enough manpower to invest just three gates and the northeast quadrant of the wall. Bohemond, who for his own reasons was the most enthusiastic to prosecute the siege, took up the key position facing the Gate of St Paul from which issued the Aleppo Road. To his right were the Northern French contingents led by Robert of Normandy and the Count of Vermandois, together with Robert of Flanders and Stephen of Blois – who watched over the Gate of the Dog. Next to them came the Provençals of Raymond of Toulouse and Bishop Adhémar. Finally, clustered around the gate which would later be called the 'Gate of the Duke' in his honour, were the 'Lotharingians, Frisians, Swabians, Saxons, Franks and Bavarians' of Duke Godfrey. Two other gates, the Gate of St George which faced west and the main river gate, the Gate of the Bridge, where a stone bridge crossed the Orontes, were left largely unattended.

The siege, at first, seemed more like an autumn holiday than a serious endeavour of war. As October passed into November, the footsore army was relieved to sit down and rest. The surroundings of Antioch were renowned for their fertility. Indeed the Orontes plain even shipped corn to Egypt in times of famine. 'We found there every abundance', said the *Gesta* knight. 'Vines full everywhere, pits full of grain, trees bent down with fruit, and many other goods useful for the body.' There were so many herds of cattle that the soldiers were not bothered to eat more than the finest cuts of meat, and threw away the rest. Others felled the orchards to make palisades to protect the camps, and the horses were given fodder without any regard for future needs.

Such prodigality could not long be sustained, and within weeks the army was having to send out the first detachments to scavenge. This was the development that Yaghi Siyan had been waiting for. The Christians' programme was altogether too slack and unhurried. They made no serious attempt to storm the walls – the task was far too daunting and there had not been enough time to construct any siege weapons – and they were even allowing detachments of Turks to emerge from the city and use the stone bridge, at first stealthily but then openly. To cross the river themselves without having to use the stone bridge, which was too exposed to enemy sorties, the Christians had lashed together a pontoon bridge of boats across the Orontes near Duke Godfrey's camp. The Turkish commander picked the day that a large force of Christians, cavalry and infantry, was observed to go off to search the countryside for food. As usual they divided into small foraging parties, and, accustomed to being left unmolested, were off guard when a strong Turkish detachment boldly crossed the stone bridge and fell upon them.

In panic the Christians ran back to the bridge of boats, hoping to cross to the comparative safety of their camp. But the pontoons were too narrow to carry the stampeding throng, and many men were pushed or jostled into the water and were drowned. By this time the knights in camp had been alerted and organised a counterattack. Hurrying to the stone bridge, they managed to intercept the Turks returning with the booty seized from the Christian foragers. As the Turks were fighting their way steadily towards the city gate, they were reinforced by the townsfolk who unbarred the gate and poured out to their help. The knights were surprised by the ferocity of the attack and were themselves driven back towards the bridge of boats. Once again there was a great deal of tumult and shoving, so that

some of the knights also, while fleeing from the pursuing foe, became so jammed together on the bridge, that they were thrown headlong into the river. Burdened with shields, breastplates, and helmets, they were swallowed up with their horses by the waters and never again appeared.

The other point of danger was the Gate of the Dog, built over a marshy patch where a small stream issued from under the city wall. The defenders had a habit of suddenly throwing open this gate, rushing across the bridge that spanned the marsh, and loosing off an arrow storm at Count Raymond's troops who were camped nearby. These impromptu attacks caused so many casualties among the Provençals that the first idea was to destroy the bridge. A call went out for mallets and iron implements, and equipped with these tools a demolition party of mailed knights went on to the bridge and attempted to prise it apart. But 'the solid masonry, harder than any iron, offered effective resistance. The citizens [of Antioch] also hindered their attempts by hurling forth stone missiles and showers of arrows.' The knights' next scheme was to close the bridge with a stout wooden tower that would be constantly garrisoned by men-at-arms. This mini-fort was constructed with great labour and hauled forward under the usual rain of rocks and darts from the city walls. But once again the Christians had underestimated the verve and dash of the defenders. The Turks launched a brisk counter-attack, surged right up to the mobile tower, and set it alight, burning it to ashes. Foiled yet again, the Provençals drew off and came up with their third plan. This time they stationed three 'engines', stone- or dart-throwing machines, in such a way as to sweep the bridge and keep up a bombardment on the city gate itself. For a while the plan worked, and as long as the machines kept up their fire, no citizen dared sortie from Antioch. But as soon as the fire slackened, when the operators lost interest or ran out of projectiles, the sorties began all over again. In exasperation Count Raymond's troops finally decided that there was nothing for it but to eliminate the gate entirely. Under covering fire from the 'machines,' the armoured knights assisted by ordinary footsoldiers rolled up huge rocks and tree turnks and piled such a mass of them against the gate that it was no longer usable.

But this was no more than self-protection. The Christians were meant to be on the attack but were behaving more and more as if they were on the defensive, and soon the inevitable shortage of food heightened this back-to-front version of a siege. Hunger began to afflict, not the Turks safe inside Antioch with their prepared stocks of provisions, but the profligate Franks outside the city walls. When the nearby countryside had been swept clean and the foraging parties had to go farther and farther afield to find increasingly meagre spoils, they were exposed to ambushes set by Turkish guerrillas. Resentment grew against the local Christians of the region, Syrians and Armenians, who profited from the army's distress by selling their produce at vastly inflated prices. Unable to find enough money, some of the poorer pilgrims died of starvation.

The army's pavilions and tents were rotting, and gave little protection from the heavy rain showers and penetrating cold. Some of the Europeans had fondly imagined that a Mediterranean winter would be mild and sunny in those regions, but by mid-December they were rudely disabused. 'Winter here is exactly the same as our winter in the West', wrote Stephen of Blois glumly to his wife. Pilgrims and soldiers had scarcely anywhere dry to sleep or keep their baggage. Their clothes, as well as the precious food, went mouldy. The camps became muddy quagmires. A pestilence broke out, and men and women, already weakened by famine and cold, died in such great numbers that 'there was scarcely room to bury the dead, nor could funeral rites be performed.'

Not surprisingly, the army began to melt away. Some fled because they feared the plague. Others simply lost heart. They headed towards Baldwin's fortress at Edessa or found their way down to the coast where – the only ray of hope in the general gloom – Christian ships had begun to appear.

But even the short trip to St Simeon, Antioch's port, was made dangerous by Turkish ambushes. Nor was it just the common folk who were absconding. William Carpenter, the high-born Viscount of Melun, quietly made off. Incredibly, Peter the Hermit went with him, the original fanatic preacher of the Crusade who had survived the massacre of the Peasants' Crusade and had attached himself to the grand enterprise. When their absence was discovered, Tancred was sent after them with his cavalry, and the runaways were overtaken and brought back in disgrace.

Then, early in February 1098 Tatikos, the Byzantine general, left. It is not clear whether he went because he thought the Christian cause was hopeless, or whether he wished to report to Emperor Alexius in person, or even whether he had been persuaded to go by Bohemond who wanted him out of the way. Whatever his reasons for leaving, Tatikos's departure had two effects: it served to encourage the flow of deserters from the camp, and it forfeited any last shred of loyalty that the westerners might still have held for the imperial cause.

Day by day conditions in the camp worsened. Life became dominated by a frantic search for food. 'The famished,' wrote Fulcher of Chartres, 'ate the shoots of beanseeds growing in the fields and many kinds of herbs unseasoned with salt, also thistles which, being not well cooked because of the lack of firewood, pricked their tongues.' The most

The siege of Antioch: Bohemond admonishes Peter the Hermit for attempting to abandon the cause.

desperate ate the skins of dogs and rats, and even picked out the undigested grains from animal droppings. As famine gnawed deeper and pestilence spread, a sense of hysteria took over. The appalling conditions were identified as God's punishment for the sins of the pilgrims. An earthquake, followed by a blood red sunset, were interpreted as signs of God's wrath. The pilgrims believed that they had forfeited His grace by their immorality. So if the Host was to be saved, it must make amends for its ungodly ways. By common consent a strict regime of penitence was devised. The camp prostitutes were expelled, and 'adultery and fornication of every description was forbidden under penalty of death, and an interdict was placed on all revelling and intoxication.' The ban extended to all 'dangerous games of chance, heedless oaths, fraud in weights and measures, chicanery of every kind, theft and rapine.' The measures were formally approved by Bishop Adhémar in his capacity as the Pope's legate, and special judges were appointed to enforce them with full powers of investigation and punishment. The one act of atonement which no one would have found difficult to observe was the call for a three-day fast so 'that, by scourging the body, they might strengthen their souls for more effective prayer.' As there was hardly any food to be had, this not only made a virtue from necessity, but was a novel way of rationing. Without a trace of irony, William of Tyre recounted that the effect of the fasting and abstinence of the army was that

Lord Godfrey who was, as it were, the one and only prop of the whole army, at once began to recover fully from the serious illness which had long troubled him, the result of a wound which he suffered from a bear in the vicinity of Antioch-in-Pisidia. His convalescence was a source of the greatest consolation to the entire army in their affliction.

This despairing reversion to their original high-minded ideals is one of the most striking developments in the story of the First Crusade. Since the original departure from their homes, there had been comparatively little evidence of extreme religious fervour as the host trudged across Europe to Constantinople, then on into Anatolia. Even the ordeals of the mountains and the crossing of the deserts had been borne without any undue calls for heavenly assistance. But now, unnerved by the steadily deteriorating conditions at Antioch, the travellers turned back to their religion for salvation and comfort. Significantly, their reformation took place at a time when several of their leaders were devising ways to reap more worldly rewards from the Crusade.

The siege of Antioch was the darkest hour of the Crusade and also its most glorious memory. It was described by every major chronicler, and their reports became the grist for all manner of ballads and stories. The suffering and eventual victory at Antioch were to be legendary. Those who came out of the ordeal well, were to join the pantheon of heroes. Those who failed or deserted were to be execrated for ever. It was here that Duke Godfrey's reputation as the peerless leader and perfect knight took hold.

Bohemond was cast by the storytellers as the warrior chief, crafty and ruthless. Bohemond's genius as a field commander was crucial. He had been complaining that he was running out of money and would have to withdraw from the expedition, and to appease him the other leaders gave him more authority on the battlefield, with immediate results. The Muslim ruler of Aleppo, Ridwan, assembled a relief force and in early

February had sent it to within fourteen miles of Antioch before it was detected. Every active knight in the Christian camp was mustered, and they rode out to meet the enemy, leaving the infantry to guard the camp. Each major leader led his own column of knights into the engagement but Bohemond was allotted the strategic reserve and decided the outcome of battle. Just as the Christian line began to buckle, Bohemond ordered his standard bearer to charge into the thick of the fighting. According to the *Gesta* knight:

That man, fortified on all sides with the sign of the Cross, went into the lines of the Turks, just as a lion, famished for three or four days, goes forth from his cave raging and thirsting for the blood of beasts. So violently did he press upon them that the tips of his renowned standard flew over the heads of the Turks. Moreover, as the other lines saw that the standard of Bohemond was gloriously borne before them, they went back to the battle again, and with one accord our men attacked the Turks who, all amazed, took to flight.

The Turks set fire to their own camp to prevent it falling into enemy hands so the loot was meagre, but the victorious knights did return to camp with some food and, equally important, a large number of remounts. To advertise their success to the disappointed garrison of Antioch, the heads of 200 Turks were impaled on stakes to face the city walls.

An Egyptian envoy who had been visiting the Christian camp and wished to return down the ambush-infested road to the port at St Simeon. The plan was that the escorting troops led by Bohemond and Raymond would then bring back additional supplies and escort new pilgrims who had arrived by sea to join the Host. Word reached camp that the supply column had been ambushed. Everywhere was consternation and doubt. No one knew whether any of the column had survived and whether both Bohemond and Count Raymond were lost. Duke Godfrey, fully restored to health, promptly instructed the herald to sound the general alarm. The entire army had to report for duty – any shirkers were threatened with death – and was divided into columns under the Duke of Normandy, the Count of Flanders, and Hugh of Vermandois. Duke Godfrey had just delivered the usual encouraging speech to the troops when Bohemond and Raymond both straggled in, to be greeted with immense relief. They approved of Godfrey's plan, which was essentially to repay the Turks in kind by setting an ambush for them along their return road to the city.

They were almost too late. The returning Turks showed up before the army was fully in position, and a furious hand-to-hand combat took place right under the city walls as the Turks tried to get back across the stone bridge. A gallery of spectators, the women and wives of Antioch, looked down from the walls. In this tournament atmosphere all the barons naturally performed splendid deeds of valour as far as the chroniclers were concerned and there was a great slaughter of the enemy all around the approaches to the bridge. But Duke Godfrey excelled. As the exhausted enemy were jostling to get back in through the gate which Yaghi Siyan had opened, the Duke performed a deed which was to become renowned in story and ballad.

Toward evening in the struggle around the bridge, he [the Duke] gave a notable proof of the strength for which he was so distinguished. . . . With his usual prowess he had already decapitated many a mailed knight at a single stroke. Finally, he boldly pursued another knight, and though the latter was protected by a breastplate, clove him through the middle. The upper part of the body above the waist fell to the ground, while the lower part was carried along into the city astride his galloping horse.

'This strange sight,' said William, recognising the birth of a legend, 'struck fear and amazement to all who witnessed it. The marvellous feat could not remain unknown, but rumour spread the story everywhere.' William was writing within the lifetime of men who had fought at the battle of Antioch, and even if the tremendous swordstroke was entirely imaginary, Duke Godfrey's reputation as the doughty warrior of Christ was assured.

That night and during the following day while the Christians celebrated their victory, burial parties crept out from Antioch to gather up the corpses of the Turkish dead and inter them in the Muslim cemetery opposite the Gate of the Bridge. It was wasted effort. The Christians decided to build a watch tower, long overdue, facing the Gate of the Bridge, and the masons pillaged the Muslim cemetery for materials, using the gravestones in the construction. The fresh graves were robbed by the soldiers, looking for jewels, weapons and gold buried with the slain, unashamed to loot infidel graves.

The skirmish: Crusader knights defeating Saracens in hand-to-hand combat.

The tide was at last beginning to turn in favour of the Franks. On payment of one hundred marks in silver, Tancred was commissioned to build a third watchtower opposite St George's Gate and make sure that no one went in or out. Now the only gate available to the garrison was a small postern which led out through a narrow defile between Mount Silpius and the adjacent peak. Though the Christians had, more or less, blockaded the city and cowed the garrison, they were no nearer to capturing Antioch. There had not been a single direct assault since the day they had taken up their positions. There had been no attempt to mine the walls or break in the gates. The defences of Antioch, among the most up-to-date in the Levant, had not been scratched.

It was left to Bohemond, once again, to devise the masterplan. Perhaps remembering the Byzantine success at suborning the garrison of Nicaea, Bohemond made contact with a disaffected captain of one of the city watchtowers, Firuz. He seems to have been a renegade Armenian Christian who had converted to Islam, but was prepared to betray his

Antioch: (left) a messenger from the traitor Firuz offers to hand over the city to Bohemond; and (right) pack trains re-supply beleaguered Antioch.

section of the wall in exchange for money and a gift of land. First, however, Bohemond called a meeting of the army council and suggested that whoever managed to arrange the capture of Antioch would be given the city. The other leaders were outraged. All had laboured for the city's fall, they said, all should share in its capture. But reports then reached them that a large Muslim army under the command of Kerbogha, Atabeg of Mosul, and was marching to the relief of Antioch. After wasting three weeks unsuccessfully besieging Baldwin in Edessa, Kerbogha's army had regrouped, picked up reinforcement from Aleppo and Damascus and was now closing in on Antioch. If the Christians failed to capture Antioch in the next few days, they would be caught between Kerbogha and the Turkish garrison and crushed. Faced with imminent and total disaster, the other leaders with the exception of Raymond were forced to agree to Bohemond's suggestion – always provided Emperor Alexius did not come to their aid – and he revealed his plan to take the city by treachery.

So came the most glamorous and daring episode of the campaign. The entire Christian army made a great show of marching out of camp as if to go off to meet Kerbogha but after setting off along the Aleppo road, it doubled back after nightfall and in the early hours of the morning was in new positions close under the city wall. Bohemond and a hand-picked band of sixty knights, including the *Gesta* knight, who reported on the whole adventure, crept their way to the base of the section of the wall commanded by Firuz. He had charge of a key post known as the Tower of the Two Sisters, and since Antioch's perimeter was so long, it was impossible for Yaghi Siyan to supervise all his sector captains all of the time. Bohemond's knights placed a single ladder against the wall, and most of the raiding party scrambled up, among them Bohemond himself and, according to some of the more colourful accounts, Duke Godfrey and the Count of Flanders. In the darkness and hurry the ladder was overloaded and broke. For one appalling moment the raiders were nonplussed. They were penned up on the parapet, and unable to descend into the city. Luckily someone found a small gate on their left which they broke open and were able to go down into Antioch. Raising a great clamour they charged down to the main gates, killing anyone in their path, and opened the city to the rest of the army.

The exulting Christians poured in and spread throughout the street, running into the buildings and putting Muslims to the sword. Some of the garrison managed to flee up the mountain and into the citadel on Mount Silpius where they bolted the gate and were safe. Another band of Turks trying to ride out over the steep crags by the northern canyon, were so hotly pursued that they were driven over the cliffs to their deaths. 'Our joy over the fallen enemy was great,' reported Raymond d'Aguilers in a grisly assessment, 'but we grieved over the more than thirty horses who had their necks broken there.' Yaghi Siyan himself managed to get out of the city on horseback, but was recognised by some Armenians when he stopped at a farm house. They killed him, cut off his head and brought it to the camp for reward.

Antioch had fallen on 3 June 1098 and just in time. Three days later the advance units of Kerbogha's relief force appeared only to find that the Christians had disappeared into the undamaged city. The besiegers had become the besieged.

CHAPTER 24

An Ambling Palfrey

An inventory of the Antioch's storehouses brought the grim news that after seven and a half months of siege the Turkish garrison had been reduced to the last scraps of their food stocks. The pilgrims found plenty of loot, 'vast supplies of gold and silver, gems, precious utensils, rugs and silken stuffs', so that 'those who had but now been hungry beggars suddenly became rich', but there was virtually nothing to eat. Dismayed, the Christians realised that their troubles had hardly changed in degree or character. In some ways their plight had actually worsened: Kerbogha's army outside the walls now cut them off from the Christian ships at St Simeon and would prevent them from foraging in the countryside for food. The Turkish-occupied citadel perched above them to their rear was watching their every move and signalling to the enemy outside the gates, and Antioch's eight-mile-long perimeter wall was too extensive for them to man effectively.

The vigour of the new Turkish army was demonstrated when, unwisely, Duke Godfrey instructed his men-at-arms to hold a blockading fort which Bohemond had built earlier outside the Aleppo Gate. But Kerbogha's troops were far too strong. They quickly overran the redoubt, and there was a dismal scene as the mob of footsoldiers fought to get back into the city and the Duke sallied out with his knights in an attempt to try to cover their retreat. He too was driven back, and scores of the Christians were either injured or taken prisoner.

The Turks in the citadel on Mount Silpius took great heart from this victory over the Duke because they had come to regard him as the chief of the Christian forces. Immediately after the capture of Antioch the

Crusaders had built a makeshift wall across the main path leading down from the citadel, and mounted several 'engines' on it to deter the Turks from launching surprise attacks downhill. But now the enemy grew audacious enough to follow secret footpaths around the wall, sneak into the suburbs and waylay Christians inside the city. Before they could be brought to battle, the Turks would scramble back up the hill and slip back into the safety of the citadel. So now, with great labour, the Christians had to dig a permanent ditch to isolate the citadel and erect a permanently manned watchtower to guard against these hit-and-run attacks. Undeterred, the Turks from the citadel tried a direct assault on the ditch and very nearly broke through. Only the last-minute arrival of the Dukes Godfrey and Robert, and the count of Flanders, prevented the defenders from being overrun.

The truth was that the Host's morale had sunk to a new low. No one could imagine how the army would ever be able to extricate itself from its new predicament. The fall of the city, followed by the massacre of the Christians, seemed imminent. 'Without was the sword, within was fear,' observed William tersely. The trickle of deserters swelled. Those who could arrange it, slipped out by the side gates. Others were lowered over the wall in baskets or slid down ropes and disappeared into the countryside.* Some deserters simply walked into the Turkish camp and gave themselves up, hoping to ingratiate themselves by reporting on conditions within the city. Several of the grandees took fright and decamped as well. William of Tyre preferred not to remember the names of all the highborn runaways and did not wish to list them in his chronicle, 'since they have been blotted out from the Book of Life, they should not be inserted in this work.'

Famine again sapped the lingering remnant of the Host's resolve. Any food that was discovered was to be shared out equally. But as supplies dried up, this policy turned into institutionalised cadging. If someone was known to have food available, he was invaded by uninvited 'guests' who demanded to be fed until forcibly turned away. The poorer pilgrims resorted to straightforward begging. They went through the streets of Antioch, knocking on doors and beseeching food. Women with babies pleaded for alms from passersby, and it was said that the older children

---

* Later they were scoffed at as 'the rope dancers'.

were simply turned out to fend for themselves, and could be seen at every crossroads supplicating for charity. Anyone who did manage to find a scrap of food, quickly took it to some private spot where he could eat undisturbed by his hungry neighbours. In their desperation the starving pilgrims dug up the corpses of dead animals and ate the putrid remains.

Hunger weakened the fighting men, and dulled their vigilance. One night a party of Turks almost repeated the Christians' success in taking the city by a very similar act of stealth. About thirty Turks managed to place a ladder against the wall close to the Tower of the Two Sisters, where Bohemond had broken in. The famished and listless garrison failed to notice the attackers, and the tower at this section of the perimeter had been left unmanned.

The Turks were already on the ramparts when they were surprised by the prefect of the watch who was making his rounds. He shouted a warning to the men in the neighbouring watchtowers, and the alarm alerted three knights, led by Henry d'Esch from Duke Godfrey's company, who ran up to the battlements and in a hand-to-hand struggle succeeded in clearing the parapet. Four of the Turks were killed and the rest tossed back over the wall. Of the knights, only Henri d'Esch came away unscathed. One of his companions was killed and the other gravely wounded.

The only outside news that filtered through was very depressing. It was learned that Kerbogha had sent a cavalry column to attack the sailors and ships waiting at St Simeon. The raid meant that the last trickle of supplies, however, inadequate they had been, was ended.

There was such an air of despondency that a group of the barons held a secret meeting to discuss how they might desert the army *en bloc*, and a sense of hopelessness infected every level of the garrison. Bohemond, who had overall command, was finding it difficult to get enough men to defend the walls, even to save their own skins. When he needed volunteers, the men skulked in their houses and refused to come out for military duties. They underestimated Bohemond's single-minded determination to retain the city he now regarded as his own. He ordered his men to set fire to the houses where the fainthearts were sheltering, and they were literally driven into the open like rats from a burning building. 'This manoeuvre was successful,' said William drily, 'for whereas before that time he [Bohemond] had been unable to procure enough men for the public service, thereafter he found all zealously anxious to perform these duties.' But neither lofty exhortations from luminaries such as Duke Godfrey and Bishop Adhémar, who persuaded the faint-hearted clique of barons not to desert, nor Bohemond's ferocious style of leadership was enough to instil in the host the fighting spirit that might break Kerbogha's stifling siege. Only a miracle could do that. Obligingly, a miracle duly took place.

On 14 June an obscure cleric by the name of Peter Bartholomew, attached to the Provençals, claimed to have discovered a fragment of the Holy Lance, the weapon that had pierced Jesus' side on the cross, lying buried under the floor of the Church of St Peter. Bishop Adhémar was sceptical that the fragment was genuine, and a number of the pilgrims thought that Peter Bartholomew was an outright charlatan. But the discovery of the Holy Lance was, for many of the ordinary pilgrims, a true miracle. It was the shining revelation that God had not forsaken them. 'I, who have written this,' claimed Raymond d'Aguilers, who was present when the Lance was being dug up, 'kissed it when the point alone had as yet appeared above the ground. What great joy and exultation then filled the city I cannot describe.' Reverently wrapped in cloth, the fragment of the Holy Lance became a totem to inspire a last-ditch effort from the weary Christians.

Just two weeks later, taking advantage of the surge in morale, the war-council leaders decided to gamble everything on a grand sortie. It was a make-or-break decision, and the entire Host knew it. All night on 27 June the priests prayed earnestly for victory, the troops sharpened their weapons and checked their armour, and the surviving horses were given a special feed to prepare them for the coming battle. At daybreak the army assembled by the Gate of the Bridge in their prearranged battle formation. They were divided into six — some accounts say as many as thirteen — battle squadrons, each under the direction of an eminent nobleman. The Normans under Hugh of Vermandois were to march out first, then the men from Flanders under their count, followed by another Norman contingent under Duke Robert; Bishop Adhémar captained the fourth group. His group carried the Holy Lance as a talisman. Duke Godfrey, according to William of Tyre, had the seventh division, and behind him came Tancred's men. Bohemond as before controlled the

Antioch: Peter Bartholomew displays the newly discovered 'Holy Lance'.

strategic reserve which he would throw into the fray when the direction of the engagement had become clear. Of the great leaders only Count Raymond was missing. He seems to have been laid low by a recurrent fever, and was obliged to stay inside the city where a minimum force of two hundred men guarded the ditch. This time William of Tyre was at pains to give the roster of names, for these were to be his Immortals – the Army of Antioch whose mailed knights who would be later sung as the paladins of Christ.

From the citadel the Turks had seen the army preparing to leave the Gate of the Bridge, and signalled to Kerbogha. He immediately despatched a contingent of horse archers to hold up the Crusaders' advance while he deployed his main force. The archers attempted to block the northern end of the stone bridge but were swept aside by Christian infantry. For a moment it seemed that the careful battle order of the knights would be squandered because the leading Frankish riders joined enthusiastically in the rout of the Turkish vanguard, chasing them back almost to Kerbogha's tent. But then the knights had the good sense to reform into their divisions and wheel into line to face the main Turkish formations. At that stage the chivalry were apparently in three main ranks, with a forward screen of footsoldiers and archers. Behind them, in readiness, was the strategic reserve under Bohemond. The army marched deliberately into the attack led by its banners and flung itself against the Turks who, unusually, stood firm to take the impact.

This was part of Kerbogha's plan. He was directing his troops from a vantage point on a nearby hillside and had already sent a large detachment of cavalry out of sight, with orders to stay hidden until they could take the Christians from behind. This force now charged the rearguard led by Bohemond. The Crusaders were lucky that the main thrust of the Turkish attack fell on their best commander who managed to blunt it until Duke Godfrey, Tancred and the rear echelons, realising the new danger, wheeled about and came to his aid. By then the melée had become widespread, and on both fronts the mailed knights were unstoppable. They ploughed remorselessly forward, many on foot and others on mules and donkeys, chopping and slashing and bludgeoning the Turkish ranks until they had driven them back or scattered them. Kerbogha tried one last stratagem. He ordered his troops to set fire to the dry grass and stubble upwind of the Christians. A pall of blinding smoke blew down on the horses and men, and allowed the Turks to return under cover of the murk and kill some of the footsoldiers. But the knights spurred their mounts clear of the smoke and returned to the task of driving the Turks from the battlefield. Seeing that the battle was lost, Kerbogha left the battlefield with is retinue and headed back to the east. Behind him the last of his forces made one brief stand on a low hill, and then trusting to the speed of their horses fled in a general retreat. Only Tancred and a few others had the energy to pursue them. But their own horses were so tired and emaciated that after three or four miles they gave up the chase and turned back.

It had been a resounding victory. The most powerful army that the Turks could bring against them had been routed, leaving behind a vast store of supplies, horses and weapons. 'It was impossible to count or measure the gold and silver, the gems, silks and valuable garments, to say nothing of utensils, most excellent in both workmanship and material.' There was a whole encampment of tents and pavilions to replace the army's old and rotting equipment. They had even captured Kerbogha's personal pavilion, a huge and splendid affair sewn from many-coloured silk, with ornamental turrets, ramparts, and a web of corridors to adjoining rooms and apartments so that it seemed like a miniature city. Best of all, the army had taken Kerbogha's entire supply train with its herds of cattle and flocks of sheep, and a great mass of foodstuffs and grain. There was enough food for everyone and 'those who had but now been in extreme destitution hardly knew what to choose.'

Ladened with their plunder, driving the captured herds with them, the exuberant army returned into the city. The ecstatic soldiers were convinced that God had indeed been on their side. Some of them swore that they had seen a heavenly troop of cavalry cantering through the hills as they marched to battle, and a light shower of rain which had sprinkled them as they advanced to the attack was identified as God's gesture to refresh them before they came to grips with the infidel. A Turkish deputation came down from the heights of Mount Silpius. They had watched the total defeat of Kerbogha's army and now offered to surrender the citadel if they would be allowed to leave unharmed with their wives and children. The army commanders were happy to see them go without a fight, and so the last Turks left Antioch.

The city was now firmly in Christian hands, and in contradiction to the view that the Crusaders were primarily interested in lining their own pockets, among the first beneficiaries of the great victory were Antioch's churches. A portion of the spoils from the battle were handed over to refurbish the interiors. Gold and silver went to make new candelabra, crosses and chalices. The fine Turkish silks were cut and sewn into priestly vestments and altar covers. These gifts were made with the knowledge that for everyone in the army the cost of the Crusade had been far greater than the value of any plunder that had been taken. The ordinary pilgrims had been destitute when the siege began. By the time it was nearing its climax nine months later a senior knight like Henry d'Esch had been reduced to such poverty that he could barely stand from hunger. Even such a great lord as Godfrey had exhausted his assets. The money he had raised by mortgaging Chateau Bouillon was gone, together with all the subventions from Emperor Alexius, and the booty captured at Dorylaeum. On his Crusade the Duke of Lorraine had beggared himself so effectively that he had ridden into the battle of Antioch on a borrowed horse.

Modern Antioch, on first impression, had very little to recall the days of the Great Siege. The plain where the Frankish chivalry defeated Kerbogha's army is covered with the standard apartment blocks of the bourgeois section of any Turkish city, featureless buildings sprouting television aerials on their roofs, and the plate glass windows of offices on the ground floor. The Orontes river was brown and smelly and jacketed between high concrete banks which made it seem like a cement drain, and the site of the Church of St Peter, where the Holy Lance was found, had been turned into a lorry park. Had we come twenty years earlier, we were told, we would have seen the original Stone Bridge where the Crusaders had fought their most savage encounters. But the bridge had been blown up to make way for the present undistinguished road bridge.

Closer acquaintance with the city, however, revealed there was a continuity about Antioch that no amount of dynamite or concrete could erase. Antioch still wore the faded garments of her glory. The splendid wall that had first defied the Crusaders and then protected them, still climbed the mountain, a triumph of engineering snaking its way up the precipitous slope until it reached the peak where the stump of the irreducible citadel could still be seen. Modern Antioch did not even fill that vast enclave. Within the city walls there were gardens and small fields, acres of wasteland and orchards. The modest houses of the townsfolk were on the lower slope of Mount Silpius, while farther down a large bazaar flourished among streets and lanes whose grid pattern loyally traced the original Roman city planning. Tucked here and there in the dim alleys among the wholesalers' warehouses, the small shops and restaurants were the remaining churches of the Armenians and the Catholics, a tiny synagogue and the mosques.

Then, too, the Antiochenes themselves were distinctive. They were livelier and less stolid than the Turks we had met elsewhere. There was much evidence of the Arab influence – darker eyes and skins, softer features, narrower faces, quicker movements and sharper, more obvious reactions, hands fluttering and gesturing frequently as men talked, and a guttural accent in their Turkish. Many were bilingual, and some citizens spoke Arabic as their mother tongue. Antioch was a cosmopolitan meeting ground for every nationality that cared to arrive there, and the city still gave the impression that it would survive invasion, betrayal, failures, earthquakes and floods with comfortable resilience.

From our strictly practical point of view Antioch's unchanged ways were an asset. The city was full of carters and carthorses, and our absolute priority was to find a replacement for poor Mystery. But first we located a makeshift stable for Szarcsa and Zippy in the suburb of Harbiye. In the time of the French Protectorate between the two World Wars, this had been a favourite holiday spot, and the Hotel de Liban had been built for the families of French civil servants and merchants who had emulated the Roman villa owners in their enjoyment of the hills overlooking the sea. Sadly reduced by the virtual closure of the coast road to Syria and the Lebanon and by Antioch's economic stagnation, the Hotel de Liban struggled on, managed by the same family that had founded it. A room, with cracked and peeling walls decorated by a sleepy lizard, was available, but there was no space for the horses. A sad-faced waiter, the very image of Peter Lorre in 'Casablanca', offered his uncle's stable across the road. His penguin waddle enhanced by his waiter's costume of white shirt, black trousers and bow tie, he led me there, to be told by the aged uncle dozing under a plane tree that his stable was too small, but a cousin opposite might help. Eventually we managed to put the horses, not into a proper stable, but into a downstairs room of a new house that had not yet been decorated or furnished. The horses were quite content to peer out of the unglazed living room windows, and Szarcsa promptly increased the rental by chewing a great notch out of the wooden frame.

The same afternoon we arrived, 19 June, Sarah and I went on a horse-hunt. Stopping the first carter we met on the road, we asked him where we could buy a working horse. He took us to the stables where all the city carters parked their horses and battered drays at night. It was in the poorest, most tumbledown section of the old town where a patch of waste ground merged into a small orchard and there was a little grazing. Three small, very ramshackle buildings were used as stables, unoccupied that afternoon except for a pair of miserable-looking, dirty nags tucked away in the dim corners, too dark to see properly and clearly dumped there out of disinterest. One of the horses was even wearing its massive ungainly pack saddle, which its owner was presumably too lazy to remove. We had not expected much of the dray horses of Antioch – to use a cart instead of a truck meant that the carters were at the bottom of the economic heap – and our misgivings were justified.

Over the next two days we patrolled the stables while a ragtag collection of carters and their animals passed before us. The carters came in all shapes and sizes – villainous with leather peaked caps, hugely obese in baggy trousers and tee shirts, neat in singlets and jeans. They had horses to match in variety and condition. There were nasty rolling eyes, wicked looks, sores, scrapes, pot bellies, swaybacks. There were stubby and heavy-legged horses, scrawny and ewe-necked horses. Sarah looked at them all and checked them over. The state of their legs, she said, was uniformly terrible, knocked about and lumpy. There were horses that were sick or exhausted or elderly. Some would have been unmanageable if they were not anchored to a rough cart, others had never been broken for riding. We looked closely at one animal, bigger and steadier than the rest, a real carthorse. But he, Sarah announced, was lazy and tank-like. He would be woodenly uncomfortable, a Carty without the Ardennes' character. At the opposite end of the scale we considered buying a flashy bay with a white snip on his nose, that had just been brought in from Iskanderun on the coast where it had been pulling a phaeton for tourists along the sea front. Although he had a terrible scar down one haunch as the result of a road accident, he was the only horse, Sarah said, with a halfway decent set of legs. It was puzzling that he was so nervous. But then someone remembered that all his life he had probably worn blinkers, and when we found and fitted an old set, he calmed down. So we gave him a trial ride, but he pranced along with a short quick stride that was fine when pulling a tourist carriage, but would have been excruciating for a long-distance rider. Also we were worried that if we took a drayhorse we could have problems with putting a saddle on a back that had not been hardened. So we rejected him. It was not that we were looking for a good horse, nor even one of medium quality. We merely wanted an animal that would have a reasonable chance of walking 500 miles to Jerusalem, not quarrel with Zippy and Szarcsa, and provide a safe and steady ride.

We were getting nowhere with the carters. Their self-appointed spokesman had a truly sinister appearance. His pinched, very dark face with its pair of glittering, close-set eyes gave him the appearance of a venomous snake, and he was very mercenary. When we had tried out the bay, he demanded money for allowing us to ride the horse. We laughed and walked away. Our lack of success was depressing. For a change we tried going out into the hills south of the city where we had been told a farmer had good pack ponies for sale. It was difficult to find the place, tucked away in broken ground near the Syrian border, and we were greeted at gun point by the farmer's three heavily armed and suspicious sons. It was evident that they were engaged in some sort of illegal activity, probably smuggling, and their pack ponies were essential to their business. So once again we drew a blank.

We returned into Antioch and were sitting in a small, scruffy office in the heart of the city, debating whether or not we would have to make an offer for the flashy phaeton horse, when our rescuer arrived in the bulky shape of a tall, heavily-built man in his mid-fifties. If the waiter previously had been Peter Lorre, here in the flesh was Sydney Greenstreet. The newcomer walked with the ponderous gait of a truly big man, and was mopping his round, pink face, with a large handkerchief. He introduced himself in impeccable old-fashioned English, enunciating with great deliberation. His name was Resit, and he had heard we were visiting Antakyah. Could he help us in any way? I explained our journey and why we were looking for a horse to continue our road to Jerusalem. With measured courtesy Resit answered that perhaps we would allow him to assist as he had good local contacts among the farmers and horseowners, being an agricultural engineer and president of the local chamber of commerce. It proved to be a splendid understatement. Resit's family had been leading citizens of Antioch and the surrounding province for the past six centuries. One ancestor had been rewarded by the Ottoman Sultan for meritorious services on the battlefield with the gift of several score of villages, many of which were still owned by Resit's family. His father had been elected one of the first Deputies to the Turkish Parliament, his wife was the daughter of another, and the family had regularly provided governors for Antakyah. His attitude was perfectly understandable. He was a grand seigneur of Antioch in the best sense, courteous, knowledgable and with a profound sense of civic responsibility. His next remark made me grin to myself. 'I think we should start by going to talk with the carters in their city stables,' he pronounced. 'Many of them are my tenants. Perhaps they will be able to help.'

Our journey back to the stables was close to being a royal progress. We climbed into Resit's large and venerable Mercedes saloon, and he drove very sedately through the narrow streets, with the window rolled down and his beefy arm resting on the door. As the vehicle nudged its way slowly through the crowds, Resit was greeted respectfully to left and right by pedestrians, shopkeepers, policemen, street vendors. Some would come running up to the car to wish him well or to ask some small favour. For everyone, whether a shoeshine man or a suited businessman with a briefcase, Resit had a polite, almost stately reply delivered in flowery Turkish, treating him as if he were a man of stature and importance. Resit appeared to know all their names, and the names and ages of their children as well. It was a *tour de force*, and by now I was looking forward to what lay ahead. The old Mercedes bumped deliberately down the rutted track that led to the carters' stables, and I saw two or three men glance up. Clearly they recognised the car, for they stopped whatever they were doing and hurried forward. He levered himself out of the driver's seat and they greeted him obsequiously. Then they saw who his passengers were, and their faces fell.

Buying a horse with Resit's aid was quite different. He stood there, majestically towering over the cluster of carters and asked in his ornate manner if they had a suitable horse for his foreign friends. Various suggestions were made. It was explained that we had tried many horses, and none had been suitable.

'Have you, by any chance, a *rahwan* horse that you could be so kind as to show them? I believe it would be what they want.'

The carters went into a huddle, and talked amongst themselves. The snake-eyed individual again took the lead. He muttered something to a colleague and the man went off to the stables. He reappeared leading the bedraggled animal that we had first seen tucked away in a dark corner of the stable. It had seemed half-dead under its enormous pack saddle, head drooping and dispirited, and we had never bothered to give the creature a second glance. In daylight the animal looked hardly any more impressive. 'A horse on pony's legs' was Sarah's immediate description.

The animal, a palomino mare, was filthy-dirty with a straggly mane, untended and uncombed. Her skin was disfigured with sores and broken scabs, and she had a scar on her face. She stood there nervously as Snake-Eyes, who turned out to be her owner, explained that he had acquired the animal only a few weeks before and was using her to carry great baskets of charcoal from the northern mountains, a five-hour journey, to the central bazaar where she was unloaded and then put in the stables and next morning ridden back up the hill to collect another load. It was

285

obvious that the pack saddle had belonged to another horse. The massive contraption, reminiscent of a huge wooden lobster pot, fitted the little mare atrociously. Wherever the holding straps touched her skin, there were great oozing red sores, and when we asked for the pack saddle to be removed, her body looked as if someone had loaded a blunderbuss with lumps of rock salt and fired it at her from short range. She was in a dreadful state, and to emphasise the fact, she now lowered her head and gave a wracking cough.

'I don't like the sound of that,' said Sarah, and went forward to feel the mare's shins. 'Lumps the size of marbles and as hard too,' she commented. 'In Europe one wouldn't look twice at such a wrecked animal but I suppose if she can walk five hours a day, six days a week, with a hundred kilos of charcoal on her back, she can endure anything.' Then she tried to sponge out the mare's dirt encrusted eyes. As Sarah raised her hand, the slumped mare went berserk, rearing and plunging in panic, scattering the onlookers. 'Someone's been thrashing her over the head until she was scared out of her mind,' Sarah diagnosed, and soothed the animal. 'Go on,' she added, 'You're the one who needs a horse. You try her.'

Snake-Eyes had run forward and was adjusting one of the cords hanging from the pack saddle so there was a loop on each side to serve as stirrups. There was no bit in the mare's mouth, just a frayed bit of string leading to a noseband. Gingerly I climbed up to perch on the uncomfortable looking lobster pot. I felt ridiculously high off the animal's back, but at least with her short legs I was not far off the ground. The little mare stood patiently until Snake-Eyes clicked his tongue, and she moved off. It was the most unexpected sensation. After riding a normal horse for two thousand miles with the usual walking and trotting action, I found myself being carried off as smoothly as if the mare was mounted on wheels. There was none of the usual staccato action of the hooves. Instead, the palomino paced out level, swerving her spine slightly from side to side but holding it completely flat and steady. The only description that I could think of was that she glided along, though technically she was an ambling or pacing horse. I was astonished and delighted.

I turned the mare – she needed just a touch of the cord on her neck – and rode back to where Resit was standing to ask him if that is what he had meant by 'rahwan' horse.

'Yes,' he said, 'it's a gait that is still quite common among horses around here, but found among pack animals, not cart horses. The farmers and carriers like it because the horse can maintain a rapid pace for hour after hour and does not tire easily.'

I confirmed that as far as I was concerned, it was perfect. 'If we can agree a price, then I'll buy the animal.'

'You must not do that directly,' he cautioned me, 'we have to employ an intermediary, a professional horse broker, and he will negotiate the price for you, for a small commission. I know such a man, and – with your permission – I will request that he look after the deal for you.'

So I was spared even the chore of haggling with Snake-Eyes. Next day the broker took me back to the stables to meet the odious character, took my hand and his, and slapped them together. The deal was done. I was now the owner of a seven-year-old, 14.1 hands high, *rahwan* palomino mare that no one had even bothered to give a name in all her life. As I confessed to Sarah later, it was not just the superb pacing gait which had persuaded me to take on a horse that looked and acted half-dead. The little mare was precisely the same age as Mystery and seemed to have the same gentle nature. Although I had promised myself after losing Mystery that I would never let sentiment play any part again in dealing with our horses, I felt that the selection of the little palomino partly compensated for Mystery's death. The palomino was being so grossly misused that she could not have lasted long with her previous owner. We had lost Mystery, but salvaged an ambling palfrey.

CHAPTER 25

Syria

We settled on Yabangı, 'Foreigner', as the name for the little mare since she was the newcomer to our group and we had never forgotten being called the Yabangı of the Taurus. When we brought her up to the stable to meet the other horses, she was nervous and frightened. A wooden box of barley was put in front of her and Yabangı plunged her head into it, bolting down the food as if she feared it would be snatched away. Calming her enough to be able to begin treating her red-raw sores was a tricky operation. She was acutely suspicious of anyone going near them, and the first time I went too close to try to puff antiseptic powder on his haunch, Yabangı lashed with a violent sideways near-horizontal kick that would have done credit to a contortionist. I was knocked flying into a corner, with a bruise that made me hobble for two days afterwards. Of course Sarah had the knack to dispel Yabangı's fear of humans and build up her confidence. This was soon extended to me, although it was many days before we could approach the palomino's eyes to clean them without her becoming hysterical. With better feeding and patient kindness, her improvement was astonishing. Most of the sores on her body dried and began to heal within a week. But the worst ones, those on her haunches, were deep gouges in the flesh, a constant lure for flies, and they mended very, very slowly. Eventually they did stop seeping and grew new skin, but the ugly pink patches embarrassed us, in case spectators might think we had been the cause of such obvious signs of abuse.

We put aside the last of the kit we hoped we would not require for the final sector of the long journey. The jeep would go back to Istanbul with the maps we no longer needed, spare clothes, sleeping bags and our wet weather gear, since it was nearly July and we did not expect to see another drop of rain before Jerusalem. Instead we would have to cope with the heat and drought of the Syrian desert, and – although we did not appreciate it then – the oven-like conditions of the deep Jordan valley close to the rim of the Dead Sea. With Resit's help we had all three horses re-shod in Antioch's bazaar and bought two extra shoes, one front and one rear, for Yabangı. They were spares in case she threw a shoe and we could not pick it up, because by my calculations we had less than a month's travel ahead of us and the horses' shoes would last that long.

On Saturday 25 June, with our kit so reduced that Zippy had barely 25 kilos on his back, we climbed out of Antioch along the winding hill road that went south towards the small border post with Syria at Kassab. The two veteran horses had to get used to Yabangı's sinuous pacing stride. The ravaged-looking palomino had just two gaits – a dull walk that was slower than either Zippy or Szarcsa and not very comfortable, or her special amble which was superbly comfortable but slightly slower than a regular trot. The awkward result was that if I allowed Yabangı to go at a pace, I was always getting far ahead of Sarah with Szarcsa and Zippy, and being grumbled at for my pains. If I slowed to Yabangı's walk, I soon fell behind. At first the difference did not matter much because Yabangı had been so poorly fed by her previous owner that she had little stamina, and after ten or fifteen miles would begin to flag. But within a week, good feeding and steady exercise meant that she could out-travel the other two horses with little effort. Even her chronic cough, the legacy of prolonged neglect, did not hold her back unduly. On steep hills she might give an occasional deep, spectacular hacking grunt, but once she had crested the slope and was on the level ground she picked up her pace and accelerated away as smoothly and as rapidly as ever. Sarah would growl at me, when she caught up, but it was only half-hearted. The stay in Antioch had helped to restore all her vitality and perkiness. She was in great spirits, and in her tee shirt and jeans looked ridiculously young and even more saucily confident than before.

I had been worrying about the Syrian border crossing. Including their winter lay-over, it was almost a year since the horses had entered Turkey, and the animals whose names had been written in my passport when we first arrived from Bulgaria had changed. Carty had been returned to his new home in Austria, Mystery had died, we had bought Zippy, and now added Yabangı. Only Szarcsa remained from the original trio. Supercilious as ever, he was in prime condition, full of vigour for his years and acting almost like a three-year-old as he scoffed down prodigious quantities of barley and chaff. I wondered what would happen if the Turkish customs officials tried to match the horses against the descriptions in the import documents. It would be difficult to persuade them that the elephantine Carty had shrunk into the tiny, twinkle-toed Zippy, though they were both about the same colour. And while Mystery and Yabangı were both seven-year-old mares, the former would have to have drastically shortened in the leg and changed colour from bay to palomino.

As it turned out, I need not have worried in the slightest. The Turkish officials in their little customs post deep in the pine woods, were amused when we announced that we were 'in transit'. We had to sketch our long zig-zag route across Turkey on the customs collector's map, describe a few of our village experiences, and then we were sent on our way. No one bothered to check the horses' documents, and it was very obvious that this particular border crossing was little used. A single car, with Lebanese registration plates, had passed us in three hours of riding on the approach road. While we chatted to the Turkish officials, one other car had passed through the border, again a large and opulent Lebanese vehicle apparently with special papers. There was no other traffic whatever until a taxi turned up, unloaded a group of four homely, Arab-looking women and two rather hen-pecked men, who all started dragging their luggage and parcels out of the boot of the taxi. After they had undergone the Turkish customs search, all the bags and packages and parcels were loaded onto a low iron-wheeled trolley, like a railway parcel trolley, and laboriously pushed under the striped guard pole and then fifty yards down the road to the Syrian side, where the process of unloading, searching and loading again went on until they could pile into an ancient taxi, which was waiting for them, and disappear. All this took place under the gaze of an armed Turkish soldier in combat smock, and was a reminder that the Turkish province of Hatay, including Antioch, was still claimed by Syria and marked on Syrian maps as such. At Kassab, the rivalry between the countries was given a high profile and trans-border traffic was discouraged, both for Turks and Syrians. Sarah and I, it was sadly evident, were entering a region where border tensions were a commonplace of life. And in another 400 miles we would have to deal with the awkwardness of passing from an Arab country into Israel.

Our reception on the Syrian side of the border succeeded in being both obliging and baffling. The kindly Irish diplomat in Damascus who had helped us to obtain our hard-won visas, now thoughtfully sent a Syrian staff member to mark our path through the thicket of entry formalities. Thus the frontier officials had been forewarned that we were arriving and were ready to help in every way they could. But on the other hand their cooperation was crippled by the fact that every step in our entry formalities – and there was a multitude – had to be taken in its proper sequence and wholly completed before we could go on to the next. There was no turning back, jumping ahead, adjustment, or flexibility. If an official was filling in a particular form and puzzled how to complete one of the blank spaces, he would telephone his superior in the nearest city, Latakia, for guidance. This meant hand-cranking the field telephone, waiting patiently for a connection, asking the question, eventually receiving an answer, hanging up, and filling in the blank. A few lines later perhaps another puzzle occurred, the telephone was lifted and cranked, a line finally obtained, the question asked and answered, the handset replaced and so forth. It all took so long that before the form could be completed, the superior at the other end of the line had gone off to lunch or to a meeting, and of course we had to wait until he returned and answered every question in its proper sequence. Finally the form was complete. Until that time we could not go on to the next step whether it be checking the passports, changing money, paying the entry tax, declaring our stock of currency or whatever. The frontier post was so small that it employed only two ranking officials and thus, although the forms changed, the officials did not. The customs collector switched to his role as baggage inspector, then to being a central bank clerk, then to money changer. The chief of police turned into an immigration officer and later had to represent the security services. All this was done with such long drawn-out formality that it was apparent that the arrival of two riders and three horses was an event to be savoured.

Only then was it discovered that our hard-won entry visas had been expired for two days, as it had taken us so long to ride across Anatolia. Permission for an extension would have to be obtained from the

Ministry. Our helper from Damascus set off to drive thirty miles to the city where he could use a more convenient telephone, and promised to return next morning. By then the extra delay hardly mattered. The local health inspector, doubling in the role of amateur vet, had inspected the animals, pronounced them fit, and filled in the forms accordingly. But we could not leave the frontier post until the papers were stamped officially. Of course the rubber stamp was in charge of someone else, and would be at least three hours reaching Kassab. Meanwhile the frontier post had to close at dusk and there was no more business until next morning.

So, officially at least, we spent the night in limbo, neither in Syria nor in Turkey. In reality we parked the horses comfortably enough in an abandoned garden by an empty house, just twenty yards from the customs post. The director of the frontier post in his role as chief-of-police assured me that I could cite his authority to trespass on the property, gather up any dried grass I needed, and sleep on the porch while Sarah took a room in town. Scarcely had I stretched out on the concrete floor of the verandah than there was a discreet cough and the glow of a cigarette end from the garden. It was the director of the post and his colleague, the head of customs. Would I care to take a stroll with them? It was a lovely evening and they would be glad of my company. The invitation was delivered in very passable English, though questions for the form filling had been delivered in Arabic, and laboriously translated. It turned out that both the director and his colleague spoke good enough English for us to chat pleasantly as we sauntered up and down the now-closed road in the gloaming. I even had to decline an offer to use the bed in the guard house explaining that I preferred to stay to keep an eye on the horses. Only two hours earlier it had been open to doubt – apparently – whether we would be allowed to stay in Syria at all.

Unlike the fairy tale, no one turned back into an official ogre with the dawn. The visa extension was granted from Damascus and the veterinary stamp appeared, brought by no less than three government vets, proper ones this time, who clustered round the horses taking their temperatures and listening to their lungs while Sarah and I prayed that Yabangı would not give her awful grunting cough which would have deafened the man on the stethoscope. To our relief, the three horses were passed as fit and well, and we were allowed to proceed. It had taken almost exactly twenty-four hours to complete our Syrian entry formalities, but by then we were no longer suspect strangers. As we were riding quietly along the road, the small bus carrying the entire complement of frontier officials, guards and clerks passed us. They had just finished their three-day shift and were heading for their homes in Latakia. The driver tooted his horn and slowed down so that all his passengers could turn round to watch us, stick their arms out of the windows and wave a happy greeting.

We left the hill town of Kassab on our right, dominated by the churches and monasteries founded by the Armenian refugees who settled there from Turkey. The town had become something of a summer mountain resort, and even this rather distant corner of Syria seemed so much more modern than the lands we had been crossing for the past three months. It was startling to see Syrians in smart jeans and blousons strolling through the streets, one young man even pushing a pram beside his wife, a sight one would never have seen in rural Anatolia. Our route still followed the line of an old Roman road, but a minor one. The main caravan trail from Antioch had always been southeast through Aleppo and not along the Mediterranean coast, but this was the way the Crusade had gone as they headed directly towards Jerusalem, their minds set on religion not commerce. We passed between steep hills densely forested with pine except for the patches where the villagers had cut out small orchards for their plum and peach trees.

We camped that night, the first spent officially in Syria, overlooking a small lake where a small cafe could provide us with a supper and, unexpectedly, a bag of barley for the horses. We had been warned that Syrian farmers were obliged to deliver their surplus grain to the government, but as usual it turned out there was a wide gap between theory and practice. The farmers were perfectly happy to sell us small quantities of food for the horses and, as for the rigamarole at the frontier, it was mostly wasted effort. Our instructions had been to preserve the dockets and receipts, the stamped and countersigned forms, passes and certificates, with the greatest care, as they would be needed at check points and inspections. Perhaps so, but in all the time we were to spend riding across Syria we were only summoned into one roadside police station. It was, admittedly, a forbidding moment. A belligerent police sergeant swaggered up and announced with sinister vehemence that we had to call on his captain who was the security chief for the district. But it turned out only that his captain had seen us passing and had been most insistent to make sure we stopped in for tea. Our first night in Syria, like most of the others, was quiet and peaceful and no one got into any trouble except for Yabangi. As we led the horses away from the café's water tap and towards their picket pins Zippy, who had been morose and glum all day, suddenly let fly a smashing double-heeled kick at the mild and unassuming Yabangi who had, in her newcomer's ignorance, walked within range behind him. The wind was knocked out of her with an audible whoof of air and she visibly staggered. But the little palomino was not hurt and as Sarah thwacked the culprit, my colleague was evidently pleased.

'I had been worrying about Zippy all day,' she remarked, 'He seemed so lacklustre that I was afraid his withers were becoming re-infected. But there's nothing wrong with the little brat.' She sighed. 'If it's not one horse to worry about, it'll always be another.'

We reached Latakia the next day, a charmless, concrete port city with an oil tank farm on the approaches and a hideous modern harbour which had smothered the graceful turn-of-the-century promenade and stranded its last few elegant houses. With the horses generously stabled by a private riding club, we paused long enough to take an excursion inland to visit the first of the chain of Crusader castles we would pass along the coast road.

These castles are monuments to later episodes in the long-running saga of the Crusaders in the Holy Land. They were built by the warlords who strove to maintain and expand the original, illustrious conquest of the First Crusaders. The vast majority of the Crusader castles, however, were constructed on sites that were already fortified by Byzantines and Arabs when Duke Godfrey and his cohorts marched that way in 1099. The castle of Qalat Saladin, for example, was built round the core of a former Byzantine stronghold. Some eighteen miles into the plateau from Latakia, Qalat Saladin or Sahyoun as the Crusaders called it, looked from a distance like a cardboard cutout of a castle, all four-square towers and crenellations and sheer walls, and lacking only the stick figures of men in conical helmets under outsize banners against the sky. The fortifications' most celebrated feature was the sheer canyon, 170 yards long and chiselled out of the rock to a depth of 75 feet, that severed the castle from the nearby spur of land. The excavation was so spectacular that one automatically wondered at the immense cost in labour to carve such a vast gash, and useless too, for the castle fell to a brisk assault on its opposite, poorly protected side. Sophisticated Chateau Sahyoun was utterly different from the plain stub of a simple round tower that Duke Godfrey had left behind him when he set out from Chateau Bouillon to march all the way to the Holy Land. At Sahyoun Godfrey's emulators had built themselves a vastly complicated structure with donjons and oil-pouring slits, re-entries, stables for horses, an enormous cistern to hold water for a prolonged siege and a drawbridge resting on a great rock spike rising from the floor of the canyon. Sahyoun was a vaunting monument to power and prestige and the desire of a handful of men to overawe. Yet one also had the feeling that it was a testimonial to a sense of insecurity and isolation. The architects who had built such an edifice were genuinely frightened of being ejected from that land, and far removed in their attitudes from the blundering, but self-confident First Crusaders who had difficulty even in making wooden siege towers. Chateau Sahyoun and the other remarkable Crusader castles belonged to a way of life, grand, gracious, and formal, that would have been beyond the imagination of the exhausted ill-prepared knights who plodded along that coast with captured Turkish horses, carrying simple, dented armour, poorly clad in the remnants of their heavy woollen garments, accompanied by a horde of dirty, tired pilgrims, footsore on the dusty path towards the Holy City.

The next day was 1 July, the beginning of the hottest month of the year, and we made a dawn start to avoid the worst of the heat. An unappealing modern dual carriageway took us out of Latakia until we could turn off and follow the old coast road again, which meandered past small farms and the occasional villa. The houses reminded us of what we had seen a year earlier in Yugoslavia, they too were unfinished, with four walls of unpainted cement, a flat roof, and the main pillars ending skyward in a fringe of steel reinforcing rods for the day when a second storey would be added. The countryside was a disappointment, dull and featureless, the shore rocky and straight, without cove or beach or headland to give it any interest. Nor could we go very far, for we saw ahead of us the distinctive silver snouts of a missile battery arranged on a low rise and pointing out to sea, and prudently gave it a wide berth, turning to ride inland.

By early afternoon we were entering the outskirts of the town of Jablé, and anxiously looking for shade for the horses, when a weird figure suddenly came into the corner of our vision, running pell-mell down the steep slope of knoll on our left. It was a man clad in a heavy white boiler suit like some engineer escaped from a nuclear power station. In that broiling heat he was wrapped from ankle to collar in white overalls tucked into white rubber boots, a broad-brimmed white hat, and white gauntlets. This bizarre figure was running with great loping strides, hallooing like a madman and waving to us. We reined the horses to a halt. Had they been less tired and hot they would have had good reason to bolt, but then this was only the latest in a series of weird apparitions that they had seen on their travels. The man in white was out of breath and nearly apoplectic with the heat. 'You must stay with me. Please, you must stay with me,' he gasped. After such an entrance we could hardly refuse, and followed him as, panting, he struggled back uphill in his rubber boots and led us to a plain square building.

His name was Wahib, he blurted out to us, and he was by profession an agricultural engineer employed to research on improved tobacco plants by the Latakia Tobacco Company. Cheerful, vivacious and eccentric, he had a mass of short dark curls, a quickness of movement, and a spontaneous grin that made him look like a handsome Italian. For three days each week he retreated to the building, which was a farm abandoned for lack of water, and there he had recently taken up the hobby of bee-keeping, hence the clothes. He had seen us passing and was eager to chat with foreigners and hear their tales. He invited us to pitch our tent in the shade of his trees though not too close to his beehives, and a little while later Wahib's two brothers arrived in a small car. They clearly indulged their unconventional brother, bringing plastic jugs of water and a stock of food, for it soon appeared that Wahib could neither cook very well nor had much success with his beekeeping. The white rig was essential because every time Wahib attended to his bees, they chased and tried to sting him, usually successfully. But he would soon get the hang of it, Wahib assured us with his flashing smile: he had a book on the subject.

He was such a charming personality and so genuinely convivial that we cancelled the rest of the day's ride and did not regret spending the rest of the afternoon in such sociable company. One brother was a lawyer, another a school teacher, and we all sat under the shade trees, discussing our trip until, inevitably, the topic turned to the fraught

296

politics of the region with remarks about Syria's colonial history, Israel, and hopes for Arab cooperation. Seeking to deflect the conversation, I enquired how they felt about the huge Crusader castles hulking along their coast, did they consider them to be relics of foreign domination? The school teacher was elected to answer. He taught history, he said, and told his students that a crusading era was only a small slice of Syria's long past. I persisted.

'What do the castles mean to you?'

'They were castles of occupation, not civilisation,' he replied, 'and with the passing of the centuries they have only become souvenirs of the past.' So how do you think your students should consider these castles? I asked. He gave a wry smile. 'The same way that the Spaniards should view the buildings the Arabs left behind in Spain,' he answered very deftly.

We were up early, leaving a drowsy Wahib and his bees undisturbed as we continued on through Jablé town, past its Roman amphitheatre and then out along the coast road. Thankfully the route was little used, and the only traffic was an occasional battered Russian-made truck or little noisy three-wheeled scooter vans. Their loads were vivid red, green and deep purple for they were servicing the market gardens that used artesian water on the sandy soil to raise peppers, tomatoes and aubergines. Occasionally we were passed by farmers travelling on their motor scooters, and sometimes their pillion passengers were women, good-looking with perfectly symmetrical faces, huge eyes and delicate features. Later we learned that throughout the region the women were renowned for their good looks, to be compared only with the fabled beauties of Aleppo. Even when we saw work squads of university-age Syrians doing their obligatory patriotic duty as street sweepers or litter-pickers, the drabbest military khaki could not disguise the stunning grace and elegance of the young women.

By noon the heat warranted a brief diversion to the seashore to cool off the horses' hooves in the shallows. It was the first time that any of them had ever seen the sea, and their reactions were typical of each animal. Yabangı skipped and danced with anxiety as the wavelets lapped around her hooves, but meekly followed instructions and stayed in the water. Zippy plodded in ten inches deep as if he was being led to the slaughter house, and stood there, eyes half-closed and wearing a put-upon expression that said 'What did I do to deserve this?' Szarcsa, ever the coward, flinched and shivered at the slightest ripple and scampered back to dry land as if chased by demons.

Detouring to avoid yet another missile battery installed along the shore, we passed a small Bedouin camp. It was a wretched collection of scruffy tents huddled together on a patch of wasteland that doubled as a rubbish tip. The tents were shabby and ill-set, and the few sheep grazed pathetically on stinking garbage. Transport was a rusty tractor with its trailer, and we were told that the Bedouin would occasionally load up and move from campsite to campsite, living off odd scraps of land. Their life seemed appallingly squalid and unhealthy compared to the free-and-easy existence of the Hatay nomads we had seen high in the *yayla* pastures of the Taurus.

From eight miles away we saw the red-and-white banded refinery chimneys poking up through the thick pollution haze which was clamped over the next town, Banyas. Here the hills pressed much closer to the shore line, pinching the already cramped coastal plain. The shoulder of the hill was an obvious site to build a castle to command the narrow waist, and here for centuries a looming castle of black basalt had stood, known as Markab, 'the Watcher'. We had been given permission to spend the night in the castle itself, and I did not wish to miss the chance of sampling the brooding atmosphere of that unique location where the self-appointed guardians of Christendom had mounted watch over the land that Godfrey and his companions had conquered. So we turned our horses for the long steep climb up to the fortress, reputedly the strongest bastion on all the coast. It took us 45 minutes to get there, walking beside flagging horses that had already covered 23 miles that day. But for the humans anyhow, the effect was worth it. We found ourselves leading the animals up the long flight of stone steps to the first gate, across the open killing space between the double walls, then through a second massive gate to clatter under the arch of the donjon and out into the broad central courtyard of the citadel. Already the last visitors had gone down the hill, and Feyyaz the resident keeper of the castle swung shut the huge gates and locked them behind us. We were left to picket the horses and camp the night where the Crusader garrison had manned 'the Watcher' seven hundred years before. The strangest sensation was to draw water for the horses from the castle's still-working reservoir, an enormous underground chamber that extended far under the broad courtyard. The crash of the bucket striking the water made a huge, hollow boom that echoed and re-echoed around the cavernous foundations of the castle, followed by the ghostly swish and dripping of the rope as we hauled the water to the surface. All around us were crumbling ruins, intermingled with portions of massive, perfectly surviving or restored architecture so that you could step from a tiny stubble field created in a derelict courtyard into a well-preserved store room, or pass under a crumbling and dangerous arch to find an entire surviving medieval lane twisting between high walls where the only light came as a shaft of late evening sunshine blazing in through an arrow slit and slanting across the gap so brightly that it seemed almost solid.

We located a corner to tie the horses; there three wild fig trees grew untended next to a small patch of grass that the groundsmen had cut and left to dry. Gathering up the ready-made hay, we left the horses happily munching after we had blocked up various lethal holes and gaps in the ground; the foundations of the castle seemed riddled with cellars and dungeons. Feyyaz the castle keeper had prepared supper in his room set high in the castle's seaward wall, where the casement window gave an eagle's view over the landing beach with its separate watch tower far, far below. Then, under a brilliant moon and stars, we pitched the tent on the edge of the great central courtyard. In the moonlight the shapes of rats scurried over the worn flagstones by the well, and it was so perfectly still and silent that when a marauding cat caught a cockroach and carried it to a nearby empty arch for its supper, the crunch of jaws on the insect's carapace was distinctly followed by the light patter as fragments of the shell fell on the flagstones like brittle petals. Lying there in the darkness I felt that this would be perhaps the last quiet, interlude in our long journey. From now onward, all throughout the Levant, there had been so many modern changes, so much development, that we would find it difficult to find the traces of those pioneer Crusaders. Nearing the end of our trek, we had achieved most of what I had set out to learn. More than seven months in the saddle, sampling the experience of the Crusade, had brought a new understanding of what went through the minds of the travellers: the fundamental change of emphasis from optimistic beginnings, through dissillusion, to a stubborn yearning to achieve the goal after so much affliction and commitment.

The enormous hollow boom of the bucket in the cistern woke us at dawn as Feyyaz drew water for his early morning tea. Rather than descend directly to the coast we decided to follow south along the shoulders of the hills until, once again, a military camp with a huge array of whirling radar dishes obliged us to rejoin the main coast road. That brought us to Tartus and the point where we knew we would have to turn aside from Duke Godfrey's trail. Already there was the tearing calico sound of war planes racing up and down the frontier, flying out to sea, wheeling and then screeching back on low-level patrols. Lebanon lay ahead, splintered by civil war. It would have been an act of complete folly to try to ride through Beirut and its suburbs, following directly in the Crusade's track, and so instead we headed for the old caravan road through Damascus, which in another 250 miles should bring us into Jordan, and then through Jericho to the Holy City.

CHAPTER 26

The Last Lap

Perversely, the Crusade frittered away nearly six months before taking the next real step along the road to Jerusalem. After the magnificent triumph of Antioch it was an extraordinary and wasteful delay. The Turks had been routed, the commissariat replenished, and after a few weeks of recuperation the mass of the pilgrims was ready to continue the march. But their leaders prevaricated. They gave all sorts of excuses: the army needed a rest, it was better to avoid travelling in the heat and drought of summer, the horses were too few and more would have to be found locally, there was a risk of plague and the army should scatter to different billets, and so forth. There was some truth to all this. A pestilence did break out, probably bubonic plague, which lingered all summer. Thousands of its victims died, and for some reason the women were particularly vulnerable. Other casualties included Bishop Adhémar, whose corpse was buried in the floor of the church where the Holy Lance had been dug up, and Henry d'Esch, the knight who had foiled the Turkish attack on Antioch's rampart. But the real cause for the delay was that the barons were busily employed in that time-honoured quarrel — the division of the spoils. The main bone of contention was Antioch itself.

By previous agreement the city was to be handed over to Emperor Alexius if he came to claim it. If not, then Antioch would belong to Bohemond who had devised the scheme to capture it. Count Raymond, who wanted the place for himself, contested the award in Emperor Alexius's name. When that device failed, he refused to move his troops out of the city, eventually making himself so obnoxious to his own men that they vitually forced him to give up his claim and the Host marched off to lay siege to the Arab citadel at Maarat an-Numan.

So a conspicuous gap was opening between the leadership and the humble pilgrims. To the rank and file Jerusalem now seemed tantalisingly close at hand, the longed-for culmination of their great journey, and as the months passed and no move was made towards it, they grew more and more disillusioned with the bickering lords. The pilgrims were fully prepared to take the matter into their own hands electing their own leader to take them onward. But they preferred to follow one of the established well-born commanders, though the list of aristocratic candidates was growing shorter by the month. Stephen of Blois had deserted during the siege of Antioch, and Bishop Adhémar was dead. Bohemond was content with Antioch, Tancred too junior, Count Baldwin was still in Edessa while Count Raymond's churlish behaviour and his unpalatable support of the Emperor was rapidly losing him popular respect. The army council briefly revived the idea that Emperor Alexius might take up the leadership, and Hugh of Vermandois and Count Baldwin of Hainault were sent to contact him. But Baldwin vanished on the road, rumoured to have been captured or killed by the Turks, and Hugh of Vermandois, after delivering his message to Alexius, took his chance to continue straight on for France. As far as he was concerned, his immediate Crusading days were over. When Alexius again refused to come eastward, the Emperor's discredit was final. The sole remaining figure of real stature was Duke Godfrey, now the leading hero of the siege of Antioch and, in the pilgrims' eyes, steadfast since the very beginning. Rightly or wrongly, popular opinion increasingly held that Duke Godfrey was the proper man who should lead the Host.

By early March 1099 the outspoken determination of the pilgrims to reach the Holy Places was compelling. Not even the strongest commander dared halt the pilgrims in their growing fervour, and so the army tramped on down the Levant coast, laying siege to a city here, bypassing a port there, making peace with a town governor or concluding a local truce as required, but never delaying long enough to lose sight of the original goal – the Holy City. They were lucky there was no real opposition to this haphazard advance which took them another three months. The Levant was a patchwork of small weak states. On the coast the Byzantines nominally still held some of the towns, and although the Egyptians had recently taken Jerusalem itself and controlled several of the port cities, they had failed to establish themselves in any strength. Inland the Turks had ravaged the great Arab capitals, leaving them in disarray.*

It was typical of the new zealotry of the Host that it should return to the controversy still raging over Peter Bartholomew and the Holy Lance. The authenticity of the relic was contested — at least one other version of the Holy Lance already existed in Europe, and there was another in Jerusalem — and the circumstances of its discovery were suspicious. Following Peter Bartholomew's directions workmen had laboured for most of the day digging up the floor of St Peter's Church in Antioch but found nothing. Several of the supervising dignitaries had left, when Peter Bartholomew threw off his coat and shoes and wearing only a shirt, himself leaped into the trench and began to pull an object from the earth which he claimed as a fragment of the Lance. Sceptics maintained that Peter Bartholomew was a charlatan and the Lance bogus. Others were equally vehement in his support. Finally, when the army was besieging the town of Arqah near Tripoli, Peter Bartholomew, pushed to the limit, offered to demonstrate the genuine properties of the Lance and his own honesty by undergoing an ordeal by fire. Two large stacks of olive wood were prepared, with a narrow path in between, and the wood was set alight. When the fire had really taken hold, Peter Bartholomew walked down the gap, holding the Lance. Among the roaring flames, said his promoters, they could detect a shadowy second figure, a saint guiding and supporting Peter. He emerged at the far end, but so badly scorched that he could barely stand, and was knocked to the ground by a mob of jubilant supporters eager to touch the Lance and acclaim its inspired bearer. Three days later Peter died of his injuries, and his detractors promptly denounced him as a proven fake. Not so, said the believers, Peter had survived the ordeal and only succumbed to the unfortunate injuries he sustained when being manhandled by his rapturous partisans who had broken his legs and back. The controversy still dragged on even as the army, abandoning the siege of Arqah, marched forward. Three weeks later, on 7 June, the walls of Jerusalem came in sight.

---

* It was said that there were 300 bakers in the city of Damascus before the Turkish attack, and only two when they left.

Thus, despite their leaders' warnings, the Host had successfully negotiated the road to the Holy City even while marching through the heat of summer. They were greatly helped by the fact that they used the coast road where the daytime temperatures were moderated by the sea breezes. Szarcsa, Zippy and Yabangı had no such relief once Sarah and I turned inland to skirt around the Lebanon. We departed from Duke Godfrey's trail shortly before reaching the spot where Peter Bartholomew had died of his burns, and rode up from the Mediterranean coast via the Crusader castles of Safita and Qalat al-Hosn, the latter better known as the Krak des Chevaliers. The castles had been built in line of sight with one another so the garrisons could signal between themselves, yet the coastal hills were so tangled that it took almost a full day to ride the intervening distance. So long as we were kept to the high ground, the temperature was reasonable, about 30 degrees at midday, and the scenery pleasantly varied, with grove after grove of olive trees planted on the rocky soil. But once we had passed through the Homs Gap, guarded by the Krak des Chevaliers, and entered on the central flatland of Syria, the temperature climbed to 40 degrees and the dust and glare became oppressive.

There was no practicable way to avoid the parching daytime conditions. The traffic made it too dangerous to ride the road after dark, and though we broke camp at first light, it was uncomfortably hot within two hours of starting to ride. The best we could do was journey very gently, resting the horses in the shade whenever possible, halting for three or four hours in the afternoon when the heat was at its worst, then riding on in the last of the evening light. We managed to give the horses two night's good rest and feeding at a riding centre in Homs and then picked up the age-old caravan track to Damascus, now a dreary motor road. That evening I misjudged the distance between settlements, built up around the former oases, and at dusk we were stranded on the bleak stone desert after twenty miles of weary slog. Not a house was to be seen, no trace of water, only the unlovely oil-streaked highway with its noisy succession of heavy trucks rumbling south, and on each side of the highway a grim moonscape of bare rock and sharp stones. We headed for a heap of ruins on a nearby hill, and found ourselves at the base of an old and crumbling watchtower that had once guarded the caravan trail. The place was tumbling to pieces, its upper storey had already fallen inwards, blocking the interior with rubble, and the sandstone building blocks were badly weathered. But the lower wall was still intact and offered a shelter from the bitter night wind of the desert. Sarah fed the horses from their nosebags while I hammered the picket pins into cracks in the wall so the animals could stand in the lee of the ancient fortification. It was impossible to drive tent pegs into the rocky ground so we attached the little bubble tent to small rocks to stop it being bowled away by the wind, and fell asleep to the sound of the tent fabric thrumming in the gusts.

We reached Damascus on 10 July, where arrangements had been made for the horses to stay at the riding club on the edge of the city. We planned for this to be their last major rest before the final push for Israel, and cautiously decided on giving the horses five full days when they could be well fed, idle, and even – in the heat of the afternoon – sprayed with water to keep them cool. Zippy and Yabangı enjoyed themselves thoroughly and perked up, but Szarcsa remained listless and dispirited. Though he had a good appetite, the flesh was melting from his bones, and he was losing condition with alarming speed. Only three weeks earlier he had been on peak form, fit and alert. Now, it seemed, his advanced years were finally catching up with him.

Beyond Damascus the signs of military tension with Israel became very evident. We were now riding parallel to the Syrian-Israeli border, with the Golan Heights in view, and every few miles there were batteries of field artillery dug into firing pits or tanks hull-down in bunkers. The slightest elevation above the monotonous flat desert was topped with arrays of radar dishes nodding like electronic imbeciles, and every second person seemed to be dressed in some sort of military uniform. The dragon-fly shapes of military helicopters clattered in and out of the folds of the hills. One helicopter pilot must have seen the three horses standing beside the long straight road, and decided to give us a fright. He dropped out of view and, keeping hidden in a wadi, circled his machine around behind us until he suddenly bobbed up a couple of hundred yards to the rear. Lining up on his target, he opened up the engines to full power and came blasting straight towards us, no more than ten feet above the ground. The shattering noise seemed to rock the horizon as the helicopter slammed over us, so close that from horseback we could almost have reached up and touched the rocket pods. If the pilot had hoped to scare the horses into bolting across the desert, he was disappointed. The three animals did not even flicker their ears.

Just how phlegmatic the horses had become was more apparent the following dawn. We had, as usual, started at six-thirty and were riding quietly out of a small, nondescript Arab village where we had spent the night. The countryside was flat and dull, a sterile expanse of seared earth and rock, devoid of any green plant at that season to brighten the monotonous duns and greys. The road was minor, a mere feeder track to the village, nevertheless we rode along it prudently, staying close to the edge of the hard surface and in single file to face any oncoming traffic. There were no other road-users, not even a pedestrian, except for a distant lorry coming towards us. As the vehicle approached, I could see that it was an elderly Russian-built truck of the type used by the Syrian army and it was rolling along at a good pace. A score of soldiers were standing in the back, hanging on to the frame for the overhead canopy. As the truck came towards us, it was apparent that the driver was steering directly at Sarah who was in the lead on Szarcsa. She saw the truck and moved Szarcsa over, nearly off the road to let it go by. Riding a few yards to the rear I saw to my horror that the truck driver had shifted his aim to continue to bear down on the lead horse. What followed was chilling, like a nightmare in which one is powerless to react to the premonition of disaster. The truck closed the gap to the horse, and perhaps – charitably – the driver had the sun in his eyes or, more likely, the steering on the hard-used vehicle was too worn and slack to be accurate. So instead of narrowly skimming the target as, I suppose, the dim-witted man at the wheel had intended, the projecting side of the truck smacked into the horse. No sound could be heard over the roar of the ancient truck engine except, incredibly, for a cheer that went up from the men riding in the back of the vehicle as Szarcsa was knocked sideways, his hindquarters slewing round as he flailed his legs to hold his balance. For a ghastly moment I thought that his side had been torn off, for a great flap had suddenly flopped down, and liquid spewed out. Then I realised that the heavy leather saddlebag had ripped open, and the liquid was the contents of Sarah's water bottle that had exploded under the impact.

I jumped down from Yabangı's saddle and ran to help Sarah from Szarcsa's back. She was shaking with shock and outrage.

'I saw it coming. I could see it, just see it,' she blurted, 'but I couldn't believe that he wouldn't swerve at the last minute. I'm alright, but another half-inch and he would have taken off my leg.'

She was not exaggerating. The well-stuffed saddle bag had projected just beyond her thigh, and if the steel edge of the truck had come a trifle closer it would have smashed her leg. The culprits had neither stopped nor slowed down. As for Szarcsa, who had every excuse to be terrified, he just stood there calmly as if being battered by a truck was an everyday event.

The constant tensions of life along the war zone, as local people preferred to call their border with Israel, seemed to have bred a manic aggression at every level. In Damascus we had been warned that we would probably be stoned by children as we rode through some villages. The children, the excuse went, had seen on television the troubles in Palestine, on the Occupied West Bank, and were merely aping the stone-throwers they saw on the small screen. Sure enough, gangs of chanting brats did assemble in several villages and flung pebbles at us, usually quite accurately. But the horses were too experienced to do more than skip and fidget as the projectiles pattered down, and the stones were too small to do any harm. But the malaise went deeper than mere mimicry, for when the Arab adults appeared from their houses to yell at their offspring to stop, the children sometimes turned and flung stones at them too.

Border living produced other, less vicious, quirks. Invited into a small and very poor house to shelter from the midday heat, we found we had arrived in the midst of a community crisis. It seemed that the village had sent a carload of young men into Lebanon to buy new radios and television sets and smuggle them back into Syria where such items were much more expensive or unobtainable. Unfortunately the car had been stopped and searched on the return journey, and most of the contraband confiscated. The crestfallen smugglers had just arrived back home, and it took us some minutes to realise why they were wistfully inspecting headphones and extension cables all dusted with white powder. They had hidden all the goods in bags of flour and only the smallest items had escaped detection. The episode finally explained to us why little Zippy had become so popular. Several times we had been stopped on the road and offered cash for the little pack pony, or while setting up camp had

307

been warned to guard him carefully at night for fear he would be stolen. We now learned that Zippy was a smuggler's ideal. Some contraband runners entered Lebanon over the mountains by mule tracks, loaded up pack animals with contraband and walked back over the mountain. If they were detected by patrols, they would turn loose the animals which often found their own way home ladened with Japanese radios and television sets, cheap watches and the tins of foreign-made cooking oil that the village housewives preferred.

As we rode down the main street of Dera'a, the border town with the kingdom of Jordan, a burly well-dressed man jumped into the street waving his arms to block our path and bellowing lustily. 'You must stay and visit the town!' He was, he told us, the Director of Tourism and he insisted that we camp overnight in his office. I protested that there was nowhere suitable to put the horses and that we should get closer to the border before stopping for the night. Not at all, he said, seizing Yabangi by the bridle, we could put the horses in a nearby park and in the morning he himself would help us with customs and immigration formalities. He was as unstoppable as a charging rhinoceros. Did we need food for the horses? Then he would find some. Had we met the local governor? Of course he would make an appointment. Ridwan had an extraordinary habit of constantly patting and pummelling his interlocutor between every burst of speech, and after an hour of his company I came to wish that, like a true Crusader, I had brought a suit of armour. But everything he suggested was carried out in double quick time and, better yet, he came with us to the frontier post the following morning.

As expected, it was a melée of cars, buses, and trucks, surrounded by a frustrated and slow-moving throng of drivers, migrant workers, Arab families, pilgrims to and from Mecca, and transients of every description. The throng was swirling from office to office trying to get documents stamped, visas checked, customs clearances and police passes issued. Into this maelstrom Ridwan hurled himself with shoulder-patting, back-slapping, elbow-nudging gusto. He thrust to the head of each queue and genially hailed the relevant official. Everyone who worked at the frontier obviously knew Ridwan, for I could see the flinch as he began his friendly pummelling. To avoid the onslaught they let him flip open the official registers and fill in the details himself, then snatch up the rubber stamp and bang it on our documents before setting off to bulldoze his path out through the waiting crowd. We were rushed out of Syria by a whirlwind force of muscle and sheer gall. Checking my watch, I saw that it had taken twenty-five minutes to complete the formalities in Ridwan's hectoring style where it had required twenty-four hours to enter at the opposite frontier. I was very grateful for the time that he had saved us. We were on the last lap now, advancing as fast as possible towards Jerusalem with three very tired horses. Every extra day we spent on the road was an increased strain on the animals, and I was worrying that we might be held up on the politically sensitive crossing from Jordan into Israeli-controlled territory.

We needed only five days to cross Jordan, but in that brief time Szarcsa's decline accelerated tragically. He walked slower and slower, and looked ever more mournfully down his aging aristocratic nose. We tried everything we could to cheer him up. We fed him titbits, rested him in the shade, gave him tonics, reduced the load in his saddlebags, sponged and cooled him, and cut back the daily distances. Yet nothing had any effect. He was wasting away before our eyes, though his appetite remained undiminished. Hoping to nurse him along the final stretch, we made a short-cut and rode cross-country directly towards the Allenby Bridge on the Jordan river, the only point where we had permission to cross into Israel. But our detour brought us to the deep trench of Wadi Zarqah and the descent to the valley floor, then the long slow climb up the other side, and this sapped the last reserves of Szarcsa's strength even though we dismounted and walked all the way uphill beside the horses, resting them at every turn. By the time we were descending into the Jordan valley itself, a thousand feet below sea level and stifling with the late July heat, Szarcsa was shuffling downhill like an old horse that had gone far enough.

By chance we found shelter that night at the farmhouse of a wealthy Jordanian landowner, a young man who owned his own horse and had to have been very fond of animals for he fed a vast collection of stray cats and their kittens on his verandah. In the distance the lights of Jerusalem twinkled so high on the Judaean hills that they might have been stars hanging low in the sky, and I began to wonder if the wisest course might be to leave Szarcsa behind as a gift for the farmer who would take care of him, rather than push him on through the heat just to make the final few miles to complete the journey. In the coolest part of the following day, before sunrise, we tried walking with Szarcsa as far as the Jordanian passport control office and knew, once and for all, that he was too stiff to keep up with Zippy and Yabangı any longer. I returned to the farm to say that we were making a present of the horse and leaving money for Szarcsa's upkeep and the cost of transport up out of the valley to higher pasture when he had regenerated. We emptied out the last of the barley from the feedbags in front of him, and Szarcsa eyed the feast when we said goodbye to him, a tall, gaunt horse so tired he could barely put one foot in front of the other.

The Jordanian army major at the military checkpoint by the bridge was dumbfounded that we had been granted official permission to take Yabangı and Zippy across the frontier.

'No animals – not even a dog or a cat – have been allowed into Israel while I have been working here,' he said. 'They are always sent back by the other side. This paper gives you permission to leave, but not to return. Are you sure you are expected.'

'Oh yes,' I said rather more confidently than I felt.

'Good luck then, and safe journey', and we plodded over the loose planks of the little bridge that spanned the insignificant, reed-choked channel of the Jordan River. A blue and white flag was hanging limply over the palm trees. An Israeli soldier in a dusty combat uniform swung up the striped pole and stared at us curiously. Then he showed us where we could tether the ponies until his superiors arrived to deal with the situation. We sat in the shade of what looked like a metal bus shelter, drank a glass of water, and hoped that a message of our impending arrival had been received by the Israeli authorities. We must have looked very insignificant indeed: two small Turkish ponies and two exhausted riders, or rather pedestrians, for it was much too hot to ride the animals and we had been travelling on foot since 4 am.

After a few minutes a taciturn Israeli officer arrived to inform us that a veterinary surgeon was on his way to check the animals. In due course a courtly Palestinian arrived and, watched by the soldiers, took blood samples, checked the ponies' temperatures and condition and informed us that we should take the animals through to Jericho where they would be held in quarantine for three days. Relieved, Sarah and I led the ponies half a mile to the spotlessly clean, air-conditioned and virtually empty customs-and-security building where every item of baggage was checked and rechecked, and even the saddles were removed and x-rayed. It was all so efficient and well-rehearsed and totally different from the world we had been living in all that summer that it produced a sense of culture shock, particularly when I was interviewed by an Israeli customs official. After tapping at his calculator he informed me that I would have to pay a hefty import duty on the two horses. It turned out that he had valued them at $2000 apiece, and it was difficult to persuade him that I had bought the horses for less than a quarter of that sum until I patiently explained that a Turkish peasant earning less than a $1000 per year was unlikely to have a pony worth twice his annual income.

We were then allowed to walk on through the killing zone, the strip sewn with mines and hung with wire to deter any raiders. It was now early afternoon, and the sun was at its fiercest, blazing down on a grotesque landscape of bone-white dunes sculpted by the wind. The temperature was 43 degrees, and the signboards beside the track read 'No Walking!' or 'Danger! Mines!'. Behind us the border post had closed for the day, and we were passed by cars, taxis and jeeps taking the staff back to a less bizarre world. An ugly vehicle like a bare truck chassis fitted with benches and a light machine gun drew up alongside and the crew, a border patrol, stared at us through the inevitable dark glasses. A few hundred yards farther on and we were walking across the bridge that spanned the anti-tank ditch, the final element of the killing zone. Despite the group of friendly and cheerful Israeli soldiers guarding the bridge, the anti-tank ditch brought to mind the rock chasm before Castle Sahyoun, the chasm dug at such enormous cost and defended 800 years earlier with what was then the state-of-the-art technology. Back in Damascus we had been told that Syria's President Assad, who had sworn to drive the Israelis into the sea as foreign invaders, thought of himself as the new Saladin. Behind his desk hung a painting of the battle at the Horns of Hattin when the power of later Crusaders had been broken. It seemed yet another contradiction in that topsy-turvy part of the world. On one hand the Crusades had been hijacked as a part of modern belligerent rhetoric, yet on the other both Arabs and Israelis had been prepared to let us ride quietly and without fuss through the turmoil and the distrust. It was a rare glimpse of tolerance in an otherwise discordant world.

CHAPTER 27

Jerusalem

We found we had entered an eerie landscape, nearly devoid of life. The Palestinians of the Occupied Territories were observing the *intifada*, the Uprising, and refusing to do anything but the most essential tasks. So there was no one working in the fields, the shops were shuttered and silent, and after an hour's slow walk, not a soul on the streets of the Arab town of Jericho. Sarah and I limped into the main square, with blistered feet and wilting under the heat. A single small car rolled quietly into view, the only sign of movement. It had been sent by the Arab vet to lead us to the quarantine which proved to be an orchard belonging to his retired assistant. There we left the ponies to begin their three-day seclusion, and an Arab driver gave us a lift up to Jerusalem so that we could check the best route to take the animals when it came to the culmination of our long trek, the day we rode into the Holy City itself and to Duke Godfrey's tomb. Our Arab driver was obliged to leave us at the city gate because the police had installed barricades and were turning away all vehicles with Palestinian registration plates. The atmosphere was tense, and Jerusalem seemed to be holding its breath, waiting for a riot. The sight of an Israeli soldier, crouching in the battlements as he surveyed the Arab quarter of the city, again recalled how many different nations' troops had watched from Jerusalem's walls – Roman, Arab, Crusader, Turk, and now Israeli – and not all of them had been facing outward to repel foreign invaders. Several had gazed inward, to spot trouble brewing in the narrow alleyways notorious for their tumults and civil strife.

I had been prepared to be disappointed with Jerusalem, particularly in such an edgy atmosphere. So much had been written about the Holy City that I imagined the place would seem stale and hackneyed. Expecting that Old Jerusalem would have been smothered by modern suburbs, it was a pleasant surprise to see how impressively the city wall still stood, clearly defining the Old City on its hill. The stonework, restored and refurbished, had been erected by the Ottomans, but their wall followed much the same line that the First Crusaders would have seen. It made a perfect frame for the jumble of spires, cupolas, towers, belfries, and roofs that were dominated by the huge glistening golden Dome of the Rock, emphasising that Jerusalem was a Holy City for Islam, as well as Jewry and Christendom.

On the battlements was a plaque which marked the section of wall where, according to the calculations of Joseph Prawer, Jerusalem's leading historian of the Crusades, the men of Duke Godfrey's brigade cracked open the city's defensive perimeter on 15 July 1099. The Duke himself was among the first to set foot on the parapet, charging across a makeshift bridge of beams which had been pushed out from his mobile siege tower. The network of lanes and city streets adjacent to the historic entry point were now virtually deserted for, by an irony of history, what had been the *Juiverie*, the Jewish Quarter, in Godfrey's day was now occupied by Arabs, and again the small shops were all shuttered, observing the *intifada*. In a museum-like hush, almost as if we were walking through the excavated streets of an archaeological site, Sarah and I found our way along the narrow streets which climbed by a succession of steps up the slope to the right. After three or four turns, we arrived at an archway carrying the sign which announced entry to the Church of the Holy Sepulchre.

Inside was a flagstone courtyard but it gave little sense of perspective. Like most of the religious buildings in the city, the great Church was squeezed shoulder to shoulder with its neighbours, and was a random collection of architectural styles and materials that accumulated over a period of 1500 years as the structure was enlarged, altered, and rebuilt after earthquake, fire or simple decay. Purists have argued over the authenticity of the site as vehemently as the debate over Peter Bartholomew's Holy Lance. But the First Crusaders were in no doubt that this was the very spot where Jesus had been crucified and then his body placed in the burial cave. So far as they were concerned this was the ultimate shrine in Christendom, the site identified by the Empress Helena when she came to Jerusalem and rediscovered the Holy Places.* Here, according to the tale, she had watched her workmen excavate three wooden crosses, the cross of Jesus and the crosses for the two thieves, as well as the superscription placed over Christ's head, and a bag of nails. The True Cross had been identified by placing a corpse upon it, whereupon the cadaver came to life. Even that location now had its own chapel, the Chapel of the Invention of the Cross, and after so many centuries the sacred ground of the Sepulchre had been so gnawed away for underground chapels and galleries, or built over and embellished with yet more chapels and oratories so that it seemed like a colony of polyps encrusting a reef.

On this first, exploratory, visit to the Church of the Holy Sepulchre, it was difficult to sense any feeling of awe, rather the reverse. We had arrived like tourists and were at once accosted by several guides, offering to conduct a tour of the building. Souvenir shops by the gate displayed, among other trinkets, replica crowns of thorns, and there was even a money changer hovering in the very courtyard, claiming he could improve on the official rates of exchange for foreign currency. Paradoxically I found these down-to-earth features reassuring, for this was precisely how the medieval pilgrims would have recognised it, with the forerunners of the same hucksters, door keepers, watchmen, vendors, importunate guides, idlers, foreign visitors, and colourful mixture of priests.

The Sepulchre was a microcosm of the variety and richness of Christianity. In Ottoman times the Church of the Holy Sepulchre had been officially given into the care of six different Christian sects, three with major responsibilities, and three with minor rights. So it was tantalising to try to identify by their individual costumes the churchmen of the Latins, Greek Orthodox, Armenian Orthodox, Syrians, Copts and Ethiopians. Each group had its own altars, special vestments, character-

---

* In 326 Helena, mother of Constantine the Great, made a pilgrimage to Jerusalem. By the end of the 4th century the story had spread in Europe that she had 'invented', i.e. discovered, the True Cross as well as identifying the site of the Crucifixion, previously covered by a pagan Roman temple.

istic styles of artwork and church furniture, and all were focused upon the central shrine, now covered by an ornate 19th-century structure to make yet another chapel, on which three lines of candles flickered, each rank of tapers lit by a different sect according to jealously guarded agreement.

Under other circumstances the miscellany and rivalry of sects could have been off-putting, but after meeting Latins, Greek and Armenian Orthodox, and Syrians in their own lands during the long ride, it seemed very natural to see them now, side by side. An Armenian priest was cleaning a chunky candelabra, his hands grimy with the rag and paste. A Coptic monk crouched in the tiniest burrow of a chapel at the back of the Tomb, a low cave scarcely bigger than a kennel, where for the payment of a small offering you could touch the bedrock close to where Christ's head had lain. In the severely modern Latin chapel of Saint Mary Magdalene a Franciscan lay helper was mopping the marble floor, while in the entrance to the Chapel of the Angel, the antechamber to the Tomb, lurked the half-seen figure of a Greek Orthodox priest standing guard, so black and still in his dark robes that he ambushed and startled the visitor with his unblinking, bearded presence. Every few paces around the Sepulchre one came to an archway or a grille or an alcove, a heavy door mysteriously closed and locked, a flight of steps leading down to an underground cellar or perhaps ascending to upper gallery. It was like wandering through a life-sized Advent calendar where a succession of paper window flaps open to reveal all manner of different tableaux – a robed door keeper, a Japanese tourist with his camera, a nun kneeling before an altar. A Roman drainpipe carried away holy water, next to an artist painstakingly restoring a Renaissance painting, and beyond him was a Greek priest on the Mount of Calvary chatting on a portable telephone, his bearded face pressed to the apparatus with its winking coloured diode lights and bright, shiny aerial in striking contrast to his grey-blue gown and tall hat. As we left the Church, an Armenian priest with heavy ringlets and a robe stained with drips of candle grease, hissed angrily at a roving cat. The animal scuttled for a few yards and then walked serenely flicking its tail. Presumably it had crossed into Greek Orthodox territory.

The Franciscans had been charged with the care of the Latin sector of the Church, and in their sacristy was the supposed sword of Duke Godfrey and his spurs. Neither sword nor spurs could have been genuine. The sword had been made at least a century after the First Crusade, and the spurs, with their spiky sunburst wheels, were very much newer than that. Folklore said that the sword would leap from its sheath to defend Christendom when mortal danger threatened. Actually the weapon was used to dub knights of the Order of the Holy Sepulchre. The cross that Duke Godfrey was said to have carried before him as the Crusade finally entered into Jerusalem had gone. Godfrey's successors in Jerusalem deemed the relic so precious that when they finally left the Holy Land, the Knights of St John took it with them to Malta and placed it in their new cathedral there (though truthfully that cross also was too new to be authentic).

But faulty provenance did not matter. It was an echo of the same extraordinary, if guileless, faith of the Crusaders which had sustained them over the long march to Jerusalem. When the host of pilgrims and footsoldiers finally came within sight of Jerusalem, they had been nearly three years on the road. Many of them must have been barely in touch with reality after the traumas of the terrible ordeals that they had undergone. They had suffered from starvation, poverty, aching cold, heat, thirst, and utter physical weariness. They had buried many of their colleagues at the roadside and seen others depart with their spirit broken by the difficulties of the road. Even without the near-run battles they had fought against the infidel, there had been enough hardship and uncertainty to have unhinged an ordinary traveller. They had needed every last vestige of their religious fervour, and the vision of Jerusalem at last, rising up on its hill, was a moment of supreme emotion. According to Albert of Aix, many of the weary pilgrims stood with the tears streaming down their faces. Others, wrote William, raised their hands to Heaven, then taking off their shoes, knelt down and kissed the ground.

On 13 June, in a surge of zeal the Host flung itself into a direct assault against the imposing walls, which were vigorously defended by troops under the Fatamid governor Iftikhar al-Dawla. Taking their timing from the inexpert advice of a Christian hermit whom they found living on the Mount of Olives, the Crusaders launched a poorly prepared assault. Their fanatic rush broke down the city's outworks, and the first few men, fighting with berserker courage managed to reach the main wall and climb to the parapet, only to fail because they had but a single scaling ladder and could not bring up reinforcements.

June and July were bad months to be camped upon the Judaean hills. The weather was much too hot, and water was very hard to come by. The only local water source was the Pool of Siloam, but that was totally inadequate for the number of people and animals. The Arabs had blocked or poisoned most of the country wells so water bags had to be sewn from the skins of freshly slaughtered buffalo and oxen, and watering parties went as far as the river Jordan, a long day's journey, to fill them. By the time the waterskins were hauled back uphill to Jerusalem their contents had turned rancid and foul in the heat. The Arabs had also driven off their flocks and herds into hiding, and bread was virtually impossible to obtain from any nearby village. Supplies of every description were scarce, and when the Franks began to build their siege engines, the quartermasters found that the scanty forests had already been denuded by the Egyptian troops who had successfully besieged the city in the previous year. But with the ultimate prize so close at hand, the Host did not slacken its frenzied preparations for a grand assault. A stock of suitable logs was laboriously brought up on camels, and a contingent of sailors arrived from the coast, bringing their ropes and axes and wedges, and under the direction of two specialist engineers two great siege towers were made. One was to the order of Count Raymond, who still had the money to pay for it. The other siege tower was for Duke Godfrey but despite the spoils of Antioch he was so short of funds that he had to raise the cost by a subscription among his followers. Meanwhile Jersualem's garrison were improving their defences. They padded the walls with straw bales and bundles of wicker and twigs to cushion the impact of the rocks hurled by the mangonels of the Franks, and hung out great beams of wood to act as buffers against battering rams and to keep the rolling towers at bay.

On 8 July, again at the instigation of the hermit on the Mount of Olives, the Host made a solemn procession around the city walls. Led by chanting priests dressed in white robes and holding sacred relics, the pilgrims walked the entire circuit of the city, singing and praying, and watched by the hooting, jeering defenders. The next day they redeployed their forces to better advantage. The weakest point in the defence had now been identified. Level ground on the northeast quadrant would allow a siege tower to be rolled forward and, once it had negotiated the ditch, it could be trundled through the gaps in the already damaged outer wall and pushed against the defences. Duke Godfrey was

317

to assault this sector, while Count Raymond would again attack the southwest corner. From his ample funds Count Raymond paid his Provençals three deniers for each rock they placed in the moat.

On 10 July the great assault began to move ponderously forward. Once again Count Raymond was unlucky in his war plan. It took two or three days of heavy labour to push, drag and lever his siege tower towards the wall, and all the while it ran into fierce opposition from the Muslim defenders who bombarded it with rocks and firebrands so successfully that they ignited the topmost of its three storeys. The massive wooden structure, burning and battered, was halted in its tracks, and the Provençal offensive lost momentum. Then, around noon on 15 July, the dispirited followers of Count Raymond saw three of Godfrey's men running towards them from the Mount of Olives, shouting that the troops of the Duke of Lorraine had broken through and were already in the city.

What had succeeded was a textbook ram-and-tower assault. Fighting day and night, Duke Godfrey's soldiers had manhandled a massive battering ram through the broken outer wall and succeeded in smashing a gap in the main wall. Behind the battering ram rolled the Duke's siege tower, with the Duke himself and his elder brother Eustace riding in the place of honour on the top floor, while a second squad of knights waited in the central floor. There had been several dangerous moments. The tower had got stuck behind the battering ram and had to be manoeuvred around it. Then the ungainly wooden structure had threatened to collapse under its own weight, and finally, when the tower was close enough to the wall, the defenders set it alight with an enormous torch made of a log filled with combustibles, most likely naphtha. Luckily the Duke's men had been forewarned by the local Christians that this device might be employed, and the flames were extinguished with vinegar. At last the scorched tower was nudged close enough to the wall for the knights in the central floor to push out some wooden beams to span the gap. Ironically, they used for this purpose the wooden baulks the Arabs had hung over the wall as fenders. Then Lietaud and Engelbert, brothers from Tournai, had the honour to be the first Frankish knights to run across the gangway and set foot on the battlements. Duke Godfrey and his brother descended from their upper floor and followed at their heels to help clear the ramparts. The Duke's standard was set up as a signal that the city's defence was ruptured, and a squad of men ran to unbar the Gate of St Stephen so 'the entire army rushed in pell-mell without order or discipline.' Soon the mass of the Norman and Lotharingian troops were racing through the narrow streets of Jerusalem, completely out of control and joined by the hysterical mass of pilgrims. In a violent catharsis of their own suffering the Host rampaged through the city, killing and pillaging indiscriminately. Only the shrewder leaders, particularly Tancred, took care to spare the more important defenders for their ransom value, and Tancred sent his troops directly to the Dome of the Rock to seize its collection of huge silver candelabra.

The mindless massacre that concluded the siege of Jerusalem appalled even their contemporaries by its gruesome excesses. Thousands of men, women and children were put to the sword. A large group of Muslims, who took refuge on the roof of the Al-Aqsa Mosque under the protection of Tancred's banner, were attacked by maddened troops who broke all pledges of safe conduct and sanctuary. Those Muslims not hacked to death, leapt to their deaths in the mosque's courtyard. Blood-spattered soldiers ran hither and thither, ransacking the houses, and the corpses piled so thickly in the streets that within days they became a health hazard as they putrefied. Arab prisoners were forced to drag the dead bodies of their co-religionists and dump them outside the city walls Exulting soldiers and pilgrims seized whichever house they fancied, murdered or drove out the occupants, and then announced their own possession by hanging some sort of symbol outside the door, a shield, a flag, or even their hat. Though William of Tyre claimed that Duke Godfrey led the first sweep through the city's streets and squares, Albert of Aix was determined to defend the good name of his hero. He insisted that the Duke was unable to restrain his troops who ran riot, for the Lotharingians were specifically identified as committing some of the worst excesses. The Duke, according to Albert, would have nothing to do with the terrible scenes within the city. He took off his armour and donned a simple woollen shift. Then he and a select band of companions walked barefoot to the Church of the Holy Sepulchre where, with tears in their eyes, they held divine service and 'thanked the Lord that he had judged them worthy to see what they had always desired.'

The day that Duke Godfrey knelt before the tomb of Christ, his

Purging a captured city of the corpses of its Muslim dead.

Crusade journey had come to an end. He was worshipping at the supreme Christian shrine that three years earlier he had vowed to liberate. To him, as to many of his companions, the success of their extraordinary mission was entirely due to divine intervention. They said that at a critical moment in the attack on the city, they had seen the figure of a heavenly warrior standing on the Mount of Olives who waved a splendid gleaming shield and beckoned them into the fray. After the fall of the city, many claimed that they saw the dead bishop Adhémar walking the streets, as well as many of their dead companions from the journey. In an ecstasy of fervour, pilgrims, soldiers and knights made solemn rounds of all the holy places, sometimes on their bare knees, and there was service after service of thanksgiving for 'this pilgrimage to Jerusalem which they were now making on earth seemed to promise a definite assurance that they would also take part at last in that future one in the life hereafter.'

The accusation that the First Crusade was largely motivated by territorial greed is contradicted by the fact that no one, not even among the barons, seemed to have any ready-made plan for Jerusalem once it was captured. There was no notion whether Churchmen or barons should be responsible for the Holy City, or who would be the overall leader. Not until a week after the fall of the city did the council assemble to choose who should hold Jerusalem. Completely out of touch with popular feeling, almost unbelievably, their first choice was Count Raymond of Toulouse who was so unpopular with the rank and file. Raymond declined the offer, ostensibly on the grounds that he had never wished to be the ruler of Jerusalem. More probably, he was undone by the vociferous opposition of his own men who offered a great many complaints about his conduct and character. The Crusade, in the form of the Host, was finally asserting its genuinely popular character. As far as the mass of the pilgrims were concerned there was only one choice for leader: Godfrey, Duke of Bouillon. It was the final recognition of his special status, and in keeping with his reputation for modesty it was later believed that when offered the crown of Jerusalem he refused it with the immortal words that 'he could not wear a crown of gold where Jesus wore a crown of thorns.' Instead he accepted the title of Defender of the Holy Sepulchre.

Duke Godfrey was now in all but name the first Latin King of Jerusalem. In the next few months he was to lead the army to victory against an Egyptian relieving force, vigorously prosecute the reduction of various Muslim garrisons on the coast, and have a difficult time in bringing to heel Count Raymond who belied his disinterest in Jerusalem by refusing to remove his troops from the city until forced to do so. Godfrey's brief tenure as Prince of Jerusalem and Defender of the Holy Sepulchre was an excuse for more legendary detail to be added to his reputation as the perfect Christian knight. A delegation of hill chieftains, ushered into his tent, was said to have found the ruler of the Franks seated on the ground with a straw-stuffed cushion as his only furniture. They were amazed that the Prince of Jerusalem used no outward show of pomp and splendour, and not even a bodyguard. It was to be reported that on the evening of his election all the nobles had gone to church to pray. As they stood before the altar with lighted candles in their hands, a great earthquake suddenly shook the building. Everyone was flung to the

The humble leader: Godfrey on campaign seated on the ground in a simple, unfurnished tent.

floor, their candles extinguished, except for Duke Godfrey's candle which shone with a ghostly brilliance. Perhaps Duke Godfrey's reputation would have been tarnished if he had lived longer, but he set the seal on his repute by disappearing abruptly from the scene. Unlike other heroes such as King Arthur or the Cid who faded in their old age, re-emerging for one last burst of glory, the Duke made his exit while still at the height of his power. On 18 July 1100 he died in Jerusalem, some said from poison but it was more likely from a fever inflicted on a body worn out by the exertions of his journey. He would have been about forty years old.

For five days the corpse lay in state and then was laid to rest at the foot of the Mount of Calvary. It was the highest honour his peers could accord him. The model for the valiant and perfect Crusader knight was dead.

The monument over Godfrey's corpse became an object of veneration. On it came to be inscribed a simple epitaph: 'Here lies the renowned Godfrey of Bouillon, who gained all this land for Christendom. May his soul rest in peace. Amen.' Next to it, eighteen years later, was placed the matching tomb of his brother Baldwin. Both monuments have now vanished. They disappeared as a consequence of a great fire that destroyed most of the Church of the Holy Sepulchre on the night of 11 October 1808. The architect commissioned the following spring to refurbish the interior of the church has been execrated ever since for his tasteless and clumsy work. Godfrey's tomb and the graves of the later Latin kings of Jerusalem were apparently broken up and either removed or the stone fragments used as building material in the renovations. A plain stone bench stands where the Defender of the Holy Sepulchre was accorded his final honour. Suitably, it is surrounded by pious tradition and sacred legends on every side. On one hand is the rock of Golgotha, the Place of the Skull, where tradition holds that Adam was buried so that the blood of Christ running down from the Cross washed away man's original sin. In the opposite direction the Stone of Unction marks the place where, again traditionally, Christ's body was anointed. A little farther on is the very Centre of the World, the navel of the medieval world image, and within sight is the candlelit entrance to the Holy Sepulchre itself.

We used the three days of quarantine for the ponies to prepare the last, small sector of our own journey. A visit to the headquarters of the State Veterinary Service brought the disappointing news that we could not accept the offer of a permanent home for the horses which had been made by a trekking centre near the Sea of Galilee. It seemed that there was too great a risk that Yabangi and Zippy might be carrying some latent equine infection, in particular the African Horse Sickness. Instead the State Veterinary Service searched around and located a kibbutz in the south of the country which was free of mosquitos of the type that would carry the Horse Sickness, and the farm cooperative arranged to send a truck to Jerusalem to collect the two animals after their last day's walk. The animals were to be a gift and they would be treated as pets for the children of the kibbutz. It seemed a suitable reward after their long trek and a considerable improvement on their earlier prospects as pack animals hauling timber and charcoal.

When the quarantine was over, we saddled up the two ponies in the orchard at Jericho, thanked their Arab guardian, and on 28 July began the long slow climb to the Jerusalem, the City on the Hill. We followed the old pilgrim road winding up the Wadi el-Qilt, past the spectacular monastery of St George, then over the same barren hills across which the Crusaders had hauled the fetid water for the siege of Jerusalem. It was a punishing ascent, and like the earlier pilgrims who had used this route we rested the ponies overnight halfway. Early next afternoon we came to the Mount of Olives, and the following morning we rode Yabangi and Zippy for the last time, down past the Garden of Gethsemane, across the Kidron valley, and up the opposite slope until we reached Herod's Gate just a few yards from the place where Godfrey had breached the wall.

Dismounting we led the two ponies in through the city gate and followed the turns and twists of the lanes we had scouted on our previous visits to the city until we came to the Via Dolorosa, and traced its Stations towards the Church of the Holy Sepulchre. There were many more people in the lanes than on our previous visits, but no one took any particular notice of two small ponies stepping gingerly on the slick polished stone blocks on their way past the shops and stalls. Yabangi and Zippy walked as placidly as well-trained dogs on their leashes, ignoring even the trays of the street vendors which set out tempting arrays of green vegetables under their noses.

'Want to sell that horse?' asked a perky trader, the proprietor of St Veronica's Gift Shop.

'How much for the horses?' asked another, and we picked up the inevitable escort of cheeky small boys, the bravest of whom reached up to pat Yabangi's pale nose.

At the point the Via Dolorosa steepened, it turned into a tunnel, with arches overhead and small shops on each side that were just opening for business. The shop keepers were emerging with long hooked poles to haul down the shop canopies and then hang up their wares from the support bars – a profusion of scarves, plastic goods and cheap clothing that dangled over our heads. We pushed on, jostling through the crowd until we came to the small open space in front of the archway to the Church of the Holy Sepulchre. A noticeboard stated that animals were forbidden from entering, so we tied the two ponies to a convenient railing, and borrowed two plastic flower tubs to fill with drinking water from them. The Arab café owner who loaned the tubs at first refused to believe that we had been allowed to cross the Allenby Bridge with the two horses. To him, that was far less likely than the fact we had ridden all the way from Chateau Bouillon. He checked the fact three times and then rushed off to spread the word among his clientele. In an hour's time, at noon, we were due to meet the lorry from the kibbutz that would carry the two ponies to their permanent home. Sarah and I walked across the courtyard and in through the great doors of the Church, scored with small crosses carved by pilgrims. Inside, the Church was almost empty. The arch of candles that marked the entrance to the Chapel of the Angel at the mouth of the Tomb twinkled in the gloom. The worn metal heels of my riding boots clacked embarrassingly on the stone floor as I crossed to the shrine and stooped to enter the low entrance of the tiny inner chamber. I felt in my jacket pocket for the three little coins which a year earlier the old peasant woman had reached up and given us as we rode through Bulgaria. 'Place them by Christ's grave', she had asked. Next to the stone slab on which Jesus's corpse was said to have been laid, was a small offertory box. I reached over and dropped in the three small coins. My own Crusade was done.

Postscript

As he lay dying, the legend goes, the Duke summoned one of his squires and gave him a casket. He was to take it back to Chateau Bouillon, to the green hills of the Ardennes, and there to open it. The knight did as he was asked. Standing on the ramparts of the castle he opened the box and the wind carried away the seeds it contained. They fell into the cracks in the courtyard flagstones, between the great stones of the outer wall and in the crevices among the rocks above the winding Semois. Every June they still bloom as small wild carnations. In Bouillon town you will be told that only in Jerusalem itself and in Chateau Bouillon grow those pale pink delicate flowers.

Bibliography

Professor Jonathan Riley-Smith in a recent work (*The First Crusade and the Idea of Crusading* Athlone Press, London 1986) lists upwards of 180 original sources and 99 secondary sources. However, for a reader, such as myself, with a practical interest, the primary choice was rather less daunting. Five main eyewitness accounts of the First Crusade were available in translation: Anna Comnena's *Alexiad* by E.A.S. Dawes (1928), the anonymous knight's *Gesta Francorum et aliorum Hierosolimitanorum* by Rosalind Hill, (1962); Raymond of Aguilers' *Historia* by J.H. & L.L. Hill (1974); Fulcher of Chartres' *Historia Hierosolymitana* by Martha E. McGinty (1941); and Peter Tudebode's *Historia de Hierosolymitano itinere* by J.H. & L.L. Hill (1968). Susan Edgington very kindly lent me her translation of Albert of Aachen's *Historia*. Many of the more colourful portions of these firsthand accounts – with other early sources – were extracted, translated, and published as an anthology *The First Crusade: The Accounts of Eyewitnesses and Participants* by A.C. Krey (1921). For Archbishop William of Tyre I used the translation of his *History of Deeds Done Beyond the Sea* by Emily A. Babcock & A.C. Krey (1943). The Archbishop established the tradition of writing splendidly readable histories of the Crusade, and this tradition was carried to a famous summit by Sir Steven Runciman's *History of the Crusades*. The first of his three volumes is devoted to the First Crusade. I was also greatly helped by Godfrey de Bouillon's biography, long overdue, written by Pierre Aube (Fayard, 1985). These works, then, were my basic guides through the story of the First Crusade, supplemented with selective reading from Professor Riley-Smith's bibliography. Of course where I have gone astray, the errors are of my own making.

327

Acknowledgements

Hospitality, generosity, enthusiasm – these were the responses that the preparation and progress of our expedition seemed most often to evoke. They made the journey to Jerusalem possible as well as pleasurable, and from thirteen different countries and a myriad of chance encounters here are the names and identities of those friends, advisors and supporters whose particular kindnesses I would like to remember with very special thanks:

In Ireland:
Terry and Carole Adams, Caroline Gallagher, John Kelly, Rex and Helen Lovell, Joe McLoughlin & Bandon Medical Hall, Sammy and Anne Mearns, the late John O'Connell, Donie O'Sullivan and family, Lib Petch, Henry Wall, Mrs Sarah Young, the staff of the Veterinary Section of the Irish Department of Agriculture as well as the Irish Department of Foreign Affairs who helped with arranging veterinary clearances across European frontiers.

In the United Kingdom:
Susan Edgington, Charlie Pinney, Professor Jonathan Riley-Smith, Andrew Wardall, Dr John France.

In France:
Cecile and Dédé Blaise, Mary Kling, Maggie Skeaping.

In Belgium:
Bernard Doffagne, Michel Frere.

In Germany:
Ulle Becker, Herbert Birk, Dr & Mrs Claus Bingold, Penny Dauster, the family Eckert, Inge and Mina Gaiser, Fritz and Helga Grauert, Annegret Loffler, Eve Ploppa, Barbara and Rolf Rohlfs, Herr Schuh, Norbert Valenta.

In Austria:
Patricia Galeitner, Martin and Christa Haller, Herr Rathammer of the Albrechtsberg Riding Club.

In Hungary:
Lajos Fulop, Professor György Györffy, Joanna Toth, Peter Toth, Adam Stang, Lazlo Varga, Steven Vargas, Josef Werle.

In Yugoslavia:
the family Bjelic, family Bogdonic, Professor Circkovic, Tomislav Jovanovic, the family Kacarevic, the family Novakovic, Radenko Raketic, Selim Selim.

In Bulgaria:
Luchezar Avramov, Valentin Bozhkov, Professor Axinia Djourova, Ludmilla Guerassimova-Lukanova, Hristo Matanov, Lyuben Nedkov, Academician Nikolai Todorov, Theodore Troev.

*

In Turkey:
Mukaddes Akça and family, Remzi Bozkurt, the family Deveci, Dr David French, Resit Kuseyrioglu, General Sadullah & Mrs Saffet Ozbakir, Colonel Jemal Tekin, Mahmut Turhanoglu, Engin Turker.

In Syria:
Tom O'Sullivan and the staff at EC Commission offices, Damascus, Najah Rafai, Dr Gabriel Saade.

*

In Jordan:
Nabil Sawalah.

*

In Israel:
George Hintlian, Professor Joshua Prawer, Dr Wahib Tarazi, Dr A. Shimshony, Malka ben-Yosef.

*

And at various times throughout the journey the television film team of Mediac International led by Ron Blythe and David Grieve.

Index

Page numbers in *italic* refer to the illustrations in the text

331

Robert Guiscard, 87
Roger I, Count of Sicily, 87
Romans, 36, 74, 76, 85–6, 167, 243
Romanus Diogenes, Emperor, 20
Runciman, Sir Steven, 23, 37, 45

Safita castle, 304
Sahyoun (Qalat Saladin), 294–5, 311
St George, monastery of, 324
Saint Hubert's abbey, 48
Saint Martin's abbey, Pannonhelm, 105–6
St Pölten, 99
St Simeon, 266, 269, 274, 276
Saladin, 311
Samuel, King of Bulgaria, 145–6
Sar, 243
Sarah: joins expedition, 37–43;
    character, 64–6, 249; accident, 186–7;
    winter rest, 196; learns Turkish, 203;
    ill health, 224–5, 226, 240; Mystery's
    death, 253–5, 258–60; Szarcsa hit by
    truck, 306–7
Sarisu river, 196, 201
Sarlopuzta, 109–11, 120
Saudi Arabia, 252
Sauer river, 70
Sava, river, 51, 128
Scandinavia, 158
Schuh, Herr (Herr Genau), 92, 94–6
Seeheim, 81
Seljuk Turks, 235; Alexius asks for help
    against, 20; ambush Peasants'
    Crusade, 173–4; siege of Nicaea,
    175–82; battle of Dorylaeum, 190–6;
    siege of Antioch, 261–73, 274–80
Selymbria (Silivri), 153
Semois river, 57, 60, 64, 326
Serbia, 128, 129–40
Severin, Tim: search for suitable horses,
    1–13, 30–3; preparations for journey,
    28–43, 52–5; trains horses, 33–5,
    36–43; departure from Bouillon,

58–62; third horse, 108–11; and
    Sarah's accident, 186–7;
    determination to finish journey, 188;
    winter rest, 188–9, 196, 197–200;
    replaces Carty, 198–9; preparations
    for second season's travel, 200–2;
    Mystery's death, 253–60; replaces
    Mystery, 282–7; forced to leave
    Szarcsa behind, 309–10; reaches
    Jerusalem, 312–16; rides into
    Jerusalem, 324–5
Sicily, 24, 87
sieges, 177–9; Antioch, 261–3, 267,
    272, 274–81; Jerusalem, 316–19;
    Nicaea, 174–80, 262, 271
Silivri (Selymbria), 153
Silk Road, 207
Siloam, Pool of, 317
Silpius, Mount, 262, 263, 271, 273,
    274–5, 280, 281
Slavonia, 87
Sofia, 142, 144–5, 146, 148
Söğütovası (Vale of the Willows),
    246–8
Sopron, 102, 105, 112
Spain, 22, 24
Sremska Mitrovic, 126
Stenay, 28
Stephen, Count of Blois, 86, 156, 162,
    176, 261, 263, 266, 302
Stojan, 136–7, 143
Struma valley, 145
Sultan Dağları, 217–19
Sviljanac, 131
Swabia, 84–6, 119–20
Swannhilde, 98
Swift, Jonathan, 112
Syria, 36, 164, 166, 188, 196, 199, 289,
    290–300, 304–9
Szarcsa: Tim buys, 110–11; character,
    112, 130; shoes, 114–15, 133–4,
    136–7; saddle sores, 123, 205;
    Sarah's accident, 186–7; winter rest,